Sustainable Energy: Resources, Technology and Planning.

ERRATUM

Sustainable Energy: Resources, Technology and Planning
By I.G. Pykh & Y.A Pykh

Due to a technical error references 158-240 are missing from this book. They are listed below. We apologise for any inconvenience caused.

[158] Messner, S., Golovin, A. & Strubegger, M. *Natural Gas in Europe.* WP-86-39. International Institute for Applied Systems Analysis, Laxenburg, Austria, 1986.

[159] Moisan, F., Bosseboeuf, D. & Lapillonne, B. *Energy efficiency policies and indicators.* Report for World Energy Council, London, 1998.

[160] Moroney, J.R. (ed), Advances in Economics of Energy and Resources, *Econometric Models of the Demand for Energy.* Vol. 5, Jai Press Inc.: Greenwich, 1984.

[161] Nakicenovic N. & Jefferson J.M. *Global Energy Perspectives to 2050 and Beyond.* IIASA Working Paper. WP-95-127. Laxenburg, Austria, 1995.

[162] Nakicenovic, N. & Grubler A. *Diffusion of Technologies and Social Behaviour.* Springer Verlag: Berlin, Germany, 1991.

[163] New Directions in Energy Modeling. ETSAP (Energy Technology Systems Analysis Programme), April 1997, ETSAP-97-1. http://www.ecn.nl/unit_bs/etsap/annex5/main.html

[164] Nilsson, H.E. Market Transformation: An Essential Condition for Sustainability. *Energy for Sustainable Development,* **1(6),** pp. 20-30, 1995.

[165] Norde, W. Energy and entropy: a thermodynamic approach to sustainability. *The Environmentalist,* **17**, pp. 57-62, 1997.

[166] Nordhaus, W. To Slow or Not to Slow: the Economics of the Greenhouse Effect. *Economic Journal,* 101 (407), 1991.

[167] Nordhaus, W. D. *Managing the Global Commons: The Economics of Climate Change*, MIT Press: Cambridge, MA., 1994.

[168] OECD. *GREEN: The User Manual.* Development Centre, OECD, Paris, 1994.

[169] OECD. OECD Economic Studies. Special Issue: *The Economic Costs of Reducing CO_2 Emissions,* No. 19, Winter 1992, Paris.

[170] OECD. *The Costs of Cutting Carbon Emissions: Results from Global Models,* OECD Documents, Paris, 1993.

[171] OECD/IEA, World Energy Outlook, 1998.

[172] Ohta, H. *Energy Technology: Sources, Systems, and Frontier Conversion*, Elsevier Science Ltd.: Tokyo, Japan, 1994.

[173] OTA, Office of Technology Assessment. *Background Paper: Studies of the Environmental Costs of Electricity.* U.S. Government Printing Office. OTA-ETI- 134. September, 1994.

[174] Parson, E.A. & Fisher-Vanden, K. *Searching for Integrated Assessment: A Preliminary Investigation of Methods, Models, and Projects in the Integrated Assessment of Global Climatic Change.* Consortium for International Earth Science Information Network (CIESIN). University Center, Mich. 1995.

[175] Pasztor, J. & Kristoferson, K. (eds.) *Bioenergy and the Environment,* Westview: Boulder, Colorado, USA, 1990.

[176] Patterson, W.C. *The Energy Alternative,* Boxtree Ltd.: London, 1990.

[177] Pearce, A. & Turner, R.K. *Economics of Natural Resources and the Environment.* Harvester Wheatsheeaf: London, 1990.

[178] Peck, S. & Teisberg, T. J. CETA: A model for carbon emissions trajectory assessment. *The Energy Journal,* **13(1)**, pp. 55-77, 1992.

[179] Penney, T.R. & Bharathan, D. Power from the sea. *Scientific American*, January 1987.

[180] Phylipsen, G.J.M., Blok, K. & Worell, E. *Handbook on International Comparison of Energy efficiency in the Manufacturing Industry,* Utrech University: Utrech, 1998.

[181] Pigford, T. H. Environmental aspects of nuclear energy production. *Ann. Rev. Nud. Science,* **24,** pp. 515-525, 1974.

[182] Pimental, D. & Hall, C. W. *Food and Energy Resources.* Academic Press: Orlando, Florida, USA, 1984.

[183] Prigogine, I. *Introduction to Thermodynamics of Irreversible Processes.* John Wiley & Sons: New York, 1961.

[184] Pringle, L. *Nuclear Energy, Troubled Past Uncertain Future*, Macmillan, 1989.

[185] Rabinovitch, J. A sustainable urban transportation system. *Energy for Sustainable Development*, **II (2)**, July, pp. 11-18, 1995.

[186] Reuter A., Voss, A., Elischer, H., Mueller, T., Saboohi, Y. & Schnabel, S. *MESAP Manual – Version 3.1*, Institute of Energy Economics and the Rational Use of Energy (IER), University of Stuttgart, 1998.

[187] Reuter, A., *MESAP Microcomputer-based Energy Sector Analysis and Planning System*, University of Stuttgart, August 1990.

[188] Rodhe, H., Langner, J., Gallardo, L. & Kjellstrom, E. Global scale transport of acidifying pollutants. *Water, Air and Soil Pollution,* **85**, pp. 37-50, 1995.

[189] Rolle, K. C. *Thermodynamics and Heat Power*, 4th ed. New York: Macmillan Publishing Company, 1994.

[190] Ross, M.H. & Steinmeyer, D. Energy for industry, *Scientific American*, September 1990.

[191] Rotmans, J. & de Vries, B., *Perspectives on Global Change. The TARGET Approach*, Cambridge Univ. Press, Cambridge, 1997.
[192] Rouhani, F. A. *History of O.P.E.C.* Praeger: New York, 1971.
[193] Rubin, R., *The EC Medium Term Energy Demand Model - Present State and Recent Results*, EUR 9011 EN, 1984.
[194] San Martin, R. L. *Environmental Emissions from Energy Technology Systems: The Total Fuel Cycle.* US Department of Energy. Spring 1989.
[195] Sandler, S. I., *Chemical and Engineering Thermodynamics.* John Wiley & Sons: New York, 1989.
[196] Sanstad, A. H., Koomey, J. G. & Levine, M.D. *On the Economic Analysis of Problems in Energy Efficiency: Market Barriers, Market Failures, and Policy Implications.* Lawrence Berkeley Laboratory. LBL-32652. January, 1993.
[197] Schafer, F. & van Basshuysen, R. *Reduced Emissions and Fuel Consumption in Automotive Engines*. Springer-Verlag: New York, 1995.
[198] Schmidt, F.W., Henderson, R.E. & Wolgemuth, K. H. *Introduction to Thermal Sciences: Thermodynamics, Fluid Dynamics, Heat Transfer.* New York: John Wiley & Sons, 1984.
[199] Schmits, K., Terhorst, W. & Voss, A., *Mathematical Modelling of Energy Systems,* Sijthoff, 1981.
[200] Schrödinger, E., *Statistical Thermodynamics*. University Press: Cambridge, 1960.
[201] Schurr, S. H. ed. *Energy, Economic Growth, and the Environment.* Johns Hopkins University Press: Baltimore, 1972.
[202] SEI: *LEAP, Long Range Energy Alternatives Planning System, User Guide*, SEI, Tellus Institute: Boston, MA, USA, July 1995.
[203] Sims, G.P. Hydroelectric energy, *Energy Policy*, october 1991.
[204] Slesser, M. *Macmillan Dictionary of Energy*. Macmillan Press, London, 1982.
[205] Smith, K.R. *Biofuels, Air Pollution and Health - A Global Review.* Plenum Press: New York, 1987.
[206] Smith, K.R. Fuel combustion: Air pollution exposures and health in developing countries. *Annual Review of Energy and Environment*, **18**, pp. 529-566, 1993.
[207] Socolow, R., Andrews, C., Berkhout, F. & Thomas, V. eds. *Industrial Ecology and Global Change.* Cambridge University Press: Cambridge, UK, 1994.
[208] Sørensen, B. A combined wind and hydro power system. *Energy Policy,* **9 (1),** pp. 51-55, 1981.
[209] Sørensen, B. Current status of energy supply technology and future requirements. *Science and Public Policy,* **14,** pp. 252-256, 1987.
[210] Sørensen, B. Energy storage. *Annual Review of Energy*, **9,** pp. 1-29, 1984.
[211] Sperling, D. *Future Drive. Electric Vehicles and Sustainable Transportation*. Island Press: Washington, DC, 1995.

[212] Tanzer, M. *The Political Economy of International Oil and the Underdeveloped Countries.* Beacon: Boston, 1969.
[213] Tester, J. W., Wood, D. O. & Ferrari, N. A. *Energy and the Environment in the 21st Century*, MIT Press: New York, 1990.
[214] UNDP/UNISE: *The UNDP Initiative on Sustainable Energy.* United Nations Development Programme (UNDP), New York, June 1996.
[215] Valero, A., Serra L. & Lozano M.A. A general theory of themoeconomics. *Proceedings ASME AES*, pp. 137-154, 1992.
[216] Van Beeck, N. *Classificationn of Energy Models,* Tilburg Univ. and Eindhoven Univ. of Technology, 1999.
[217] Van der Mensbrugghe, D. *GREEN: The Reference Manual.* OECD Economics Department Working Papers, No. 143, Paris, 1994.
[218] van Wees, M.T. & van Wisk, A.J.M. *Long Term Prospects of Energy Technologies: the SYRENE Programme Summarized*, Utrecht University, Netherlands, September 1995.
[219] Vogely, W. A. Energy Modelling and Policy Making: A Review. *Energy Modelling.* Special Energy Policy Publication, reprint 1976.
[220] Voinov, A.A. Paradox of Sustainability. Institute for Ecological Economics, Solomons, MO 20686, USA, 1997.
[221] Voss, A., Reuter, A., Elischer, Mueller, H. T., Saboohi, Y. & Schnabel, S. *Validation of the Integrated Energy Planning System MESAP* - A Country Case Study, University of Stuttgart, May 1990.
[222] Wagner H. M. *Principles of Operations Research with Applications to Managerial Decisions,* Prentice-Hall: Englewood Cliffs, NJ, U.S.A., 1969.
[223] Walker, J.F. & Jenkens, N. Wind Energy Technology. Wiley: West Sussex, England, 1997.
[224] Wark, K. *Thermodynamics,* 4th ed. McGraw-Hill Book Company: New York, 1983.
[225] WEC (World Energy Council). *Energy for Tomorrow's World.* Kogan Page, St. Martin's Press: New York, 1993.
[226] WEC (World Energy Council). *Efficient Use of Energy Utilising High Technology: an Assessment of Energy Use in Industry and Buildings.* London, UK, 1995a.
[227] WEC (World Energy Council). *Energy for Tomorrow's Wold - The Realities, the Real Options and the Agenda for Achievements,* Kogan Page; London, UK, 1992.
[228] WEC (World Energy Council). *Global Transport Sector Energy Demand Towards 2020.* London, UK. 1995b.
[229] WEC (World Energy Council). *New Renewable Energy Resources - A Guide to the Future.* Kogan Page: London, UK, 1994.
[230] Weinberg, C.J. & Williams, R. H. Energy from the sun. *Scientific American*, September 1990.

[231] Wene, C. O. Using a comprehensive model for community energy planning. *Spatial Energy Analysis, Models for Strategic Decisions in an Urban and Regional Context,* eds. L. Lundqvist, L. G. Mattsson, E. A. Eriksson, Avebury, Aldershot, U.K., pp. 271-295, 1989.

[232] Werko-Brobby, Ch.Y. & Hagen, E.B., *Biomass Conversion and Technology*. Wiley: West Sussex, England, 1996.

[233] WHO (World Health Organisation). *Health and Environment for Sustainable Development*. WHO, Geneva, 1997.

[234] Wilson, D. & Swisher J. Exploring the gap: Top-down versus bottom-up analyses of the cost of mitigating global warming. *Energy Policy,* **21(3),** pp. 249-263, 1993.

[235] World Bank. *Computer Tools for Comparative Assessment* (1999) http://www.worldbank/org/html/fpd/em/power/EA/methods/

[236] World Energy Conference. *Energy Terminology - A Multi-Lingual Glossary*. 2nd Edition, Pergamon Press: London, 1986.

[237] World Energy Prospects to 2020 (1998) International Energy Agency. http://www.iea.org/g8/world/index.htm

[238] Ybema, J.R., Lako, P., Gielen, D. J., Oosterheert, R. J. & Kram, T. *Prospects For Energy Technologies in the Netherlands*, ECN-C-95-002 (Vol. 1) and ECN-C-95-039 (Vol. 2), ECN, NOVEM: *SYRENE, Opting for Sustainable Energy Management Priorities for Research and Development*, Utrecht, Netherlands, March 1996.

[239] Yoneda, F. *Brief Sketch of New Earth 21 Model*, presentation to the CERT, IEA, March 1997.

[240] Zweibel, K. *Harnessing Solar Power: The Photovoltaics Challenge*. Plenum Publishing: New York, 1990.

Sustainable Energy: Resources, Technology and Planning

I.G. Malkina-Pykh
Center for International Environmental Cooperation,
Russian Academy of Sciences, Russia
&
Y.A. Pykh
Center for International Environmental Cooperation,
Russian Academy of Sciences, Russia

WIT*PRESS* Southampton, Boston

I.G. Malkina-Pykh
Center for International Environmental Cooperation,
Russian Academy of Sciences, Russia

Y.A. Pykh
Center for International Environmental Cooperation,
Russian Academy of Sciences, Russia

Published by

WIT Press
Ashurst Lodge, Ashurst, Southampton, SO40 7AA, UK
Tel: 44 (0) 238 029 3223; Fax: 44 (0) 238 029 2853
E-Mail: witpress@witpress.com
http://www.witpress.com

For USA, Canada and Mexico

Computational Mechanics Inc
25 Bridge Street, Billerica, MA 01821, USA
Tel: 978 667 5841; Fax: 978 667 7582
E-Mail: info@compmech.com
US site: http://www.compmech.com

British Library Cataloguing-in-Publication Data

A Catalogue record for this book is available
from the British Library

ISBN: 1-85312-939-9
ISSN: 1476-9581

Library of Congress Catalog Card Number: 2002110764

No responsibility is assumed by the Publisher, the Editors and Authors for any injury and/or damage to persons or property as a matter of products liability, negligence or otherwise, or from any use or operation of any methods, products, instructions or ideas contained in the material herein.

Printed in Great Britain byIBT Limited, London.

Contents

Preface

This book discusses some of the fundamental considerations associated with energy sustainability. It gives a broad introduction into major aspects of energy: the history of energy use by people, evolution of energy science, ideas and concepts, energy technology, energy economics and energy interlinkages with society. Global aspects of energy and sustainability issues receive special attention in the book.

Almost every individual, organisational, and societal activity is linked to, and dependent on, the use of one or more forms of energy. The development of a nation and the quality of life of its population are closely related to the amount and types of energy consumption. Therefore, energy use is a key requirement for achieving and sustaining the development of not only a modern society, but also a just society. In the face of an increasing world population, improving the standard of living in the developing countries, as well as maintaining the levels that have been reached in the advanced industrialised countries, will require a considerable increase in the world's use of energy. The challenge is to make this use compatible with sustainability. After receiving scant attention in Agenda 21, energy has emerged as one of the priority issues in the move towards global sustainability.

This volume contains eight chapters. Chapter one deals with energy through history, its development, energy scientific principles, and a brief overview on what is sustainable energy. Chapter two provides a description of systems analysis application to energy systems studies. Systems analysis is a multidisciplinary problem-solving approach that has evolved to deal with complex problems. The solution of the global energy problem cannot be postponed until a proven scientific solution is found, especially since such a solution may never emerge. In this situation systems analysis, based on energy models and various types of indicators and indices, may help in making the necessary decision. However, models and indicators will not lead to correct or validated results, but to reasonable suggestions or educated estimates.

Chapter three presents the important subject of energy resources and its distribution. This discussion is significant in that sustainable development requires depleting non-renewable energy resources at a slow enough rate so as to ensure the high probability of an orderly society transition to renewable energy sources.

Chapter four is devoted to the main aspects of energy technology. Many of the technologies needed for an energy revolution are virtually available but the pace of change will be heavily influenced by the ability of societies to overcome the policy barriers that remain.

Chapter five discusses the subject of energy economics. Subsidies to energy production and consumption, especially to fossil fuels and nuclear energy, constitute serious barriers to sustainable energy paths. Many obstacles persist in attracting private investment to sustainable energy. Energy has to be dealt with within the framework of a market economy but recent negative trends are often due to the globalisation and deregulation that impede or completely block sustainable energy initiatives, investments and policies.

Chapter six presents the main aspect of energy policy and planning. Energy supply and consumption are not ends in themselves. What people want is not energy but the benefits that energy provides: domestic needs (cooking, heating, lighting); community needs (clean water, sanitation, safe storage of food); and the productive sector (industry and agriculture, commercial transportation, communication and other economic activities). Making these three levels of energy services accessible worldwide implies that decision-making and change in energy policies should also come from each of these three levels, integrating supply and demand constraints into a sustainable pattern where efficiency and renewable sources play a decisive role.

Chapter seven provides a discussion of energy-society interlinkages. To promote sustainable development, energy systems should be environmentally, economically and socially sustainable. In practice, not all of these can be accommodated at the same time and trade-offs will often be necessary. Trade-offs should be determined through a multi-stakeholder process seeking the agreement of interested and affected parties.

Chapter eight concentrates on the main impacts of energy on the global environment as well as on the future global aspects of energy. The application of the principles of sustainable development to climate change has placed energy in the limelight. The direct links between energy and major global issues can be identified in at least three main areas: human development (poverty, population, health); environmental sustainability (climate change, acidification, land degradation, waste, competitive use of land for food and energy); and economic and geo-strategic issues (investment, foreign exchange impacts, R&D, fossil fuel reserves, energy imports, nuclear proliferation).

The volume also contains a Glossary of Energy terms that could be useful for all readers.

This text is written for both advanced undergraduates and first year graduate students in energy resources, technology and planning and such related areas as energy economics, energy - society links and energy impacts on global environment.

The book should also be attractive to the many professionals in industries concerned with energy technology, management and energy systems sustainability. These includes professionals in such diversified areas as energy project management, energy information systems, systems analysis and simulation of energy systems.

Irina G. Malkina-Pykh & Yuri A. Pykh
St. Petersburg, 2002

Chapter 1
History and Introduction

1 Energy Through History

Energy is inseparable from human life. The history of human civilisation began with the utilisation of tools and energy. In the early times, mankind led a life in harmony with the environment, without threatening the health of the earth's ecological system. However, with the advent of the industrial revolution, human consumption of energy, primarily of fossil fuel, has been on the increase. The sharp increase in energy consumption particularly in the past several decades has raised fears of exhausting the globe's reserves of petroleum and other resources in the near future. The huge consumption of fossil fuels has caused visible damage to the environment in various forms, for example, by giving rise to acid rain and the greenhouse effect. In today's modern industrial civilisation, which depends heavily on energy, humankind is confronted with an ambivalent situation. The more people seek to improve their standard of living, the greater the risk of destroying civilisation itself. As well, the risk is not only for human civilisation but also for all other forms of life.

Before the Industrial Revolution of the 1890s, human beings had only a moderate need for energy, which was met by their own physical strength.

About a million years ago, humans first learned to make and control fire and began to use it for cooking food and warming their dwellings.

Thousands of years ago, human beings also learned to use wind as an energy source. Wind is produced by an uneven heating by the sun on the surface of the earth because of the different specific heats of land and water. Hot air is lighter than cold air and the convection currents resulting from the difference in density produce wind.

By about 1200 BC Polynesians began to use sails to get wind energy to move their boats.

About 5000 years ago, magnetism was discovered in China. Magnetic force acts on certain materials such as iron. The magnetic compass became a useful instrument in navigation.

Electric energy was discovered by a Greek philosopher named Thales, about 2500 years ago. Thales found that, when rubbing fur against a piece of amber, a static force that would attract dust and other particles to the amber was produced which now we know as the "electrostatic force".

Around 1000 BC, the Chinese found coal and started using it as a fuel. It burned slower and longer than wood and gave off more heat. It served as an excellent fuel and continued to be used for centuries thereafter. When Marco Polo returned to Italy after an exploration to China in 1275, he introduced coal to the Western world.

1600s

The Netherlands was the first country to find coal in Europe, and it provided the fuel to England and other nearby countries. In the 17th century, England started producing coal on its own and supplying it to other countries.

During this period, Europeans also learned to capture solar heat in a closed room made out of glass (a greenhouse) to grow plants with the indoor warmth even in the cold weather.

1700s

Because most of Europe, especially England, had considerably diminished its forests by this century, it relied extensively on coal for fuel. Another of the main causes of the considerable demand for coal was the invention of the steam engine. Coal mines were often filled with water that leaked in from the surface and had to be removed by means of lifting up a bucket attached to a rope in order to proceed with the mining. Seeing the inefficiency of the operation, Captain Thomas Savery invented a steam engine in 1698. Its purpose was exclusively to extract water out of the coal mines. His steam engine operated by means of the pressure of the atmosphere and is therefore called an atmospheric engine. It worked by filling a cylinder with steam and then pulling the water when the steam condensed with cooling.

In 1712, Thomas Newcomen invented a more effective steam engine. Like the Savery steam engine, it was an atmospheric engine and was made for pumping water out of coal mines. However, it was simpler and more effective than the previous one. Instead of making the water from the mine directly fill the cylinder of the engine, the Newcomen engine pumped the water indirectly with exterior pumps. It was a powerful and economical engine that had the capacity of up to 4.7 million foot-pounds of work per bushel of coal. Later, its efficiency was increased to 9 million foot-pounds/bushel of coal by J. Smeaton.

A superior steam engine was developed by James Watt in the 1770s. Unlike the two previous engines that relied on only one operating cylinder, Watt's engine had two and operated with the flow of heat between the two cylinders rather than using the pressure of the atmosphere. Its efficiency was up to 20 million foot-pounds/bushel of coal, doubling the capacity of the

Newcomen-Smeaton engine. Watt's steam engine was not only to be used in pumping water out of mines. It soon proved to have the greater significance of being the driving force of the Industrial Revolution.

1800s

The Amazing Picture Machine During the 19th century, the world went through a great change as the Industrial Revolution that started in England spread to the rest of Europe, North America and other parts of the world. Characterised by mass production aided by machines and the supply of much clothing, furniture and many other products, the demand for energy increased remarkably. Also, new means of transportation were developed with the application of the new technology such as the construction of the first steam boat in 1807 and the first locomotive in 1804. This situation required the invention of more effective engines and cheaper energy sources.

While coal was being used extensively by the industrial movement, some scientists were already becoming concerned about the exhaust from combustion of the fossil fuel. Some of these scientists started developing natural energy sources as an alternative to coal. The energy sources include solar energy, hydroelectric energy, and geothermal energy.

An engine driven by solar energy was first developed by Mouchout of France in 1860. His solar engine consisted of a glass-enclosed iron cauldron with reflectors that concentrated solar radiation to boil water and to operate a small steam engine with the steam produced. After observing this engine, William Adams improved the solar engine by reflecting solar radiation with several mirrors to a copper boiler elevated on a tower. With a configuration of 72 mirrors it was possible to produce 3 times as much power as the Mouchout solar engine. Several other modifications made by Charles Tellier, John Ericsson, Henry E. Willsie, Eneas, and Shuman considerably improved the performance of the solar engines, but the engines failed to commercialise because of the widespread and relatively cheaper use of coal.

Small hydroelectric power plants were also constructed in the 19th century. Windmills that until then were used for pumping water or grinding crops were also developed in an attempt to produce electrical power. Geothermal energy began to be used to heat up houses and, by the end of the century, to produce electricity.

Another big change occurred when Colonel Edwin Drake managed to drill and extract crude petroleum oil out of the ground in Titusville, Pennsylvania. It was discovered that several useful products could be produced from petroleum, including kerosene, a gas that was ideal for lighting purposes, and gasoline, and a fuel that could be used for locomotive purposes. With the invention of internal combustion engines mounted on automobiles, petroleum gradually began to dominate coal in the energy industry.

The most fundamental driving force for the Industrial Revolution was the steam engine invented by J. Watt (1736-1819). The invention of a condenser, which separates the steam (working substance) from cooling water, contributed to decisive increases in the efficiency of steam engines (1769).

The energy resource in eighteenth century was firewood which occupied more than 95% in 1850. With the spreading of the steam engine, demands on iron rapidly increased and firewood, from which charcoal is manufactured, would be exhausted. Abraham Darby tried to utilise coke as an alternative to charcoal and succeeded in 1709. Since that time coal became the main energy resource of industries, because charcoal can be manufactured from coal.

1900s

Watt's engine had spread rapidly all over the world and small-sized engines were required by many kinds of industries. In 1887, Otto's four-stroke engine was developed, it was fuelled by gas and was so economical and much quieter that many inventors also tried to invent small-sized engines. Meanwhile, G.Daimler and C.Benz, independently, had invented engines with greater speeds that were fuelled by liquid fuel in 1883.

These events marked the start of the petroleum age, a commodity whose value was yet to be fully realised.

G.S. Ohm (1784-1854) discovered "Ohm's law" in 1826 and shortly afterwards J.R. Joule (1818-1889) found a numerical value for the mechanical equivalence of heat, in 1841, which was succeeded by J.R. von Meyer (1814-1879), who established the first thermodynamical law defining energy conservation in 1842. This period was full of interest and investigations into energy science and technology.

S.F.B. Morse (1791-1872) invented the telegraphic instrument which was the pioneering technology of the information age. Communications between England and Europe started in 1851 with submarine cables. On the other hand, J.C. Maxwell published his theory of electromagnetic waves in 1855, and 33 years later H.R. Hertz (1857-1894) carried out experiments demonstrating wireless telecommunication by electric waves.

The applications of electricity are thus classified into two groups. One is energy utilisation and another is communication. Of the two, energy application advanced rapidly. Examples include the invention of the battery in 1868 by G. Leclanche (1839-1882), establishment of the power generating station in 1881 by T. Edison (1847-1931), the A.C. generating station by Westinghouse Co. Ltd. in 1886, and three phase A.C. current with 10 kW capacity transmitted in 1887.

Industry utilised a large amount of electrical energy in electric lamps, electric motors, telephones, and aluminium manufacturing.

Beside these energy related industries, photographic technology, ammonia synthesis and cement manufacturing were also developed.

The French inventor Lenoir invented an internal combustion engine that used gasoline as fuel. It was a big relief for the oil companies since petroleum was not a preferred automobile fuel. Henry Ford later put automobiles into mass production, and the car started to become a common means of transportation.

The Wright brothers invented the first airplane with a gasoline engine, which ushered in an era of faster and cheaper transportation.

Modern Times

The frontiers of technologies in the twentieth century can be classified into three categories: (1) energy, (2) material, and (3) information. The most remarkable demand on energy at the beginning of the twentieth century was the rapid increase in utilisation of gasoline and oil due to the widespread use of vehicles. For example, the first jetplane flew only 34 years after the Wright brothers invented the First airplane. The rise of airplane transportation is one of the most distinctive developments of twentieth century civilisation. This was due to the invention of light and strong materials like duralumin (1907) and heat-proof alloys such as Inconel 700 and 713C.

More than 70% of the world's primary energy of world demands were met by coal in 1925, while petroleum and gas occupied more than 50% of world needs in 1950. It can be said that the twentieth century was the century of coal —> petroleum and iron —> plastics.

A few new materials that arrived in the twentieth century include Bakelite (invented in 1907), Acetate (1913), Polyethylene (1934), Nylon (1938) and other complex materials. All of them are manufactured from fossil fuels, but recently several ceramics have been recovered from the stone age to play important roles in frontier technologies. Glass-fibre is also indispensable in laser communication technology. These ceramics cannot be manufactured unless enough electrical energy is provided.

In 1942, the first nuclear reactor was successfully operated in E. Fermi's laboratories in Chicago. Since then nuclear energy has increasingly contributed to the generation of electric power. At the end of June 1991, there were 422 nuclear power stations in the world, and their generated electrical power totalled 343.41×10^6 [kW], which accounts for 16,470 of the world's generated power.

Kondratiev (1986) noted an interesting trend concerning the rise and fall of new technologies. A new technology gains more commercial acceptance and reaches a maximum if the technology succeeds in overcoming all difficulties and is welcomed by society. Then as it is gradually replaced by newly developed technology its amount of commercial trade tends to zero about 45 - 55 years after it was first introduced. This cycle is called "Kondratiev's cycle". It is often cited when discussing innovation and frontiers of technologies (Ohta, 1994).

The traditional relationship between technology and civilisation was established during this century. The term "traditional" means that the technologies that survived won the day without any restriction or constraint. Research and development were performed in every effort to invent cheaper and more convenient technologies and discover more abundant and economical resources. Such traditional principles as described above are believed to yield to Kondratiev's cycle.

However, it can be said that free competition cannot exist in the future as mentioned previously. Thus we can hardly predict the tendency of the cycle after 2000.

As the depletion of fossil fuels and the environmental damage caused by the pollutants produced become notable, scientists began to seek alternative sources of energy. Some of the types of energy sources that are becoming popular are solar, wind, hydroelectric, biomass and geothermal energy. Many of them had already been developed nearly a century ago, but are only now coming into widespread use. Nuclear energy is widely used today. Its potential is very attractive but the disposal of radioactive waste that is harmful to the environment is the main concern.

As we look over our energy's history, one thing is clear; the energy sources that have sustained human civilisation so far, namely fossil fuels, have been abused and are now rapidly becoming depleted. It is important for us to learn that whatever the energy source of the future turns out to be, we must learn to conserve and value it.

One of the most feasible developments for frontier technology in the twenty-first century which requires little energy and materials will bc life technologies such as genetic engineering. We expect that the trend of technology development and the supporting energies will be directed towards environmental protection and resource management, placing the preservation of life at their centre. The frontiers of development will be those described in this text.

2 Scientific Principles

2.1 Basic Energy Principles

The term "energy" was derived from the Greek "ergon" meaning "work". Ergon signifies not only work but also vital power, vitality, and vigour. The term energy is still often used to describe such a vigorous state. The Greek term "aergon" used to express depressed state yielded the name of the element "argon", one of the inert gases.

The word "energy" belongs to our daily vocabulary and usually refers to the ability to perform work. This is, as will be explained later, just one appearance of energy. It is not easy to give a precise definition of energy; it is a rather abstract notion. Each object ("system" in thermodynamic language) contains a certain amount of energy. Moreover, since Einstein's $E = mc^2$ it is recognised that matter and energy are equivalent. It is, however, impossible to determine the energy content of a given system and, therefore, ignorance remains about the energy of a system. This is not much of a problem; it is more important that changes in the energy content can be determined exactly. Such changes may result from two types of processes: (1) by performing work on the system or letting the system perform work and (2) by exchanging heat between the system and the environment (= rest of the universe).

Thermodynamics is a basic science that formulates the rules for the conversion of energy and matter from one form into another. It sets the physical limits for the evolution of and the developments in the world around us. In contradiction to the mechanical approach, thermodynamics indicates that economic growth leads to increasing disorder. More specifically, increasing the flows of energy and matter through society, as happens in the process of ongoing industrialisation, leads to progressive depletion of available energy and matter or, otherwise stated, to increased entropy. Excessive entropy production is reflected in natural disorders such as the greenhouse effect, ozone holes, environmental pollution, etc. Sustainable development can only be approached by imposing a close to steady-state lifestyle on mankind.

Energy is the driving force for the universe. Energy is a quantitative property of a system which may be kinetic, potential, or other in form. There are many different forms of energy. One form of energy can be transferred to another form. The laws of thermodynamics govern how and why energy is transferred. Before the different types of energy resources and their uses are discussed, it is important to understand a little about the basic laws of energy.

Thermodynamics, in general, is concerned with those physical and chemical phenomena which involve heat and temperature. From the practical definition, thermodynamics is the phenomenological theory of converting heat to work and understanding the role of energy and other properties of matter in this conversion process.

Thermodynamics - a system of rules and constraints describing energy conservation and energy transformations in macroscopic matter - originated as a practical science during the industrial revolution of the early nineteenth century. Thermodynamics was a useful guide during the industrial revolution. Today, we need to consider methods of energy production and the pollution they inevitably entail. The waste or exhaust heat guaranteed by the second law is unavoidable thermal pollution from all forms of energy generation. Other forms of pollution (such as greenhouse gases from fossil fuels) may contribute to climate change within your lifetime.

There are three laws of thermodynamics. *The First Law of Thermodynamics.* Toward the middle of the 19th century heat was recognised as a form of energy associated with the motion of the molecules of a body. Speaking more strictly, heat refers only to energy that is being transferred from one body to another. The total energy a body contains as a result of the positions and motions of its molecules is called its internal energy; in general, a body's temperature is a direct measure of its internal energy. All bodies can increase their internal energies by absorbing heat. However, mechanical work done on a body can also increase its internal energy; e.g., the internal energy of a gas increases when the gas is compressed. Conversely, internal energy can be converted into mechanical energy; e.g., when a gas expands it does work on the external environment. In general, the change in a body's internal energy is equal to the heat absorbed from the environment minus the work done on the environment. This statement constitutes the first law of thermodynamics, which is a general form of the law of conservation of energy.

Fermi (1936) asserts that "the first law of thermodynamics is essentially the statement of the principle of the conservation of energy for thermodynamical systems". As shown by both Poincaré and Carathéodory, in order to derive the first law, heat (Q) and work (W) must be initially defined, and equality of temperature must be assumed (Keenan & Shapiro, 1947). Poincaré uses these definitions to develop his statement of the first law: "in a cyclic process the net heat is proportional to the net work." This statement provides the basis for the existence of a property known as energy, whose change is defined as $dE = dQ-dW$.

The Second Law of Thermodynamics. A cyclic process is one that returns the system, but not the environment, to its original state. A closed cycle consisting of two isothermal and two adiabatic transformations is called a **Carnot cycle** after the French physicist Sadi Carnot, who first discussed the implications of such cycles. During the Carnot cycle occurring in the operation of a heat engine, a definite quantity of heat is absorbed from a reservoir at high temperature; part of this heat is converted into useful work, but the balance is expelled into a low-temperature reservoir and thus "wasted". The greater the temperature difference between the two reservoirs, which in a steam engine are represented by the boiler and the condenser, the greater the fraction of absorbed heat that is converted into useful work. It is, however, theoretically impossible to convert all the heat extracted from the reservoir into useful work.

In general it is impossible to perform a transformation whose only final result is to convert into useful work heat extracted from a source that is at the same temperature throughout. This statement is Lord Kelvin's version of the second law of thermodynamics. Another version of this law, formulated by R.J.E. Clausius, states that a transformation is impossible whose only final result is to transfer heat from a body at a given temperature to a body at higher temperature; in other words, the spontaneous flow of heat from hot to cold bodies is reversible only with the expenditure of mechanical or other nonthermal energy. These two versions of the second law of thermodynamics can be shown to be entirely equivalent.

The second law is expressed mathematically in terms of the concept of entropy. When a body absorbs an amount of heat Q from a reservoir at temperature T, the body gains and the reservoir loses an amount of entropy $S=Q/T$. Thus, in a reversible adiabatic process (no heat change) there is no change in the total entropy. If an amount of heat Q flows from a hot to a cold body, the total entropy increases; because $S=Q/T$ is larger for smaller values of T, the cold body gains more entropy than the hot body loses. The statement that heat never flows from a cold to a hot body can be generalised by saying that in no spontaneous process does the total entropy decrease.

In all real physical processes entropy increases; in ideal reversible processes entropy remains constant. Thus, in the Carnot cycle, which is reversible, there is no change in the total entropy. The engine itself experiences no net change in entropy because it is returned to its original state at the end of the cycle. The entropy gained by the low temperature reservoir is equal to the entropy lost by the high temperature reservoir. However, according to the formula $S=Q/T$, less heat need be expelled into the low temperature reservoir than is extracted from the high temperature reservoir for equal and opposite changes in entropy. In the Carnot cycle this difference in heat appears as useful mechanical work.

Just as the primary outcome of the first law is the definition of energy, the second law displays the existence of stable equilibrium states. Gyftopoulos and Beretta (1991) present three statements of the second law, each of which elucidate a different consequence of it.

Clausius (1850): "No process is possible in which the sole net effect is the transfer of energy from a system in a stable equilibrium state with a lower temperature to a system in a stable equilibrium state with a higher temperature."

Kelvin-Planck (1897): "It is impossible to construct an engine that will work in a complete cycle and produce no effect except the raising of a weight and the transfer of energy out of a system in a stable equilibrium state."

Carathéodory (1909): "In the neighbourhood of any given stable equilibrium state there exist stable equilibrium states that cannot be reached by any weight process that starts from the given state."

The Third Law of Thermodynamics. The so-called Third Law of Thermodynamics does not seem to some physicists as secure as the other two.

A postulate related to but independent of the second law is that it is impossible to cool a body to absolute zero by any finite process. Although one can approach absolute zero as closely as one desires, one cannot actually reach this limit. The third law of thermodynamics, formulated by Walter Nernst and also known as the Nernst heat theorem, states that if one could reach absolute zero, all bodies would have the same entropy. In other words, a body at absolute zero could exist in only one possible state, which would possess a definite energy, called the zero-point energy. This state is defined as having zero entropy.

The Third Law becomes important when we investigate the connection between thermodynamic quantities and the equilibrium constant for a chemical reaction.

When put together, these laws state that a concentrated energy supply must be used to accomplish useful work.

Many of us commonly think of energy as the ability of a system to do work. **Work** is said to be done when a force applied to an object, moves the object over a certain distance in the direction of the force, such as pulling or pushing a wooden block across your desk. Your muscles do work when they facilitate body movement. Units of work and energy are joules (J). One joule equals one newton meter (N.m).

Energy is a generic term for the faculty, power or capacity for doing "work" possessed by a body or a system of bodies. If the term "work" in this definition implies physical work, then the energy is scientifically defined. However, the exact meaning of energy was not established until the middle of the nineteenth century when kinetic energy was introduced. This is the easiest to understand. G.W. Leibniz (1647-1716) first proposed the concept that a moving body of mass *m* possesses "energy" by expressing

$$E = mv^2$$

instead of the term vital power used up to that time.

T. Young (1773-1829) subsequently published a book entitled *A Course of Lectures on Natural Philosophy* (1807) in which he stated "The term energy may be applied, with great propriety, to the product of mass or weight of a body: into the square of the number expressing its velocity". He recognised Leibniz's hypothesis very well.

A more advanced account of kinetic energy is due to G.G. Coriolis (1772-1843). His expression is

$$E = (1/2)mv^2$$

This was one of the most important steps in the establishment of the physical concept of energy.

During the development of modern physics, two remarkable innovations of the energy concept have been realised. One is the concept of energy quanta proposed by M.L. Planck (1858-1947) in 1900. He discovered that the energy of monochromatic light with frequency v has an energy

$$E = \mathrm{n}hv$$

where n is an integer and h is Planck's constant ($= 6.626 \times 10^{-34}$ Js). It exists in five kinds of energy among which only light energy has a special characteristic different from the other kinds, that is to say, the energy magnitude of monochromatic light varies discontinuously from nhv to (n ± m)hv, where m is also an integer.

Another important discovery was due to A. Einstein (1879-1955). In 1922, as a result of the theory of special relativity, equivalence between mass and energy was proposed through the relationship

$$E = mc^2$$

where c is the velocity of light ($= 2.99 \times 10^8$ m/s). This equation shows that the sum of mass and energy must be conserved in any energy conversion process, so that the sum of mass and energy in the universe remains constant forever.

By definition, work is an energy requiring process. So, how do you describe energy? Energy is not a substance that can be held, seen, or felt as a separate entity. We cannot create new energy that is not already present in the universe. We can only take different types of materials in which energy is stored, change their state, and harness the energy that escapes from the system in order to use it to do work for us. If the released energy is not used, it will escape and be "wasted" usually as heat.

Heat is a form of energy associated with random or *thermal* motion of atoms and molecules. At absolute zero, a system has no heat energy. Heat is additive. If two masses with heat energies of 5 joules and 10 joules are added together, the added masses will have a total heat energy of 15 joules. Heat and temperature should not be confused.

Temperature is an intrinsic property of a system. When a temperature of a system is equal to the temperature of its surrounding, it is thermal equilibrium. The amount of heat transferred, Q, when temperature in not equal is $\dot{Q} = mc(dT/dt)$, where m and c are the mass and heat capacity of the system, T is the temperature and t is time.

Temperature is not additive. Putting two metal blocks that are 75° C together will leave the new system at the same temperature. Putting two masses that are 50° C and 100° C will make the new system somewhere between 50° C and 100° C. The temperature of the combination would be dependent on the masses and heat capacities of each added element.

When a fast-moving molecule collides with other molecules, it loses some of its kinetic energy to those surrounding molecules. Those molecules now have more energy than they had before. This extra energy is manifested as vibrations within the molecule. Thus, the temperature of the substance being hit will increase.

Consider the explosion of gasoline in your car. The spark ignites the gas, causing combustion. Combustion of gas is the rearrangement of the carbon and hydrogen atoms in gasoline and oxygen in air into more stable forms, carbon dioxide and water vapour. The energy left over from forming CO_2 and H_2O propel these molecules to move faster, causing the gas to expand. The expansion of the gas causes the movement of the pistons in your car engine, which turns the crankshaft, which turns the wheels. The fast-moving gas molecules collide with the wall of the cylinder and transfer their energy to it. This energy makes the metal atoms of the cylinder vibrate faster or in other words heat up. The engine walls must be cooled to make it safe to operate. Oil and water from the radiator cool the walls of the cylinder. Air from the fan cools the water in the radiator, which is released into the environment as wasted energy. Wasted energy causes the efficiency to be much less than 100%.

Energy **efficiency** is the amount of useful energy extracted from a system divided by the total energy put into a system. It may also be thought of as the efficiency with which we are capable of utilising a resource. If we don't use the energy released from the chemical bonds in a resource, the energy goes into waste heat, sound, thermal vibrations, or light. The more energy conversion steps there are in a process, the more energy you lose as waste heat. For example, in order to run your car, the **chemical potential energy** in the gas must first be converted into thermal energy (or **heat energy**) by igniting the fuel. The thermal energy is converted to mechanical energy to make the engine run. This three-step process has an overall maximum efficiency of about 30%. That means that 70% of the energy initially stored in the gasoline was lost as waste heat, mostly in the form of thermal vibrations to the surrounding materials. This illustrates the importance of learning about energy and trying to find better ways to responsibly use the resources available to us.

To determine the efficiency of a process, a way must be used to measure energy. You cannot pick up energy, turn it around in your hands to describe it, or put it under your pillow to see how long it'll stay there. We do not use mechanical measurements (like how much of a certain resource is needed to make your car go so many miles at such speed) because different pathways and different machines have very different efficiencies. If we tried to quantify it mechanically, we may never know just how much absolute energy is in the resource itself. Therefore, we use the "heating value" of fuels: how using so much of a certain resource (rearranging its bonds into a more stable state) converts to so much heat (motion of molecules).

We all hear every day about counting calories. What is a calorie? A calorie (cal) is defined as the amount of heat needed to raise the temperature of one gram of water by 1° C. A food calorie actually consists of one kilocalorie, or 1000 calories. Why do we worry about calories in relation to our weight? Energy conservation! If you feed your body with more calories than it can use, it will store the energy in a stable state like body fat for you to use and lose later.

Energy is measured in other units as well. A common one is the British Thermal Unit, or **BTU**. One BTU is the amount of energy required to raise the temperature of one pound of water by 1° F. One gallon of gasoline contains about 125,000 BTU (see Table 1). A related unit is the THERM, or 100,000 BTU. Another unit familiar to physicists is the joule (J), equivalent to 0.239 calories or 9.47×10^{-4} BTU. Most systems of measurement throughout the world use joules to measure energy, even in food. When we speak in terms of energy, we often use the unit of **Quads**, which equals 10^{15} BTU. Another way energy content is often quantified is by converting the amount of energy of different sources to the amount in one barrel (42 gallons) of crude oil. Because the values are usually quite large, the equivalence is usually compared to so many *million* barrels of oil per day (MBPD). Burning 500 million tons of coal a year would be approximately 6 MBPD of oil for a year.

Energy has been the most important and useful concept to the study of physics and chemistry since the start of modern science. Lagrange's equation in mechanics, the Hamiltonian operator in quantum mechanics, and Gibb's or Helmholtz's in chemistry are typical examples. Natural phenomena occur along a path, which minimises the overall energy necessary for the process.

Table 1: The average energy contained in or consumed by some common items

Items	Average Energy In Btu
A Matchstick	1
An Apple	400
Making A Cup Of Tea	500
A Stick Of Dynamite	2,000
A Loaf Of Bread	5,100
A Pound Of Wood	6,000
100 Hours Of Television	28,000
A Gallon Of Gasoline	125,000
20 Days Gas Cooking Range	1,000,000
Food For 1 Person For Year	3,500,000
Apollo 17 To The Moon	5,600,000,000
Hiroshima Atomic Bomb	80,000,000,000
1000 Transatlantic Jet Flights	250,000,000,000
1 Year Energy 30 African Countries	1,000,000,000,000,000
Energy Used By World 1993	343,000,000,000,000,000

* Note that 10^{15} BTU = 1 QUAD

On the other hand, the concept of energy in society seems to be quite independent of scientific energy; it concerns the problems of petroleum, coal, natural gas, nuclear energy, and hydroelectric power, etc., from an economic point of view. Recently global air pollution, including climatic change, became a new energy problem. The primary solution to these problems is undoubtedly energy conservation, whose leading principle can be derived only from physics and chemistry. Associating the social energy problem with physics and chemistry is becoming more and more important but it does not always draw people's attention.

Three classifications of energy are possible. The first is based upon the behaviour, or state, that results from physical or chemical energy, such as electromagnetic energy.

The second characterises the energy systems used in society, that is to say, the sub-system of primary energy (energy resource) composed of fossil fuel, nuclear energy, and natural energy.

Secondary energy is the genetic name of energy that is processed (oil refining, conversion to electric energy, etc.) to be easier and cleaner to utilise. The main source of secondary energy is different in each country, i.e., about 40% electrical power in Japan, more than 40% in USA, and maybe about 10% in China, as of 1991. The share of electrical energy as a source of secondary energy has been increasing more and more. This trend shows that energy conversion to electrical energy is becoming increasingly important.

Utilisation systems are multifarious and technological improvements in energy efficiency are urgently needed. It should be stressed that one must select the energy source which is most appropriate to the utilisation purpose. Energy systems will be discussed in more detail in the next section.

The third kind of classification results from the primary energy source (resources). Energy resources are (1) fossil fuel (petroleum, coal, natural gas, tar sand, oil shale, and so on), (2) nuclear energy (nuclear fission, nuclear fusion), and (3) natural energy (biomass, hydropower, geothermal, ocean tide, ocean thermal, solar photovoltaic, solar heat, wind power, and so on). In 1992, the world's primary energy sources consisted of petroleum (38%), coal (30%), natural gas (20%), hydropower (7%), nuclear energy (5%), and other contribution (below 1%). However, these statistics do not include non-commercial fuels such as biomass in the underdeveloped countries. Each percentage is calculated based on its generated energy.

The classifications of energy could be as follows:

(1) Mechanical Energy: (a) Kinetic energy; (b) Potential energy; (c) Energy of fluid (gas and liquid).
(2) Energy of Electrical and Electromagnetic Systems: (a) Electrostatic energy; (b) Energy of parallel plate condenser; (c) Energy of electromagnetic induction; (d) Energy of electromagnetic wave; (e) Magnetic energy.
(3) Chemical Energy: (a) Cohesive energy of materials; (b) Density energy.
(4) Heat (thermal) energy.
(5) Photon energy (energy of light).

Table 2 gives different types of energy along with their definitions.

Table 2: Forms of Energy

Energy form	Definition
Chemical Energy	Energy stored in chemical bonds of molecules
Thermal or Heat Energy	Energy associated with the heat of an object
Mechanical Energy	Kinetic or potential energy
Potential Energy	Energy stored in a body or a system as a consequence of its position, shape, or state. This includes gravitational energy, electrical energy, nuclear energy and chemical energy
Kinetic Energy	Energy possessed by a material body by virtue of its motion
Electrical Energy	Energy associated with the movement of electric charge
Radiant Energy	Energy that is radiated. For example, the energy from the sun is radiant energy
Nuclear Energy	Energy found in the nuclear structure of atoms

2.2. Chemical Energy Basics

When we use a resource, such as coal, to produce energy, we are breaking the chemical bonds within the substance and rearranging them into more stable bonds. This change results in the formation of different products, such as carbon dioxide and water in the case of combustion, and a release of energy.

That may sound complex, but this analogy makes it really simple. Picture an old-fashioned water well. The molecule is at the bottom of the well. It takes energy to bring it to the top of the well (winding up the bucket). Think of the molecule as now being broken up into its atoms - the energy that was expended to do that is its binding energy, or the energy holding the atoms together in a molecule. One way to measure binding energy is the heat of formation. Now those independent atoms (at the top of the well) combine into other molecules that are even more stable. Combining means that they fall back down into a couple of new wells. These wells are deeper than the original well - there is more binding energy in these new molecules. When the atoms "fall down" into the new wells, becoming new molecules, energy is released. The hand-crank spins wildly as the bucket falls to the bottom. To figure out how much net energy is released, just compare the depths of the new wells to the old one.

A numerical example may help explain this. The combustion of methane to form carbon dioxide and water is represented by the following chemical reaction:

$$CH_4 + 2O_2 + \text{spark} \longrightarrow CO_2 + 2H_2O + \text{heat}$$

The heat of formation of CH_4 is -17.88 kcal/mol. The heat of formation of O_2 is defined as 0 kcal/mol. The sum of the heats of formation of the reactants (-17.88 kcal/mol + 0 kcal/mol) is the sum of the depths of the original wells in the previous example. Adding a spark to the left side of the reaction is analogous to cranking the bucket to the top of the well and expending energy.

Carbon, hydrogen, and oxygen atoms are now at the top of the well. They then combine into other molecules, namely CO_2 and H_2O. In combining, the molecules fall into new "wells" whose depths correspond to the heats of formation of the new molecules. The well for CO_2 has -94.1 kcal/mol, and the well for H_20 has 2(-57.8 kcal/mol) because there are two moles of water formed for each mole of methane burned.

With numbers, the equation above looks like:

$$-17.88 \text{ kcal/mol} + 0 \text{ kcal/mol} = -94.1 + 2(-57.8) \text{ kcal/mol} + \text{heat}$$

Now rearrange:

$$\text{heat} = -17.88 \text{ kcal/mol} + 94.1 \text{ kcal/mol} + 2(57.8) \text{ kcal/mol}$$
$$= +191.82 \text{ kcal/mol methane burned}$$

This means that there is 191.82 kcal per mole that is now expressed as heat and the motion of the products, CO_2 and H_2O.

2.3. Radioactivity Basics

The reader is undoubtedly familiar with the periodic table of the elements. When you read the atomic weight of an element on the chart, such as carbon at 12.01 g/mol, you are not reading the absolute atomic weight of the element. Instead, you are reading the *average* of the naturally occurring isotopes of carbon, some of which include radioactive isotopes. Remember that an isotope of an element has the same number of protons and electrons as the other isotopes, but has a different number of neutrons in the nucleus. This sometimes causes the isotope to be unstable and to radiate energy, or be radioactive. The **half-life** of a radioactive substance is the amount of time it takes for the substance to emit one half of its radioactivity.

Radioactivity is all around you, from the food you eat to the bricks in the buildings surrounding you. Radioactive elements that occur naturally are considered part of background radiation. Background radiation comes from anything that is part of the natural world that is around *all the time*. Because of this, you can easily conclude that *all* radioactivity is not bad. Rather, your body is bombarded with radioactivity every minute of every day, especially if you get lots of exposure to the sun. Several every day ordinary food objects are slightly radioactive, including table salt substitute and bananas. Check it out the next time you take your Geiger counter to the grocery store! Another common radioactive object sold in stores is the Coleman Lantern mantle, which contains thorium.

The "dangerous" radiation comes in eating or otherwise ingesting radioactive elements which occur in large concentrations, or from external sources which give a high dose.

Radiation is generally measured in units of **rads**, or radiation absorbed dose, which is equivalent to 0.1 J of energy emitted per kg of isotope. Another common unit of measure is the **rem,** or radiation equivalent for mammals, which is equal to a rad in most cases. To give you some qualitative idea, a dental x-ray produces the equivalent of 1 **millirem**. The natural background level of radiation you receive is approximately 200 to 300 millirem per year, depending on where you live. "Natural background" is composed of radiation from cosmic rays, the ground, bricks, stone in buildings, radon gas, medical procedures, and potassium in your body. The government limit of acceptable radiation for the general public is 500 millirem in a year, not counting what a doctor may prescribe for you. The first medical sign of radiation sickness occurs after a single dose (all at once) of 25 rem (25,000 mrem), although lower levels may increase the risk of developing cancer at some point in life.

Several types of radioactive decay occur to make an unstable nucleus more stable. **Alpha emission** is the loss of a helium nucleus (2 protons and 2 neutrons) which carries away a mass of four atomic mass units. The charge of the alpha particle is +2.

During alpha emission, the atomic mass decreases by four and the atomic number decreases by two. Alpha decay usually occurs in elements with atomic numbers greater than 82 which do not contain enough binding energy to hold together the massive nucleus. A typical alpha emission is the decay of a heavy isotope such as plutonium-239 to uranium-235.

Excess binding energy is given off by the kinetic energy of the alpha particle and sometimes by the emission of gamma energy. Gamma energy is emitted as photons and is a type of electromagnetic radiation.

Elements below atomic number 40 generally have stable nuclei with an equal number of protons and neutrons (1:1 ratio). As the atomic number increases from 40 to 108, the stable neutron to proton ratio increases toward 1.5 neutrons to 1 proton. **Beta decay** is the loss of an electron from the nucleus. Usually there are no electrons in the nucleus. During beta decay one of the numerous neutrons changes into a proton and an electron. This electron from the nucleus is called a beta particle and is ejected from the nucleus. During beta decay, the number of neutrons decreases by one and the number of protons increases by one. The atomic mass remains the same. Also note that the overall charge is conserved.

$$n^o = p^+ + e^-$$

The decay of carbon-14 into nitrogen-14 and a beta particle is an example of this type of decay.

Another form of radioactive decay is positron emission, the loss of a positron (positive electron) from a nucleus that has an excess number of protons. Elements that have a higher proton to neutron ratio than normal can decay by positron emission. Here a proton splits into a neutron and a positron (e^+). During positron emission the atomic number decreases by one and the number of neutrons increases by one as a proton is converted to a positron and a neutron. The atomic mass remains the same, and the overall charge is again conserved.

$$p^+ = e^+ + n^o$$

The decay of carbon-10 to boron-10 is an example of this type of reaction.

Gamma emission refers to the discharge of high-energy electromagnetic radiation from an atom. Energy loss in the form of gamma emission occurs when the nucleus is in an excited state and returns to its ground or normal state by releasing a gamma particle, or high-energy photon. During gamma emission, neither the atomic mass nor the atomic number change.

An example of this reaction is the emission of gamma radiation from barium -137m. The "m" stands for "meta stable", which means it is stable only for a limited time.

The type of radioactive decay which occurs in nuclear reactors is induced by particle bombardment and is called transmutation. This concept is the basis of fission splitting of the nucleus; and fusion joining of two nuclei.

Neutron bombardment is the process of "hitting" a nucleus with a free thermal neutron (one with the correct amount of energy) in order to split it into lighter products. Several products are possible when splitting the nucleus of an atom. A common example is the fission of ^{235}U in a nuclear reactor. Free neutrons are almost always among the products, which propagate the reaction with other nuclei, called a **chain reaction**. When ^{235}U is bombarded with very low energy free neutrons, a fission reaction occurs where the products may be krypton-92, barium-141, three neutrons, and possibly gamma radiation.

Many different products could have occurred as a result of the breakdown above. The criterion is that the numbers of amu's, protons, and neutrons of the products add up to that of the reactants, much like a chemical reaction. Note that the amu's add up: $235 + 1 = 92 + 141 + 3$, as well as the number of protons: $92 + 0 = 36 + 56 + 0$ and neutrons: $143 + 1 = 56 + 85 + 3$.

Another way to induce decay is by striking the nucleus with a helium nucleus, or **alpha bombardment**. When an alpha particle reacts with a nitrogen-14 atom, an oxygen-17 atom forms and the energy is released as a hydrogen-1 atom and gamma radiation.

Bombarding an aluminum-27 atom with an alpha particle produces phosphorus-30 and a neutron.

Proton bombardment is the bombardment of the nucleus with a proton. When lithium-7 reacts with a proton, two helium-4 atoms are produced.

3 What Is Sustainable Energy?

Until the last ten or twenty years, sustainable energy was thought of simply in terms of availability relative to the rate of use. Today, in the context of the ethical framework of sustainable development, other aspects are equally important. These include environmental effects and the question of wastes, even if they have no environmental effect. Safety is also an issue, as well as the broad and indefinite aspect of maximising the options available to future generations.

There are many who, at the dawn of a new century, see no realistic alternative to pushing sustainable development criteria into the front line of energy policy. However serious the greenhouse effect (which has taken on a political life of its own, regardless of the science), there is clearly growing concern about how we address energy needs on a sustainable basis.

A number of factors are indisputable. The world's population will continue to grow for several decades at least. Energy demand is likely to increase even faster, and the proportion supplied by electricity will also grow. However, opinions diverge when it comes to satisfying that electricity demand. Will it continue to be served predominantly by massive grid systems, or will there be a strong trend towards generation close to the points of use. It is a fascinating question, but either way, more large-scale grid-supplied power will be needed over the next several decades, especially in urban areas.

The key question is how we generate that electricity. Today, worldwide, 64% comes from fossil fuels, 16% from nuclear fission and 19% from hydro, with very little from other renewables. There is no prospect that we can do without any of these.

The term "sustainable energy" embraces a number of practices, policies, and technologies which seek to provide us with the energy we need at the least financial, environmental, and social cost. It could be divided into two major groupings: energy efficiency and renewable energy.

Energy efficiency encompasses the policies or practices which help to evaluate the full cost of our energy choices and which help us get more output from a unit of energy. Energy efficiency includes:

1. Demand-side management (practices or policies undertaken by energy planners that encourage users to employ energy more efficiently.

2. Integrated resource planning (practices that help energy planners and regulators evaluate the total costs and benefits of both supply-side (generation) and demand-side (end-use efficiency) options, in order to employ the mix which will provide energy at the least financial and environmental cost.

3. Generation, transmission, and distribution efficiency (practices and technologies that improve the efficiency with which electricity is generated and delivered to end-users. This category includes co-generation and efficient natural gas-burning turbines, among other technologies.

4. End-use efficiency (these are technologies or practices that improve energy efficiency at the level of the final user. This category includes nearly all electricity-using and thermal technologies, such as motors, lighting, heating, ventilating, air conditioning, and appliances. It also includes technologies that help conserve or better use energy, such as insulation and controls.

Renewable energy includes sources of power that are replaceable and often locally accessible. Renewable energy includes: Solar power (Solar power includes active, passive, and photovoltaic technologies and practices. Active and passive solar technologies use the sun's energy for cooking, space heating, and water heating. Photovoltaic cells convert solar energy into electricity); Biomass power (Biomass refers to biological sources of energy like wood and agricultural waste). Biomass energy technologies may burn these fuels for heat or power generation, or convert them to liquids (such as alcohol) or gas (such as methane) for later combustion. Also included under renewables are wind power, hydroelectric generation, and geothermal power.

Harnessing renewable energy must be the first consideration in sustainable development, but it cannot be the only option. We can certainly make much more use of solar energy, for direct application (hot water etc) and for conversion to electricity. However, the very fact that we seek the sun for our summer holidays testifies to its low intensity. Similarly, bad weather and night time underline its short-term unreliability. These two aspects offer a technological challenge of some magnitude. It requires collecting energy at a peak density of about 1 kilowatt (kW) per square metre when the sun is shining to satisfy an electricity demand which requires a relatively continuous and large-scale supply.

The criteria for any acceptable energy supply will continue to be cost and safety, as well as environmental considerations. Addressing environmental effects has cost implications, as the current greenhouse debate makes clear. But low cost electricity with acceptable safety and minimal environmental impact will depend substantially on harnessing technology.

Manufacturing high-efficiency solar cells is not a cottage industry; nuclear energy has obvious high-tech requirements for reliability and safety; and even burning coal becomes a high-tech operation under efficiency and greenhouse constraints.

Fuel cells promise to extend significantly the effectiveness of solar energy collection. But they are at an early stage of technological development and still require substantial, research and development input, although. they will be an important technology in the future. Because they depend on hydrogen fuel, which will probably be extracted from water, a considerable increase in electricity demand is foreseeable. However, this need not be continuous base-load supply as hydrogen can be accumulated and stored, and solar or wind generation may well serve the purpose. Even so, the safety implications of a hydrogen economy (which would maximise the use of fuel cells) still need to be addressed in the public arena.

The key word is transition: firstly, a transition from current wasteful practices to cleaner production and consumption patterns using energy-efficient technology; transition from dependence on fossil fuels to an environmentally friendly mix of carbon-free and renewable sources; and transition from the predominant supply-driven approach to a demand-side or "energy services" approach which emphasises issues like quality, affordability, reliability, safety and accessibility.

Efficient use of energy is the cornerstone of a more sustainable energy system. In order to hold carbon emissions to about the current level in 2025 and then cut them substantially, the world will need to double the current level of global energy productivity over the next four to five decades. Rapidly advancing technologies in areas such as lighting, glazing, refrigeration, electronic controls, and synthetic materials will help speed the pace of efficiency improvements.

Many of the technologies needed for an energy revolution are virtually ready to go. But the pace of change will be heavily influenced by the ability of societies to overcome the policy barriers that remain. The needed policy changes number in the hundreds, but most fall into one of following four categories:

1. Reducing fossil fuel subsidies and raising taxes on them to reflect environmental costs. Energy price reform is a prerequisite to the development of a sustainable energy system. In 1991, direct fossil fuel subsidies totalled some $220 billion a year worldwide. World Bank economists estimate that gradually

removing such subsidies worldwide would cut carbon emissions in 2010 to 7 percent below the projected level. The next step in energy price reform is to ensure that fossil fuel prices reflect their full environmental costs. One of the best ways to incorporate these into day-to-day economic decisions is to levy energy taxes so that the environmental cost is roughly embodied in the price consumers pay.

2. Focus research and development spending on critical new energy technologies. Nuclear energy and fossil fuels have traditionally dominated the portfolios of government research efforts. In the past, R&D funds for alternative energy were wasted on large, premature demonstration projects, but most governments now seem to recognise that smaller efforts to advance key technologies and cost-shared commercialisation efforts with private companies are more effective.

3. Accelerating investment in the new devices. The expansion of commercial markets for technologies such as efficient electric motors, wind turbines, fuel cells, and a host of other innovations is a key goal for policy makers who must catalyse market-driven, multi-year purchases so that manufacturers can scale up production. A government strategy to promote continuing development of new technologies can rely either on direct purchasing programs or on partnerships with private industry.

4. Channelling international energy assistance to developing countries. Most of the increased demand for energy over the next three decades is expected in developing countries so turning the energy market toward new technologies there is critical. The large energy assistance programs that earlier pushed them down the fossil fuel path need to be redirected. Some changes have begun at the World Bank. In recent years, for example, the organisation has increased its support for natural gas, apparently at the expense of electric power projects.

Many of the measures will require recasting the role of government. In most areas, greater reliance on the market and less direct government involvement are called for, although in a number of cases governments will need to set the rules, focusing on ways to ensure that environmental costs are considered when economic decisions are made.

Sustainability must be monitored "horizontally" on the ecological, social, economic, technological and cultural/political dimensions. But it also has to be checked "vertically" since energy sustainability criteria must address the whole energy cycle, from extraction to waste disposal.

Energy supply and consumption are not ends in themselves. What people want is not coal or oil, or even gasoline or electricity. They want the services that energy provides, basic components of human well-being and development.

It is, therefore, essential to focus on the end-uses of energy and energy services. Among these energy services one should include:

- energy services that correspond to domestic basic needs (cooking, heating, lighting)

- energy services that correspond to community needs (clean water, sanitation, safe storage of food)
- energy services for the productive sector (motive power for industry and agriculture, energy for commercial transportation, for communication and other economic activities).

Making these three levels of energy services accessible worldwide implies that decision-making and change in energy policies should also come from each of these three levels, integrating supply and demand constraints into a sustainable pattern where energy efficiency and renewable sources play a decisive role.

Wastes are a major concern in any consideration of sustainable development. In the case of solar energy, wastes are mainly confined to manufacturing the conversion equipment, and there are established methods for dealing with these. Burning fossil fuels produces primarily operational wastes, and, as yet, there is no satisfactory way to avoid or dispose of the greenhouse gases which result from this combustion. Nuclear energy produces both operational and decommissioning wastes. Although experience clearly shows that there is no technical problem in managing any civil wastes without environmental impact, the question has become political, focusing on final disposal. In fact, nuclear power is the only energy-producing industry which takes full responsibility for all its wastes, and costs this into the product - a key factor in sustainability.

Ethical, environmental and health issues related to nuclear wastes are topical, and their prominence has tended to obscure the fact that they are a declining hazard, while other industrial wastes retain their toxicity indefinitely.

Regardless of whether particular wastes remain a problem for centuries or millennia or forever, there is a clear need to address the question of their safe disposal. If they cannot readily be destroyed or denatured, this generally means their removal or isolation from the biosphere. An alternative view asserts that indefinite surface storage of wastes under supervision is preferable because progress towards successful geological disposal would simply encourage continued use and expansion of nuclear energy. It is often evident that ideological opposition to nuclear energy is more important to its detractors than dealing effectively with wastes to achieve high levels of safety and security. The wider question of alternative low-CO_2 means of producing base-load electricity tends not to be addressed.

In a 1999 OECD article, Long-term management of radioactive waste, ethics and the environment, Claudio Pescatore outlines some ethical dimensions of this question. He starts on a very broad canvas, quoting four fundamental principles proposed by the US National Academy of Public Administration. They resulted from a request by the US Government to elucidate principles for guiding decisions by public administrators on the basis of the international Rio and UNESCO Declarations which acknowledge responsibilities to future generations:

- The Trustee Principle: "Every generation has obligations as trustee to protect the interests of future generations".
- The Sustainability Principle: "No generation should deprive future generation of the opportunity for a quality of life comparable to its own".
- The Chain of Obligation Principle: "Each generation's primary obligation is to provide for the needs of the living and succeeding generations," the emphasis being that "near-term concrete hazards have priority over long-term hypothetical hazards".
- The Precautionary Principle: "Actions that pose a realistic threat of irreversible harm or catastrophic consequences should not be pursued unless there is some countervailing need to benefit either current or future generations".

From a national perspective, the security of future energy supplies is a major factor in assessing their sustainability. Whenever objective assessment is made of national or regional energy policies, security is a priority.

France's decision in 1974 to expand dramatically its use of nuclear energy was driven primarily by considerations of energy security. However, the economic virtues have since become more prominent. The EU Green Paper on energy security in 2000 put forward coal, nuclear energy and renewables as three pillars of future energy security for Europe.

During the 1990s the United Nations organised a number of major conferences on global issues directly or indirectly related to energy. In 1990, the Second World Climate Conference discussed the First assessment report of the Intergovernmental Panel on Climate Change (IPCC) paving the way for the Rio summit of 1992 also known as the Earth summit. In 1992, the UN Conference on Environment and Development (UNCED) held in Rio de Janeiro, became a bench-mark establishing for the first time at the global level the conceptual framework and the comprehensive strategy for action on sustainable development.

Following the Earth Summit, other global conferences reflected further on global issues completing this conceptual framework. The World Conference on Human Rights in Vienna (1993), the International Conference on Population and Development in Cairo (1994), the World Summit for Social Development in Copenhagen (1995), the Fourth World Conference on the Rights of Women in Beijing (1995) the Solar Summit in Zimbabwe and the Second Conference on Human Settlements (Habitat II) in Istanbul (1996) all these global conferences have discussed and agreed upon, linkages, principles and objectives that are related explicitly or implicitly to sustainable energy.

The Earth Summit, held in Rio de Janeiro in 1992, attracted wide international attention and brought together an unprecedented number of world leaders adopting Agenda 21, a program of action to be implemented by Governments, development agencies, UN organisations and independent groups in every area where human activity affects the environment. The issue of energy did not manage to reach strong consensus and concrete commitments at the Earth

Summit. A positive step towards the right direction was however initiated by Chapter 9 of Agenda 21 ("Protecting the Atmosphere: Making the Energy Transition"), which correctly points out that "much of the world's energy is currently produced and consumed in ways that could not be sustained if technology were to remain constant and if overall quantities were to increase substantially". Still, there were no strong enough arguments in favour of the need for a radical change in the field of energy. The Framework Convention on Climate Change (UN FCCC) signed by 154 countries in Rio and presently ratified by 164 (as of December 1996), echoed this rising awareness of decision makers and governments. During the first two conferences of the Parties (COP 1 and 2) more evidence was brought to the negotiations' table. Still, despite this growing evidence concerning the scientific knowledge in the area, the progress at the political level has not been sufficient. The Third Conference of the Parties (COP-3) to the United Nations Framework Convention on Climate Change (FCCC) was held from 1-11 December 1997 in Kyoto, Japan. Over 10,000 participants, including representatives from governments, intergovernmental organisations, NGOs and the press, attended the Conference, which included a high-level segment featuring statements from over 125 ministers. Following a week and a half of intense formal and informal negotiations, including a session on the final evening that lasted into the following day, Parties to the FCCC adopted the Kyoto Protocol, in which the parties agreed to binding limitations of greenhouse gases for the 38 developed countries and economies in transition (former Communist nations). A number of specific issues were clarified and finalised at the next (4th) Conference of the Parties (COP-4) in Buenos Aires, Argentina, 2-13 November, 1998.

After receiving scant attention in Agenda 21, energy has emerged as one of the priority issues in the move towards global sustainability. The application of sustainable development principles to the climate change issue has turned the spotlight on the contribution of fossil fuels to the creation of greenhouse gases. However, this is only one factor in the complex equation required to move society to sustainable patterns of energy production and consumption.

Chapter 2
Systems Analysis of Energy Systems

1 Introduction

Energy is an important factor in the world economy. Energy supply has an enormous impact on the environment, primarily through emissions, such as CO_2, SO_2 and NO_x. The fossil fuels oil, coal and natural gas dominate the global energy supply. In the developing countries, the demand for energy and the use of fossil fuels are increasing due to population growth and industrialisation. Fossil and nuclear fuels are finite resources and unreliable foundations for energy supply in the long run. A long-term environmentally sustainable energy system can only supply an energy demand that is low enough not to drain the world's natural resources. The energy system may be based on renewable energy sources, such as biofuels, solar energy, and hydroelectric and wind power. In many regions, there may be competition for land use between biofuel, timber and food production.

This would require a significant reduction of the resource consumption in the industrialised countries, which initially may be realised through more efficient utilisation of the resources, but a decrease in the material standard of living may be necessary. If the values of a clean environment and, possibly, global justice are considered, the total experienced benefit might, however, not need to decrease. Global justice requires that everybody only uses a fair share of the limited resources on earth. Each individual should ideally occupy an *environmental space* (cf. e.g. Alcantara & Roca 1999) in the form of resource consumption and environmental impact that does not exceed what nature can withstand and that does not intrude on the supplies for other human beings of current or future generations. The internalisation of external costs and profits may be a means to manifest the total gains of a sustainable course in monetary terms, which makes the phenomena obvious for managers and politicians. The exhausting of terrestrial reserves is an unfavourable foundation for long-term economic wealth. The development and manufacturing of technologies that are means to achieve a sustainable development may promote economic growth and industrial prosperity.

Today, a major trend in the industrialised world is market liberalisation. Like in many other areas of society, the currently increasing competition in the energy field may enhance the power of money at the expense of public influence, especially if utilities are privatised and merged. Free markets also for grid-based energy carriers, such as gas, electricity and district heating, may reduce popular influence on energy supply on local, regional and national levels. The circumstances, concerning which politicians can only *argue* increase at the expense of those that democratic bodies can *govern*. A public utility may be a political instrument to control heat and electricity supply and if it is sold, the elected assembly dispose of a means to govern energy supply. Instead, a special, separate interest gains influence.

Energy may be supplied in various ways. In a global context, it is essential to reduce the consumption of natural resources and to decrease the environmental impact of human activities. From a more narrow viewpoint, it is important for nations and companies to have cost-effective energy systems in ever more competitive surroundings. Measures that are taken to achieve these two aims may be synergetic or conflicting.

Centralisation of energy conversion required for heating and cooling to district heating or cooling plants may be environmentally and economically favourable because professional supervisors can control the operation of large, efficient units, and emissions of harmful substances may be reduced. District heating systems and industrial heat and steam demand may serve as heat sinks for co-generation of heat and electricity, which is more efficient than condensing power production. Energy-conservation measures may reduce the need for final-energy supply. Load management decreases the instantaneous electric power demand, which may stop the commitment of expensive and polluting, peak production units, such as gas turbines and condensing power plants in bad condition.

Sustainability requires a moderate energy demand. Through systems analysis, resource utilisation that nature can withstand may be found. Systems analysis may help finding energy systems that best satisfies the aims and increases often the understanding of complex systems. Through systems analysis, it may be determined how the available resources within a system boundary should be utilised to satisfy the aims in the best possible way. An unbiased comparison of alternatives ought to be performed. To be successful, a systematic method must be accepted as a relevant tool.

Planning should comprise goal definition, problem identification, information gathering including input-data collection for models, identification and comparison of alternatives (probably model calculations and result interpretation), reporting and decision making. However, the goals may be unclear, contradictory and shifting from time to time. Decisions may be made for indistinct reasons, and alternatives may be disregarded due to misjudgements.

By operational research, alternative actions in complex, uncertain situations, often concerning long-term planning, are evaluated and certain measures are recommended (Wagner 1969). However, a long time horizon for one kind of study may be a short time horizon for another type of analysis. Carbon dioxide reduction studies may be classified as short-, medium- and long-term if they comprise 15-20, 35-60 and 100 years, respectively. The short- and medium-term analyses concern primarily the transition of an energy system, whereas the long-term studies focus on the desired final system (Beaver 1993). But long time horizons are problematic. What appears correct today may turn out to be wrong tomorrow. There are fundamental limits to scientific findings, such as future prices and technological development (Groscurth & Schweiker 1995).

Models may be advantageous compared to human thinking alone because complex linkages between phenomena can be described and large amounts of data can be processed and, more or less, easily be updated and changed. Model building often reveals relationships that are not apparent, which results in a greater comprehension of the modelled object. In systems that involve large investments and environmental pollution, model computations may be especially beneficial because unfavourable installations and operations may cause immense negative consequences. In models, it is normally assumed that people behave completely rationally and that a perfect market exists, which is absolutely transparent and lacks monopolies and bureaucratic distortions (Groscurth & Schweiker 1995). Models may facilitate the understanding of correlations between system parameters (Hake et al. 1994). Due to frequently changing conditions and uncertain future circumstances, multiple computations with alternative input data scenarios should be performed. The effects of alternative values for uncertain parameters should be evaluated to find robust strategies, which are favourable in several scenarios.

Computer models can treat complex correlations between phenomena and helps in finding beneficial system designs. By model construction, the important parameters and their relations must be known and assumed to remain valid. The input must be complete, correct and consistent. It must be scrutinised that the output is reasonable. Energy models may reflect the planned economy of a single utility or many consumers that may find energy conservation, energy carrier switching and load management profitable compared to the energy supply cost. Environmental impact can be represented by emission limitations and uncertain external costs. Energy system optimisation models can consider many component combinations and present the system design and operation that best serve the objective, normally minimum cost for satisfying useful energy demand. Through scenarios and sensitivity analyses, the influence of varying conditions should be analysed and robust strategies may be found. It should be easy to test unlikely conditions that may show favourable but not obvious solutions, such as co-operation beneficial to many actors. Besides results, modelling gives insights to the involved persons and improves the understanding of system behaviour, which may be more valuable than the, after all, uncertain result numbers. Long-term studies are problematic because the foundations for costs may include new elements (e.g., environmental externalities) and discounting reduces the importance of future activities. A model must prove to be an adequate tool but many factors outside models must be considered by decision making.

In models there are factors that cannot change (constants), can *change* (parameters) and can *be changed* (decision variables) (Wilson & Swisher 1993). By computations, constants and parameters are supposed to be known whereas decision variables are unknown. Models mostly assume perfect foresight (clairvoyance) of future conditions but probabilistic models include stochastic variables. A computer-model designer must specify the subsystem to examine, select the appropriate aggregation level, as well as determine what parameters to consider and their interrelationships. One must have sufficient knowledge of the conditions, be aware of the governing parameters, and assume that they remain valid during the time period considered to design meaningful models (cf. Groscurth & Schweiker 1995). A good model should be easy to understand. It should be easy to detect errors and to compute the solution. Irrelevant details, which hardly influence system performance, should be omitted because they would make the model cumbersome. Very aggregated models may, on the other hand, neglect determinative details, such as time dependencies. In a large model, it may be difficult to comprehend the relations between the system components, and a simplification may facilitate the interpretation of awkward results. A too large model that is tiresome to use, and whose computations take a long time, may make the analyst reluctant to test conditions that he/she considers unlikely and fruitful but unorthodox system configurations may thereby be overlooked.

An absolute validation of a model is often not possible because there are uncertain input data and partially subjective assumptions, which are influenced by personal views. The model must correspond to the real system. Data, assumptions and relations must be complete, correct and consistent. The results should be an answer to the posed questions and show plausibility and consistency. It should be assessed if the outcome is reasonable, in view of historical experience among other things. Model behaviour under extreme conditions should be examined (Wagner 1969, Hake et al. 1994).

Systems analysis may be seen as a means of understanding situations rather than a technique for solving problems. The insights that are gained by modellers and decision makers during the modelling process are at least as important as the numbers the model produce. A model can be seen as an instrument for learning and may help suggest courses of action that might not otherwise be evident. Models may give reasonable qualitative suggestions rather than correct and validated quantitative results. Model results may help the understanding of system behaviour under certain conditions rather than being directly implemented (Wene & Rydén 1988, Williams 1993, Groscurth & Schweiker 1995, Grohnheit 1997).

Data quality must be assessed, as well as the goals and knowledge of people who collect and supply the data. Even if many input data are uncertain, it may be better to find the most accurate result that is possible to calculate with current knowledge than to make no quantitative assessment at all.

It is necessary to keep in mind to which systems a model is applicable. A model is a simplified representation of reality, but it is easy to believe that model results are as exact and true as they seem. One must guard against thinking of a model as being reality. Model results very seldom are in perfect harmony with the client's existing attitudes (Wagner 1969). Recommendations that are based on model results should be one of many means to support decisions. There are many aspects that cannot be included in a model (e.g., human behaviour) and that have to be considered before measures are implemented.

2 Classifications of Energy Models

In recent years, the total number of available energy models has grown tremendously not in the least because of the expanding computer possibilities. As a consequence, these models vary considerably and the question arises which model is most suited for a certain purpose or situation. A *model* is defined as a mathematical description – usually in the form of a computer algorithm – of a real system and the ways that phenomena occur within that system, and an *energy* model is a model with its focus on energy issues (van Beeck, 1999).

There are general characteristics which are shared by all models. For instance, any model will always be a simplification of reality and includes only these aspects that the model developer regarded as important at that time. Furthermore, Grubb et al. (1993) mention that any model dealing with future situations unavoidably makes use of estimates and assumptions which may or may not turn out to be valid under certain circumstances, but will at the time of application inevitably be uncertain.

The problem with classifying energy models is that there are many ways of characterising the different models, while there are only few models – if any – that fit into one distinct category. An example of a classification is given by Hourcade et al. (1996) who distinguish three important ways to differentiate energy models, namely regarding the *purpose* of the models, regarding their *structure*, and regarding their *external or input assumptions*. On the other hand, Grubb et al. (1993) use six dimensions to classify energy models, including 1) top-down vs. bottom-up, 2) time horizon, 3) sectoral coverage, 4) optimisation vs. simulation techniques, 5) level of aggregation, and finally 6) geographic coverage, trade, and leakage. Other ways of classification include (among others): the applied mathematical techniques, the degree of data intensiveness, the degree of model complexity, and the model flexibility (van Beeck 1999).

The nine possible ways of classifying energy models nine ways are representations of the main model distinctions found in the literature (see, for instance, Vogely (1974), Meier (1984), APDC (1985), Munasinghe (1988),

Kleinpeter (1989), World Bank (1991), Grubb et al. (1993), IIASA (1995), Kleinpeter (1995), Hourcade et al. (1996). The nine ways include:

1. General and Specific Purposes of Energy Models
2. The Model Structure: Internal Assumptions & External Assumptions
3. The Analytical Approach: Top-Down vs. Bottom-Up
4. The Underlying Methodology
5. The Mathematical Approach
6. Geographical Coverage: Global, Regional, National, Local, or Project
7. Sectoral Coverage
8. The Time Horizon: Short, Medium, and Long Term
9. Data Requirements

1. General and Specific Purposes of Energy Models

General purposes are the purposes that reflect how the future is addressed in the model. Hourcade et al. (1996) identify three general purposes of energy models:

a. *To predict or forecast the future*

Because prediction is based on extrapolation of trends found in historical data, forecasting models are usually only applied for analysing relatively short-term impacts of actions. A prerequisite for such an extrapolation is that critical underlying development parameters (e.g., elasticities) remain constant.

This approach requires an endogenous representation of economic behaviour and general growth patterns and is most often found in short-term, econometrically driven economic models.

b. *To explore the future (scenario analysis)*

Exploring the future is done by scenario analysis, in which a limited number of "intervention" scenarios are compared with a "business as usual" reference scenario. The alternative intervention scenarios are only relevant in the context of the reference scenario and rely on assumptions rather than parameters extracted from past behaviour. Generally, assumptions must be made about economic behaviour, physical resource needs, technical progress, and economic or population growth. Economic behaviour is usually represented or simulated either by a "least cost optimisation" (utility) approach or in terms of technology adoption processes. Sensitivity analyses are crucial to provide information on the effects of changes in the assumptions. The scenario analysis approach can be used in the so-called "bottom-up" models as well as the "top-down" models.

c. *To look back from the future to the present ("backcasting")*

The purpose of backcasting models is to construct visions of desired futures by interviewing experts in the fields and subsequently look at what needs to be changed to accomplish such futures. This approach is often used in alternative energy studies and can also be seen as a separate methodology. However, it is possible to use this methodology as an analytical tool for assessing the long run (economic) consistency of the alternatives. This way, the "bottom-up" models can be linked with the "top-down" models.

More specific or concrete purposes of energy models are the aspects on which the models focus, such as energy demand, energy supply, impacts, or appraisal.

a. *Energy Demand Models*

Demand models focus on either the entire economy or a certain sector and regard demand as a function of changes in population, income, and energy prices.

b. *Energy Supply Models*

Supply models focus mainly on the technical aspects concerning energy systems and whether supply can meet a given demand, but may include financial aspects using a least-cost approach.

c. *Impact Models*

Impacts can be caused by using certain energy systems or enact certain policy measures. Impacts may include changes in the financial/economic situation, changes in the social situation (distribution of wealth, employment), or changes in health and the environment (emissions, solid or liquid waste, biodiversity). Impact models assess the consequences of selecting certain options.

d. *Appraisal Models*

If there are several options they need to be compared and appraised in order to select the most suited option. Even if there seems to be only one option to be appraised there will always be the other option of *not* selecting the option which has consequences as well. The consequences or impacts of each option are compared and appraised according to one or more preset criteria of which efficiency (technical as well as cost) is the most commonly used.

Although there exist models that focus on one aspect only (such as some utility expansion models or environmental impact models) recent models generally have an integrated approach in the sense that they combine several specific purposes. Demand-supply matching models and impact-appraisal models are common examples of integrated models, but an integrated approach is also required to study energy-economy-environmental interactions. Also, almost all models include some indication of costs as a means for appraisal. Some models are constructed as a modular package, which enables the user to select only those modules (submodels) that are relevant.

Another aspect concerning the purpose is what form of energy the model addresses. Not all models include all forms. In fact, there exist many models which focus on electricity exclusively. On the other hand, some models that address "energy" as a whole, can not differentiate between different forms of energy and thus do not deal with the fact that not all energy forms are suited for certain purposes (e.g., there is no use in supplying more heat to the end-users if people want to use more electrical appliances.

2. The Model Structure: Internal and External Assumptions

Besides the purpose of models, the models can also be distinguished according to their structure, more specific the assumptions on which the structure is based. For each type of model, a decision has to be made on which assumptions will be embedded in the model structure (the implicit or internal assumptions) and which are left to be determined by the user (i.e., external or input assumptions). Hourcade et al. (1996) distinguish four independent dimensions with which the structure of models can be characterised:

a. *The degree of endogenisation*

Endogenisation means the attempt to incorporate all parameters within the model equations so as to minimise the number of exogenous parameters. Predictive models have endogenised behaviour, while exploring or backcasting models use external (or input) assumptions about behaviour which make them more suited to simulate the effects of changes in historical patterns.

b. *The extent of the description of the non-energy sector components of the economy*

Non-energy sector components include investment, trade, consumption of non-energy goods and services, income distribution, and more. The more detailed the model's description of the non-energy sectors, the more suitable the model is for analysing the extent to which energy policy measures affect the entire economy.

c. *The extent of the description of energy end-uses*

The more detailed the model's description of energy end-uses, the more suitable the model is for analysing the technological potential for energy efficiency.

d. *The extent of the description of energy supply technologies*

The technological potential for fuel substitution and new supply technologies can best be analysed if the model allows for a detailed description of technologies. Most models with an economic background represent technology only in a highly aggregated manner, treating it as a black box. This makes them less suited for analysing different supply technologies.

For each of the four dimensions there is a range from "more" to "less" and each energy model can be ranked somewhere on that range. Hourcade et al. state that, because the dimensions are independent, it is practically impossible to classify existing models in only one classification scheme or dimension that uses only one range.

As far as parameter values are not assumed within the energy model, the model users themselves will have to make external assumptions about these parameters. According to Hourcade et al. (1996), external assumptions often include assumptions about:

a. *Population growth*

Other things being equal, population growth increases energy demand.

b. *Economic growth*

Economic growth generally causes an increase in activities for which energy is needed (this does not have to imply, however, that energy demand increases because energy efficiency might increase at the same time). Another consequence of economic growth is that it reduces the economic lifetime of energy-using equipment.

c. *Energy demand*

Energy demand is influenced by structural changes in an economy because different sectors have different energy intensities. Furthermore, the choice of technology and the associated energy efficiency affect the demand for energy.

d. *Energy supply*

Energy supply is determined by the short-term availability of alternative resource supplies as well as by backstop technologies which give an indication of the cost at which an infinite alternative supply of energy becomes available (and thus provide information on the maximum cost of a policy).

e. *Price and income elasticities of energy demand*

Elasticities measure the relative change in energy demand, given relative changes in energy prices and in incomes. Higher elasticities imply larger changes in energy use.

f. *Existing tax system and tax recycling*

Taxes can have large impacts on the total costs of energy systems.

If all the parameters of a model have to be determined exogenously, the model would be no more than a computational device, albeit an extremely flexible one. On the other hand, there will always have to be at least one external parameter. In practice, energy models will be placed somewhere between these two extremes.

3. The Analytical Approach: Top-Down vs. Bottom-Up

The distinction between top-down and bottom-up models is particularly interesting because they tend to produce opposite outcomes for the same problem. Hourcade et al. (1996) and in particular Grubb et al. (1993) provide useful information on this subject. According to Hourcade et al., the differences in outcomes of top-down and bottom-up models stem from the distinct manners in which these two types of models treat the adoption of technologies, the decision-making behaviour of economic agents, and how markets and economic institutions actually operate over a given period of time.

Grubb et al. (1993) state that the top-down approach is associated with –but not exclusively restricted to – the "pessimistic" *economic paradigm*, while the bottom-up approach is associated with the "optimistic" *engineering paradigm*. Therefore, the latter is also referred to as the *engineering approach*.

Economics regards technology as a set of techniques by which inputs such as capital, labour, and energy can be transferred into useful outputs. The "best" or most optimal techniques (defined by efficient markets) determine the so-called economic "production frontier" which can be constructed by observing actual behaviour. No investments are possible beyond this frontier. However, it is possible to move the frontier towards the origin by means of technological progress.

A purely economic model has no explicit representation of technologies, but uses elasticities which implicitly reflect the technologies. Hourcade et al. (1996) state that technological change in most economic models is represented by the "autonomous energy efficiency index" (AEEI) and the "elasticity of substitution" between the aggregate inputs to households and firms. Stated otherwise, technology is treated as a black box, which makes it difficult to convert detailed technological projections into the production functions of these models.

Engineering studies, on the other hand, are independent of observed market behaviour. They describe the techniques, the performances, and the direct costs of all technological options in order to identify possibilities for improvement. In practice, the technological potential differs from the "best" technologies that represent the economic production frontier in economic models. The difference arises due to the fact that the engineering approach tends to ignore existing constraints, while the economic production frontier is based on market behaviour. According to Grubb et al. (1993), these constraints include hidden costs, costs of implementation measures, market imperfections, macro-economic relationships (multiplier effects, price effects), and macro-economic indicators (GNP, employment). Market behaviour can be regarded as a result of the existence of these constraints. Therefore, models which are based on data derived from actual behaviour are believed to automatically include existing constraints. However, promoters of the bottom-up approach argue that appropriate policy measures would reduce the constraints substantially, making existing consumer behaviour no longer an adequate measure.

Another characteristic of top-down models is that they use aggregated data to examine interactions between the energy sector and other sectors of the economy, and to examine the overall macro-economic performance of the economy. This is done by endogenising behavioural relationships as much as possible.

Past behaviour can then be extrapolated into the future, which makes top-down models suitable for predictive purposes on the short term.

In contrast, bottom-up models usually focus on the energy sector exclusively, and use highly disaggregated data to describe energy end-uses and technological options in detail. According to Hourcade et al. (1996), bottom-up models can be further subdivided into descriptive and prescriptive models.

Descriptive models try to provide a practical estimate of the technology mix that would result from actual decisions, based on factors such as complex preferences, intangible costs, capital constraints, attitudes to risk, uncertainty, and market barriers. Prescriptive studies, on the other hand, provide an estimate for the technological potential by examining the effects of acquiring only the most efficient existing technologies (or of minimising explicit costs for a given service at a system level). As a consequence, descriptive models are typically less optimistic than prescriptive studies. In a sense, the purpose of descriptive models tends towards prediction and it can be seen as an attempt to bridge the gap between the engineering paradigm and the economic paradigm, while the purpose of prescriptive models tends more towards exploration.

So, as Hourcade et al. summarise (1996), in general top-down models can only be used "if historical development patterns and relationships among key underlying variables hold constant for the projection period" i.e., there is no discontinuity in historical patterns. Bottom-up models, on the other hand, are suited only "if there are no important feedbacks between the structural evolution of a particular sector in a strategy and the overall development pattern" i.e., if interactions between the energy sector and the other sectors are negligible.

The very first energy models for policy making were probably of a highly aggregated top-down kind with a purely economic approach used for predictive purposes. The production functions which were used in these models dealt with technology as a black box and included only a general variable to represent energy demand. As a response, the early bottom-up models were developed specifically for purposes that could not be performed by the early top-down models, such as simulation and backcasting. These bottom-up models are assumed to originate from the engineering models that were used by utilities for planning their energy production. Regarding the model structure, early top-down models score typically high on the dimensions I (degree of endogenisation) and II (description of other sectors), while early bottom-up models score high on dimensions III (description of energy end-use) and IV (description of energy supply technologies). Today, the clear distinction between top-down and bottom-up is diminishing as more "hybrid" models become available in which the two approaches have been merged. For instance, many top-down models now also allow for simulations. This implies that different outcomes must then be ascribed to differences in external or input assumptions rather than differences in model structure.

Concluding, the distinction between top-down and bottom-up can generally be typified as the distinction between aggregated and disaggregated models respectively, or as the distinction between models with a maximum degree of endogenised behaviour and models with a minimum degree. Furthermore, (early) top-down models are generally used for prediction purposes, while bottom-up models are mainly used for exploring purposes. The different aspects associated with top-down and bottom-up models are summarised in Table 3.

4. The Underlying Methodology

Methodologies used for the concrete development of energy models can be found in, among others, APDC (1985), Grubb et al. (1993), IIASA (1995), Kleinpeter (1995), Hourcade et al. (1996). Below, an overview is given of commonly used methodologies found in the above literature. These methodologies include 1) econometric, 2) macro-economic, 3) economic equilibrium, 4) optimisation, 5) simulation, 6) spreadsheet, 7) backcasting, and 8) multi-criteria methodologies. In practice, the distinction is not always clear.

Table 3. Characteristics of top-down models and bottom-up models (van Beeck, 1999).

Top-Down Models	*Bottom-Up Models*
use an "economic approach"	use an "engineering approach"
give pessimistic estimates on "best" performance	give optimistic estimates on "best" performance
can not explicitly represent technologies	allow for detailed description of technologies
reflect available technologies adopted by the market	reflect technical potential
the "most efficient" technologies are given by the production frontier (which is set by market behaviour)	efficient technologies can lie beyond the economic production frontier suggested by market behaviour
use aggregated data for predicting purposes	use disaggregated data for exploring purposes
are based on observed market behaviour	are independent of observed market behaviour
Disregard the technically most efficient technologies available, thus underestimate potential for efficiency improvements	disregard market thresholds (hidden costs and other constraints), thus overestimate the potential for efficiency improvements
Determine energy demand through aggregate economic indices (GNP, price elasticities), but vary in addressing energy supply	represent supply technologies in detail using disaggregated data, but vary in addressing energy consumption
Endogenise behavioural relationships	assess costs of technological options directly
Assumes there are no discontinuities in historical trends	assumes interactions between energy sector and other sectors is negligible

For instance, the literature make a distinction between simulation, optimisation, and spreadsheet methods usually only when referring to bottom-up models, while recent economic top-down models use optimisation and simulation techniques as well. On the other hand, econometric, macro-economic, and economic equilibrium methods are generally only applied in top-down models, although there are exceptions here also.

a. *Econometric Models*

Econometrics is defined as "applying statistical techniques in dealing with problems of an economic nature" (Kleinpeter 1995). Econometric methodologies are methodologies that apply statistical methods to extrapolate past market behaviour into the future. They rely on aggregated data that have been measured in the past to predict the short- or medium-term future in terms of labour, capital, or other inputs. They are also frequently used to analyse energy-economy interactions. So, generally, the purpose of econometric models is to predict the future as accurately as possible using measured parameters. Although early energy (demand) models were purely econometrics based, nowadays econometric methodologies are mainly used as parts of macro-economic models.

A disadvantage of this methodology is that it does not have a representative set of technology options, in fact it does not represent specific technologies at all. Also, since variables are based on past behaviour, a reasonable stability of economic behaviour is required. Finally, Munasinghe (1988) as well as the APDC (1985) state that econometric models can only be used by experienced econometricians and have rather high data requirements. Long term effects can only be addressed by increasing the aggregation level in order to reduce the fluctuations over time.

The APDC (1985) mentions another methodology similar to the econometric one, namely "trend analysis". Trend analysis also extrapolates past trends of energy-economic activity and energy per capita ratios but has less stringent data (and formal) requirements. However, trend analysis is not suited for policy analysis partly due to the fact that it requires highly aggregated data (to reduce fluctuations in behaviour over time) and does not allow for energy-economy feedbacks. It cannot capture structural change and does not explain determinants of energy demand.

b. *Macro-Economic Models*

The macro-economic methodology focuses on the entire economy of a society and on the interaction between the sectors. It is often applied in energy demand analysis when taken from a neo-Keynesian perspective (i.e., output is demand determined). Input-Output tables are used to describe transactions among economic sectors and assist in analysis of energy-economy interactions. The Input-Output approach can be used only when the assumptions of constant returns to scale as well as the possibility of perfect aggregation hold. Macro-economic models are often developed for exploring purposes, using assumed parameter and scenarios which do not necessarily have to reflect reality.

Often macro-economic models do not concentrate on energy specifically but on the economy as a whole, of which energy is only a (small) part. Therefore, some do not regard macro-economic models as energy models.

Similar to the econometric methodology, the macro-economic methodology has the disadvantage that it does not represent specific technologies and requires a relatively high level of expertise. Also, effects of intertemporal preferences and long-term expectations are not taken into account, which results in a rather static representation of technical change.

c. *Economic Equilibrium Models*

Where econometric and macro-economic methods are mainly applied to study the short or medium term effects, economic equilibrium methodologies focus on the medium to long term. They are used to study the energy sector as part of the overall economy and focus on interrelations between the energy sector and the rest of the economy. Economic equilibrium models are sometimes also referred to as resource allocation models.

There is a distinction between partial equilibrium models on the one hand, and general equilibrium models or optimal growth models on the other. Partial equilibrium models only focus on equilibria in parts of the economy, such as the equilibrium between energy demand and supply. General equilibrium models are particularly concerned with the conditions which allow for simultaneous equilibrium in all markets, as well as the determinants and properties of such an economy-wide set of equilibria. According to Slesser (1982), general equilibrium models consider simultaneously all the markets in an economy, allowing for feedback effects between individual markets. Economic equilibrium methodologies are used to simulate very long-term growth paths and do not systematically rely on econometric relationships but are instead benchmarked on a given year in order to guarantee consistency of parameters. They rely on (neo-classical) perfect market equilibrium assumptions; output is determined by supply and markets "clear" (there exists no structural unemployment). The disadvantage of these models is that they do not provide adequate information on the time path towards the new equilibrium, implying that transition costs are understated.

d. *Optimisation Models*

Optimisation methodologies are used to optimise energy investment decisions endogenously (i.e., the results are directly determined by the input). The outcome represents the best solution for given variables while meeting the given constraints. Optimisation is often used by utilities or municipalities to derive their optimally investment strategies. Furthermore, in national energy planning, it is used for analysing the future of an energy system. Underlying assumption of optimisation methodologies is that all acting agents behave optimally under given constraints. According to DHV (1984), disadvantages are that optimisation models require a relatively high level of mathematical knowledge and that the included processes must be analytically defined. Optimisation models often use linear programming techniques.

By optimisation, there is a quest for the best system design or operation according to some criterion, for example, minimum cost, emissions, or oil supply. Optimisation enables a simultaneous consideration of the multitude of component configurations that may be constructed with the available menu of equipment, and the best system subject to the defined aims can be found. An energy system optimisation model has an objective function, which may be minimised, and mostly great technical detail of energy sources and supply and demand-side technologies but does not consider economic effects outside the energy sector. Normally, the cost for satisfying the useful-energy demand is minimised but emission or primary-energy minimisation can be made with some models. Such objectives may be supplemented by a cost limitation to produce realistic results.

Kram (1994) made an overview of MARKAL (e.g., Kram & Hill 1996), which largely is generally applicable to energy system optimisation models that use linear programming for cost minimisation and that can include emission limits. Other models of this sort are MODEST (Henning 1998), EFOM (e.g., Grohnheit 1997) and TIMES (ETSAP 2000). In these kind of models, technologies and operation are selected according to least total cost as long as constraints, such as capacity and emissions limitations, are satisfied. Seasonal and diurnal fluctuations are sometimes considered in detail, for instance in MODEST (Henning 1998).

Energy system optimisation models are often used to find least-cost strategies for providing energy services. The analyses consider alternatives that can change energy supply and demand and recommend the implementation of new technologies that are economically beneficial (Wilson & Swisher 1993). Normally, higher energy costs do not cause reduced energy-*service* demand. That is, useful-energy demand is fixed but final-energy demand may be reduced through technical energy conservation and energy carrier switching. Energy-conserving measures with various costs and potentials may be considered. At higher energy supply costs, more costly efficiency improvements would be profitable. The purpose of the energy use is assumed not to be influenced by these measures.

An energy system optimisation model may reflect a perfect, planned economy or a perfect, free market. In the first case, there is an administrative body that knows everything about the energy system and all potential actions, that makes the optimal kinds of investments at the right occasions and to the correct extent, and that controls the systems to achieve its optimal operation. In the latter case of perfect competition, all energy suppliers and users are assumed to be aware of the their current cost for energy supply and use, as well as the costs and characteristics of their own abilities to influence energy supply and use, and they take all measures at the times and to the extents that are most profitable for themselves. Supply and demand-side measures are, thus, in both cases assumed to be taken rationally. The planning situation applies when the energy supply of a single utility is studied and the market interpretation is preferable when the supply side comprises many actors or demand-side measures (energy conservation, energy carrier switching and load management) are considered.

The demand-side measures can also, with a planning-oriented perspective, be viewed as demand-side management (DSM), that is, as measures that are introduced through initiatives from the utility that supplies energy. In this case, the demand-side measures may even be paid by the utility because this expenditure would reduce its total costs. In a deregulated market however, a utility may help consumers to change their demand, just like any other consultant, but it would be risky for a utility to invest in demand-side measures, from which the utility would not benefit if the consumer changes supplier (cf. Bakken & Lucas 1996). If utilities do not implement DSM, demand-side measures may be introduced by the consumers because they find it profitable compared to the energy supply cost. Here, the demand-side measures may also be viewed as price-induced reduction of the demand for energy (conservation), a certain energy form (energy carrier switching) or electric power (load management). The consumer experiences an energy price that makes it profitable to change the energy use. The information on energy cost is transmitted to every part of the model and may be obtained as marginal costs (shadow prices, e.g., Andersson 1994, Andersson & Karlsson 1996). Although a global optimisation is made, the decision to take a measure may be interpreted as being made at the point where the cost is apparent and the measure works. For instance, a house-owner decides to buy a wood-fired boiler instead of an electric one.

e. *Simulation Models*

According to the World Energy Conference (1986), simulation models are descriptive models based on a logical representation of a system, and they are aimed at reproducing a simplified operation of this system. A simulation model is referred to as static if it represents the operation of the system in a single time period; it is referred to as dynamic if the output of the current period is affected by evolution or expansion compared with previous periods. Simulation models are especially helpful in cases where it is impossible or extremely costly to do experiments on the system itself. A disadvantage is that simulation models tend to be rather complex. They are often used in scenario analysis.

f. *Spreadsheet Models (Tool Boxes)*

In the literature the spreadsheet methodology is often mentioned as a separate (bottom-up) methodology (see, for instance, Grubb (1993), Hourcade (1996)). Although the models all make use of spreadsheets (as the term suggests), this term may cause some confusion because other methodologies also frequently use spreadsheet programs as a basis. What is meant by spreadsheet models is a highly flexible model which, according to Munasinghe (1988) is actually more like a software package to generate models than a model per se. The World Bank (1991) refers to spreadsheet models as "tool boxes" which often include a reference model that can easily be modified according to individual needs.

g. *Backcasting Models*

The backcasting methodology is used to construct visions of desired futures by interviewing experts in the fields and subsequently by looking at which trends are required or need to be broken to accomplish such futures. This approach is often used in alternative energy studies. For instance, the Dutch interdepartmental research program Sustainable Technological Development (STD) uses backcasting to explore the (technological) requirements for certain desired futures (STD, 1998).

i. *Multi-criteria Models*

The multi-criteria methodology can be used for including other criteria than just economic efficiency alone. It enables you to include quantitative as well as qualitative data in the analysis. This approach is not yet widely applied in energy models. Two examples of application can be found in studies conducted by Georgopoulou (1997) and Georgopoulou (1998).

5. The Mathematical Approach

At the level of concrete models, a further distinction can be made regarding the mathematical approach or procedures applied in the models (see, for example, IIASA (1995), and Kleinpeter (1995)). Commonly applied techniques include linear programming, mixed integer programming, and dynamic programming. Of course, combinations of techniques within a model are also possible. Mathematical techniques that only recently have been applied to energy planning, such as multi-criteria techniques and fuzzy logic, are not addressed here.

a. *Linear Programming (LP)*

Linear programming is a practical technique for finding the arrangement of activities which maximises or minimises a defined criterion, subject to the operative constraints (Slesser 1982). All relationships are expressed in fully linearised terms. Linear Programming can be used, for instance, to find the most profitable set of outputs that can be produced with given type input and given output prices. The technique can deal only with situations where activities can be expressed in the form of linear equalities or inequalities, and where the criterion is also linear. LP is a relatively simple technique which gives quick results and demands little mathematical knowledge of the user.

Disadvantages are that all coefficients must be constant and that LP results in choosing the cheapest resource up to its limits before any other alternative is used at the same time for the same item (World Bank 1991). Also, LP models can be very sensitive to input parameter variations. This technique is used for almost all optimisation models, and applied in national energy planning as well as technology related long-term energy research.

b. *Mixed Integer Programming (MIP)*

Mixed Integer Programming (MIP) is actually an extension of Linear Programming which allows for greater detail in formulating technical properties and relations in modelling energy systems. Decisions such as Yes/No or (0/1) are admitted as well as nonconvex relations for discrete decision problems. MIP can be used when addressing questions such as whether or not to include a particular energy conversion plant in a system. By using MIP, variables that cannot reasonably assume any arbitrary (e.g., small) value – such as unit sizes of power plants – can be properly reflected in an otherwise linear model (World Bank 1991).

c. *Dynamic Programming*

Dynamic programming is a method used to find an optimal growth path. The solution of the original problem is obtained by dividing the original problem into simple subproblems for which optimal solutions are calculated. Consequently, the original problem is then optimally solved using the optimal solutions of the subproblems.

6. Geographical Coverage: Global, Regional, National, Local, or Project

The geographical coverage reflects the level at which the analysis takes place, which is an important factor in determining the structure of models. Models range in coverage from global, regional, national, to local coverage. Yet two global models, for example, may examine different sub-regions and may make different trade and technology transfer assumptions. Non-global models of course vary among each other, but also vary based on the assumptions made within the model about the capabilities and reactions of the world outside the model's coverage. Some models are ***generic*** and can be customised for a specific region.

The global models describe the world economy or situation, the regional level frequently refers to international regions such as Europe, the Latin American Countries, South-East Asia, etc., although the literature uses the term "regional" in some cases to refer to regions within a country. In this paper, we will use the term "local" in these cases. National models treat world market conditions as exogenous, but encompass all major sectors within a country simultaneously, addressing feedbacks and interrelationships between the sectors. Examples of national models are econometric models for the short term and general equilibrium models for the long term. The local level is subnational, referring to regions within a country. The project level is a somewhat special case. It usually refers to a subnational level focusing at a particular site. However, the project level can also encompass a project on a national or even international scale, although specific "project models" generally do not focus on these large scale projects.

The comprehensiveness of models focusing on the global, regional, or national level generally requires highly aggregated data and models focusing on one of these levels often include all major sectors and macro-economic linkages between those sectors, implying a considerable simplification of the energy sector.

Local and project models, on the other hand, usually require a bottom-up approach using disaggregated data.

7. Sectoral Coverage

A model can be focused on only one sector, as many early bottom-up models do, or include more sectors.

How the economy is divided into certain sectors is crucial for the analysis. Multi-sectoral models can be used at the international, national, as well as subnational level and focus on the interactions between these sectors. Single-sectoral models only provide information on a particular sector (in our case the energy sector) and do not take into account the macro-economic linkages of that sector with the rest of the economy. The rest of the economy is represented in a highly simplified way. Nearly all bottom-up models are sectoral, but not all sectoral models use bottom-up methodologies. For instance, top-down partial equilibrium models focus on the long-term growth path of a distinct sector.

8. The Time Horizon: Short, Medium, and Long Term

In this context, short, medium, and long time horizons describe how a model accounts for the introduction and evolution of energy technologies. Short horizons may consider changing energy prices, supplies, and demands, but do not include any significant technological change since they span such a short time period. In the medium term (about 2010-2030), the technology mix may change, but only to include technologies that are already deployed or have reached the final stages of development. Over long time horizons (beyond about 2030), new technologies may play a significant role even though they have not yet been completely developed today. Resource depletion, population growth, and greenhouse gas accumulation, as well as research and development investment, are driving factors behind technology change.

There exists no standard definition of the short, medium, and long term. However, Grubb et al. (1993) mention a commonly noticed period of 5 years or less for the short term, between 3 and 15 years for the medium term, and 10 years or more for the long term. The time horizon is important because different economic, social, and environmental processes are important at different time scales. Thus, the time scale determines the structure and objectives of the energy models. Long run analyses may assume economic equilibrium (i.e., resources are fully allocated or markets "clear"), while short run models need to incorporate "transitional" and disequilibrium effects (e.g., unemployment).

9. Data Requirements

Models require certain types of data. For instance, most models will require data of a quantitative, cardinal type, some even require aspects to be expressed in monetary units. However, sometimes data are not available or unreliable (for instance in developing countries), in which case it might be important that the energy model can handle qualitative or ordinal data as well. Furthermore, data may be aggregated or disaggregated. Long-term global and national models will necessarily need highly aggregated data with little technological detail. Great detail in representing energy supply and consumption is only possibility in models that are specific for the energy sector.

Energy systems are socio-techno-economic systems that involve various sciences. Computer simulation makes it possible to consider many different configurations and facilitates the finding of beneficial measures. Energy demand and other parameters may be defined according to societal sector, geographic region and time. A trade-off between sectoral, spatial and temporal resolution may be necessary. Possibilities to influence energy use should be considered, such as energy conservation that reduces final-energy consumption, energy carrier switching, and load management that alters the time of energy supply. Technical progress may be represented by decreasing costs and increasing efficiency. *Experience curves* can reflect the fact that early investments in emerging technologies are necessary to enhance performance and reduce costs of the equipment. In such a model with *learning rates*, the technology characteristics improve with installed capacity rather than with time (Mattsson & Wene 1997).

Sensitivity analyses should be performed to predict the probable consequences of various conditions. There are many parameters that ought to be varied, such as fuel availability, electricity prices and demand. An analysis of an energy system that comprises many actors should be studied from a public-economy viewpoint, whereas a study of a nation-wide or local energy system that is controlled by a single actor (e.g., a utility) should be analysed from a business-economics point of view. The two approaches primarily differ concerning system boundaries and cost representation. In the former case, those measures should be found that are beneficial for the energy-carrier supplier *and* consumer from a common system perspective. By *integrated resource planning* (IRP), the social cost, including external environmental costs, for the provision of energy services is minimised. Supply possibilities and demand-side measures are compared on equal terms and quantified (e.g., Bakken & Lucas 1996).

Energy-economy equilibrium models often have no explicit technologies. Transformation of the capital stock (e.g., power plants) into new installations and the substitution between goods, such as energy forms, can be described as more or less difficult and costly. In these models, a price increase can reduce energy-service demand. Thus, the benefit of energy use is decreased. *Autonomous energy-efficiency improvement* (AEEI) is considered in many energy-economy models and occurs because new, more energy-efficient equipment replaces old units and due to the movement from energy-intensive manufacturing towards service business (Beaver 1993). Another important parameter is ESUB, the price elasticity of substitution between capital, labour and energy.

Aspects of Energy System Analysis

For energy systems, desired aims may include reduced primary-energy consumption and emissions, as well as enhanced utilisation of renewable energy sources. Problems arise when such aims conflict with the usual quest for low costs. In addition, administrative divisions may stop beneficial measures from being implemented. As an example, separate organisations for electricity and district-heating supply may obstruct introduction of combined heat and power production. Energy planning should focus on exploiting synergies, which may require co-operation between different organisations, and system objectives, such as environmental control (cf. Wene 1989).

Economic energy models may predict future market behaviour based on historical relationships. The assumed values for GNP (gross national product) growth, AEEI (energy intensity decrease) and ESUB (price elasticity) are determinative for model results. (Wilson and Swisher 1993). AEEI and ESUB are difficult to estimate even for today.

Energy system optimisation models may rest on an implicit assumption that the world can be changed. They mostly have the advantage that the properties of potential installations may be given as input without requiring a previous judgement of their size, profitability, or suitable time of introduction. A great number of technologies can normally be represented in such models. Even equipment that seems unlikely to be beneficial should be considered because it could be included in component combinations that are not obvious at first sight. It may be appropriate to restrict investments in long-life equipment to reserve capital for new technologies.

Various scenarios ought to be studied and the robustness of solutions should be tested through sensitivity analysis. If conditions are very uncertain, it may be favourable to perform a study of an energy system for one year, rather than determine a desired development path for several decades. If the future energy system will exist for a much longer period than the transition phase, it may be more important to find the optimal final system than the best path to reach it. Groscurth and Schweiker (1995) also suggest that in long-term energy modelling, it is preferable to seek a physically optimal system with respect to primary-energy consumption or pollutants instead of minimising uncertain costs. We may then ask whether we can and want to pay for the resulting energy system, or if we must find a compromise.

3 Descriptions of Energy Models

We include in this paragraph the short descriptions of the most well-known and widely used energy models.

CO_2DB

The IIASA CO_2 data bank (IIASA 1992a,b; Messner & Strubegger 1991) is a software system for collecting data on technologies related to the CO_2 problem. It predefines the information to be entered into the data bank, structures it according to sector and type, and supports the evaluation of chains of energy conversion and utilisation technologies. The database has been specifically designed to provide a uniform framework for the assessment of the ultimate reduction potential of greenhouse gases resulting from the introduction of new technologies over different time frames in different regions.

The database contains over 1400 technologies in the fossil, renewable, zero carbon and scrubbing, end-use, transportation, and other sectors.

Technical descriptions include the physical energy flows in the process (quantity and quality of energy inputs and outputs), material requirements, information on the unit size, technical and average availability, construction time, and plant life.

Economic descriptors consisting of investment, fixed and variable operating and maintenance costs, fuel costs, and decommissioning costs are collected for each technology.

Environmental data on quantities of major pollutants emitted or extracted.

CO_2DB includes information concerning the potential introduction, penetration, and transfer of certain technologies.

The data bank facilitates aggregation and evaluation of a consistent set of data on technologies relevant for CO_2 reduction and removal. It serves as a unified framework to data collection, structures the information, and defines the format.

The CO_2DB was used in the *Global Energy Perspectives to 2050 and Beyond.*

DECADES

The DECADES project (IAEA 1995a,b) is carried out jointly by the EC, the Economic and Social Commission for Asia and the Pacific (ESCAP), the IAEA, IBRD/World Bank, IIASA, NEA, OPEC, UNIDO and the WMO. The DECADES project focuses on producing a technology inventory including complete life cycle analysis, developing computer software to use the data in electricity system analysis and expansion planning studies, reviewing and documenting methodological approaches, and carrying out case studies illustrating the use of data and tools.

The overall objective of the DECADES project is to improve the abilities for comparative assessment in the process of planning and decision making for the electricity sector. Even though the relatively short time horizon of the DECADES project prevents significant analysis of technology change over time, its incorporation of all steps in the fuel cycle from mining to waste disposal is noteworthy.

The model can conduct comparative studies for various supply-side expansion strategies within a time frame of up to 30 years. The DECADES project aims to establish three main types of data bases: technology inventory, toxicity of pollutants, and impacts from electricity generation systems. The user supplies system load, general, and economic data. The user defines constraints with regards to first date of availability of new technology, and penetration rates of new technologies.

Within the DECADES project, the software package DEPAC was developed. DEPAC is designed for use together with the DECADES databases. DEPAC links the databases with the following electricity system analysis/planning modules: Electric System Analysis Module, Primary Energy Supply Analysis, and Environmental Analysis Module.

The DECADES project main driving forces are exogenous variables. The user supplied data on economic growth, as well as future technical characteristics, will be the main determinants in predicting penetration rates of climate friendly technologies.

Energy 2020

Energy 2020 (Backus et al. 1993) is a disaggregated energy model used for energy scenario analysis within any adequately defined region. It dynamically simulates changes in energy demand, supply, and fuel prices each year through 2020. The model is forward-looking. Its structure, scope, assumptions, and level of detail are customised for each user. Several Eastern European governments and North American utilities and regulators use Energy 2020 as their primary forecasting and policy analysis tool.

Energy 2020's main distinction is the attention it gives to modelling decision-making at consumer and producer levels. Other important characteristics are its degree and flexibility of technological detail, and its integration with macroeconomic and sensitivity analysis packages.

Demand and supply sectors are flexible depending on user requirements and limitations. Interactions between sectors vary to simulate real-world relationships. Detailed pricing, finance, expansion, and production data are generated in each sector. Peak load is considered in decisions to add new capacity. There is also a pollution sector used to quantify emissions, effluents, and constraints.

The need to replace retired capital stock and add new capacity drives technology change in Energy 2020. Consumers and producers determine which fuel and technology to use for new investments based on perceptions of cost and utility. Marginal trade-offs between changing fuel costs and efficiency determine the capital cost of the chosen technology. These trade-offs depend on perceived energy prices, capital and operating costs, risk, access to capital, regulations, efficiency, and other non-price factors.

Since decisions are assumed to be made based on imperfect information, simulated investors do not always choose the "best" technologies. More expensive or otherwise less preferred technologies may still achieve some market penetration over time. In general, however, technology mix will change in favour of more preferred characteristics including higher efficiency and lower cost.

The evolution of price and non-price characteristics of supply technologies are exogenous. Changes in fuel prices are endogenous. As much as possible, Energy 2020 bases rates of change on historical data.

E3Net

E3Net (Energy, Economy and Environment Analysis based on NetWorks) is a multi-period intertemporal linear optimisation model. It was developed by the Institute of Energy Economics and the Rational Use of Energy (IER) of the

University of Stuttgart. In the E3Net model the energy system is represented by an oriented network in which the energy, starting in a form of primary energy, is flowing and is gradually transformed to final energy and then further down to useful energy and energy services. The model is used to create process-engineering representations of energy systems. The objective functions of the energy model can be, for example, the minimum of total system costs or the lowest emissions of the whole energy system.

Because of its flexible structure E3Net can be used to model local, regional, national or multinational energy systems. E3Net has further the capability of a high and flexible time resolution.

E3Net was built to permit policy assessment in the field of energy and environment. The possibility to consider energy systems in a high level of technological detail allows to describe and analyse energy systems, to compute prime and side effects of policies, and to identify "best" policies in respect of objectives and criterions within the framework of selected cases.

E3Net is the energy system optimisation module of MESAP (Modular Energy System Analysis and Planning Environment). MESAP is a tool for integrated energy and environmental planning (Voss 1994). It integrates on a personal computer different modular energy planning models through a central database system called NetWork.

To account for the interactions between the energy system and the rest of the economy, E3Net is coupled with a macroeconomic growth model. As a general equilibrium approach E3MACRO integrates the technological detail of E3Net with a general description of the economy. Another extension refers to Mixed Integer Programming (MIP). An extended version of E3Net is planned with fuzzy optimisation to represent uncertainties in energy system models.

E3Net is an extension of EFOM-ENV which was developed for the European Community.

Therefore E3Net is an intertemporal optimisation model of the energy system. The time horizon is divided into time periods. The time periods (also called sub-periods) of a case study are entirely defined by their first and last years. Intertemporal conditions exist between these milestone years. In contrast to EFOM-ENV, E3Net allows a subdivision of a model period in as many seasons and daily time segments of a load curve as necessary. Furthermore it offers a flexibility concerning the regional and sectoral aggregation level of a model. The degree of detail in the representation of the energy system can be adapted to the objective of the case study.

Further E3Net has the capability to solve mixed integer problems (MIP). The improvement consists in a definition of unit sizes for certain technologies that can only be built in large units.

This is especially important for applications to small regions (Regional and Local Energy Planning). Another extension to EFOM-ENV is that E3Net can be applied to problems with a partly non-linear objective function or with non-linear constraints (E3Net-NLP). E3MACRO was developed in order to consider the feedback between the energy sector and the rest of the economy.

E3Net focuses on competition between technologies. It optimises the technology mix with regard to an objective function. Important parameters of the model in order to describe the energy system are, for example, the operating costs of technologies, the capital requirements for investments, the fuel prices and the emission factors. Costs and energy requirements are represented in equations for each supply and demand technology. In addition, constraints such as the emission levels can be used in the model. In order to find the optimal technology mix the model uses normally linear programming methods.

As a technology mix optimisation model, the E3Net database can contain a large number of supply and end-use technologies in order to describe production, conversion, transmission, and use of energy. Important parameters of the model system are the operating costs, the construction costs, efficiencies, and emission factors. The German database contains some 10,000 descriptive pieces of data.

Because the demand vector of the E3Net model is an exogenous input data, there is no feedback between the technology mix and the technology drivers. This feedback can only be considered in the E3MACRO approach.

IKARUS

IKARUS (Instruments for Reducing Greenhouse Gas Strategies) (IER 1995; Katscher 1993) is an energy modelling and database system developed by the Federal Republic of Germany to assist in formulating strategies to reduce their greenhouse gas emissions. The system projects German energy, economic, and emissions activity in the years 2005 and 2020. It consists of a technology oriented optimisation model, several dynamic simulation models representing individual sectors, a macroeconomic model, and technology and economic databases. The models are not linked together, but serve to generate input for each other and to compare results for consistency.

The system attempts to integrate results from three distinct modelling methods - optimisation, simulation, and input-output. The technology model contains a high level of technical detail, while the macroeconomic input-output model is more aggregated. The simulation models help the user gain insight into economic and market effects predicted by the other two models. Projections into the 2020 depend on the characterisation of the technologies found in the database, and the economic results from the macroeconomic model.

The IKARUS technology database characterises over 2000 technologies in terms of cost, efficiency, emissions, and other relevant factors, as they are predicted to appear in 2005 and 2020. The technology model attempts to find the lowest cost energy system possible under a given constraint such as CO2 emissions. Ten sectors and several subsectors interact in the optimisation process. Some of the subsectors within the technology model, such as space heating, are also modelled separately in individual simulation submodels.

LEAP

The Long-range Energy Alternatives Planning system (LEAP) (SEI 1995, LEAP 1990) is a commercial software package developed by the Stockholm Environment Institute (SEI) with support from the United Nations Environment Programme (UNEP). It simulates energy supply and demand within a generic user-defined region and time horizon. The user also defines the specific demand and transformation technologies and their interactions. Government agencies and research institutions in over 30 countries use LEAP for energy and environmental policy scenario analysis.

LEAP is a scenario development tool, rather than a formal model. It focuses on flexibility, user-friendliness and use of transparent calculations. It avoids commitment to hard-wired endogenous relationships, but does not preclude such at the user's discretion. Therefore, the user defines almost every aspect of the energy system - costs, technologies, interactions - and how these are expected to change over time. Users may also choose to use default data gathered for certain regions and technologies. LEAP provides a method and structure for incorporating these details into a simulation model.

LEAP is driven by demand assumptions. Transformation (supply) attempts to match demand, but may not always succeed depending on the assumptions used. Energy prices do not adjust in response to market imbalances.

LEAP incorporates data and methodology for performing full fuel cycle analyses on the scenarios run. Users may incorporate externality costs of fuels and processes into their analyses. LEAP also provides economic, instead of accounting, cost and benefit output. These features are intended to assist policy makers in evaluating the social impacts of energy policy decisions.

MARKAL/MARKAL-MACRO

The International Energy Agency (IEA) developed the Market Allocation Model (MARKAL) to project optimum mixes of energy supply and demand technologies under different scenarios and objectives (ETSU 1994, Manne, Wene 1992). Continued use and development is occurring under the ETSAP implementing agreement. MARKAL serves as a framework for expressing energy technology interactions, and as a mathematical tool for optimising technology mixes to meet specified objectives such as least cost or lowest emissions. For this reason, MARKAL is termed an "optimisation" model. Policy analysts use MARKAL to frame energy policy and evaluate options based on their projected financial and environmental effects. MARKAL covers a generic geographic region over 45 years in nine, five year intervals. Supply always adjusts to meet aggregate demand, and supply capacity takes into account peak demand.

To enable macroeconomic feedback, MARKAL has been integrated with the MACRO economic model (IEA 1992). Even though much of MARKAL's description remains unchanged, MARKAL-MACRO does have some significant differences. The time horizon is broken into four, ten year intervals.

Furthermore, energy demand becomes an endogenous calculation based on production functions similar to those found in pure economic models.

MARKAL focuses on competition between technologies. Since the model varies the technology mix to optimise with respect to a set of objective functions, assumptions used in calculating those objectives, such as technology cost and efficiency improvement rates, discount rates, and fuel prices, play key roles.

The distinguishing feature of the MARKAL model is its optimisation capability. Policy analysts may define many kinds of objectives or combinations of objectives including lowest cost, fossil fuel use, renewables use, and emissions targets. Costs and energy requirements are represented in equation form for each supply and demand technology. In addition, constraints such as the rate of technology penetration, emission levels, and plant utilisation are programmed into the model. Once the entire set of required data has been added, the model uses linear programming methods to solve for the technology mix that best meets the specified objectives.

Generality and flexibility are also important aspects of MARKAL. Definition and description of technologies are limited only by the modeler's preferences. A single energy system may contain definitions of several hundred technologies that contribute to supply, demand, efficiency, production, or any relationship defined by the modeler.

Even though MARKAL-MACRO will still be considered an optimisation model, economic feedbacks between the two sub-models, such as technology and energy prices, cause model results to resemble those of economic models. MACRO sets energy demand based on macroeconomic factors and activity within MARKAL adjusts to meet those demands with maximum utility.

MIDAS

MIDAS is a large-scale energy system planning and forecasting model developed by National Technical University of Athens (Capros & Mantzos 1992). It performs dynamic simulation of the energy system, which is represented by combining engineering process analysis and econometric formulations. The model is used for scenario analysis and forecasting. Each national application of MIDAS is a simultaneous system of more than 2500 equations solved dynamically over a period of 20-25 years. The MIDAS model building project was funded by the Joule Programme of DG XII and by DG XVII, of the European Commission. MIDAS covers the whole energy system and ensures, on an annual basis, the consistent and simultaneous projection of energy demand, energy supply, energy pricing and costing, so that the system is in both quantity and price-dependent balance. The model output is a time-series of detailed EUROSTAT energy balance sheets, lists of costs and prices by sector and fuel, and a set of capacity expansion plans including emission data. The MIDAS database uses the following sources: EUROSTAT detailed energy balances (SIRENE), OECD/IEA energy prices and taxes, EFOM model database, UNIPEDE/Eurelectric data, BP database, MURE, FRET and DERE databases of DG XII, KRONOS (macroeconomic indicators) and several national sources for mining, refining, power generation, coal statistics, natural gas, crude-oil production and transmission.

NE21

The Dynamic New Earth 21 (NE21) model (Fujii & Yamaji 1997; Yoneda 1997) is a technologically detailed model which covers all the regions on the globe. It makes a comprehensive assessment of the technological measures for limiting the atmospheric CO_2 concentration at a level that would prevent dangerous anthropogenic interference with the climate system. The model can develop desirable future energy systems incorporating CO_2 abatement technologies for different scenarios.

The Dynamic NE21 model is a system engineering model, it solves for a multi-period intertemporal non-linear optimisation problem with inequality and equality linear constraints. The NE21 model seeks the optimal solution for the future world energy system at intervals of 10 years to 2050, and at intervals of 25 years to 2100. World energy demand is exogenously set for each scenario. The reference scenario for the CO_2 study was derived from the IPCC emission scenario of IS92a, also known as the "Business as Usual Scenario". Global energy demand is disaggregated into four types of secondary energy carriers: gaseous fuel, liquid fuel, solid fuel, and electricity. Energy supply and demand systems are divided into 10 regions. The 10 regions are linked to each other by energy exports and imports. NE21 can explicitly analyse the role of processes of CO_2 recovery, disposal, and storage.

The Dynamic New Earth 21 Model is a multi-period inter-temporal non-linear optimisation problem with inequality and equality linear constraints. The constraints represent supply-demand balances, energy and CO_2 balances, and inter-temporal constraints such as growth rate limitations. The objective function is defined as the sum of fuel production costs, levelized plant construction costs, fuel transportation costs electricity transmission costs, and other supply costs.

The constraints represent regional supply-demand balances, mass and energy balances, intertemporal restrictions, and world trade balance constraints. The NE21 model contains over 15,000 variables and 8000 constraints.

Energy efficiency is aggregated, and is incorporated in a top-down approach. There are two main factors driving energy saving behaviours, autonomous energy efficiency improvements (AEEI) and the energy saving encouraged by the CO_2 abatement policy. The effects of AEEI have assumed to already be incorporated in the BAU scenario. Due to the top-down approach used in this model, explicit technological improvements in end-use sectors are not represented The production costs of fossil fuel energy supply technologies are expressed as five-step linear functions of their cumulative productions by region. The supply costs of renewable energy sources are expressed as non-linear functions of their annual productions. The input data was derived from studies made by the World Energy Conference, IIASA, Solar Energy Research Institute, and additional sources. Daily load duration curves for each global region are accounted for with three time periods: peak, intermediate, and off-peak.

NEMS

The National Energy Modelling System is a computer-based, energy economy modelling system of US energy markets (EIA 1996a,b,c). NEMS is used by the Energy Information Agency to project the energy, economic, environmental, and security impacts on the US of alternative energy policies and of different assumptions about energy markets. NEMS was built to support energy policy analysis and to serve as a resource for the development and analysis of the impacts of alternative energy policies on key US markets and economic growth. It provides a consistent framework for representing the interactions of supply and demand in the US energy system.

NEMS is an integrated modular system that achieves a supply/demand balance in the defined end-use demand regions for the mid term period of 1990 through 2015. The model achieves a balance in the separate demand regions by solving for the prices of each energy product that will balance the quantities producers are willing to supply.

The system is composed of four separate supply modules, four demand modules, two conversion modules, an international energy module, a macroeconomic activity module, and the integrating module. The modularity of the NEMS design provides the flexibility for each component of the US energy system to use the methodology and coverage that is most appropriate.

The integrating module controls the NEMS solution process as it iterates to determine a general equilibrium across all the modules. Each module is called in sequence and solved, assuming that all other variables in the energy markets are fixed. The modules are called iteratively until the prices and demanded quantities remain constant within a specified tolerance. The solution procedure for one iteration involves the execution of all the component modules, as well as the updating of expectation variables for use in the next iteration. The order of execution of the modules may affect the rate of convergence but will generally not significantly alter the results.

The system defines many key parameters internally. Any one of several hundred exogenous variables are specified to create a new case. Two major classes of assumptions characterising a case are assumptions concerning economic growth in the US and assumptions about foreign oil supply and demand and their influence on world oil prices.

PRIMES

PRIMES, the Price Inducing Model of the Energy System (EC 1995a), is a price-clearing partial equilibrium model that is designed to examine current and future trends in energy markets across the European Union. PRIMES calculates price equilibrium in each energy market. The high level of technological detail in PRIMES makes it a good tool for the analysis of research and design strategies, the prospects and economics of new energy technologies, environmental policy options and instruments, and externalities associated with energy production and use. PRIMES is a continuation of the modelling work of the EFOM and MEDEE energy models. It is a prototype model which is still under development.

PRIMES explicitly represents the price clearing behaviour of competitive energy markets for the years 1990-2030 at five year intervals. It considers both national energy systems and the overall European energy market. There is a high degree of disaggregating detail about technologies in both the supply and demand sectors. Technology is considered explicitly in all demand and supply sub-models. This data is drawn from EFOM and MIDAS, and is supplemented from the EC's MURE and THERMIE projects.

The main constraints for PRIMES are that the total available electric power (imports plus production) meets or exceeds local demand. PRIMES also represents constraints on fuel and plant capacity and transport. Major macro-economic inputs into PRIMES include: GDP, industrial activity, income, inflation, exchange rates, interest rates, techno-economic characteristics costs, technical progress, abatement costs, global fuel prices, policy constraints for taxes, standards, and permits parameters in energy pricing policies, base year existing capacities in energy supply and demand, and planned decommissioning and forced investments in the beginning of the simulation period.

POLES 2.2

POLES 2.2 (Prospective Outlook on Long-Term Energy Systems) is a disaggregated economic model used for energy and emissions policy analysis in fourteen global regions and twelve subregions (EC 1996a). It dynamically simulates changes in energy supply, demand, and prices annually through 2030. Activity in each region is governed by four modules: Final Energy Demand, New and Renewable Energy, Electricity and Transformation System, and Oil and Gas Production. Global activity is co-ordinated using the International Energy Prices Module. POLES 2.2 was developed under the European Commission's JOULE program to analyse world energy issues and policy tools.

POLES 2.2's primary distinctions are its independent treatment of new and renewable technologies and its hierarchical structure. GDP growth and technological advance are key parameters.

European Energy to 2020

European Energy to 2020 (EC 1996b) takes a scenario-based approach to aid in the development of energy policy. The scenario approach allows for analysis over a variety of possible future changes in an objective way.

The study looks outwards to the year 2020, exploring different scenarios. Four scenarios were developed to reflect different societal and economic trends. These scenarios were translated into detailed macroeconomic indicators which reflected the scenario circumstances. Detailed econometric and simulation modelling was undertaken for the European countries in 5 year increments. A simplified analysis of the world was also completed for 10 year time periods.

Global Energy Perspectives to 2050 and Beyond

The Global Energy Perspectives to 2050 and Beyond study (IIASA 1995) was conducted by IIASA for the World Energy Council. It expands the conclusions of "Energy for Tomorrow's World" (WEC 1993), which concluded that the world would have to rely on fossil fuels through 2020 with relatively few opportunities for alternatives. This study considers what the implications for the global energy system will be after 2020.

The study utilised 6 scenarios spanning the time horizon 2020-2050, with some preliminary results to 2100. The scenarios covered three alternative high growth cases, one modest growth and technological improvement case, and two cases which assume high growth and innovation rates, coupled with aggressive international co-operation focused on environmental protection and international equity. All 6 scenarios started from base year 1990. The scenarios covered energy demand and supply characteristics for 11 world regions. The regional differences in energy intensities incorporated anticipated future technological characteristics and improvements in performance, cost, and diffusion of new technologies. The main exogenous variables concerning population growth and economic growth were derived from a World Bank scenario.

The IIASA Global Energy Perspectives project pooled all the available technology data into a single data bank, extracted medians and ranges for specific technological input. The database includes over 1500 technologies that cover the whole energy system, with data drawn from an extensive review of cost studies. For example, costs for solar generating technology were derived from 45 independent estimates.

The scenarios have different learning curves effects for various individual and generic technologies reflecting different priorities for research and development, socio-economic development, and energy system requirements. In all cases, energy options which are not feasible today are excluded (e.g., nuclear fusion).

Technology costs and performance characteristics improve with experience. New or emerging technologies initially are deployed in niche markets. Significant improvements in performance and economics then need to be made to reach commercialisation. Overall, research and development spending helps create a "supply push" for new technology, increasing the experience with the new technology. Such supply pushes when combined with demand pulls (in both niche applications and through overall policy driven actions) lead to a pattern of diminishing costs with increasing experience for climate friendly technologies.

The Global Energy Model is actually a series of scenario analyses calculated from several linked models. The principal exogenous variables are population growth by region and per capita economic growth by region. Levels of primary and final energy consumption were derived using a IIASA developed model labelled Scenario Generator ("SG"), essentially a combination of an extensive data base of historic data on national economies and their energy systems and estimated equations of past economic and energy developments.

For each scenario, SG generated plausible future paths of energy use consistent with historical data and the specified features of each scenario. The paths generated were then checked for internal consistency with two formal models. A modified version of Global 2100 (Manne 1993), was used to check for consistency between a region's macroeconomic development and it's energy use. Estimates of energy demand and supply was provided by MESSAGE III, a dynamic linear optimisation model (similar to MARKAL) that calculates the supply structure with the lowest cost that meets demand for useful energy, subject to constraints of resource availability, and the menu of given technologies.

SYRENE

SYRENE is used to give recommendations with respect to the prospects of long-term technological developments that can contribute to a sustainable energy system to prioritise research and development efforts (Ybema et al. 1995; van Wees & van Wisk 1995). To address this objective, technology characterisations, energy sector analysis and an integral analysis were carried out to develop general conclusions with regard to the long term prospects of energy technologies in the Netherlands.

SYRENE covers three periods, the present period, the period 2010/2015, and the mid/long term period 2030/2040. This is a time frame in which most of the technologies and productions processes can be renewed, but is not too far away to make reasonable estimates for technology development.

SYRENE incorporates data for over 400 technologies for electricity and thermal energy production, end use and energy conversion. The data inputs for technology characterisation were supplied by expert analysis and by literature surveys combined to give an estimate. These inputs were then reviewed by two or more experts to incorporate into the final technology characterisation and data sheets. These technology characterisations provide data on energetic performance (conversion efficiency, heat losses), economic parameters (investment and O&M costs, lifetimes), and environmental effects.

The model was run for four primary cases: renewables, increased energy efficiency, nuclear, and CO_2 capture technologies. Each case was examined under high and low energy price scenarios.

The SYRENE model incorporates information on energy technology data, technology preference, discount rate regimes, environmental constraints, and scenarios for differing energy prices and demand levels. It then generates a baseline energy system and a CO_2 constrained energy system and can provide information on technology assessment based on comparing cost effectiveness for the alternate scenarios.

ENPEP

ENPEP is a set of micro-computer based energy planning tools that are designed to provide an integrated analysis capability developed by International Atomic Energy Agency (Buehring et al. 1991). ENPEP begins with a macroeconomic analysis, develops an energy demand forecast based on this analysis, carries out an integrated supply/demand analysis for the entire energy system, evaluates the electric system component of the energy system in detail, and determines the impacts of alternative configurations. Also, it explicitly considers the impacts the power system has on the rest of the energy system and on the economy as a whole.

Data requirements include: 1) base year energy balance - user selected level of detail; 2) base year energy prices; 3) energy technology performance; 4) energy technology costs; 5) international energy price projections; 6) electric system load characteristics; 7) local environmental coefficients - optional.

Local, regional, national scales possible.

Time horizon could be: 1. Short (1-3 years) to long-term (50 years maximum); 2. Annual time steps in Total Energy; 3. Annual, seasonal, monthly in Detailed Electric System Analysis.

Objectives of the ENPEP are: energy policy analysis; energy tariff development; energy project investment analysis; electric system expansion planning; environmental policy analysis (for energy system).

ENPEP doesn't present any macroeconomic model, but provides interface to external macroeconomic model(s).

ENPEP presents the total energy system analysis which includes:

1. Demand analysis: Detailed evaluation of composition of demand by sector, subsector, fuel, useful energy. Growth of demand determined by macroeconomic variables and/or other user-specified parameters. Energy conservation and demand side management analysis capabilities;
2. Resource analysis: Representation of depletable resource availability and cost; Representation of renewable resource availability and cost;
3. Supply side analysis: Detailed evaluation of supply system configuration, both current and future. User-defined structure and level of detail;
4. Supply/demand balance: Non-linear, equilibrium solution for total energy system. Energy policy constraints can be imposed.

ENPEP presents the detailed electric system analysis which includes:

1. Load curve: Computed from total energy system analysis or input separately by user;
2. Load characterisation: Analysis of historical load data to develop hourly, seasonal and annual load characteristics;
3. Generation expansion analysis: Least cost optimisation of system expansion plan (WASP III plus).

All environmental burdens computed as uncontrolled emissions, with alternative control equipment, under alternative environmental regulations, and with incremental cost of control.

The Asian-Pacific Integrated Model

Japan's National Institute of Environmental Studies (NIES) pursues collaborative research on global environmental change with other ministries, universities, and international research institutes (1998, http://www-cger.nies.go.jp/ipcc/aim/). NIES' centre for Global Environmental Research, in collaboration with Kyoto University, has developed the Asian-Pacific Integrated Model (AIM) to study impacts of mitigation and adaptation scenarios in the Asia-Pacific region.

AIM comprises three interlinked modules: an emissions module, a climate module, and an impacts module. The emissions module consists of three separate country models for Indonesia, China, and Japan, which are then combined with an aggregate model of emissions in the rest of the world. These regional models determine anthropogenic greenhouse gas emissions using regional assumptions on population, technological, and economic growth to obtain estimates of energy consumption and land-use changes. Because the regional models are still under development, a more aggregate working version of the emissions module based on the Edmonds-Reilly-Barns model is being used until that work is completed.

Climate scenarios are produced using a variety of existing simple reduced-form models and results from prior Global Circulation Model (GCM) runs. Impacts of climate scenarios are estimated for agriculture, sea-level rise, water resources, public health, regional economics, and natural ecosystems. Impacts are represented spatially using a Geographic Information System (GIS).

TARGETS

The TARGETS model (Tool to Assess Regional and Global Environmental and health Targets for Sustainability), the other major integrated-assessment modelling project under way at RIVM, seeks to study not just climate change, but broad issues of global change and sustainable development (Rotmans & de Vries 1997). TARGETS will include five interlinked "horizontal" modules representing population and health, energy and economics, biophysics, land and soils, and water. Cutting across each horizontal module will be a consistent framework representing dynamics within four "vertical" modules that describe the state and dynamics of the system, the pressures on it, the resultant impacts, and the range of policy responses. The initial version of TARGETS employs a global scale, while subsequent versions will disaggregate the world into six regions.

IMAGE 1.0

Since 1990, a series of dynamic simulation models for integrated assessment of climate change has been developed in Europe, with support from the EC Commission and participation from several institutions. Leadership on a number of these projects has been with RIVM, the Dutch Institute for Environment and Public Health. The first of these projects was IMAGE 1.0

(Integrated Model to Assess the Greenhouse Effect), the first model to attempt to integrate the climate-change system from emissions to impacts.

In part inspired by the highly successful RAINS model for integrated assessment of acid rain in Europe, IMAGE was a deterministic, global, dynamic simulation model based on the systems-dynamics approach to modelling. It worked in one-year time steps from 1900 to 2100. It originally used four external emissions scenarios for CO_2, CH_4, N_2O, and CFCs, and was subsequently modified to use the Edmonds-Reilly-Barns (ERB) energy-economic model to generate emissions. The global emission model was coupled to global atmospheric chemistry and climate models and to regional impacts models that projected sector-specific impacts for the Netherlands. The first impacts modules concentrated on sea-level rise and coastal defence, and allowed calculation of optimal policy response in the form of optimal time-paths for dike raising and dune strengthening. IMAGE also included a module that calculated impacts from increased ground-level UV radiation as a consequence of emissions of ozone-depleting substances development (Rotmans & de Vries 1997).

IMAGE 2.0

Another team of researchers from RIVM, the Dutch Institute for Environment and Public Health, has developed IMAGE 2.0 (Integrated Model to Assess the Greenhouse Effect). Though sharing a name with IMAGE 1.0, IMAGE 2.0 differs in several fundamental respects. In particular, IMAGE 2.0 is the first integrated assessment model to represent environmental phenomena at a fine spatial scale. IMAGE 2.0 consists of energy-industry, terrestrial environment, and atmosphere-ocean submodels.

The energy-industry model is based on highly detailed bottom-up regional representation of technologies and their emission characteristics in 13 world regions, with very little modelling of behaviour. The terrestrial environment model represents land-use, soil type, element fluxes and certain classes of impacts and land-use change on a worldwide grid at 0.5-degree resolution, and permits vivid high resolution display of emissions, land use, and certain impacts on global maps. The atmosphere-ocean module uses a two-dimensional atmospheric energy model and a separate two-dimensional ocean model. The computational demands of all these models are large, yielding run times from several hours to a day. Consequently, the uncertainty analysis performed with them is limited to comparison of large discrete policy futures or scenarios (Alcamo 1994).

The PAGE Model

PAGE (Policy Analysis for the Greenhouse Effect) was developed with European Union support. PAGE focuses on simplicity and ease of use, and allows extensive specification and propagation of uncertainty.

PAGE models four world regions and represents emissions of CO_2, CH_4, CFCs, and HCFCs from 1990 to 2100. Emission projections are not modelled but are specified by the user. The model then generates emission-reduction costs from a set of regional no-cost emission paths for each gas, and marginal costs and break-points for a piecewise linear abatement cost function.

Emissions drive an atmospheric model that represents atmospheric lives of each gas and resultant time-paths of radiative forcing and global-average temperature. Impacts are assumed to be zero if the time-path of future temperature lies below a specified trapezoidal curve defined by an initial limit on the rate of temperature increase on total temperature change. If the temperature path passes above this region, sector- and region-specific costs are defined proportional to the excess. In all illustrative runs presented so far, though, the parameters of this time-path of "tolerable" temperature change have been fixed at zero so that costly impacts begin with any temperature change.

The richest part of the PAGE model is its treatment of uncertainty. All major parameters on the emissions, atmospheric, and impacts side are represented by triangular probability distributions whose parameters can be set by the user, and uncertainty is propagated throughout the model. No other distribution forms than triangular are available, however (Hope, Anderson & Wenman 1993).

The DICE Model

The DICE model, developed by William Nordhaus (1991), is a dynamic integrated model of climate change in which a single world producer-consumer makes choices between current consumption, investing in productive capital, and reducing emissions to slow climate change. Population growth and technological change yielding productivity growth are both externally assumed to decline asymptotically to zero, eventually yielding stabilised population and productivity.

The single consumer maximises discounted present value of utility of consumption, subject to a Cobb-Douglas production function that includes damages from climate change. Emissions per unit output are assumed to decline exogenously at a fixed rate, and can be further reduced by costly emission-control measures. An increasing, convex emission-control cost function is estimated from prior studies, in which reducing emissions 50 percent from the prevailing level at any time costs about 1 percent of the world economy. Current carbon emissions add to atmospheric concentrations via a fixed retention ratio, and realised temperature change is modelled by a three-box model representing the atmosphere, mixed-layer upper ocean, and deep ocean. Damage from climate change is a quadratic function of realised temperature change with a 3-degree change calibrated to cause a 1.3 percent world GNP loss. A detailed description of the DICE model, including derivations of model equations, results, and sensitivity analysis can be found in Nordhaus (1994).

In an earlier analysis, Nordhaus developed an estimate of the sensitivity to climate change of the US economy by looking separately at each major sector. His best estimate for the impact of an equilibrium 3-degree global temperature change was a loss of 0.25 percent of GNP. Judgementally incorporating cross-sectoral linkages or other overlooked damages, he estimated that 1 to 2 percent of GNP was a plausible upper-bound for the cost of climate change of this magnitude. Several researchers developing other integrated-assessment models use points from Nordhaus' estimated damage range to calibrate their damage functions.

Two extensions of the DICE model have recently been developed. RICE, developed by Nordhaus and Yang, includes multiple regions and decision makers, to permit analysis of more strategies and protocols. RICE exists in six-region and 10-region versions. The six regions are the United States, Japan, China, the European Union, the former Soviet Union, and the rest of the world; the 10-region version separates the rest of the world into five groups clustered by size. RICE has been used to analyse the implications of three broad international policy approaches: "do nothing" (the market solution); an efficient solution ignoring distributional effects (the co-operative solution); and a solution in which each nation chooses the best policy for itself (the nationalistic solution). PRICE, under development, will include uncertainty in some key parameters.

CETA

CETA is a model developed at the Electric Power Research Institute (EPRI), which contains a single world region. The model draws on a major energy-economic model, Global 2100, a previous EPRI project. Global 2100 modelled five world regions with moderately detailed energy sectors and a single representative consumer-producer in each (Manne & Richels 1992). CETA collapses the Global 2100 world into one region and adds simple illustrative representations of the carbon cycle, global-average temperature change, and damages due to warming. In CETA, the world's single consumer-producer now optimises present value utility of consumption net of loss from climate change. Illustrative damage functions are defined that express climate-change damage at any time as an increasing function of the realised change in global-average temperature. These functions are calibrated to be consistent with Nordhaus' upper-bound estimate of 2 percent GNP loss from an equilibrium 3-degree Celsius temperature change, and the implications of different forms of damage function passing through this point (linear, quadratic, etc.) for the optimal emissions trajectory are explored. CETA has also been used for separate analyses of the effect of making damage depend on the rate of temperature rise and of varying parameter values. More recent analyses with the model redivide the world into two regions and consider the effect of different levels of co-operation on optimal emission paths (Peck & Teisberg 1992).

MICRO-MELODIE

MELODIE (Devezeaux et al. 1989) is a French macroeconomic model with a detailed technological description of the energy sector, especially in the electricity sector. The model also computes polluting emissions such as: NO_x,

SO_2 and CO_2. Economy, energy and environment are then described in a single framework, but for each topic a specific methodology has been developed. MELODIE is adapted to measure any energy policy modifying the cost structure of electricity supply.

Data requirements include: 1) Input/Output tables at current and constant prices; 2) Economic accounts of the Institutional sectors; 3) Technological and economic data on the electricity sector including fuel cycle; 4) International economic data; 5) Energy balances in physical and monetary units; 6) Environmental data (polluting emissions).

Spatial coverage is at national level.

Time horizon includes medium (1-5 years) and long run (40 years) term.

The main objective of the model is the analysis of macroeconomic-energy and environment linkages. Basic approach is a macro econometric model with technical representation for the energy sector.

The model is providing macroeconomic analysis (country specific econometric model, total energy system analysis), demand analysis (analysis of energy requirements for households, and industrial sectors using econometric estimation of transfer cost and utility functions), resource analysis, supply side analysis (technological representation of the electricity sector including a full representation of coal, gas, oil and nuclear fuel cycles), supply/demand balance (price equilibrium) and some other kinds of analysis.

The model already has been adapted to different countries (Algeria, Morocco, Jordan and Tunisia).

MESSAGE III

The MESSAGE modelling system is generally used for the optimisation of energy supply systems developed by the International Institute for Applied Systems Analysis (IIASA) (Messner & Strubegger 1990). However, other systems supplying specified demands of goods that have to be processed before delivery to the final consumer could be optimised. MESSAGE consists of a demand data module, supply data module, optimisation module, results module and supporting programs.

Data requirements include: 1) technology database, e.g., efficiency, costs, emissions, etc.; 2) energy prices; 3) resource bases; 4) import/export constraints; 5) technology penetration; 6) rates and constraints; 7) optimal load curves.

Spatial coverage depends on user's choice.

The time horizon is divided into periods, the number of years aggregated into a period depends on the problem to be solved. The number of years within a period can vary over the planning horizon.

MESSAGE is an instrument for medium- to long-term dynamic planning of the operation and expansion of energy systems. The objectives include: resource extraction analysis; import/export of energy; energy conversion analysis; energy transport and distribution analysis; final energy utilisation by consumers analysis; environmental protection policy; investment policy; opportunity costs (shadow prices, marginal costs).

MESSAGE III evaluates energy systems costs and capital requirements for energy planning (scenario development) and CO_2 tax impacts on energy mix.

MESSAGE III presents demand analysis (incorporates useful energy, final energy, secondary energy, energy efficiency, fuel substitution, energy conservation, energy/economy elasticity (optional)); resource analysis (fossil fuel resources are given by various cost categories, domestic renewable energy potentials and costs); supply side analysis (detailed evaluation of supply side configurations); supply/demand balance (optimisation of energy balances in dynamics); detailed electric system analysis (load curve: typical days (e.g., winter, summer and intermediate season's day) are used to describe load curves; load characterisation: each typical day is described by three parameters - night, peak, and the remaining day load); generation expansion analysis (electricity generation is controlled by technology penetration parameters and demand constraints); transmission (simple analysis includes costs and energy flows); environmental analysis.

MESAP

MESAP is a modular energy planning package with the specific needs of developing countries in mind. It is designed as a flexible planning package providing energy analysts and planners with tools to perform complex energy analysis. It consists of: basic techniques for energy planning, a set of tested energy modules, and data management and processing software. At the heart of MESAP is a network oriented database (Reuter 1990).

Data requirements includes: 1) base year energy balance, base year economic activities; 2) energy technology characteristics; performance, costs, investments; 3) technological, environmental, political constraints; 4) world energy prices (imports); 5) resources, potentials, restrictions; 6) optional: emission factors.

Spatial coverage is regional or national (investment calculation program - INCA is local). Time horizon is mid to long term.

Resolution: year, split in seasons; simplified load duration curves. Steps: monthly or yearly in INCA; yearly in WASP and MADE; yearly or per period in LP.

The main objective of the model is energy and environmental policy analysis and planning.

Issues addressed are macroeconomic analysis (country-specific econometric model), total energy system analysis, demand analysis (analysis of energy requirements at the useful energy level, or optionally, on the final energy level; choice of econometric and process engineering methods, user specified sectors and fuels considered; level of calculation is specified by the user - model can be expanded until the resource level (simulation model)); resource analysis (simple representation of depletable and renewable resources; different grades and resource limits can be specified by user); supply side analysis (either a simulation program or a LP-package (MESSAGE) is available. Both models are technology-oriented), detailed electric system analysis, environmental analysis.

Structure of energy systems can be adapted to statistical data available. Level of detail of analysis is user-defined. Analysed system can be expanded to cover non-energy sectors, too. User programs can be incorporated.

MERGE

MERGE is a regionally disaggregated integrated-assessment model, whose development was supported by the Electric Power Research Institute. MERGE is based on Global 2200, a dynamic general equilibrium model with five world regions and a single consumer in each region who makes both savings and consumption decisions. A simple climate model represents atmospheric lifetimes of CO_2, CH_4, and N_2O, which yield global change in radiative forcing, and equilibrium and realised global-average temperature change. Illustrative impact functions are defined separately for market and non-market components. Market impacts are modelled as a quadratic function of realised temperature change, calibrated to pass through a judgemental point estimate that is consistent with the estimate of Nordhaus. Non-market impacts are modelled as a worldwide public good, for which each region's willingness to pay to avoid a specified temperature change is an S-shaped function of regional income.

A reduced-form Excel-based version of MERGE, called MiniMERGE, has recently been developed by EPRI to permit testing of alternative inter-regional burden-sharing schemes in a simplified environment. MiniMERGE allows the user to choose one of two discount rates and to specify one of four policy objectives for global emissions: business-as-usual; stabilise emissions at 1990 levels; stabilise CO_2 concentrations at 550 ppm; or optimise emissions to minimise the present value of damages. Then, region-specific costs can be calculated under a user-specified assumption of how fast the allocation of global emissions shifts to equal per-capita entitlements.

GREEN

The GeneRal Equilibrium ENvironmental model, hereafter referred to as GREEN, was developed by the OECD Secretariat in order to assess the economic impacts of imposing limits on carbon emissions (Burniaux et al. 1992). The model was developed in the period 1991-92 and has been used extensively for a wide variety of analyses including the impacts of emissions constraint in the OECD, global agreements, tradable permits, transfer mechanisms, and comparisons with other carbon abatement models.

GREEN is a recursive-dynamic global computable general equilibrium (CGE) model with a special focus on energy production and consumption. The model is calibrated on a 1985 data set, and is calibrated dynamically to produce an exogenously given path of real GDP growth and population growth.

Global economic activity is divided into twelve regions, each one modelled similarly, albeit with a different base data set and a different set of parameters. Economic activity is initially divided into eight sectors, with seven energy backstop substitutes introduced in later years. The initial sectors include five energy-based sectors, and three other sectors. The energy sectors are coal, crude oil, natural gas, refined petroleum products, and electricity (which for - data reasons - also includes gas and water distribution). The remaining sectors are agriculture, energy-intensive industries, and all other goods and services.

The model incorporates energy backstop substitutes. These are sources of energy that are expected to be available in the future. There are seven backstop energies. Coal, crude oil, and natural gas, are each assumed to have two substitute fuels - one that is carbon intensive, such as tar sands, and one that is carbon-free, such as biomass. Electricity has one backstop energy substitute, which is assumed to be a carbon-free source, such as fusion, solar, wind, etc.

GREEN is a recursive dynamic model, i.e., each period of the model is solved as a single period model, with backward looking transition equations linking the individual periods together. The key transition equations include labour growth, capital accumulation, fossil fuel resource depletion, and energy and factor efficiency improvements.

The model has three kinds of factors of production: labour, capital, and sector-specific fixed factors. There are two main characteristics of the production structure in GREEN - the putty/semi-putty specification of production, and the multi-level nesting of the inputs of the production structure.

Each region has one representative consumer (household), which receives all the income generated by value added, i.e., both labour and capital income (including income generated by the sector specific fixed factors).

There are three final demand activities other than households: government expenditure on goods and services, labour, and capital; investment final demand; and change in stock levels (which is assumed to be at a zero activity level after the base year).

Trade is modelled using the so-called Armington assumption. Each commodity is assumed to be differentiated by its region of origin.

There are three closure rules in GREEN - the net government balance, investment-savings, and the trade balance. GREEN computes carbon emissions that are generated by the consumption of carbon-based fuels - coal, crude oil, natural gas, refined oil, and the carbon-based backstops.

GREEN has three sources of technology changes: labour, capital, and energy. Changes in labour efficiency are assumed to be exogenous, and they are specified by the user. Changes in energy efficiency are also exogenous, and obviously represent a key component in determining the level of energy use and emissions. This parameter, sometimes referred to as the Autonomous Energy Efficiency Improvement (AEEI) parameter, is implemented as specific to the region, the sector, the capital vintage, and time. For tractability (and comparison with other models), a uniform value of 1 per cent has been chosen for the reference simulation.

The capital efficiency parameter is calibrated in the business-as-usual simulation in order to insure that the model generates balanced growth, i.e., the capital-labour ratio (in efficiency terms) remains constant. Another way of looking at this dynamic calibration procedure is to think in terms of targets and instruments. The target is a specified growth rate of real GDP. This factor has been chosen as the instrument to achieve the exogenously specified growth rate. In all policy simulations, the capital efficiency parameter is exogenous.

GEM-E3

GEM-E3, namely General Equilibrium Model for Energy – Economics - Environment, is a multinational, multi-sector general equilibrium model developed by the European Commission (Capros et al. 1997). It includes detailed representation of the energy supply, of the energy consumption, of the polluting emissions related to the latter and of the damages to environment that the emissions generate. It also provides links with details sectoral energy models.

The GEM-E3 model intends to deal with the general subject of sustainable economic growth, in a way to support concrete policy analysis issues. Sustainable economic growth refers to tightly linked environmental and energy related strategic objectives that have to be considered in the same time as prerequisites and conditions for achieving stability and economic development. A particular subject, which encompasses almost all aspects and interactions within the objective of sustainable economic growth, is the greenhouse problem and the analysis of related policies. In fact, in order to reduce greenhouse gas emissions, in particular CO2 emissions, it is necessary to achieve substantial gains in energy conservation and in the efficient use of fossil fuels in electricity generation, as well as to perform important fuel substitutions throughout the energy system (for instance in favour of natural gas). Within the increasingly liberalising markets, the effective carriers of such a policy can mainly be the carbon-related taxes, the pollution permits and other instruments, which certainly have significant macroeconomic effects. The efficient use and production of energy, as well as the fuel substitutions, induced by the greenhouse targets, have also beneficial effects on other types of pollution and direct impacts on the international energy markets. Thus, all three systems, namely economy, energy and environment, are interrelated. Is it possible to achieve economic growth that will not be altered by environmental problems (e.g., greenhouse) or energy shortages, and at which economic or social cost? This is the general type of questions to be analysed by GEM-E3.

The model addresses an important additional issue, so as to support the policy analysis needs of the Commission. This is termed "burden sharing" and concerns the distributional effects of efforts towards sustainable economic growth. Distributional effects are considered in two senses: distribution among European countries and distribution among social or economic groups within each country. This concerns the particular allocation of taxation between nations, producing sectors and consumer groups.

Closely related to the previous subjects are the restructuring the energy system in Europe and changes in the conditions of energy provisions. These two subjects emerge as a consequence of both the European unification and the evolution in eastern European countries. The former subject includes in particular the deregulation of the energy sectors which may change electricity and gas supply patterns in Europe. The latter subject includes the "energy charter" and its follow-up, which may induce a new situation in natural gas provisions in Europe.

The GEM-E3 Europe and GEM-E3 World model

The GEM-E3 Europe model is a full scale general equilibrium model for the EU, consisting of 14 inter-linked country-modules. An extension to the newly associated countries and to Switzerland is foreseen in a current EU research project. A world version of GEM-E3, with 18 region-modules, has also been developed following the same general structure as the GEM-E3 Europe model and based on GTAP database. The model results from a collaborative efforts by a consortium, involving the National Technical University of Athens (NTUA), the Centre for Economic Studies of the Katholieke Universiteit Leuven and the Centre for European Research (ZEW) as the core modelling team. Other participants in current projects for a further developing of the model are ERASME (Ecole Centrale de Paris), MERIT (University of Maastricht), the Paul Scherrer Institute (PSI) and the University of Budapest of Economic Science. Its development has mainly been financed by the European Commission through research projects within the Joule programme and the 5th Framework Programme.

The GEM-E3 model has been frequently used in the past by the project partners for policy-oriented research activities for National Authorities and for Directorate Generals of the European Commission. The new model developments foreseen in projects financed under the European Union 5th Framework Programme (TCH-GEM-E3 and GECS) will further widen the scope for interesting issues. The multi-purpose nature of GEM-E3 (national, EU-wide, world wide applications, endogenous innovation, alternative assumptions about expectations of agents, new instruments etc.) makes it an appropriate tool for the evaluation of policies in many domains, also outside energy and environment. At EU level, the focus of policy analysis to be undertaken with GEM-E3 will be on climate policy, both at world and EU level, for the Kyoto and post Kyoto period, and on the implications of research and development expenditure for growth and environmental policies.

GEM-E3 provides details on the macro-economy of the EU countries/World regions and its interaction with the environment and the energy system. It is an empirical, large-scale model, written entirely in structural form, which has the following characteristics:

- it considers explicitly market clearing mechanisms, and related price formation, in the economy, energy, environment economy markets; prices are computed by the model as a result of supply and demand interactions in the markets, in which economic agents are price takers; through its flexible formulation, it also enables the representation of hybrid or regulated situations, as well as perfect competition.
- it formulates separately the supply or demand behaviour of the economic agents in the individual optimisation of their objectives, and makes them compete within markets cleared by prices that achieve global equilibrium.
- its scope is general, in other terms global, in two senses: it includes all simultaneously clearing inter-related markets, and represents the system at the appropriate coverage level, with respect to geography, the sub-system (energy, environment, economy) and the dynamic mechanisms of agents' behaviour, including expectations;
- although global, the model exhibits a sufficient degree of disaggregating detail concerning sectors, structural features of energy, and policy-oriented instruments (e.g., taxation, subsidies, environmental permits).
- as it includes multiple countries/regions, industrial sectors and economic agents, it allows a consistent evaluation of distributional effects of policies.

GEM-E3 is a dynamic, recursive over time, model, involving dynamics of capital accumulation and technology progress, stock and flow relationships and backward looking expectations. The results of GEM-E3 include projections of full Input-Output tables by country, national accounts, employment, capital, financial flows, balance of payments, public finance and revenues, household consumption and welfare, energy use and supply, and atmospheric emissions. The computation of equilibrium is simultaneous for all domestic markets and their interaction through flexible bilateral trade flows.

The G-CUBED Model

The G-Cubed model was developed by Warwick McKibbin and Peter Wilcoxen (1995a,b). The model has been constructed to contribute to the current policy debate on environmental policy and international trade with a focus on global warming policies, but it has many features that will make it useful for answering a range of issues in environmental regulation, microeconomic and macroeconomic policy questions. It is a world model with substantial regional disaggregation and sectoral detail. In addition, countries and regions are linked both temporally and intertemporally through trade and financial markets.

G-Cubed contains a strong foundation for analysis of both short run macroeconomic policy analysis as well as long run growth consideration of alternative macroeconomic policies. Intertemporal budget constraints on households, governments and nations (the latter through accumulations of foreign debt) are imposed. To accommodate these constraints, forward looking behaviour is incorporated in consumption and investment decisions. G-Cubed also contains substantial sectoral detail. This permits analysis of environmental policies which tend to have their largest effects on small segments of the economy. By integrating sectoral detail with the macroeconomic features of the MSG2 model, G-Cubed can be used to consider the long run costs of alternative environmental regulations yet at the same time consider the macroeconomic implications of these policies over time. The response of monetary and fiscal authorities in different countries can have important effects in the short to medium run which, given the long lags in physical capital and other asset accumulation, can be a substantial period of time. Overall, the model is designed to provide a bridge between computable general equilibrium models and macroeconomic models by integrating the more desirable features of both approaches.

EPPA

The MIT Emissions Prediction and Policy Analysis (EPPA) model is used to analyse the processes that produce greenhouse-relevant emissions, and to assess the consequences of policy proposals intended to control these emissions. It is a global, applied general equilibrium model of economic growth, international trade, and greenhouse gas emissions (CO_2, CO, CH_4, SO_2, NO_x, N_2O, CFC_s) from a set of trade-linked economic regions (Babiker et al. 2001). The model also includes consideration of sulphates and non-methane volatile organic carbon gases, which are important inputs to the atmospheric chemistry-climate component of the IGSM.

The EPPA model is used to compute predictions of anthropogenic emissions of the key gases from twelve economic regions, and converts them into distributions by latitude where needed. Special provision is made for analysis of uncertainty in key influences, such as the growth of population and economic activity, and the pace and direction of technical change. Further, EPPA has been formulated to support analysis of a variety of emissions control policies, providing estimates of the magnitude and distribution among nations of the costs, and clarifying the ways that changes are mediated through international trade.

The Emissions Prediction and Policy Analysis (EPPA) model is used to calculate paths of future greenhouse emissions, and to provide economic analysis of proposed control measures. It is a model of economic growth, international trade, and greenhouse gas emissions.

Examination of human influence on future climate begins with the prediction of future levels of emissions of greenhouse gases and aerosols. At the same time, it is necessary to address future economic and technological change in some detail. Because many of the important chemical species that determine atmospheric levels of pollutants and greenhouse gases exist only for a short time in the atmosphere, the Program's approach is to predict economic development and the resulting emissions of trace gases as functions of geographic location as well as time. For example, our predictions of sulphate aerosols and ozone take account of expected shifts of emissions during the next century from Europe and North America to China and Southern Asia. For this purpose, and for policy analysis, the IGSM includes a global economic development model that addresses economic growth, technological change, and the resulting changes in the magnitude, composition, and location of future anthropogenic emissions.

Previous research at MIT on greenhouse gas emissions and their control resulted in the development of the EPPA model, which is built on a comprehensive energy-economy data set developed by the Global Trade Analysis Project (GTAP) that accommodates a consistent representation of energy markets in physical units as well as detailed accounts of regional production and bilateral trade flows. In addition, estimates of non-CO_2 gases and sinks have been introduced in the calculation of least-cost abatement. The emissions coefficients and the sectors and activities to which they are attached in EPPA have been updated to reflect current inventory estimates, which have significantly improved as a result of the improved monitoring, estimation and reporting of emissions by country and sector, as required under the Framework Convention on Climate Change. The EPPA model was initially based on the General Equilibrium Environmental (GREEN) model developed by the Organisation for Economic Co-operation and Development (OECD), but has been significantly modified and extended in its development at MIT.

The EPPA model takes account of the supply of input factors available to a region: labour, capital, imports, and natural resources. These are matched with the demand from various sectors. Demand for the output of the producer sectors comes from a set of household, government, investment and export sectors, and are paid for with income earned from the provision of the input factors, taxes and foreign exchange. Savings by consumers affect future economic output through the accumulation of capital. Because of its importance for greenhouse gas emissions, the energy sector includes separate treatments for oil, gas and coal, and fossil and non-fossil fuel technologies that might replace conventional sources in the long term. The model takes account of estimated in-ground resources in the different regions, and their depletion as production proceeds over time. It separately identifies the electric sector, and accounts for its input fuels, including nuclear and other non-fossil technologies, for example, wind and solar. Greenhouse- and pollution-relevant gases resulting from the economic activities considered in the model are predicted for each economic region, and then used as inputs to the climate model.

EFOM-ENV

The EFOM-ENV models are national dynamic optimisation models (employing linear programming) representing the energy producing and consuming sectors in each Member State (de Kruijk & van den Broek 1993). They optimise the development of these sectors under given fuel import prices and useful energy demand over a pre-defined time horizon. The development of national energy systems can be subject to energy and environment constraints like availabilities of fuel supply, penetration rates of certain technologies, emission standards and emission ceilings. The model data bases contain a wide range of conversion and end use technologies such as conventional technologies, renewables, efficient fossil fuel burning technologies, combined heat and power and energy conservation measures in the demand sectors.

Data requirements include: 1) energy balance in a base year; 2) projections of useful energy demand and fuel prices; 3) investment and operating costs, availability and efficiency of energy production, transformation and the technologies; 4) energy and environmental constraints, where relevant (e.g., development of nuclear power, availability of renewable resources, emission standards, etc.); 5) emission factors (SO_2, NO_x, particulates, CO_2); 6) load duration curves for electricity and heat demands.

Spatial coverage is within a country.

Time horizon is from medium to long-term. Length of period (in years) chosen by users.

The main objective of the model is the energy and environment policy analysis and planning. In particular, cost-effectiveness analysis of energy policy options for reducing pollutant emissions (so-called "bottom-up" approach of emission reduction objectives).

Issues addressed include macroeconomic analysis, total energy system analysis, demand side analysis (analysis of energy requirements at the useful energy level or on the final energy level. Also the levels of activity of options including energy saving measures are investigated), resource analysis, supply side analysis (all energy flows entering the system are represented, either as import or extraction of energy carriers. Also renewable energy like wind, sun or hydro energy are defined), supply/demand balance (detailed electric system analysis), environmental analysis.

E3ME

The Energy-Environment-Economy Model of Europe (E3ME) model has been built by a European team under the EU JOULE/THERMIE program as a framework for assessing energy-environment-economy issues and policies. The model has been used for general macro analysis and for more focused analysis of policies relating to greenhouse gas mitigation, incentives for industrial energy efficiency and sustainable household consumption (Barker 1998a,b). Its pan-European coverage is appropriate for an increasingly integrated European market. E3ME provides a one-model approach in which the detailed industry analysis is consistent with the macro analysis: in E3ME, the key indicators are modelled separately for each sector, and for each region, yielding the results for Europe as a whole.

The model provides annual comprehensive forecasts to the year 2012: for 19 European regions including the EU15 (plus north/south Italy and east/west Germany), Norway and Switzerland for industry output, investment, prices, exports, imports, employment and intermediate demand at a 32-industry level including nine service industries for consumers expenditure in 28 categories.

- Full macro top-down and industrial bottom-up simulation analysis of the economy, allowing industrial factors to influence the macro picture.
- An in-depth treatment of changes in the input-output structure of the economy over the forecast period to incorporate the effects of technological change, relative price movements and changes in the composition of each industry's output.
- Dynamic multiplier analysis, illustrating the response of the main economic indicators, industrial outputs and prices to standard changes in the assumptions, e.g., changes in world oil prices, income taxes, government spending, and exchange rates.
- Scenario analysis, across a range of greenhouse gas mitigation policies, including carbon taxes and permit trading.

E3ME is intended to meet an expressed need by researchers and policy makers for a framework for analysing the implications of long-term E3 policies, especially those concerning R&D and environmental taxation and regulation. The model is also capable of addressing the short-term and medium-term economic effects as well as, more broadly, the long-term effects of such policies.

Most conventional macroeconomic models which are operational in government describe short and medium-term economic consequences of policies but with a limited treatment of long-term effects, such as those from the supply side of the labour market, and this limits their ability to analyse long-term policies. In contrast, Computable General Equilibrium (CGE) models, have been widely used to analyse long-term E3 policies. CGE models specify explicit demand and supply relationships and enforce market clearing, and are therefore seen as characterisations of long-term outcomes in which markets are assumed to be in equilibrium; for this reason they have been developed particularly in the US for the analysis of environmental regulation. However, CGE models are not generally estimated by time-series econometric methods and so have not typically been subjected to historical validation, either in terms of the values of the model's parameters or, more broadly, the underlying assumptions with respect to economic behaviour. They also have no treatment of the dynamics of model solution, and so cannot be used for historical validation of the overall model or for analysing the short- and medium-term impacts of policy changes. Their use in forecasting is limited.

E3ME combines the features of an annual short- and medium-term sectoral model estimated by formal econometric methods with the detail and some of the methods of the CGE models, providing analysis of the movement of the long-term outcomes for key E3 indicators in response to policy changes. It is essentially a dynamic simulation model estimated by econometric methods.

The econometric model, in contrast with some macroeconomic models currently in operation, has a complete specification of the long-term solution in the form of an estimated equation which has long-term restrictions imposed on its parameters. Economic theory, for example the recent theories of endogenous growth, informs the specification of the long-term equations and hence properties of the model; dynamic equations which embody these long-term properties are estimated by econometric methods to allow the model to provide forecasts. The method utilises developments in time-series econometrics, with the specification of dynamic relationships in terms of error correction models (ECM), which allow dynamic convergence to a long-term outcome. This is therefore a relatively ambitious modelling project that expands the methodology of long-term modelling to incorporate developments both in economic theory and in applied econometrics, while at the same time maintaining flexibility and ensuring that the model is operational.

E3ME is a detailed model of the 25 Nace-Clio sectors expanded to 32 sectors with the disaggregation of energy and environment industries, in which the energy-environment-economy interactions are central. The model is designed to be estimated and solved for 19 regions of Europe chosen for the project (the EU-15 member states plus Norway and Switzerland, with Germany divided into east and west and Italy divided into north and south), although eastern Germany is excluded from the econometric estimation.

This one-model approach is distinguished from the multi-model approach, which is a feature of earlier model-based research for the EU. In principle, linked models (such as the DRI or the HERMES-MIDAS system of models) could be estimated and solved consistently for all the economies involved. However, in practice, this often proves difficult, if not impossible, and considerable resources have to go into linking. Even if the consistency problem in linkage can be solved by successive iterative solutions of the component models, there remains a more basic problem with the multi-model approach if it attempts to combine macroeconomic models with detailed industry or energy models. This problem is that the system cannot adequately tackle the simulation of "bottom-up" policies. Normally these systems are first solved at the macroeconomic level, then the results for the macroeconomic variables are disaggregated by an industry model. However if the policy is directed at the detailed industry level (say, a tax on the carbon content of energy use), it is very difficult (without substantial intervention by the model operator) to ensure that the implicit results for macroeconomic variables from the industry model are consistent with the explicit results from the macro model. As an example, it is difficult to use a macro-industry two-model system to simulate the effect of exempting selective energy-intensive industries from the carbon/energy tax.

The detailed nature of the model allows it to represent fairly complex scenarios, in particular scenarios that are differentiated according to sector and to country. Similarly, the impact of any measure can be represented in a detailed way.

The econometric grounding of the models gives it a better capability in representing and forecasting performance in the short to medium run. It therefore provides information which is closer to the time horizon of many policy makers than pure CGE models.

An interaction (two-way feedback) between the economy, energy demand/supply and environmental emissions is an undoubted advantage over other models which may either ignore the interaction completely or only assume a one-way causation.

WEM

The world energy model (WEM, http://www.iea.org/weo/) is a tool to analyse:

- Global energy prospects: trends in demand, supply availability and constraints, international trade and energy balances by sector and by fuel to 2020.
- Environmental impact of energy use: CO_2 emissions from fuel combustion are derived from the detailed projections of energy consumption, while emission trading among countries is simulated to arrive at a optimal price for tradable permits.
- Effects of policy actions or technological changes: scenarios to analyse the impact of policy actions and developments in technologies, such as in: electricity generation, transportation and fossil fuel supply, and in the overall energy supply/demand balance.

The WEM is a mathematical model made up of four main submodels: final demand, power generation and other transformation, fossil fuel supply and emission trading. The main exogenous assumptions are GDP, population, international fossil fuel prices and technological developments. The level of electricity consumption and electricity prices link the final energy demand and power generation modules. Primary demand for fossil fuels serves as input for the supply modules. Energy balances are calculated using the outputs of the three modules for each region. CO_2 emissions can then be derived using implied carbon factors. The emission trading module uses marginal abatement cost curves, obtained by an iterative process of running the WEM with different carbon values.

The final energy demand module is based on the sectoral breakdown. In the standard model, nine sectors are modelled: Industry (Iron and Steel, Chemicals, Other Industries), Transport (Road, Aviation, Other Transport), Other Sectors (Residential, Commercial and Services, Agriculture). Total final energy demand is the sum of energy consumption of each sector. In each sector six types of energy are identified: coal, oil, gas, electricity, heat and renewables. Within each sector, whether substitution between fuels is considered or not, fuel consumption is estimated in a more or less aggregate way. If aggregated, the consumption is split between fuels mainly by relative fuel prices as well as other market determinants, such as capital stock turnover. If fuels are estimated separately, total final consumption is calculated as the sum of each component.

In most of the equations, energy demand is a function of the following explanatory variables:

- Economic activity: This is represented in general by GDP or GDP per capita. In several sectors, a specific activity variable is used. For example, in the steel industry, final energy demand is a function of steel production. In the transport sector, vehicle stock, passenger-kilometres or tonne-kilometres are used.
- Price: End-user prices are calculated from the exogenous international energy prices. They take into account both variable and fixed taxes, and also transformations and distribution costs. For each sector, a representative price (usually a weighted average) is derived. This takes account of the product mix in final consumption and differences between countries. This representative price is then used as an explanatory variable directly, lagged or as a moving average.
- Other variables: Other variables are used to take into account structural and technological changes, or saturation effects.

The purpose of the power generation module is to calculate the following:

1. Amount of any new generating capacity needed.
2. Type of any new plant to be built.
3. Amount of electricity generated by each type of plant.
4. Fuels consumed to generate the previously determined level of electricity demand.
5. System marginal cost of generation.

The model uses 11 different technological types of plant:

1. Steam boiler
2. Combined cycle gas turbine (CCGT)
3. Open cycle gas turbine (GT)
4. Integrated gasification combined cycle (IGCC)
5. Nuclear
6. Biomass
7. Geothermal
8. Wind
9. Hydro (conventional)
10. Hydro (pumped storage)
11. Solar

For each region, sector and fuel, CO_2 emissions are calculated by multiplying energy demand by an implied carbon emission factor. Implied emission factors for coal, oil and gas differ between sectors and regions, reflecting the product mix.

Oil module. The purpose of this module is to determine the level of oil production in each region. Production is split into three categories: non-OPEC; OPEC; unconventional oil production. OPEC conventional oil production is assumed to fill the gap between non-OPEC and unconventional production and total world oil demand. Total oil demand is the sum of regional oil demand, world bunkers and stock variation. The derivation of conventional and unconventional non-OPEC production uses a combination of two different approaches. A short-term approach estimates production profiles based on a field-by-field analysis. A long-term approach involves the determination of production according to the level of ultimate recoverable resources and a depletion rate estimated using historical data. Ultimate recoverable resources depend on a recovery factor. This recovery factor reflects reserve growth, which results from improvements in drilling, exploration and production technologies. The trend in the recovery rate is, in turn, a function of the oil price and a technological improvement factor.

Gas module. The gas sub-module is similarly based on a resources approach. However, there are some important differences with the oil sub-module. In particular, three regional gas markets - America, Europe and Africa, and Asia - are considered, whereas oil is modelled as a single international market. Two country types are modelled: net importers and net exporters. Once gas production from each net importer region is estimated, taking into account ultimate recoverable resources and a depletion rate, the remaining regional demand is allocated to the net exporter regions with exogenous assumptions on their respective shares.

Coal module. Sufficient reserves of coal exist to meet world demand and coal reserves are generally much more evenly distributed throughout the world than oil and gas reserves. Because of the wide diversity of existing and potential coal suppliers, security of coal supply is not an issue. The current WEM does not, therefore, model coal supply explicitly but information on coal production prospects is provided in the regional chapters.

4 Energy Indicators

The indicators are designed to show the key energy trends. By watching them closely, we can gain an understanding of where we are and make better decisions about where we want to go. In some cases, the indicators combine energy, economic, or demographic information to create an index that illustrates energy intensity. For example, indicators for the residential, commercial, industrial, and transportation sectors illustrate energy consumption and expenditures relative to an appropriate economic factor for each sector. Other indicators are designed to show key energy trends by breaking down energy consumption and prices by type of energy or end-use sector.

The effective indicator has to meet characteristics reflecting the problem and criteria to be considered. Its purpose is to show how well the system is working. Indicators are strongly dependent on the type of system they monitor.

It is known that any numerical number, semantic expression or mathematical sign is information. Also, positive or negative sign of the variable are also information. Collecting information and its processing will convert them into data. So, the data represent agglomerated information, which are partially or finally processed .

In order to use the data for the assessment of the respective system, it is necessary to convert them into an indicator. So, the indicator represents the measuring parameter for the comparison between different states or structure of the system. Also, we can evaluate different structures, of the systems by the indicator. In this direction is the assessment of intelligence use in the improvement of the system compatibility with its surrounding measured by the respective indicators.

Good indicators show the basic and fundamental relationships between energy and the long term quality of life. They must be understandable and useful to policy makers and the public. They must be measurable. Consistent and reliable data must be available to create the indicators.

Many systems of energy indicators and indices exist. Their exact properties depend on the objectives of the study and the requests of the users. For example, the selected energy performance indicators fall into two groups: overall indicators to show consumption, price, renewable energy, and energy emission trends and indices to show energy performance and intensity.

Overall Indicators

- Energy Consumption by Major Fuel: Consumption trends by major fuel (petroleum, natural gas, electricity and coal).
- Energy Consumption by Sector: Consumption trends by end-use sector (residential, commercial, industrial and transportation).
- Average Energy Prices: Average energy prices for natural gas, electricity, gasoline, and distillate oil and overall Washington State energy prices compared to national prices.
- Greenhouse Gas Emissions: Carbon dioxide emissions from energy sources indexed to 1990 levels.
- Energy Intensity Indices.
- Energy and the Economy: Energy expenditures and consumption relative to gross state product with comparison to national values.
- Energy Consumption per Capita: Annual energy consumption per Washington resident.
- Residential Indicators: Residential energy expenditures and consumption per household.
- Commercial Indicators: Commercial energy expenditures and consumption relative to commercial employment.
- Industrial Indicators: Industrial energy expenditures and consumption relative to industrial activity.
- Transportation Indicators: Highway transportation energy expenditures and consumption relative to vehicle miles travelled.

In this chapter we present in more details two systems of energy indicators: energy systems sustainability indicators and energy efficiency indicators. We select these two systems for description because they reflect the core issues of our study on energy sustainability.

4.1 Energy System Sustainability Indicators

The criteria for the energy system sustainability assessment have to reflect four aspects, namely: resource aspect, environment aspect, social aspect and economic aspect (Afgan et al. 1998). In this respect, the sustainability assessment of an energy system will comprise the evaluation of those parameters which are a reflection of the integral concept of sustainability. As any other complex system the energy system is defined with constraints which reflect its function, technology, geography, property and capacity (Afgan et al. 2000).

In the definition of sustainability criteria for the energy system the following aspects were taken into consideration in the definition of the criteria (Geiz & Kutzmark 1998):

- It should reflect sustainability concept. This will imply that the indicators for the criteria represent quantities, which have relevancy to the sustainability. This will imply that the energy system dematerialization in the design may be seen as the introduction of knowledge based systems, use of virtual library, digitalised video, use of on-line diagnostic systems, development of new sensor elements and development of new combustion technologies.
- It will be defined with indicators which can be measured as physical parameters and are available as the data which are possible to obtain in quantitative or qualitative form.
- It should be based on timely information. Indicators have to be the information which is relevant to the time. This will mean that the energy system and its subsystems have to meet sustainability through every stage of the life cycle. It is known that the energy system work under different conditions in order to meet load change, environment change, social change. It is obvious that there will be different cycles for each of the mentioned time scale.
- It is based on the reliable information. In this respect the indicators have to be the data which you must trust because they may be the milestone for the important decision to be made.
- It reflects a strategic view. Since the sustainability is not a quick fix of current problems and it is a way of choosing actions today that will cause problems tomorrow. As regards the energy system, it may be interpreted as: mixed energy concept with optimisation of local resources, urban and industrial planning with transport optimisation and use of renewable energy sources.
- It gives possibility to perform optimisation of the system to minimise energy cost, available material, government regulations, financial resources, protection of the environment, together with safety, reliability, availability and maintainability of the system.
- It reflects longevity of design. Complex energy system is commonly composed of different subsystems and individual equipment elements. It has been recognised that the life of the elements and subsystems is not equal. In this respect optimal selection of the life cycle for elements and subsystems may lead

to the retrofitting procedure that will reflect need for the sustainable criterions application.

Measuring sustainability is a major issue as well as a driving force of the discussion on sustainability development. Developing tools that reliably measure sustainability is a prerequisite for identifying non-sustainable processes informing design-makers of the quality of products and monitoring impacts to the social environment. The multiplicity of indicators and measuring tools being developed in this fast growing field shows the importance of the conceptual and methodological work in this area (Voinov 1997).

In order to cope with the complexity of sustainability related issues for different systems the indicators have to reflect the wholeness of the system as well as the interaction of its subsystems. Consequently, indicators have to measure the intensity of the interactions among elements of the system and system and its environment. In this view, there is a need for the indicator sets related to the interaction processes that allow an assessment of the complex relationship of every system and its environment. This will imply that complexity indicators will be defined reflecting links among internal parameters and external parameters of the system. This may be interpreted in the thermodynamic vocabulary as the intensive and extensive parameters of the system (Afgan et al. 2000).

In order to quantify the criteria for the sustainability assessment of any design of energy system the indicators are defined to meet this requirement. In this respect, the efficiency of resources use and the technology development are of fundamental importance. The efficiency of energy resource use is a short term approach which may give return benefit in the near future. As regards the technology development, a long-term research and development is needed. In some cases it will require respective social adjustment in order to meet requirements of the new energy sources.

For the sustainability assessment of energy system the following indicators are used.

1. Resource indicator - RI.
2. Environment indicator - EI.
3. Social indicator - SI.
4. Efficiency indicator - FI.

The resource indicators (Pearce & Turner 1990) for the energy system will comprise four elements, including: fuel resources; stainless-steel resource; copper resource and aluminium resource. The indicators reflecting individual elements of the resource indicator are defined as the total amount of the respective material resource used in the design of the system divided by the total annual energy production. This means that the following elements will compose the resource indicator.

Table 4. Energy systems sustainability indicators (Afgan et al. 2000)

	Name	Definition	Unit
Resource indicators			
RI(fuel)	Fuel resource indicator	The amount of fuel consumed in tons divided by the energy produced in lifetime	kg/kWh
RI(cs)	Carbon steel resource indicator	The amount of carbon steel in tons used in the construction of the plant divided by the energy produced in lifetime	kg/kWh
RI(coop)	Copper resource indicator	The amount of copper in tons used in the construction of the plant divided by the energy produced in lifetime	kg/kWh
RI(al)	Aluminium resource indicator	The amount of aluminium in tons used in the construction of the plant divided by the energy produced in lifetime	kg/kWh
Environmental indicators			
EI(CO_2)	Carbon dioxide Environment indicator	The amount of carbon dioxide in tons produced by the plant divided by the energy produced in lifetime	kg/kWh
EI(NO_x)	Nitrogen oxide Environment indicator	The amount of nitrogen oxide in tons produced by the plant divided by the energy produced in lifetime	kg/kWh
EI(SO_2)	Sulphur dioxide Environment indicator	The amount of sulphur dioxide in tons produced by the plant divided by the energy produced in lifetime	kg/kWh
EI(waste)	Waste environment indicator	The amount of waste in tons produced by the plant divided by the energy produced	kg/kWh

		in lifetime	
Social indicators			
SI(job)	New job indicator	Number of paid hours per kWh produced in lifetime	hours/kWh
SI(inv)	Capital indicator	The amount of capital per kWh produced in lifetime	USD/kWh
SI(div)	Diversity and vitality indicator	Number of respective entity per kWh produced in lifetime	Number/kWh
Economic indicators			
EcI(effic)	Efficiency economic indicator	The efficiency of the system divided by the energy production	1/kWh
EcI(inv)	Capital investment indicator	Amount of USD invested in the respective option divided by the energy production in lifetime	USD/kWh
EcI(com)	Community economic indicator	Gain of GNP for the community per unit kWh	USD/kWh

The fuel indicator will comprise the total organic fuel needed for the annual energy production including fuel consumption for energy production and energy needed for the respective materials production

The environment indicators are composed of three elements, namely, CO_2, NO_x, SO_2 indicator.

The social indicators reflect the social aspect of the options under consideration. It will comprise the following three indicators: job indicator, standard indicator and community indicator. The job indicator element represents the number of new jobs to be opened corresponding to the respective option. The standard indicator element reflects the potential increase of the standard of living in the community. The community indicator element takes into consideration the community benefits due to individual option.

Economic indicators are based on the elements, including: effectiveness indicator, investment indicator, energy unit cost indicator. The effectiveness indicator element is defined as the thermodynamic efficiency of the system. It will include the energy efficiency conversion from the energy resources to the final energy. The investment cost indicator is aimed to obtain valorisation of the investment per unit power. The energy unit cost indicator will comprise the cost of the energy per unit kW production.

The definitions of resource, environment, social and economic indicators are shown in Table 4.

Sustainable energy development is the ultimate goal of modern society in order to meet the ever growing demand for new energy resources. In particular it was recognised that the complexity of the global system will require special attention to the interaction between life support systems. There is the possibility to define the consistent set of sustainability indicators to be used in the assessment of energy system.

4.2 Energy Efficiency Indicators

Energy efficiency continues to be a vital component of the energy strategy. Since most greenhouse gas emissions result from the use of energy, managing greenhouse gas emissions implies managing energy use. Energy-efficient technologies, renewable energy, and other clean technology are paths that can be taken to mitigate the effects of greenhouse gases.

Those involved in negotiating international agreements (binding or voluntary) and other decision makers need to have an understanding of energy usage. They need a clear, comprehensive picture of the actual effects to date, as well as potential effects in the future, of technological advances whose design and/or ultimate effect is to improve energy efficiency. It is also important to understand how efficiency improvements interact with other social, economic, and behavioural trends that may be reinforcing or counteracting the effects of efficiency. It is important to measure these effects by means of aggregate energy-usage indicators, energy-efficiency indicators, and CO_2 emissions indicators.

Since 1992, 15 national agencies in charge of implementing energy efficiency and environmental policies have developed a monitoring tool for energy efficiency assessment called "ODYSSEE". To monitor trends of energy efficiency and CO_2, a set of comparable energy efficiency indicators and CO_2 indicators among countries has been commonly defined, calculated and interpreted by participants (Bosseboeuf et al. 2000).

Since the first oil shock, various policies and measures (PAM's) on energy efficiency have been set up in Europe with different amplitudes and timing. They have been reinforced with a new legitimacy with the rise of climate change concerns. Ministries, energy and environmental agencies or organisations in charge of the implementation of the programs are directly concerned by the question of the evaluation of their actions. Among the different methodologies, macro-sectoral energy efficiency and CO_2 indicators are helpful to monitor and evaluate energy efficiency and CO_2 trends and policies.

Energy efficiency and CO_2 indicators have been developed with several objectives:

- definition and monitoring of the targets set at the national and international levels of energy efficiency and CO_2 abatement programmes;
- evaluation of the energy efficiency programmes that have been implemented;
- planning tool of future actions, including R&D programs;

- feeding the energy demand forecasting models and improving the quality of forecasts;
- and, finally, to enable cross-country comparisons, a crucial issue in connection to international negotiation on climate change.

Energy efficiency indicators considered in the "ODYSSEE" project are macro-indicators, defined at the level of the economy as a whole, of a sector or of an end-use: industrial process, mode of transport, or energy service in the household or service sectors. Three types of indicators are considered to describe and characterise energy efficiency and CO_2 emissions trends:

- Economic ratios, relating an energy consumption or CO_2 emissions to a macro-economic variable ("energy intensities, carbon intensities");
- Technico-economic ratios, relating an energy consumption or CO_2 emissions to an indicator of activity measured in physical terms ("unit" or "specific consumption"): litre of motor fuel or gram of CO_2 per veh-km, ton oil equivalent or ton of CO_2 per ton of cement, kWh or gram of CO_2 per refrigerator or per dwellings etc.;
- Finally energy savings or CO_2 abatement indicators, that provide an assessment of quantities of energy or CO_2 saved, in absolute values (e.g., Mtoe) or in relative terms.

Macro economic indicators such as energy intensities or carbon intensities are favoured by economists to assess the energy efficiency or CO_2 trends at the level of the whole economy or at the sectoral levels. They are also mostly used by decision makers and for international comparisons. But, their high level of aggregation unfortunately limits the interpretation. In particular, they do not indicate to which extent changes in these indicators result from voluntary actions towards energy savings or from other factors, not necessarily linked to energy (e.g., structural changes, increase of product value added). Therefore, intensities are also calculated at constant structure to leave out the influence of structural changes in the economy or in the international trade and provide a better indication for actual overall efficiency (from a policy viewpoint).

Greenhouse Gases inventories gather data on emissions. They are not sufficient to identify the impact of measures implemented in each sector. Economic growth, exceptional climate conditions have influence on the level of emissions and may hide the real impact of policies and measures, at least on the short term. The evolution of sectors emissions result from several driving forces (mainly the level of activity and its structure and the specific carbon efficiency).

The monitoring of PAM's should rely on specific indicators more directly connected with their immediate impact with the following caution of interpretation:

- several measures could be focused on the same impact, for example voluntary agreements with cars manufacturers and tax on motor-fuel have, both, an impact on emissions from cars;

- some measures could also be designed to have an impact on activities itself (modal shift in transportation for example);
- other sectoral policies (transport policy etc.) could also have impacts on EEI trends.

Taking into accounts these observations, "ODYSSEE" indicators can be organised into 3 categories:

- Energy efficiency indicators that can be directly linked to energy efficiency policies.
- CO_2 indicators that will differ from the EEI by including the impact of the energy mix.
- Finally, indicators of diffusion of clean and efficient equipment and practices.

Indicators are not sufficient to assess by themselves the real impact of a specific measure, but reveal to which extent a set of measures implemented towards a source of GHG emission is efficient. The indicators identified below are suited to monitor the main driving forces responsible for emissions trajectory to 2010 and related to the most common measures implemented. Some other indicators can be identified to capture the longer term inflexions in emissions trajectories (change in urbanism, land planning...).

CO_2 emissions ratios by sector or end-uses are calculated in two ways in "ODYSSEE":

- Direct emissions, from the consumption of fossil fuels (as in the IPCC methodology)
- Total emissions, including the CO_2 content of the electricity consumed, so as to show the exact contribution of the sector or the end-use in the total emissions.

The final energy intensity of industry (final consumption of industry per unit of industrial value added) gives a preliminary global indication of energy efficiency changes in industry. The final energy intensity at constant structure of the industrial GDP provides a more precise insight on energy efficiency trends related to PAM's, since it leaves out the impact of structural changes within the industry sector (delocalisation, shift from intensive industries towards lighter industries).

Energy consumption or GHG emissions per unit of product or per unit of value added for other industries are best suited to interpret detailed policies impact. In some cases, a third type of indicator showing the share of the most efficient process (electric steel, dry process for cement etc) is necessary to improve the detailed sectoral evaluation. For the steel industry, different trends can be observed depending whether the appraisal is made in terms of energy efficiency or in terms of CO_2. This mainly reflects the impact of the CO_2 content of the electricity (if total emissions including those for electricity generation are considered) and the share of electric steel. In the cement industry, the convergence of performances across country is due to the adoption of the dry process for the clinker production.

These indicators can be used to monitor negotiated agreements between governments and industry in the large consuming sectors. These indicators address also other measures implemented in the industry sector such as carbon or energy taxes, incentives for investment in efficient technologies (as fiscal incentives), and audits.

In the residential sector, CO_2 emissions are mainly due to two main end-uses of energy: heating of dwellings (and water heating) and electrical appliances.

Space heating: Indicators of specific energy consumption of dwellings for heating per m^2 encompasses the combined impact of a shift between house and flat, the preference for larger dwellings, as well as energy efficiency improvements. Conversion in carbon emissions indicators account for the nature of the energy consumed (gas, oil, electricity…). It is necessary to separate indicators by type of dwellings because EE policies and measures are different according to whether they address new dwellings or the overall stock of dwellings.

The specific energy consumption for space heating of new dwellings reflects the effectiveness of thermal regulations of new dwellings (buildings codes) implemented in all European countries. The impact of the measure is growing with the rate of construction of dwellings.

The specific carbon emission or energy consumption for space heating of dwelling reflects the impact of several measures :

Thermal regulation on new or refurbished buildings, certification and standards on components used in refurbishing (double windows, insulation, boilers…);

Incentives for energy efficiency investments of households (insulation, efficient boilers, energy regulation equipment…);

Carbon or energy taxes on fuels for heating;

Information dissemination and subsidies for diagnosis to promote investments changes.

These indicators cannot monitor each one of these measures individually but assess the overall efficiency of dwellings for heating.

Electrical appliances: Trends in specific electricity end-use is growing rapidly everywhere, linked to the increased welfare of households. The growing equipment ownership, including multi-ownership, the preference for bigger appliances and new services are factors pushing the electricity consumption upwards, partly compensated by technical improvements. Energy efficiency policy implemented in this area is mainly the European Directive for the labelling of domestic appliances, which can be monitored through the market share of efficient equipment.

The specific consumption of electrical appliances can be used to monitor the combined impact of all measures and more generally of DSM policy or technological procurement.

In this sector, despite a worse data coverage, similar indicators to the ones presented for dwellings are performed. The unit carbon emission or energy consumption for heating in service sector buildings enable to monitor the measures implemented:

- thermal regulation of new buildings
- incentives for energy efficiency investments
- carbon or energy taxes.

Building codes vary significantly among European countries, even when compared at normalised climate.

The specific electricity is also growing rapidly over all Europe due to a rapid penetration of offices electrical equipments. As a consequence, the electricity consumption per employee is increasing everywhere in Europe; this is certainly linked to the labour productivity improvement. However the link between this indicator and measures (labelling of offices appliances, DSM etc.) is not easy to assess due to the relative weakness of the measures implemented in that sector.

In the transport sector, trends in CO_2 emissions or energy efficiency result from three driving forces:

- the mobility demand for passengers and transport requirement for freight;
- the energy and carbon efficiency of each transport mode and vehicle type;
- the shift between different transport modes (road versus railway for example).

Usually the measures address one of these driving forces. For example, voluntary negotiated agreements with car manufacturers will have an impact on car efficiency but neither on mobility nor on mode shifting (at first approximation). Some measures, however, address several driving forces (fuel taxation will have an impact on cars efficiency, mobility and transport mode shifting).

Measures dedicated to increase the efficiency of new cars could be monitored through a specific indicator of emissions (in CO_2/km) or of efficiency (in l/100 km). This indicator enables us to monitor the impact of several measures such as the voluntary agreement of car manufacturers, taxes on car purchase or ownership, taxes on motor-fuel, incentives for buying more efficient cars. In addition, an indicator of diffusion can be monitored, such as the penetration of clean and fuel efficient vehicles or small cars.

For the total stock of cars, there is a growing discrepancy between the level of emissions as measured on new cars and the observed level of emissions due to the real conditions of use. The indicators used (in gram of carbon/kilometre or litres/100 km) address the evolution of global efficiency of the fleet and takes into account not only the energy or carbon efficiency of new vehicles but also the traffic conditions and the drivers behaviour. It also captures the fuel mix impact. The following measures can be monitored through these indicators:

1) Measures to improve the behaviour of drivers and the maintenance of cars, such as information dissemination or mandatory controls of motors.

2) Measures dedicated to increase the efficiency of new cars.

3) Measures dedicated to reduce the use of cars for bad traffic conditions (small journeys…).

For freight transport, the same kind of indicators can be defined, although indicators in l/100 km are difficult to obtain. To evaluate the effect of policies in that sector, particularly the shift from road transportation towards railways on large distances, is a major issue. The ratio of "ton per kilometre" of goods transported by railway versus road could be used to monitor measures dedicated to promote modal shift towards railway :

1) measures dedicated to internalise the real cost of road transport (taxes on diesel or on vehicles, speed limits of trucks, regulation on maximum driving time)

2) measures dedicated to improve the traffic of railways for freight (public support for infrastructures, negotiated agreements with transport companies clients…).

These indicators encompass the major measures implemented in the transport sector and can report on the major driving forces of emissions. Indicators on mobility itself (passenger per km or tons per km) could also be used to monitor the global evolution of transport demand (passenger and goods) but the impacts of measures on mobility demand (such as urban planning) will only be relevant at long term and/or local level.

The summary of the indicators described are given below.

Measures	Emissions sources	Indicator
Transport		
Voluntary agreement of car manufacturer	New Cars	1. l/100 km 2. gCO_2 per km 3. % of small cars
Voluntary agreement of car manufacturer Taxes on vehicle Taxes on motor fuel Mandatory technical control Traffic regulation	Stock of cars	1. l/100 km 2. gCO_2 per km 3. % of small cars
Tax on motor fuels Speed limits for trucks Control enforcement	Trucks long haulage	1. koe/tkm 2. gCO_2 per km 3. % tkm by trucks

Residential and Services		
Thermal regulation of new buildings	Space heating for new building	1. toe/dwelling, toe/m^2 2.tCO_2/dwelling, CO_2/m^2
Standard on building components window, Boilers etc. Technical control on boilers Tax on heating fuels Support for diagnosis	Space heating for existing	1. Toe/dwelling, toe/m^2 2.tCO_2/dwelling, CO_2/m^2
Labelling Norms Efficiency standards Target value	Electrical appliances consumption	1. kWh per new appliances, Kwh per appliances 2. Toe/dwelling, toe/m^2 3. t CO_2 per appliance
Industry		
Tax on energy/CO_2 Support for diagnosis Voluntary agreement Support to R&D R&D demonstration Fiscal incentives	Energy intensive industries	1. Toe per ton of output 2. tCO_2 per ton of output 3. % of efficient process
Tax on energy/CO_2 Support for diagnosis Voluntary agreement Support to R&D R&D demonstration Fiscal incentives	Energy light industries	1. Toe per V.A. 2. tCO_2 per V.A. 3. % of efficient process

Many more detailed indicators can be considered to provide a better link between individual measures and CO_2 but increasing the number of indicators is an obstacle to a synthetic and common appropriation by policy makers among the various countries.

On the one hand, a broader use of indicators requires transparency in the methodology including data collection, definition of indicators etc. On the other hand, their use will increase in relation to their ability to correctly interpret the policies impact. Both these two objectives mutually reinforced. Other indicators could be identified to assess longer term emissions trajectories such as public investments in collective transports, sustainable urban planning.

Chapter 3
Energy Resources

1 Fossil Fuels

Fossil fuels are coal, oil, and natural gas. We call them fossil fuels because all of them in some way originated from the decomposition of organic matter in or on the earth. Each provides a unique source of energy that humans have taken advantage of over thousands of years. Approximately 90% of our energy consumption comes from fossil fuels. Approximately 50% of the fossil fuels humans have consumed throughout history were used in the last 20 years. The scary fact is that we cannot make more. In other words, our fossil fuel reserves are finite. Humans have used most of our reserves in a 200 year period. We will need to change over to the most plentiful fossil or non-fossil fuel sources over the next hundred years in order to meet the world's growing energy needs.

1.1 Coal

Coal has been used as a fuel since about 1000 B.C. Although coal is abundant in most parts of the world, it was not used extensively for fuel until the industrial revolution. The transition from wood as the main source of fuel to coal which occurred at this time was a result of dwindling fuel-wood supplies and the superior energy content of coal. It was the need to pump water out of coal mines that resulted in the first use of the steam engine. From that point until the end of the 19th century when oil and natural gas came on the scene, coal was the fuel which powered the industrial revolution.

Coal is a combustible, black sedimentary rock composed predominantly of carbon. It is formed out of plant matter that accumulated at the bottom of swamps millions of years ago, during the Carboniferous Period. At this time, the earth's climate was extremely favourable for plant growth. Organic matter accumulated in stagnant swamps which were low in oxygen and thus inhibited decomposition. Eventually, seas rose or the land subsided and the swamps were submerged. Sand, clay and other debris buried the organic material. Over thousands of years, the organic material was compacted under the weight of the overlying sediments and was transformed into coal. Coal deposits are now found buried beneath layers of sandstone, limestone and shale all over the world. Several different types of coal can be found depending on the depth and location of the seam. The four main types of coal, which differ by carbon content are shown in Table 5.

Table 5: Types of Coal by Carbon Content

Type of Coal	Carbon %	Energy Content (Btu/lb)
Lignite	30	5000-500
Subbituminous	40	8000-10,000
Bituminous	50-70	11,000-15,000
Anthracite	90	14,000

Lignites are the "youngest" coals, which have high water content and low heating values. The heating value of a fuel is used to quantify the useful energy content in it. Lignite usually has many impurities and is therefore not a preferable type to use. Subbituminous coal is cheaper to mine because it is not as deep as bituminous coal and contains less sulphur than lignite. Bituminous coal is the most abundant type of coal. It has a high heating value, but it also has a high sulphur content. Anthracite coal is a very hard coal which burns longer, with more heat and with less dust and soot than the other types of coal. These qualities make anthracite a popular home heating fuel.

Not all plant material turns into coal; some eventually becomes graphite, and a tiny amount is compressed into diamonds. Coal is burned in power plants to produce heat which is used to change water into steam. This steam turns a large fan-like structure called a turbine which is coupled to an electric generator that generates electricity.

Total recoverable reserves of coal around the world are estimated at 1088 billion tons - enough to last another 210 years at current production. Although coal deposits are widely distributed, 60 percent of the world's recoverable reserves are located in three regions: the United States (25 percent); Former Soviet Union (23 percent); and China (12 percent). Another four countries - Australia, India, Germany, and South Africa - account for an additional 29 percent. In 1996, these seven regions accounted for 81 percent of total world coal production.

Quality and geological characteristics of coal deposits are other important parameters for coal reserves. Coal is a much more heterogeneous source of energy than is oil or natural gas, and its quality varies significantly from one region to another and even within an individual coal seam. For example, Australia, the United States, and Canada are endowed with substantial reserves of premium coals that can be used to manufacture coke. Together, these three countries supplied 85 percent of the coking coal traded worldwide in 1997.

At the other end of the spectrum are reserves of lignite or "brown coal." Coal of this type is not traded to any significant extent in world markets, because of its relatively low heat content (which raises transportation costs on a Btu basis) and other problems related to transport and storage. In 1996, lignite accounted for 19 percent of total world coal production (on a tonnage basis). The top three producers were Germany (206 million tons), Russia (106 million tons), and the United States (88 million tons). As a group, these countries accounted for 41 percent of the world's total lignite production in 1996. With respect to the heat content, lignite deposits show considerable variation. Estimates by the International Energy Agency for coal produced in 1996 show that the average heat content of lignite from major producers in countries of the Organisation for Economic Co-operation and Development (OECD) varied from a low of 4.3 million Btu per ton in Greece to a high of 12.3 million Btu per ton in Canada.

Coal is commonly recovered from the earth by two methods. Surface mining or strip mining, is preferred due to cost and safety factors. Strip mining usually occurs on flat land. Hilly or steep terrain requires contour mining. Deep mining involves digging shafts and tunnels to gain access to the coal seam. The coal can then be excavated from the seam with only some columns of earth left behind for support. Deep mining is unappealing because of safety hazards in the tunnels and health hazards like black lung disease. However, deep mining has become more acceptable due to automation. On the flip side, the negative effects of mining are the intense, irreversible damages inflicted upon the environment.

Coal gasification is a process by which coal is converted into a synthetic fuel, natural gas. The process basically adds hydrogen to the carbon in coal. In order to change the carbon to hydrogen atomic ratio from 12 to 1 in coal to 1 to 4 in natural gas, several steps must be carried out. First the coal is brought into contact with high-pressure, high-temperature steam in the gasifier. The heat for the reaction from coal to "synthetic gas" is provided by introducing some oxygen, which causes some of the coal to burn. In the second stage, the C:H ratio is increased by further addition of steam, which increases the heating value of the fuel. The resulting mixture is then purified and converted to methane in the presence of a nickel catalyst. The methanisation is an exothermic reaction, in which lots of low temperature heat is lost, therefore making the process inefficient. Synthetic methane is the resulting fuel.

Coal liquefaction converts coal into synthetic crude oil, or syncrude. This process also involves adding hydrogen to heated coal and then separating the gas and liquid product. The hydrogen is added to coal in a slurry at elevated temperatures and pressures. The high temperature breaks the carbon bonds, which produces a liquid phase product due to the high pressure.

Economic considerations hinder the further development of coal gasification and liquefaction systems. It has been neither economical nor efficient to produce synthetic fuels from coal on a large scale basis. The production facilities are more expensive to run and maintain than simply buying the oil or natural gas itself. It is important, however, that the processes are maintained and improved even at a slow rate. As our reserves of crude oil are depleted, the price of oil will probably increase dramatically, making the use of synthetic fuels more economical.

In the past, coal was burned for a variety of purposes. These included heating, cooking, mechanical power, transportation (steam trains and ships) and heat for manufacturing processes. In 1937 coal accounted for 74% of worldwide energy consumption. Since that time, cheap supplies of oil, a more convenient fuel, and natural gas have replaced coal in many of these applications. Today, with a few exceptions in the developing world where it is still used for home heating and cooking, coal is predominantly used for generating electricity and for providing process heat in some industries. Coal's share of world energy use has since declined to 30% but the amount of coal consumed is higher than ever and increasing.

If electric power is generated using coal combustion, the cost per [kW-hJ] is cheaper than that for oil generation only when no extra provisions are made for removing pollution. China is the world's largest coal user, accounting for 27% of world production. More than 70% of the country's energy is generated from coal. For example, the degree of cleanliness of the exhaust gas from coal combustion was 48% and 25% for USA and China, respectively, compared to Japan in 1990. If we can devise an inexpensive, but cleaner method of coal combustion, then the energy problem will be solved by the stability provided by the coal resources.

There are problems with the use of this form of fossil fuel. First, the extraction of the coal from the ground can be very expensive. Most coal deposits lie well below the surface of the earth which means that special drilling, the creation of mine shafts, and the shoring up of these shafts must be paid for. In addition, there is the danger of mine explosions when deposits of natural gas or finely powered coal dust undergoes combustion resulting in an explosion. Breathing of coal dust by the miners leads to a condition known as "black lung". This adds to the cost of the coal mining industry for the need of mine safety, and insurance and medical costs for the miners. Once the coal reaches the surface of the ground it must be transported by railroad or ocean going ships. This is an expensive undertaking. Once it reaches its destination for burning of the coal, one has to make sure that sulphur deposits and other elemental trace amounts are extracted from the coal which is expensive in and of itself. If this is not done then a number of other things are possible.

Other major difficulties associated with coal utilisation include the following: the "air pollution" problem caused by the exhausted gas of coal combustion. More than three times the amount of SO_x gas are exhausted compared to oil combustion. Another problem concerns the disposal of the remaining ashes.

1.2 Oil

Since "rock oil" was discovered near Titusville, Pennsylvania, in 1859, by a man drilling for water, crude oil, also called Petroleum, has become the world's foremost source of energy, and the backbone of the industrial society. Oil accounts for 38% of energy use worldwide. Oil's liquid form, high energy density, and relatively clean burning nature make it the most versatile of all fuels. When oil was first discovered, it was primarily used in the form of kerosene for lamps and stoves. Since that time, inventors have developed hundreds of new uses for oil, with the most prominent being the internal combustion engine.

Oil is mainly formed by the deposition of dead plant, animals, and marine microorganism matter in or near marine sedentary basins. Once the matter is buried at about 450 meters, the temperature and pressure begin to cause the rearrangement of matter. The newly-formed liquid molecules migrate through porous rock formations such as limestone and sandstone until they are trapped by a non-porous rock barrier. Crude oil, also called petroleum, is a complex mixture of carbon and hydrogen (hydrocarbons), which exist as a liquid in the earth's crust. On average, crude oil is made up of 83% carbon (C) and 12% hydrogen (H), with the remainder being sulphur, oxygen and nitrogen. Crude oil found in different locations is never exactly the same. Some is black, thick and tar like, while other crude oils are lighter in colour, thinner and more volatile. The carbon and hydrogen in crude oil are thought to have originated from the remains of microscopic marine organisms that were deposited at the bottom of seas and oceans. After having been buried under huge layers of other sediments, the organic material is transformed at high temperature and pressure into crude oil and natural gas. The oil and gas are then squeezed out of the marine shales in which they were deposited, and make their way into porous sedimentary rocks such as sandstones and limestones. This oil and gas migrates upward through the porous rock, as it is less dense than the water which fills the pores. Unless it reaches an impermeable layer of rock, the hydrocarbons will make their way to the surface and evaporate. For oil and gas to be trapped in quantities large enough to allow humans to recover them, these migrating hydrocarbons must reach a layer of impermeable rock through which they can't flow. Several different types of oil and gas "traps" exist. Crude oil is "mined" by drilling a hole into the reservoir rock (sandstone, limestone etc.). Often, the oil is under pressure and will come out of the hole on its own. In some cases, pumps and other more complicated procedures are required to recover crude oil from the ground.

Petroleum is usually recovered by drilling wells down through the non-porous rock barrier under which the oil is trapped. There are three types of oil recovery. Primary oil recovery occurs as the oil flows out of a well by its own pressure or is pumped out. This removes about 30% of the oil. Another 10% is removed by flooding the well with high pressure water or gas, a method of **secondary** recovery. Some methods of tertiary recovery have been developed in which the oil is heated (by burning some underground detergents or the oil itself) to scrub it out. This only removes another 10%, however, and requires energy to do so. Therefore, about half of the oil is left trapped in this rock with no economical means for its recovery.

Unconventional oil recovery entails obtaining oil from oil shale. Oil shale is a material with hydrogen content between that of coal and crude oil due to the fact that it was never buried deeply enough or heated enough to form crude oil. The concentration of oil in this material is quite low, and it is chemically bonded to the shale. The maximum amount of recoverable oil is one barrel per 2.4 tons of sand or 1.5 tons of rock. Enormous problems also occur with extraction of oil from oil shale. The potential amount of oil contained in oil shale is greater than the known and unproved crude oil resources in the world, which would add approximately 40 years to the projected time before oil will be exhausted. The dilemma is that it takes about half the energy contained in the shale to extract the oil. Recovery of oil from oil shale is therefore not economically feasible at this time.

Once crude oil is extracted from the ground, it is "refined" into many different products. Refining separates the "lighter" components of the crude oil, such as gasoline, from the "heavier" components such as fuel oil and lubricants. However, crude petroleum has to be processed before we can untap that energy locked up into its molecular structures. Crude petroleum is refined by fractional distillation. This means that the distillation process occurs with successive separations carried out at increasingly higher temperatures. The condensed vapours are collected in several portions, or fractions, the first fractions being richest in low boiling point components. These include gasoline, kerosene, furnace oil, naphthas (liquid hydrocarbon mixtures), and lubricating oils. The heavy residues left over are used as asphalt and residual oil. The second step in oil refining is conversion, or cracking, of the molecules in order to squeeze out a higher percentage of lighter, low boiling point products like gasoline from each barrel of oil. The last step, treatment, or enhancement, increases the quality of the product by such means as removing sulphur from kerosene, gasoline, and heating oils. About 15% of crude oil goes into non-energy products such as plastics and paints, while the rest is eventually used for combustion in one form or another.

The classifications and heat energy densities of several petroleum fuels are as follows. Kerosene: 40,850 [kJ/kg] (= 9739 [kcal/kg]), burner oil: 42,680 [kJ/kg] (= 10,160 [kcal/kg]), heavy oil: 45,740 (= 10,900 [kcal/kg]), heavy oil (0.3% sulphur): 43,850 (= 10,440 [kcal/kg]). Because the density of kerosene is about 0.8 [kg/kl], its energy density per unit volume is about 12,160 [kcal/kl].

There are several advantages that crude petroleum has over coal use. First, the crude petroleum is a liquid with dissolved gases and suspended solid matter. Most of it is a liquid and as such, can be brought to the surface under pressure. Once at the surface of the Earth, the crude petroleum can be transported to its destination via pipeline to awaiting ships. The transportation and mining costs are much reduced.

However, gasoline and diesel fractions do have their own disadvantages. They form toxic products that exit the exhaust pipe. Some of these exhaust gases can be easily converted to harmless gases by the use of a catalytic converter. This device causes the decomposition of Nitrogen Oxides formed as a result of high temperatures and the presence of Oxygen and Nitrogen gases in the atmosphere. These oxides can be very toxic, but the catalyst will aid in the decomposition of the Nitrogen Oxides back into harmless Nitrogen and Oxygen gases.

Other problems have resulted because of additives like Lead Tetraethyl that was added before the 1970s. The Lead Tetraethyl did cause the gasoline fraction to burn more efficiently adding as much as a 10-20 to the Octane Rating. However the extreme heats in the combustion chamber of the internal combustion engine would result in the decomposition of the Lead additive and the entrance of Lead into the atmosphere. Lead is a very toxic substance. They have banned Lead in paints because the ingestion of Lead can cause dementia and other forms of mental illness.

Oil was plentiful and cheap throughout most of the twentieth century, resulting in patterns of transportation and land use based upon the private automobile. Oil was also extensively used for heating homes and generating electricity; and since oil was so cheap, it was not used very efficiently. The world's romance with oil came to a crashing halt in 1973, when OPEC (Organisation of Petroleum Exporting Countries) unilaterally raised prices and cut production. Oil prices skyrocketed, there were huge lineups for gasoline in the US, and oil suddenly became a political issue. More recently, dwindling supplies in the industrial world and concerns over global warming are also beginning to change the world's oil consumption patterns.

There exist two kinds of world reserves for petroleum. One is the confirmed reserves (C.R.) and another is the ultimate reserves (U.R.). In 1985, British Petroleum Co. published a figure of 1113×10^8 [kl] as C.R. As regards the U.R., most authorities published somewhat different values. For example, the value of U.R. was estimated to be 4093×10^8 [kl] by the World Energy Conference of 1980, 2731×10^8 [kl] by the 11th World Petroleum Conference, and 3145×10^8 [kl] according to Japan Petroleum Society's data in 1986. As a general trend, we may estimate that the U.R. of petroleum is ca. 3180×10^8 [kl], approximately 2×10^{12} [B] (barrel, 1 [B] = 0.159 [kl]). The petroleum resources are unevenly distributed. The confirmed reserves in the world are estimated at about 1110×10^8 [kl] and these reserves are geographically distributed as shown in Table 6. It is obvious that about 57% of the confirmed oil reserves exist in the Middle East.

Table 6. Distribution of confirmed oil reserves (Ohta 1994)

Area	Oil Reserves (10^8 kl)	%
North America	54.5	4.9
Middle & South America	332.2	12.0
Europe	42.3	3.8
Asia & Oceania	42.3	3.8
Africa	90.0	8.2
Russia	129.0	11.6
Middle East	631.0	56.8
Total	1,110	100

Oil and its derivatives are used for a multitude of different tasks; but, worldwide, over half of the crude oil used for energy is used in the transportation sector. Prior to the invention of the internal combustion engine by August Otto in 1876, mechanised transportation was provided by the steam engine. Steam engines using coal or wood as a fuel were used to power ships and trains; but they were too large and cumbersome for use in smaller applications. The gasoline powered internal combustion engine was able to deliver much more power from a compact design, making it an ideal match for many types of vehicles, including the automobile and later the airplane. At the present time, oil provides the energy for over 95% of the world's transportation needs.

When oil was cheap, it was often used to generate electricity, especially in remote locations such as islands which did not have access to hydroelectric power or coal. Oil was well suited for electricity generation in such applications because it is easy to transport and store. Today, oil is still used to generate electricity in many of these places, simply because the power plants are already in place. Since the "oil-crisis" of 1973, oil has been an increasingly expensive fuel for generating electricity.

Oil fired power plants operate in the same way as those fuelled by coal. Oil is burned producing heat, the heat boils water, and the steam produced is used to spin a turbine. In this type of power plant only about 35% of the energy originally in the oil is converted into electrical energy. The rest is lost to the environment as heat.

The final major use of oil is for space heating in residential and commercial buildings. After coal was determined to be too dirty, and before natural gas was widely available, oil was a very common fuel for heating homes. Fuel oil was easily distributed by trucks to customers homes, and safely stored in tanks for use as needed. Oil furnaces have traditionally not been very efficient; but newer models are capable of very high efficiencies in the range of 90%. Like all other uses of oil, home heating with oil became more expensive after 1973, prompting many homeowners to convert to natural gas.

As world supplies of oil become more scarce, there is a feeling that oil is too valuable a resource to be used for processes such as heating and generating electricity, which can be easily accomplished by other means. Using our supplies of oil more efficiently is another possible method of extending the lifetime of the world's oil supplies. Automobiles in Canada, for example, average about 8 kilometres per litre, while test vehicles achieving over 32 km/litre have been built by many of the major car manufacturers. Similar improvements can be made to most other vehicles that use oil as a fuel, such as trucks, buses and airplanes.

The use of oil has two distinct types of environmental impacts. The first occurs during oil production, while the second occurs at the point of end use. Exploration for oil, oil production and oil transportation all have negative environmental impacts on the environment. Ecosystems in areas of oil exploration and production are often damaged by the heavy equipment required for the job. An example of this is the oil exploration currently taking place in Alaska, which is threatening caribou on a national wildlife preserve. Off-shore oil drilling has also resulted in severe oil spills which have damaged marine ecosystems in many locations.

The transportation of oil from the well to the end user can also damage the environment. Everybody is familiar with oil tanker spills such as the Torrey Canyon and the Exxon Valdez, which have shown the world what kind of damage can be caused to marine life by oil spills. New tanker designs with double hulls can prevent some of these spills; but the added costs of building these ships have prevented widespread use. Pipelines that carry oil to either shipping terminals or refineries can also disrupt ecosystems. The effects of the Alaska Pipeline, which crosses the permafrost in Alaska, were not known when it was built, and are still poorly understood.

The final environmental impact related to the production of oil is indirect, and related to the important role oil plays in the world economy. It is an undeniable fact that one of the reasons that tensions are so high in the Middle East is the value of the oil reserves in that region. Many people believe that one of the main motivations behind the "Gulf War" in 1991 was the world's need for reliable and inexpensive sources of oil. The Gulf War resulted in damage to the marine environment of the Persian Gulf, atmospheric pollution from burning oil wells, and damage to desert ecosystems by tanks and other heavy equipment.

The combustion of oil releases carbon dioxide (CO_2), which is a greenhouse gas responsible for global warming, as well as sulphur dioxide (SO_2) and nitrous oxides (NO_x), which result in acid rain. Currently, oil directly used for transportation is responsible for about 25% of the world's CO_2 emissions. Each average North American car will spew out more than its own weight (1500 kg) of CO_2 during its lifetime. Oil use overall is responsible for about 40% of humankind's CO_2 emissions. Similarly, the burning of oil products in vehicles and other applications is one of the largest sources of NO_x, which cause acid rain. Finally, the incomplete combustion of oil, especially in transportation fuels, results in increased levels of carbon monoxide (CO), unburned hydrocarbons and ultimately ground level ozone. These all have impacts on human health and the environment.

1.3 Natural Gas

Natural gas is a gaseous mixture of light hydrocarbons, which is found underground in sedimentary rock formations, often in the same location as crude oil. The most clean burning of all the fossil fuels, natural gas is now widely used for space heating as well as electricity generation. Until the past few decades, natural gas encountered while drilling for oil was often simply burned off, because the infrastructure necessary to capture the gas and transport it to potential users was not available. Today, natural gas pipelines are in place to serve a large portion of the industrialised world. Now natural gas is seen as an important economic factor in drilling for oil; and natural gas itself supplies 20% of the world's commercial energy needs.

Worldwide supplies of natural gas are reasonably widespread and should last for 60 years at current rates of production. Environmental concerns such as global warming have resulted in calls for increased use of natural gas. This is because natural gas gives off only one half as much carbon dioxide (CO_2) per unit of energy produced as does coal, and 25% less than oil. Natural gas is made up predominantly of methane (CH_4), which itself is a greenhouse gas if it is released into the atmosphere. Leaks from natural gas pipelines and storage facilities may release enough methane to counteract its CO_2 emission benefits. For this reason, although natural gas may be the fuel of choice in the coming decades, more research is needed into its environmental impacts.

Natural gas is a mixture of light hydrocarbons including methane, ethane, propane, butanes and pentanes. Other compounds found in natural gas include CO_2, helium, hydrogen sulphide and nitrogen. The actual process of natural gas formation is not fully understood. The carbon and hydrogen in natural gas are thought to have originated from the remains of microscopic marine organisms that were deposited at the bottom of seas and oceans. After having been buried under huge layers of other sediments, the organic material is transformed at high temperature and pressure into crude oil and natural gas. The oil and gas are then squeezed out of the marine shales in which they were deposited, and from there go into porous sedimentary rocks such as sandstones and limestones.

Natural fuel gases can be classified into two kinds according to whether they are produced coincident with crude oil in oil fields or are produced independent of oil. Some gases which are produced along with crude oil also exist everywhere on the earth's surface. Methane is a typical gas of this kind. Methane, ethane, propane, *n*- or *iso*-butane, and other gases are known as "petroleum gas", because they are yielded along with crude oil.

Ethane, propane, and butane are usually used in LPG (liquefied petroleum gas, or often propane gas) as a substitute for gasoline or kerosene. These gases are very cheap at the oil fields, hence most of them are burned out on site. The majority of LPG imports are due to Japan, where many homes use LPG instead of city gas.

The disadvantage of using LPG is that the raw petroleum gases are difficult to obtain, not enough to meet demands, whenever OPEC (Organisation of Petroleum Exporting Countries) undertakes a policy of reducing oil output.

The confirmed world reserve of methane gas is estimated at about 100×10^{12} [m^3] which is equivalent to 1050×10^8 [kl] of oil, a quantity roughly equal to the confirmed oil reserves. The production rate of methane gas was 1.7 $\times 10^{12}$ [m^3/Y] in 1985 (not so much different from today), so that a simple estimation of the lifetime is 58.8 [Y].

LNG is liquefied natural gas. Almost all of the manufactured quantities are imported by Japan. A major investment is necessary to construct a liquefaction facility and therefore it is impossible economically to have LNG plants in gas fields with few reserves.

This gas migrates upward through the porous rock, as it is less dense than the water which fills the pores. For gas to be trapped in quantities large enough to allow humans to capture them, these migrating hydrocarbons must reach a layer of impermeable rock through which they can't flow. Several different types of gas "traps" exist. Natural gas is captured by drilling a hole into the reservoir rock. Most often, the natural gas is under pressure and will come out of the hole on its own. In some cases, pumps and other more complicated procedures are required to remove the natural gas from the ground.

Natural gas is either found mixed in oil or it is released from coal. It is measured in **cubic feet**, ft^3. The energy content in 6000 ft^3 of natural gas is the equivalent of one barrel of oil. When it is removed from a reservoir, natural gas can either be pumped to the processing station for removal of liquid hydrocarbons, sulphur, carbon dioxide, and other components, or stored in large caverns underground until it is needed. Pipelines are the principal method of natural gas transportation. Because natural gas was not highly valued in the early half of this century, the expansion and development of the pipeline system did not occur until about 1940. In addition, natural gas deposits were often burned off when they were found mixed in oil deposits. Today gas pipelines cover the United States, Canada, Western Europe, and Russia. Transporting it overseas has been made more economically expedient by liquefaction techniques, but it is still quite expensive. The price of oil has been a key factor in determining the development of transportation facilities for natural gas.

As of January 1, 1999, proven world natural gas reserves, as reported by Oil & Gas Journal, were estimated at 5145 trillion cubic feet, 58 trillion cubic feet higher than the estimate for 1998. Most of the increase in reserves is attributed to the developing countries, with a small increase in reserves of the industrialised regions and virtually no change in the reserves of Eastern Europe and the former Soviet Union (EE/FSU). In the industrialised regions, the decrease of 12 trillion cubic feet between 1998 and 1999 in Western Europe's natural gas reserves was offset by the doubling of Australia's reserves (from 19 to 45 trillion cubic feet) in industrialised Asia. In the developing countries, reserves in Central and South America declined by 3 trillion cubic feet between 1998 and 1999, but in every other region of the developing world, reserves increased. Proven reserve estimates increased by 13 trillion cubic feet for Africa, by 16 trillion cubic feet for Asia, and by 24 trillion cubic feet for the Middle East.

About 72 percent of the world's natural gas reserves are located in the FSU and countries of the Middle East. Russia and Iran alone account for almost one-half of the world's gas reserves. In the industrialised world, reserves have remained fairly stable over the past 20 years. Reserves of the industrialised countries declined every year between 1993 and 1998, but in 1999 they increased by 10 trillion cubic feet because of the addition of 24 trillion cubic feet in Australia's proven reserves. Reserves in the EE/FSU and the developing world have, in contrast, more than doubled over the past 24 years, although since 1994 reserves in the EE/FSU have remained flat.

Worldwide, natural gas reserves are more widespread geographically than oil reserves. Outside the EE/FSU and the Middle East, reserves are fairly evenly distributed, except for industrialised Asia. Moreover, despite high rates of increase in gas consumption, particularly over the past decade, most regional reserves-to-production ratios have remained high. Worldwide, the reserves-to-production ratio is estimated at 64.1 years. Central and South America has a reserves-to-production ratio of about 72.7 years, the FSU about 86.2 years, and the Middle East and Africa both more than 100 years.

Natural gas is a very versatile fuel that can be used for space and water heating, process heat for industry, electricity generation, cooking, mechanical power and transportation. Heating and electricity generation have traditionally been the predominant uses of natural gas, representing about 75% and 15% of natural gas use respectively. In the future, increasing concerns about urban air pollution may lead to increased use of natural gas as a transportation fuel.

Furnaces which burn natural gas to provide space heating and hot water for homes and businesses are the largest users of natural gas. Ultra high efficiency gas furnaces can convert over 90% of the potential energy in natural gas into useful heat. The high efficiency of gas furnaces and the low price of natural gas have made it the most popular heating fuel in cities where there are distribution networks. Natural gas can also be converted into a liquid form such as propane, which can be stored in tanks and used for heating in areas where gas pipelines are not available. Unfortunately, filling the tanks and transporting them to a site significantly increases heating costs. In the future, gas driven heat pumps promise to deliver even higher efficiencies than are achieved by today's best furnaces, and gas fired "chillers" will allow air-conditioning demands to be met by natural gas rather than electricity.

The generation of electricity is the other main use of natural gas. Producing electricity from natural gas is generally more expensive than using coal, because of increased fuel costs. Natural gas fired power plants are very versatile, however, and can be turned on and off much more quickly than large coal fired or nuclear plants. For this reason, many electric utilities use natural gas to generate electricity during periods of "peak" demand, while supplying the "base-load" electricity demand with other alternatives such as coal or nuclear power.

Natural gas is the cleanest burning fossil fuel. When natural gas is burned, it gives off less CO_2 than oil or coal, virtually no sulphur dioxide, and only small amounts of nitrous oxides. CO_2 is a greenhouse gas, while sulphur and nitrous oxides produced by oil and coal combustion cause acid rain. Natural gas is mostly composed of methane (CH_4) and other light hydrocarbons. Both the carbon and hydrogen in methane combine with oxygen when natural gas is burned, giving off heat. Coal and oil contain proportionally more carbon than natural gas; therefore giving off more CO_2 per unit of energy produced. Natural gas gives off one half the CO_2 of coal and 25% less CO_2 than oil, for the same amount of energy produced. CO_2 is the most important greenhouse gas, contributing to global warming. Heating a home with natural gas rather than electricity generated by coal can result in greenhouse gas emissions up to 5 times lower, depending upon the efficiencies of the gas furnace and the coal power plant.

As alluded to earlier, reduced CO_2 emissions may not be the end of the story when it comes to natural gas and global warming. Methane is itself a greenhouse gas, which molecule for molecule can trap more heat than CO_2. While it is known that leaks occur in natural gas distribution networks (pipelines etc), the total volume of methane leaking into the atmosphere from natural gas installations is unknown. This may counterbalance the CO_2 benefits of burning natural gas instead of oil and coal. Before large amounts of money are spent converting our energy consumption patterns from oil to natural gas, more research into the effects of methane leakage should be undertaken.

Concerns about acid rain and global warming will no doubt result in increased use of natural gas in the future. Two areas which could see expanded use of natural gas are fuel cells and transportation. Fuel cells are used to generate electricity, and operate something like a battery. The difference is that the energy for fuel cells comes from hydrogen, which can be made from natural gas. Fuel cells eliminate the need for turbines and generators, and can operate at efficiencies as high as 60%. Fuel cells also operate at low temperatures, thus reducing emissions of acid rain causing nitrous oxides, which are formed during high temperature combustion of any fuel.

Concern over urban air pollution may lead to increased use of natural gas as a transportation fuel in the future. Natural gas burns far more cleanly than gasoline and diesel fuel, producing fewer nitrous oxides, unburned hydrocarbons and particulates. Natural gas vehicles require large storage tanks for their fuel. Therefore, the main market may not be for private automobiles, but rather buses and trucks which are used within cities.

Worldwide crude oil distribution and trade occurs mainly by sea. This presents a potential problem in the form of oil spills in the oceans, threatening coastal and marine plants and wildlife in addition to coral reef degradation by anchoring tankers.

In the past decade there has been a movement to expand natural gas usage for several reasons. There are greater domestic reserves of natural gas, and it is the cleanest-burning fossil fuel because it contains the least amount of carbon and virtually no sulphur. Since natural gas is a clean burning fuel, some new cars are designed to use it. Natural gas costs about two-thirds as much as gasoline per BTU, and it is in comparatively plentiful supply. However, in order to convert to natural gas use for transportation, fuel tanks would have to be pressurised, making them heavier and larger. Cars would also need to be refuelled about every 100 miles because natural gas has a lower energy density than gasoline.

2 Nuclear Energy Resources

As the reserves of fossil fuels continue to diminish, alternative energy resources are being developed. Nuclear power is one example of an alternative energy resource and belongs to fission energy. Fission is the splitting of certain nuclei that are capable of undergoing this fission process. Not all nuclei can undergo this process. Uranium 235 and Plutonium 239 are two isotopes that are fissionable.

The set of activities required for producing nuclear power, from the mining and processing of uranium to its use in reactors and final disposal, is known as the nuclear fuel cycle. The mining of uranium is similar to the mining of many other ores; but miners must also be protected against radioactive dust and radon, a radioactive gas. Uranium ores occur naturally in many parts of the world, but the uranium extracted from them must often be "enriched" before it can be used as fuel in a nuclear reactor. This is because naturally occurring uranium contains about 99.3% uranium-238, a non-fissionable isotope of uranium, and only 0.7% of the fissionable uranium-235. Uranium enrichment increases the proportion of uranium-235 in the mixture, enabling it to sustain a fission reaction. Such uranium fuel is placed in the core of a nuclear reactor, and the heat given off by the fission chain reaction is captured to produce electricity.

Like any other fuel, enriched uranium eventually becomes exhausted. This occurs after all the readily fissionable isotopes in the fuel have been used up. The fuel has now been changed into a mixture of fission products and other non-fissionable material such as uranium-238, which has been subjected to a massive bombardment by neutrons. As a result, spent fuel is a very hot and highly radioactive waste, which must be removed from a reactor and disposed. Some of the radioactive waste produced by fission reactors will remain highly radioactive for thousands of years, and is a potential source of the material required for the production of nuclear weapons. At the present time, there is no agreed upon method of permanently disposing such wastes, and they are piling up in temporary holding tanks. Plans are underway to bury these wastes deep underground in rock caverns; but to date no such facilities have been approved.

The atom is composed of subatomic particles called **protons, neutrons,** and **electron**. There is a force called the strong force that holds protons and neutrons together at very small distances. The electrons are "bound" to the nucleus by electric charge because the unlike positive and negative charges of the protons and electrons, respectively, attract.

Two isotopes of an element contain the same number of protons and electrons, but a different number of neutrons in the nucleus. An isotope with more neutrons is called "heavy" in comparison with the "lighter" isotope (of the same element) with less neutrons. Take, for example ^{235}U and ^{238}U (read "Uranium 235" and "Uranium 238"). Both consist of 92 protons and electrons, which makes them Uranium. The difference is that ^{235}U has 143 neutrons (235-92) whereas, ^{238}U has 146 neutrons (238-92). Therefore, ^{238}U is heavier than ^{235}U.

Nuclear energy may be defined as the energy found within an atomic nucleus or as the nuclear **binding energy**. If we take the helium nucleus, the mass of its parts (two protons and two neutrons) is less than the mass of the nucleus itself. Using Einstein's equation $E = mc^2$ (where c is the speed of light) we can see that a tiny bit of mass can make an enormous amount of energy.

In a nuclear reaction, an unstable nucleus will become more stable by emitting particles and rearranging the neutrons and protons into more stable nuclei. A stable atomic nucleus does not undergo nuclear reactions unless bombarded with nuclear particles such as protons, neutrons, or alpha particles a process called nuclear bombardment.

Another type of induced nuclear reaction is nuclear fusion. Fusion joins together two small nuclei. Fusion reactions supply the power needed for our sun to shine. The principle behind fusion is that in fusing two small nuclei like deuterium (^2H, or one neutron and one proton), a great deal of energy is released. Deuterium (^2H) and tritium (^3H) are both isotopes of hydrogen which are obtainable in normal water. The reaction of deuterium and tritium follows:

Note that 17.6 million electron volts of energy is released per ^4He produced. This is due to the difference in the atomic energies of the reactants and products. Conditions needed for fusion are high concentration of fusing elements, high temperature, and high density. It has been estimated that, reacting only 1 gram of deuterium will release an amount of energy equivalent to 2400 gallons of gasoline.

Energy from nuclear reactors is considered to be "clean" energy, as carbon and nitrogen oxides as well as smoke and soot are not released into the atmosphere. The disadvantages of nuclear energy include the high cost of building nuclear power plants, finding politically acceptable ways to dispose of the radioactive wastes including the spent fuel rods, the risk of radioactive release, and the cost of shutting down a nuclear power plant at the end of its useful life.

The resource for nuclear fission energy is Uranium 235 which can be manufactured by condensing natural uranium using the centrifugal method. The total amount of Uranium in the world is considerable because even seawater contains uranium with a density of 3.3×10^{-6} [kg/kl]. However, the investment for a condensation facility for seawater is too great to be a practical application. The amount of uranium resources is a function of the price. The confirmed reserves (C.R.) which can be provided with the price under US $80/kg is about 3.1×10^6 [t] and with the price under US$130/kg is 5.2×10^6 [t] in C.R. and 13.27×10^6 [t] in U.R. The price of US$ 80/kg is considered equivalent to oil when both fuels are applied to generating electric power in a power station.

The life cycle model of the uranium fuel is not so simple to evaluate as fossil fuels because an explicit form of the function for the production rate and C.R. with the time and the price are not definite, however, we may infer that the U.R. which can compete economically with oil is comparable or less than that of oil.

3 Renewable Energy Sources

A renewable resource is a fuel source that can provide energy for man forever if man takes care of it. There are many types of renewable resources that man has learned to take advantage of, ranging from solar power to biomass and geothermal to wind power. With these resources, man has utilised the power of the sun, wind, and the earth itself. The efficiency varies with the resource, however.

Renewable power is energy (usually in the form of electricity) produced using fuel resources that don't run out, or are quickly renewed through natural processes. These resources include (see Table 7): 1) Solar Energy; 2) Wind Energy; 3) Hydropower; 4) Geothermal; 5) Biomass; 6) Ocean Energy; 7) Tidal Power.

Table 7. Resource capacity of natural energy in the world (Ohta 1994)

Classification	Capacity	Kind of energy
Solar energy (absorbed in the atmosphere)	0.4×10^{14} kW	Photon and heat energies
Hydropower	3.0×10^{9} kW	Kinetic energy
Wind power	9.7×10^{9} kW*	Kinetic energy
Geothermal	4.0×10^{17} kJ	Kinetic energy
Tide energy	6.7×10^{7} kW	Kinetic energy

* This value is the USA only.

Choosing renewable power can provide many benefits, such as:

- Making use of secure, indigenous, and replenishable natural resources.
- Helping to keep our air clean.

- Potential to reduce the production of carbon dioxide - a leading contributor to global climate change.
- Helping to create jobs for local workers.
- Nation-wide, reducing dependence on imported oil.

In the new competitive market, the responsibility lies with consumers to choose renewable power over conventional power, thus helping existing facilities to continue to operate and ensuring that new renewable power facilities continue to be developed.

Renewables can be more expensive because the price we pay for conventional power does not reflect the full cost of its environmental impacts. At the same time, renewable power provides benefits that are not priced in the market. By purchasing renewable power, you can send an important message to the market: that you value and are willing to pay for the benefits provided by renewable energy. As more consumers like you purchase electricity generated from renewable resources, the costs of these technologies may become more competitive with conventional technologies.

3.1 Solar Energy

Solar power may be the energy of the twenty-first century. At the present time solar power is quite limited. Solar power can be broken down into two categories: 1. Passive solar and 2. Active Solar.

Passive solar energy is making direct or indirect use of the thermal energy from the sun. Indirectly, we can take advantage of the fact that a southern exposure guarantees the maximum exposure of the sun's rays. Architects can take advantage of that fact when they build structures where the windows utilise the sun's thermal energy during the winter. Special metal leaf covering over windows can block out the sun during the summer months. Special thermal solar collectors can circulate water through the collection unit that collects the sun's thermal energy for the purpose of heating the water for use. More expensive units can use the thermal energy of the sun in a heat exchange pump for the air conditioning of small buildings. These thermal solar collectors have been coming down in expense but are limited by the geographical setting where the sun's energy is at its maximum.

Active solar energy is the direct use of the sun's electromagnetic radiation in generating electrical energy. Technically, this is accomplished by the use of semi-conductor Silicon Boron solar chips. The problem with these solar chips is that they have a low efficiency ratio and can only be used in supplying the energy needs of small devices like calculators, watches, radios, or as a limited power source in satellite systems. However the present technology does not allow the use of these solar chips to supply the power needs for whole communities. Perhaps in time, autos will be supplied electrical energy by solar conversion. Active solar power could be a power source for the near future.

The nuclear fusion reactions in the sun yield a huge amount of energy which is estimated at 3.47×10^{24} [kJ] per unit time. This value is comparable with the revolving kinetic energy of the moon around the earth. Of this huge amount of emitted energy, only a small part, 5×10^{-11}, is irradiated onto the earth's surface. The incident solar energy is distributed into many branches. Solar energy is said to be clean and undepletable. It is true that solar energy is harmless to living bodies on the earth's surface because the harmful short wavelength ultra-violet rays are absorbed by the stratospheric ozone layers and weakened by the air and moisture in the atmosphere. However, if the ozone layers are destroyed by artificial chemical substances such as flon CFC (Chlorofluorocarbon), living bodies will be subject to serious effects and human beings especially will be prone to skin cancer.

Solar energy activates the atmosphere thus generating climatic phenomena, but the balance of the energy is absorbed by molecules of the materials on the earth and converted into heat at low temperature. This is an example of the entropy increasing process of nature. It is reasonable to plan to actively utilise the sun's photon - and high temperature heat-energies before they decay to produce entropy.

3.2 Wind Energy

Not only does the sun supply the earth with direct radiant energy, but it also heats the gases of the atmosphere, which produces wind. Wind power uses energy from the moving air to turn large blades on windmills. In the past, the motion of the blades was used to grind flour or pump water, but now the blades turn turbines, which rotate generators in order to produce electricity. Wide open windy spaces are needed in order for this system to be efficient. Wind energy produces no air or water pollution, involves no toxic or hazardous substances, and poses no threat to public safety. The major problem with wind power is the limited ability of sites with steady wind and the lifetime of the wind power generator units.

The windmill is one of the most traditional and oldest of human technologies. It is inferred that the invention of the windmill on which white sails are stretched occurred about 2000 B.C. where it was utilised on the Aegean islands and on Crete. The spreading of windmills was most lively in the Netherlands, Denmark, and Northern Germany where there are low lands.

In the 1880s the use of windmills was a common sight on the country landscape. These paddle wheel devices were used to harness the wind to pump water up from beneath the ground for cattle to drink. Such windmills were also used to mill grain at the granaries. The windmills died out in the latter half of the twentieth century only to be revived in the 1970s in the form of huge bladed machines that are moved by the gentlest of wind of less than 3 mph. These wind machines have been used to power small dwellings. The biggest disadvantage of this source of energy is its limited geographical setting. It can only be taken advantage of where the wind moves continuously as you would have at the coast or in vast flatlands. Perhaps in the future there will be efficient wind machines that will be banked together and supply enough wind power to supply the energy needs of a whole city.

In 1992 the world output from installed windmills was about 2.22×10^6 [kW]. The distribution of these windmills is shown in Table 8. However, at the end of 1993, wind farms built in California have 19,000 windmills generating 190×10^6 [kW].

Table 8. Distribution of windmills in the countries of IEA (1992)

Country	**Capacity (10^3 kW)**	
	Working	under construction
USA	1600	260
Denmark	410	100
Germany	100	0
Netherlands	80	10
England	10	131
Sweden	6	4
Canada	5	10
Italy	2	20
Japan	2	2
Norway	0	2
Total	2200	572

Basic classification of windmills are horizontal axes such as sail wing, propeller, multi bladed, Netherlands type and vertical axis such as paddle type, savonious, gyromill, and darrieus.

The many kinds of windmills include propeller and other axial-flow turbines, as well as radial systems mounted on vertical axes. Most modem windmills have two or three blades which have the highest efficiency under most climatic conditions. In order to generate alternating current electric power with a constant cycle, the windmill must be operated at a constant angular velocity over a wide range of wind speeds. In addition, other contrivances are necessary, for example, an energy storage battery system is necessary when no wind comes, automatic stopping systems are needed when too strong a wind comes, and so on.

Windmill power generation has many problems such as spoilage by salty wind and attachment of ice and snow on the blades. Technologies for manufacturing blades using new materials made of glass fibre, carbon fibre, and so on, which avoid such damage, are important. Computer applied control is another necessity.

The social problems of windmills are, for example, that the electro-magnetic waves for TV, radio and other communications are disturbed by the spinning rotors; counterplans are necessary.

One of the benefits of wind generated electricity is that it avoids most of the traditional environmental impacts associated with electricity generation. Wind power has none of the greenhouse gas and acid gas emissions which result from the combustion of fossil fuels such as coal, oil and natural gas, the traditional sources of electrical power. Similarly, wind power obviously does not result in the risks of radioactive exposure associated with nuclear power plants. Although use of the wind for generating electricity would help reduce the problems of global warming and acid rain, no source of energy is totally without environmental impacts.

The main environmental concerns surrounding the use of wind energy are impacts on land use, noise, effects on wildlife and disruption of radio transmissions. Since the available wind resource is so spread out, vast areas of land are required to provide significant amounts of electricity. Wind turbines can however be placed on areas used for grazing of animals, or land of marginal value. The aesthetics of wind farms has also been questioned, but the public seems to accept the thousands of electricity transmission towers which dot our landscape.

The noise of wind turbines has also been cited as a negative impact of wind turbines. It is true that wind turbines create increased noise levels, but the decibel level of wind turbines drops quickly with distance from the turbine. At a distance of 300 m from the average wind turbine, the ambient noise level is similar to that in a library. Turbines are generally located at least this far away from human activity for safety reasons. Similarly wind turbines can disrupt radio signals and therefore can't be located near airports or other sources of important radio transmissions.

Naturalists have always been concerned that wind farms would have a negative effect on bird populations. These fears may not be justified however, as recent studies by the Royal Society for the Protection for Birds have shown wind turbines to have very little effect on bird populations. The damage to wildlife habitat caused by traditional fossil fuel electricity generation has a much greater impact on wildlife than wind turbines.

3.3 Hydropower

Hydroenergy is the energy of moving water. People since the time of ancient Egypt to the present have used flowing water to do work. Moving water turns a wheel attached to a shaft. The rotating shaft is used to do work.

The first water wheels were used to grind grain or to move irrigation water. Water still does those jobs in many parts of the world. In industrialised countries, the most important use of hydro power is to generate electricity.

The first hydroelectric plants in British Columbia were built in 1897 at Bonnington Falls near Nelson, and in 1898 at Goldstream near Victoria. Today

95 per cent of B.C.s electricity comes from hydropower. In other parts of the world, much less of the electricity comes from hydroelectricity.

Hydroelectricity requires water to fall on a turbine and make it rotate. The water is collected behind a dam in a reservoir. The water then flows downhill in a pipe called a penstock. The falling water turns a turbine and creates electricity. The electricity is taken to the users by transmission lines. The water returns to the river below the dam.

Large dams on big rivers can create huge amounts of electricity. In British Columbia, big dams on the Peace River and the Columbia River provide power to the whole province. At Kitimat, a large hydro dam provides electricity to an aluminium smelter.

Even small streams can be used for hydroelectricity. In China, over 86,000 small dams serve local districts. In North America, small-scale hydro projects power individual houses or small communities.

Hydropower systems use the energy in flowing water for mechanical purposes or to produce electricity. The head and the flow are two variables that essentially determine the potential efficiency of a site for a hydropower system. The height of the falling water is called the head. The greater the head, the higher the velocity of the water falling will be, and hence the greater the pressure with which it hits. The flow is the total amount of water moving. The advantages of using water for a power source are that the resource is free, and it can be stored effectively and put to use quickly. Water for hydropower may be stored in a reservoir or above a dam forming a lake. The mechanics of the hydropower system are very similar to the wind power system, the only difference being water turning the blades instead of wind. The turning wheel can also drive a shaft to produce mechanical energy, which may be used to perform simple tasks, especially for agricultural applications such as sawing wood or grinding grain.

Most sites available for large scale hydroelectric plants have already been developed. Therefore, new developments in hydroelectric generation are small scale. Small scale hydropower systems are quite efficient when used to supply local needs. The Hoover Dam is an example of a large scale hydroelectric plant still in use in the United States today. The United States and Canada have the greatest number of hydroelectric plants. Virtually every other country in the world has some development of hydropower plants. **Hydroelectricity** is the power source of choice for many developing countries. However, the development of hydroelectricity is quite expensive as well as site-dependent. There are some concerns over the detrimental environmental effects of hydroelectric power. Environmental problems include siltation and erosion, the breaking up the free passage between oceans and rivers, weed growth, disease spread by small organisms that live in stagnant water, and floods due to dam failures.

According to Lvovitch (Russia), the world's total annual rainfall is, on average, 108.4×10^{12} [t/Y], of which 12×10^{12} [t] are absorbed into the ground,

25.13×10^{12} [t] are carried away to the sea, and 71.27×10^{12} [t] are evaporated. If the quantity of rain water described above falls from a height of 1000 [m] above the earth's surface, then a kinetic energy of 1062.32×10^{15} [kJ/Y] is imparted to the earth every year. Some of this huge energy is stored at dams, constructed in mountain valleys, confining the potential energy so that one can utilise it to generate electric power sufficient for their needs. Such a system is called the "dam system". There also exists another system called the "flow system" or "river system". The latter system utilises the kinetic energy possessed by the flowing water of a river, and is constructed in the river. This system consists of the intake of river water, a precipitation area where muddy water is purified, and intake pipes leading to the water turbines. The water head is not so large as that of dam power systems.

A typical river system power station is the Bonneville power station existing on the Columbia river along the boundary between the states of Oregon and Washington in the U.S.A. This power station has a capacity of ca. 1.06×10^6 [kW]. Beside the Bonneville station, there exist four more large river system power stations. The total sum of their outputs is over 8.4×10^6 [kW].

Dam system power stadons can hardly find suitable sites in developed countries, while large reserves of river system power remain untapped in the underdeveloped countries.

The world's reserves of hydro power for both types of power generating system are estimated to be about 20×10^8 [kW], only about 10 to 15% of which are developed while the remainder exist in developing countries such as China, India, South America, Siberia, and Canada. Most of them are of the river system type. In 1991, China proposed the construction of the Chang Kiang river dam that is 2 [km] long, with a 200 [m] height between the highest water level of the upper stream and the power station site. This dam can store 730×10^8 [t] water and has the capacity to generate 25×10^6 [kW] of power, the largest in the world. It is said that more than one million people had to move from the dam sites.

Another example of the social problem accompanying dam construction is that of Narmada river dam in India where more than one hundred thousand people were forced to move. Such a problem is, more or less, typical of any dam construction.

A new type of hydropower station is the pumping dam, which has been invented as a storage method of electrical energy. Being different from oil-, coal-, and gas-fired plants, it is barely possible (actually impossible) to quickly alter the output of a nuclear reactor. Therefore the output from an atomic power station is usually constant even at midnight or on holidays. Thus it is necessary to construct a facility for storing electrical energy when nuclear power plants are constructed.

The mechanism of energy storage in a pumping dam is obvious. The surplus electrical energy drives motors to pump water up from a pond to a dam located a few hundred meters higher than the pond. Then, when electrical energy is needed, the water is released and hydropower drives turbines to generate the needed power. It is an advantage that the pumping motor can be used also as a generator. The system efficiency of the pumping dam is about 30%. In 1990 Japan had a pumping station capacity of 5.63×10^6 [kW] while that of its other hydropower stations was 20.30×10^6 [kW].

Water power is renewable. Rivers will continue to flow. But hydroelectricity can be produced only at special sites that usually require a dam and reservoir. Over time, the reservoirs fill in with sediment deposited by the water. Some reservoirs in Africa may fill in less than 50 years, although most B.C. reservoirs will last over 200 years. The sites can be used only once and are not renewable. So hydroelectric energy is not a completely renewable resource.

Advantages of hydroelectricity:

- Water is a renewable resource.
- Hydroelectric generators are clean and nonpolluting to operate. The water is not destroyed, consumed or polluted by generating electricity.
- Flowing water is free and reliable. Seasonal changes in water supply are fairly predictable. The water stored in the reservoir provides a continuous supply, even during dry weather.
- Once a dam is built, it costs very little to operate. Dams and generators require little maintenance and are very reliable. The direct cost of hydro-electricity is very low. Hydroelectricity is the least expensive source of electricity in large quantities.
- Small-scale hydro is simple and inexpensive. Individual homes and small communities can get electricity from local streams.
- Hydro reservoirs can also be used to control flooding, for irrigation and for recreational activities such as boating and fishing.

Disadvantages of hydroelectricity:

- Large dams are expensive and slow to build. It can take over ten years between the decision to build one and the time the electricity flows.
- There are few sites for building large dams. In North America, most sites suitable for large dams are already used. The sites that are left are mostly in the far north.
- Dams disrupt the natural flow of water and disrupt ecosystems upstream and downstream. Creatures that live in the water and animals that live on land can be seriously harmed by changes in the flow of the river.
- Reservoirs flood people's homes, forests and farmland. The people who live in the settlements and who use the forests and land may not want a reservoir there, even if they want electricity.

3.4 Geothermal energy

Geothermal energy originates from the inner core of the earth. Geothermal energy is evident on the earth's surface in the forms of volcanoes, geysers, and hot springs. Even though the amount of energy within the earth is basically infinite, our ability to use it is limited by site considerations. Favourable sites for geothermal energy extraction are rare and occur where magma, or hot molten rock of the earth's mantle, has been pushed up near the earth's surface through faults and cracks in the crust. The resulting "hot spots" 2 to 3 km from the surface naturally heat water that leaks in. From there, the steam and hot water may be used directly to turn turbines or to heat homes. As the steam and hot water is expelled from the hot spot, cooler water runs back down, and the cycle continues.

For thousands of years, humans have used naturally occurring hot springs for bathing. More recently, geothermal energy has been used to generate electricity, and to provide heat for homes and industries. Geothermal energy is a versatile and reliable source of heat and electricity which generally produces none of the greenhouse gases associated with the combustion of fossil fuels. Unfortunately, the best geothermal resources are concentrated in areas of volcanic activity and are not widely distributed. California, Iceland, Italy, New Zealand and Japan are all areas where geothermal energy is used on a significant scale.

The high temperatures in the earth's core are a result of heat trapped during the formation of the earth approximately 4.7 billion years ago, as well as the decay of naturally occurring radioactive elements. The rate of heat flow out of the earth is about 5000 times smaller than the rate of solar energy reaching the earth's surface. Solar radiation therefore controls the surface temperature of the planet; but a few meters below the earth's surface, temperatures are governed by the internal heat of the earth. Geothermal energy is often considered a renewable source of energy. This is not strictly true, because human uses of geothermal generally remove the heat from a location faster than it is replaced. The magnitude of the geothermal resource is so large, however, that on a human time scale it may be considered as a renewable energy source.

The temperature of the earth's crust rises as the depth from the surface increases, all over the world. In some places the rate of this increase in temperature, the "geothermal gradient", is higher than in others. These areas tend to be located in regions that are geologically active, where sections of the earth's crust are either colliding or moving apart. Due to this fact, the most promising geothermal resources are located in areas of volcanic activity. The higher the geothermal gradient, the less expensive it is to extract heat from the earth, due to drilling and pumping costs. In the ultimate case, the gradient may be so high that naturally occurring surface waters have been heated to a useful temperature. This is the case with hot springs and geysers.

Geothermal energy can be usefully extracted from four different types of geologic formations. These include hydrothermal, geopressurised, hot dry rock and magma. Each of these different reservoirs of geothermal energy can potentially be tapped and used for heating or electricity generation. Different extraction and processing techniques are required for the different sources of geothermal heat. In addition to the above, heat pumps can be used to extract low temperature heat from shallow depths. Such heat pumps are similar to the air-to-air heat pumps commonly used to heat homes, and will not be examined in detail.

Hydrothermal reservoirs contain hot water and/or steam trapped in fractured or porous rock formations by a layer of impermeable rock on top. Hydrothermal reservoirs have been the most common source of geothermal energy production worldwide. Geopressurised resources are from formations where moderately high temperature brines are trapped in a permeable layer of rock under high pressures. These brines often contain dissolved methane which can potentially be extracted for use as a fuel.

Hot dry rock is another potential geothermal resource. Hot dry rock reservoirs are generally hot impermeable rocks at depths shallow enough to be accessible (600°C).

The theoretical potential of the world's geothermal energy resource is enormous. There is enough heat in the earth's core to provide all of the world's energy needs for thousands of years. Unfortunately, most of this heat is at such great depths below the surface that it is extremely expensive or impossible to extract. Accessible geothermal energy is also not evenly distributed around the globe. For instance, here in Canada, the only area with geothermal resources that can be economically extracted at the present time is British Columbia.

The result of the above facts is that geothermal energy is currently being exploited only in those regions where heat is available near the surface, such as "The Geysers" in California where 1866 million watts (MW) of electricity are generated. Other locations with extensive use of geothermal energy include Reykjavik and Rotorua in Iceland where shallow reservoirs of subterranean steam are tapped to provide heating and hot water for many buildings. In all cases, individual reservoirs from which heat is extracted will eventually cool to the extent that they are no longer useful. This forces new or deeper wells to be drilled, increasing the costs of geothermal energy.

Geothermal resources are abundant. Since the oil crises of 1973 and the 1980s, more power plants have been developed; we currently have about 4 $\times 10^6$ [kW] as the total world capacity of the approximately 100 electric power plants' output.

3.5 Biomass Energy

Biomass is the most important source for energy production supplied by agriculture. Biomass energy refers to fuels made from plants and animal wastes. The most common kinds of biomass are wood and wood chips, animal manure and crop wastes.

Wood is one of the oldest forms of biomass energy. Wood is still gathered from forests and burned for fuel around the world. In British Columbia, wood chips are burned to boil water to make steam used in pulp and paper mills.

In this century, scientists have developed new ways to use biomass. Animal manure is decomposed by bacteria to make methane gas. It is called biogas. The gas is burned for heating and cooking and is used as a vehicle fuel. It is also burned to create steam to generate electricity. Biogas is used in places where there is a large amount of animal waste. India and China have thousands of biogas plants.

Field crops or the stems of plants left after a crop is harvested can be processed with yeast to make liquid alcohol fuels. The alcohol is either burned or mixed with gasoline to make a fuel often called gasohol. In British Columbia, the Mohawk Oil Company adds alcohol made from wheat to some of its gasolines.

Animal wastes are gathered in a sealed vessel where natural processes convert them to methane gas that can be drawn off and used for fuel.

Biomass materials are the remains of animal or plant life that have not been subjected to the tremendous heat and pressure that formed the fossil fuels. Biomass materials such as wood, dried dung, animal wastes, and even garbage can be used as renewable sources of energy to heat homes, cook food, and even produce electricity. The energy produced when wood is burned was originally stored in the bonds of the glucose formed during photosynthesis in the leaves of the tree. As the wood is burned, energy is required to break the bonds in the cellulose. As the carbon dioxide and water are formed, more energy is released than was initially required to break the bonds. Thus, net energy is released. Examples of widely-used biomass energy systems are ethanol in gasoline, anaerobic digestion of municipal waste water or swine waste to produce methane gas, and incineration of garbage.

There are several other applications of biomass fuel. Ethanol is presently used in gasohol (10% ethanol, 90% gasoline), resulting in a cleaner burning fuel, which emits an average of 20% less carbon monoxide than unblended gasoline. Swine farmers collect the manure and add methane-producing bacteria called methanogens in a controlled environment. The methane is collected and burned to produce electricity for the hog confinement buildings. Municipal waste water treatment plants use a two stage process to separate the waste into two parts. One converts waste sludge into a variety of organic acids and carbon dioxide; the other reacts the waste with the methanogens to produce methane. The forest industry now burns much of its waste to provide heat and electricity.

The biomass resource can be considered as organic matter in which the energy of sunlight is stored in chemical bonds. When the bonds between adjacent carbon, hydrogen, and oxygen molecules are broken by digestion, combustion, or decomposition these substances release stored energy. Biomass is made available on a renewable basis through natural processes, or it can be made available as a by-product of human activities. Biomass energy is generated when organic matter is converted to energy.

Biomass energy is a form of solar energy. During the photosynthesis reaction, organic materials are produced from carbon dioxide and water by the energy of light. Photosynthesis typically converts less than one percent of the available sunlight to stored chemical energy. Although the process of photosynthesis is not very efficient in converting solar energy into chemical energy, the produced energy is relatively inexpensive and produced in large quantities over wide land areas. A sort of "low-cost solar collector" is naturally provided by the land surface on which plants grow. When the sun is not shining this chemical energy is also stored in the chemical bonds of the produced biomass (such as plants). Overall biomass resources are quite significant, as approximately 100 terawatt-years of chemical energy are stored in plants each year (an amount of energy equivalent to ten-times that of humanity's current energy needs).

In lesser-developed countries, many people rely on biomass energy in the form of wood fuel for cooking. Nearly two billion people are totally reliant on biomass fuels for their energy needs. Wood, a form of biomass, provides for three quarters of all the energy used in sub-Saharan Africa. In Ethiopia and Nepal, nearly all energy is derived from biomass. India derives one-half of the country's energy from biomass. In Asia, nearly one-third of China's energy needs are met by biomass. In South America, biomass is used to meet one-quarter of Brazil's energy needs. In the Middle-East, one-fifth of Egypt's energy is supplied by biomass. In the 1980s, biomass energy accounted for 1% (or less) of the total energy use in developed countries, while in the lesser-developed countries biomass accounted for approximately 43% of the total energy use. Globally, biomass resources supplied approximately 14% of total energy used during the last decade.

In developed countries, biomass energy is often closely associated with agriculture and forestry activities. Biomass resources are used in the form of solid fuels (such as pellets), gaseous fuels (such as methane), and liquid fuels (such as ethanol). Biomass energy carriers in the form of solid, gaseous, and liquid fuels can also be used to generate electricity. In addition, the manufacture of liquid fuels from biomass resources is feasible and in some cases preferable to using fossil-based liquid fuels. Biomass material typically has less ash and sulphur than coal, and its looser molecular structure allows it to be gasified at temperatures lower than coal. Therefore, biomass resources can act as an alternative feedstock for fuel production. Biomass derived energy can play many roles in meeting our present and future energy needs.

Examples of Biomass Energy Use:

- Direct combustion of biomass for heating and cooking energy.
- Biomass derived solid fuels for conversion to energy.
- Biomass derived liquid fuels for conversion to energy.
- Biomass derived gaseous fuels for conversion to energy.
- Generation of electric energy from biomass derived fuels.
- Biomass derived fuels for transportation energy.

• Biomass derived aqueous chemicals for feedstocks in fuel and chemical production.

There is a consensus amongst scientists that biomass fuels used in a sustainable manner result in no net increase in atmospheric carbon dioxide (CO_2). Some would even go as far as to declare that sustainable use of biomass will result in a net decrease in atmospheric CO_2. This is based on the assumption that all the CO_2 given off by the use of biomass fuels was recently taken in from the atmosphere by photosynthesis. Increased substitution of fossil fuels with biomass based fuels would therefore help reduce the potential for global warming, caused by increased atmospheric concentrations of CO_2.

Unfortunately, things may not be as simple as has been assumed above. Currently, biomass is being used all over the world in a very unsustainable manner, and the long term effects of biomass energy plantations has not been proven. As well, the natural humus and dead organic matter in the forest soils is a large reservoir of carbon. Conversion of natural ecosystems to managed energy plantations could result in a release of carbon from the soil as a result of the accelerated decay of organic matter.

An ever-increasing number of people on this planet are faced with hunger and starvation. It has been argued that the use of land to grow fuel crops will increase this problem. Hunger in developing countries, however, is more complex than just a lack of agricultural land. Many countries in the world today, such as the US, have food surpluses. Much fertile agricultural land is also used to grow tobacco, flowers, food for domestic pets and other "luxury" items, rather than staple foods. Similarly, a significant proportion of agricultural land is used to grow feed for animals to support the highly wasteful, meat centred diet of the industrialised world. By feeding grain to livestock we end up with only about 10% of the caloric content of the grain. When looked at in this light, it does not seem to be so unreasonable to use some fertile land to grow fuel. Marginal land and under-utilised agricultural land can also be used to grow biomass for fuel.

Acid rain, which can damage lakes and forests, is a by-product of the combustion of fossil fuels, particularly coal and oil. The high sulphur content of these fuels together with hot combustion temperatures result in the formation of sulphur dioxide (SO_2) and nitrous oxides (NO_x), when they are burned to provide energy. The replacement of fossil fuels with biomass can reduce the potential for acid rain. Biomass generally contains less than 0.1% sulphur by weight compared to low sulphur coal with 0.5-4% sulphur. Lower combustion temperatures and pollution control devices such as wet scrubbers and electrostatic precipitators can also keep emissions of NO_x to a minimum when biomass is burned to produce energy.

The final major environmental impact of biomass energy may be that of loss of biodiversity. Transforming natural ecosystems into energy plantations with a very small number of crops, as few as one, can drastically reduce the biodiversity of a region. Such "monocultures" lack the balance achieved by a diverse ecosystem, and are susceptible to widespread damage by pests or disease.

Biomass currently supplies 14% of the world's energy needs, but has the theoretical potential to supply 100%. Most present day production and use of biomass for energy is carried out in a very unsustainable manner with a great many negative environmental consequences. If biomass is to supply a greater proportion of the world's energy needs in the future, the challenge will be to produce biomass sustainably and to convert and use it without harming the natural environment. Technologies and processes exist today which, if used properly, make biomass based fuels less harmful to the environment than fossil fuels. Applying these technologies and processes on a site specific basis in order to minimise negative environmental impacts is a prerequisite for sustainable use of biomass energy in the future.

3.6 Ocean Energy

Two-thirds of the Earth's surface is covered by oceans. These bodies of water are vast reservoirs of renewable energy. In a four day period, the planet's oceans absorb an amount of thermal energy from the sun and kinetic energy from the wind equivalent to all the world's known oil reserves. Wave energy, ocean current energy, and ocean thermal energy belong to this realm. There is no practically applied example in this field yet, although the energy resources are numerous.

(1) Wave energy. The energy density of ocean waves ranges widely, from 10^{-3} to 10^{3} [kW/m], where the energy unit shows the energy per 1 [m] of coastline.

The total amount of wave energy in the world has been studied by many authors. Their results suggest that the total resources are of the order of 10^{9} [kW]. This numerical value can be confirmed by integrating over all the coastlines in the world. This integral gives 2.7×10^{9} [kW].

There are a several kinds of effective energy conversion systems, from wave energy to electrical energy. Among them, the most popular method is to activate air turbines. If a pipe equipped with an air turbine at the upper end is fixed in the sea water near a coast, the wave motion periodically raises and lowers the water level in the tube. Accordingly the air is either pressed out or drawn in as the water level rises and falls. Thus the turbines are activated to generate electric power.

The sea waves is not always constant so that the generated electrical energy can hardly have a constant cycle. The energy density of a sea wave is not high, on average, while a conversion facility requires a big investment. Hence, it is not easy to develop a wave power plant that is practical.

(2) Ocean current energy. The solar energy falling upon the tropical zone is so intense and plentiful that the sea water is warmed and becomes a warm current that flows towards the southern and northern poles. The warm current is

cooled by ice in the Antarctic and Arctic seas and flows back to the tropical sea. This is the heat cycle of tropical solar energy. Both currents flow along nearly the same path every year. Therefore we may extract kinetic energy using water turbines that are fixed in the sea (e.g., moored between islands). It is probably not feasible to construct power plants utilising such ocean currents as the investment would be too great.

(3) Ocean thermal energy. As described above, the two kinds of ocean currents exist, one being warm and the other cold. Dr. A. d'Arsonval, a French physicist, first proposed an energy conversion system using the temperature gradient between them and his student, G. Claude, made a preliminary experiment as early as in 1881.

The principle is simply described as follows. A heat medium liquid such as CFC (Chlorofluorocarbon) or ammonia is cooled to the liquid state by deep sea water at a temperature of 5-10°C. The liquid is then pumped up from the deep sea and vaporised by the warm surface current where the temperature is 20 - 25°C. The resulting vapour pressure is used to drive a gas turbine. This system is called OTEC (Ocean Thermal Energy Conversion).

The electric power generated in this system can be used to electrolyse sea water to generate hydrogen which can then be easily transported, instead of using direct electrical transmission which is difficult in mid-ocean.

Despite its low energy efficiency, this ocean system has another merit of pumping up nutritious deep sea water to support the on-site fish culture.

3.7 Tidal Power

Tides are the movement of the coastal waters caused by the gravitational forces of the moon upon the earth. Since the creation of the Earth, tidal forces have been with us. The movement of the water at the coastal front is kinetic energy that can be tapped into. The French have been experimenting with tidal basin near Marseilles on the Mediterranean coastline. The water as it moves motivated by the gravitational pull of the moon on the earth will run past tiny turbine blades that create electrical energy by electromagnetic induction. This produces enough electrical energy to supply the partial power of the city of Marseilles. Tidal electrical generators have not been used by people in this country yet, but it represents a limited potential source of energy.

The differences between the sea levels of ebb tide and high tide vary from coast to coast. The largest head observed thus far is about 16 [m] at Fandy bay on the east-southern coast of Canada. The only realised practical power plant is the Ranee power station in France where the largest head is 13.5 [m] and the high tide visits every 6 hours and 12 minutes.

In coastal areas with large tides, flowing tidal waters contain large amounts of potential energy. The principal of harnessing the energy of the tides dates back to eleventh century England when tides were used to turn waterwheels, producing mechanical power. More recently, rising and falling tides have been used to generate electricity, in much the same manner as hydroelectric power plants.

Although ocean tides contain extremely large amounts of energy, it is only practical to generate electricity at sites with exceptionally high tides such as the Bay of Fundy in Atlantic Canada which, at up to 17 metres, has the highest tides in the world. Tidal energy is an essentially renewable resource that has none of the typical environmental impacts of other traditional sources of electricity such as fossil fuels or nuclear power. Changing the tidal flow in a coastal region could, however, result in a wide variety of impacts on aquatic life, most of which are poorly understood.

Tides, the daily rise and fall of ocean levels relative to coastlines, are a result of the gravitational force of the moon and sun as well as the revolution of the earth. The moon and the sun both exert a gravitational force of attraction on the earth. The magnitude of the gravitational attraction of an object is dependent upon the mass of an object and its distance. The moon exerts a larger gravitational force on the earth because, although it is much smaller in mass, it is a great deal closer than the sun. This force of attraction causes the oceans, which make up 71% of the earth's surface, to bulge along an axis pointing towards the moon. Tides are produced by the rotation of the earth beneath this bulge in its watery coating, resulting in the rhythmic rise and fall of coastal ocean levels.

The gravitational attraction of the sun also affects the tides in a similar manner as the moon, but to a lesser degree. As well as bulging towards the moon, the oceans also bulge slightly towards the sun. When the earth, moon and sun are positioned in a straight line (a full or new moon), the gravitational attractions are combined, resulting in very large "spring" tides. At half moon, the sun and moon are at right angles, resulting in lower tides called "neap" tides. Coastal areas experience two high and two low tides over a period of slightly greater than 24 hours. The friction of the bulging oceans acting on the spinning earth results in a very gradual slowing down of the earth's rotation. This will not have any significant effect for billions of years. Therefore, for human purposes, tidal energy can be considered a sustainable and renewable source of energy.

Certain coastal regions experience higher tides than others. This is a result of the amplification of tides caused by local geographical features such as bays and inlets. In order to produce practical amounts of power (electricity), a difference between high and low tides of at least five metres is required. There are about 40 sites around the world with this magnitude of tidal range. The higher the tides, the more electricity can be generated from a given site, and the lower the cost of electricity produced. Worldwide, approximately 3000 gigawatts (1 gigawatt = 1 GW = 1 billion watts) of energy is continuously available from the action of tides. Due to the constraints outlined above, it has been estimated that only 2% or 60 GW can potentially be recovered for electricity generation.

Tidal power has the potential to generate significant amounts of electricity at certain sites around the world. Although our entire electricity needs could never be met by tidal power alone, it can be a valuable source of renewable energy to an electrical system. The negative environmental impacts of tidal barrages are probably much smaller than those of other sources of electricity, but are not well understood at this time. The technology required for tidal power is well developed, and the main barrier to increased use of the tides is that of construction costs. The future costs of other sources of electricity, and concern over their environmental impacts, will ultimately determine whether humankind extensively harnesses the gravitational power of the moon.

Chapter 4
Energy Technology

1 Energy Systems

The term "energy system" is ambiguously used to depict a total system combining elemental subsystems, such as the search for primary energy resources, and its subsequent development, refining, conversion, transportation storage, distribution, utilisation, security, pollution problems, and so on. Accordingly the energy system has been regarded as a kind of economic system attaching importance to the distribution system rather than an object of science and technology.

An outline of energy flow is shown as a system in Figure 1. Primary energy (fossil fuels, nuclear energy, renewable energy) is transported, stored, and converted to secondary energy (electrical power, city gas, gasoline, light oil, kerosene, etc. The secondary energy is transported (or transmitted), stored and converted to a more convenient energy with high quality. By quality of energy we mean, for example electrical energy with constant voltage and frequency, city gas with constant pressure and caloric density, gasoline with high octane and no impurity. The term "tertiary energy system" is applied to the most convenient utilisation system.

The energy flow is accompanied by unavailable and dispersed energy that can be referred to as "losses". Such multistage energy utilisation is a noticeable trend in the energy saving age, and can be a primary object of energy system science. The losses in transport and storage are unavoidable. For example, oil or gas transportation by a pipeline system needs energy to compress the fluid, which is one kind of loss. The effective utilisation of energy resources is one of the most important tasks for energy engineering, because it provides for the conservation of resources and the reduction of global environmental problems. This system is shown for the five kinds of energies in Table 9.

Unavailable energy is usually able to generate a useful secondary energy, while dispersed energy is not. For this purpose, multistage energy conversion technology has been developed. The present object is to utilise effectively the unavailable (wasted) energy so that the overall successive conversions makes the efficiency very high.

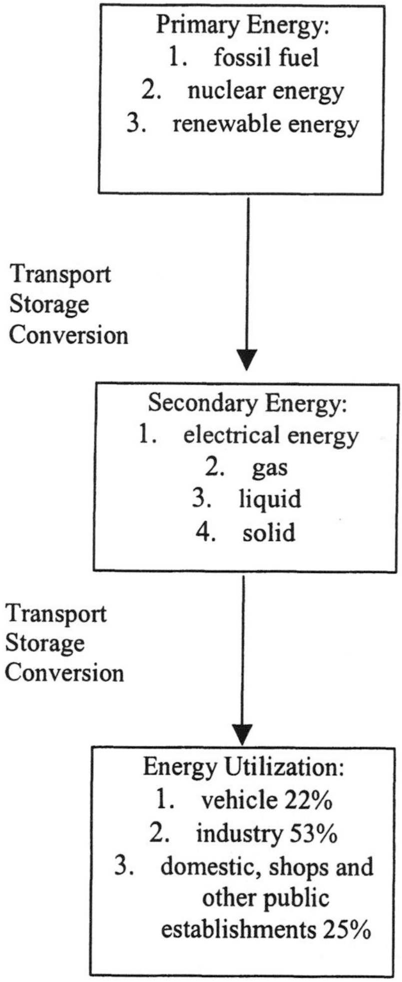

Figure 1. Energy System

Primary energy is selected in expectation of its terminal utilisation. In other words, the most adequate primary energy is chosen and supplied to the final consumption system. For example, coal is for iron and steel manufacturing, heavy oil is for ships (waterway), hydrogen is for rockets, solar energy is for domestic heating and air conditioning, and wind and hydro power are for agriculture.

Electrical power should be applied to communication, TV, radio, fax, telephone, train, motor, and other applications exclusively driven by electrical energy. Electrical and electronic machines have high efficiency and low unavailable energy. Electrical energy is precious because it is generated and transmitted by many processes. The electrical energy of 1 [kW-h] has a caloric equivalent of 860 [kcal], but to generate 1 [kW-h] of electrical energy by a heat engine requires more than 2530 [kcal] input heat.

Table 9. Energy conversion and unavailable energy

Energy	Resource	Conversion	Unavailable	Dispersed
Mechanical	Hydropower wind power	Turbine propeller	slower-motion	friction viscosity
Electromagnetic	no available resources	Generator	Recovered	joulian heat discharge
Photon (particle beam)	solar beam (nuclear energy)	Solar cell, photo-chemical reaction	longer (shorter) wavelength	heat
Chemical	fossil fuel density gradient	Electrolysis, chemical reaction	lower temperature, chemical product (low grade)	heat, unneeded-product
Heat	Nuclear fission, Fossil fuel, Wood, geothermal, solar, ocean thermal	Combustion collector, heat pump	lower-temperature	near the environ-mental temperature

2 Energy Conversion

There exist two kinds of energy conversions. The first is called direct energy conversion. The initial type of energy is directly converted to the final one without any mediated energy; for example, there is thermoelectric conversion (from heat to electricity), fuel cell (from chemical energy to electricity), solar cell (from photon energy to electrical energy), thermoionic conversion (from heat to electricity), magneto hydrodynamic conversion (from heat to electricity) and so on. In these conversions, no third kind of energy is mediated.

Direct energy conversion has, in principle, a relatively high efficiency and produces less entropy and is therefore recommended for future technology.

Table 10. Matrix of energy conversion

	Mechanical Energy	Electrical Energy	Chemical Energy	Photon Energy	Heat Energy
Mechanical Energy	Torque converter Flywheel	Generator Piezo electricity M.H.D.*	Mechano chemical effect Metalhydride	Tribo-luminescence	Friction Collision Metalhydride
Electrical Energy	Motor Linear Motor Magneto-electro striction	Transformer Invertor Microwave transmission	Electrolysis Electro-chemical reaction	Electro-luminescence Laser	Joulian heat Peltier heat Microwave absorption
Chemical Energy	Mechano chemical effect Explosion Super expansion Metalhydride	Primary battery Secondary battery Density gradient power generation	Chemical reaction	Chemical Luminescence Chemical laser	Combustion Dilution heat Metalhydride
Phoon Energy	Light pressure Photon rocket	Photoelectric effect Solar cell	Photo chemical reaction Photo electrode reaction	Maser Fluorescence Phosphores-cence	Absorption Norbor-nadiene
Heat Energy	Heat engine Convection Shape memory Metalhydride	Seebeck effect A.M.T.C.** Thermo electron emission Thermo dielectric conversion	Thermo-chemical reaction Distillation Metalhydride	Radiation	Heat pump

* M.H.D. - magnetohydrodynamics generator
** A.M.T.C.- Alkali Metal Thermoelectric Conversion

The second kind of energy conversion is called indirect energy conversion. Mechanical energy and electrical energy can be converted with mutually high efficiency, because this energy conversion does not always accompany entropy production. Therefore, in order to get electricity, one may convert the initial energy to the mechanical energy and then obtain electricity from a power generator. In typical fire powered plants, the chemical energy of the fossil fuel is changed to heat, then this heat makes water vapour that activates a turbine to generate electric power. That is, the following process: initial chemical energy —> heat —> mechanical —> final electrical energy, is realised. On the other hand, a fuel cell has the process: initial chemical energy —> final electrical energy.

Entropy production is appreciable in the conversion of chemical energy to heat and from heat to mechanical energy, and therefore the fuel cell is preferred.

As has often been mentioned, there are five kinds of energies so that at least twenty-five kinds of energy conversions exist. These are arranged in Table 10 as a matrix. The elements of the matrix are examples of conversion phenomena or technologies. Most of them are familiar to the readers. However, some of them are curious and their explanations are presented later.

Some of the elements represent direct energy conversions, but others do not.

(a) Tribo-luminescence. This effect has an alternative name of tribo thermal luminescence which means that the heat caused by the mechanical energy of friction gives rise to luminescence. However, the impulse or the friction may directly cause this effect although the mechanism is not clear yet

(b) Mechano chemical effect. If the application of an impulse, or pressure to a chemical system initiates its reaction, then such an effect is called the mechano chemical effect. The reverse effect is also possible.

(c) Super expansion. Wood expands by absorbing water. The water molecules enter the spaces in the network structure of the wood's molecules. Agar and jelly also have large molecules and a network structure that can appreciably expand by absorbing water. They are called gels. If polyacrylamide (a polymer of C_3H_5NO) is submerged in alcohol or acetone, then it assumes a jelly-like state and under some conditions achieves an extraordinary expansion. For example, a polyacrylamide specimen submerged in an aqueous solution of acetone makes an extraordinary contraction to below 1/350 of its original volume when the density of acetone increases to 42%. Then, if the temperature rises from water temperature to 22°C, while maintaining a 42% acetone density, it rapidly returns to the original volume. This extraordinary expanding phenomena can also be controlled by applying an electrical voltage instead of temperature.

(d) Primary- and secondary-battery. Batteries are indispensable in the age of modern electronics. Primary batteries are the most widely used. Common examples of this type are zinc-carbon and alkaline-manganese dry cells. These are not designed to be rechargeable. A secondary battery can be recharged. Common examples of this type are lead-acid and nickel-cadmium batteries, which are widely used in conjunction with internal combustion engines.

(e) Norbor-nadine (C_7Hg). When irradiated with light, the norbor-nadine isomerises to quadricylene which has the same molecular formula but a different molecular structure. However, if a catalyser is present, the deformation is recovered giving off the potential energy.

(f) Shape-memory alloy. These alloys memorise their shapes above or below a critical temperature so that the original shape can be repeatedly reproduced from any shape deformed below or above the critical temperature. Applications of these alloys are multifarious. For example, we shall show a heat engine. Consider two kinds of shape memory alloys whose critical temperatures are different from each other. One of them is higher than and another is lower than room temperature, respectively. If these two kinds of alloy are connected to a rotary disk, then by heating the system the alloy-bar A will recover its original length pushing the disk from right to the left (in the direction of the arrow), while alloy-bar B is pressed and deformed. Next, if the system is cooled down, then alloy-bar B will recover its original length pushing the disk from left to right. Thus the disk makes a forward and return motion.

Besides the energy conversion described above, we have many other applications which are important in modern technologies. We shall name them according to the matrix in Table 10: (i) Flywheel, (ii) M.H.D. (magneto hydro dynamics), (iii) Metal hydride, (iv) Electrolysis, (v) Solar cell, (vi) Photo electrode, (vii) AMTEC (Alkali Metal Thermoelectric Conversion), (viii) Thermo dielectric conversion, (ix) Density gradient power generation.

3 Energy Storage

Energy storage as well as its transport plays an important role in energy systems in order to supply a stable amount of secondary energy, because primary energy resources are unevenly distributed and the need for the secondary energy is subject to heavy fluctuation.

Energy storage is most conveniently done by use of potential energy. Potential energy has two kinds of aspects, one of which is microscopic and the other macroscopic. The chemical cohesive energy of substances like fossil fuels and biomass fuels belong to the former. The chemical energy stored inside the fuels is the best way to store energy. The latter applies to dams, springs, electric or magnetostatic energy, etc.

The most difficult kinds of energies to store are photon and electromagnetic waves, the storage of which is usually carried out by conversion to other kinds of energy. Dynamic electric energy and heat energy are usually stored by conversion to mechanical potential energy (water pumping dam system) or chemical energy (water electrolysis). Storage using superconducting coils is under development. The storage and transport of heat energy is basically difficult, because heat disperses by heat conduction, radiation and convection.

However, excellent heat insulators, and materials that have very high reflection coefficients have been invented and apply to heat transportation for a distance as long as 10 km. Moreover, heat pipes have been developed so that heat is effectively transported.

The ranking of the kinds of energies that are adaptable to storage is as follows: chemical energy, mechanical potential energy, electromagnetic potential energy, electric current, heat, electromagnetic wave, and photon energy.

Common fundamental conditions for storage and transport are as follows.

1) Prevention of any chemical reaction. Fuels placed in contact with an atmospheric environment sometimes change in quality by oxidisation or other reaction.

2) Minimisation of the energy loss due to dispersal processes (entropy production) generated by friction, discharge, radiation from a hot body, and other phenomena.

3) Prevention of the efflux of energy carrying materials (fossil fuels, heat medium, electric charge, etc).

All of these conditions are needed to minimise entropy production. This goal is difficult because the required technology is severely set against the second law of thermodynamics (entropy increasing law). Representative practical facilities for energy storage are closely related to the strength of the constructing materials of storage vessels or instruments.

We shall survey energy storage systems or materials in which the storage densities are appreciable. Storage systems have relatively small energy density and many of them are of small (S) and middle (M) scale except for pumping hydropower dam and compression gas systems (L).

Condensers, springs, spiral springs, and organic elastomers have too low an energy density to be used in actual macro-energy systems. Batteries, primary and secondary, are suitable for application to electrical and electronic equipment and necessities.

(a) Mechanical energy. There exist two kinds of mechanical energies that can be stored. One is kinetic and the other is potential energy. It could be stored by (i) Flywheel. (ii) Pumping up hydropower dam. (iii) Gas-compression. (iv) Metal hydrite. (v) Cryogenic storage.

(b) Electrical energy. Electrical energy is stored as chemical energy in batteries. Batteries are classified into two groups, one of which is the primary battery and another is the secondary battery. The former is not rechargeable, while the latter is rechargeable. The fuel cell is sometimes included as a secondary battery, however, it is actually a kind of generator having no storage function of electrical energy.

(c) Heat energy. Heat energy is determined by the temperature difference between the heat medium and the environment. Higher temperatures as well as lower temperatures are the object of heat energy storage. Heat with higher temperature tends toward equilibrium with the environment by the processes (i) radiation, (ii) convection, which is realised in fluids, (iii) heat conduction that occurs in any material except for vacuum.

A typical heat storage vessel is the "thermos flask" (vacuum bottle) structure. Heat insulation is devised by providing the double structure, i.e., the inner bottle is suspended by heat insulating thin supports and the space between the inner bottle and the inner wall of the outer bottle is evacuated. In addition, both surfaces of the inner bottle and the inner surface of the outer bottle are plated with silver giving a high reflective coefficient. As a result of such a design, escape of heat is prevented in three ways to stop the heat dispersion described in (i), (ii), and (iii) above. A thermos flask represents the principle of heat storage.

However, strictly speaking, the term "heat" used above means sensible heat. Heat is most conveniently stored by using latent heat.

Energy storage is an essentially important factor in energy systems and the examples of the pumping up dam, flywheel, elastic body, gas-compression, oil, batteries and others have been discussed so far. Storage is carried out by either materials, such as the case of heat storage, or structures, as a pumping dam, flywheel, etc. States of energy storage are in a non-equilibrium state, that is to say, an energy storage system is a sustainable structure of materials or structures in an unstable state. Chemical energy is exceptionally adaptable to storage because chemical substances have cohesive energies that are confined stably within them. These are obtained out by a relatively small ignition energy.

The general rules that govern the structure or vessel of energy storage are as follows:

(1) The total amount of storable energy is determined by the mechanical strength of the material that composes the structure of the storage system.

(2) The storable amount of energy is independent of the scale of storage structure for a fixed quantity of the structure. This rule states that the ratio of the quantity of the storage structure material to the stored energy is constant, being independent on the structure scale, if the maximum energy is stored.

(3) The quantity of component material of the energy storage structure is proportional to the storable energy and the proportional coefficient is constant or nearly constant.

4 Energy Transport

The types of energy and transport means are shown in a matrix in Table 11. Important transport means are the tanker, pipeline, utility power line, and heat pipe. These facilities have been put into practical use in order to support daily life. Other than these, optical fibers have been widely applied to transport laser light, but the main aim here is not energy transport but signal transmission. The USA, Japan and Europe have been connected using undersea optical cable and important information can now be rapidly exchanged.

The main methods of energy transport are: electric power line system, pipeline system, and container batch system.

Table 11. Transport of each kind of energy (Ohta 1994)

Energy	Batch	Conveyer, belt, chain	Pipeline	Electric powerline	Optical fibre
Mechanical	weight, flywheel, fluid	weight	gas compress, liquid pumping	-	-
Electro-magnetic	coil, condensor, electric tray	van de Graff accelerator	-	A.D. D.C.	-
Chemical	fuel	fuel	fuel	-	-
Photon	-	-	-	-	maser laser
Heat	latent & sensible heat (material)	Latent & sensible heat (material)	heat pipe (latent heat) sensible heat	-	-

To summarise the effectiveness of energy storage and transport in practical systems are as follows:

(i) Energy density. Two kinds of energy density are introduced. They are volume density [kg/m^3] or [kcal/*l*] and weight density [kJ/kg] or [kcal/kg]. The former is more important for energy stations. The criterion of the effectiveness is taken as oil which has 9.8×10^6 [kJ/m^3]. No facility exists that has more capacity except for nuclear fuels, which have about 10^6 times the energy density of oil in uranium. However, the storage and conversion facilities are very complicated and expensive and are therefore not deemed superior to oil. A hydrogen-air fuel cell has an output density a little smaller than oil. The energy density of a fly-wheel is also a little less than oil, but is not stable for long periods.

In the case of vehicles (rocket, airplane, train, automobile), weight density is rather more important. Liquified hydrogen is the best fuel.

(ii) Time factor (theory of pipeline). The time factor is rather important in energy storage. Storage for too long a period yields unnecessary chemical reactions. The leaking of energy carriers is especially appreciable in the case of liquified fuels at very low temperatures.

The temperatures of liquified hydrogen (which is sometimes denoted LH_2) and liquified methane (LNG) are 20.3 K and 111.8 K, respectively. These are much too low to completely prevent vaporisation. A device for recovering the vaporised LNG is equipped to LNG tankers and uses the recovered gas to drive electric power generators.

To minimise the vaporisation of liquified fuels, the ratio of surface area to container volume should be minimised, that is, the vessel must be a sphere. On the other hand, spherical containers do not always utilise space efficiently. Some contradictions will always exist between economical and scientific requirements, but safety and environment should always be considered first.

5 Power Plants

5.1 Conventional Power Plants

In conventional power plants, pulverised coal is fed into a boiler, where it is burned to produce heat. The heat is used to vapourise water, creating steam. The steam is passed through a turbine attached to an electric generator (Figure 2). Coal-fired power plants of this configuration often generate over 1000 MW (1MW = 1 million watts) of electricity. Like any fossil fuel fired thermal power plant, only about 35% of the potential energy in the coal is converted into electricity. The remaining energy is released into the environment in the form of heat.

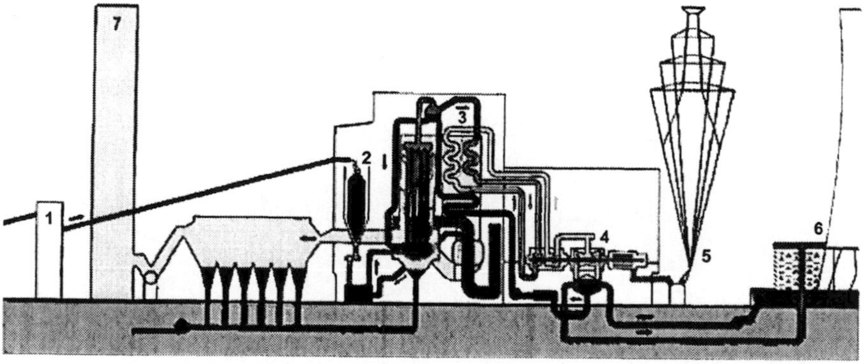

Figure 2. Coal-fired power station: 1 – delivering the coal; 2 – preparing the coal; 3 – inside the boiler; 4- generating electricity; 5 – transmitting electricity; 6 –recycling the water; 7 – protecting the atmosphere.

Source: http://www.energyed.ergon.com.au/educatio/coal/tour.htm

Attempts are being made to increase the efficiency of coal-fired power plants. One method of doing this is to have smaller coal-fired power plants located in a region where there is a demand for heat. Waste heat from a power plant can be captured and used to provide process heat for industries or space heating for any type of buildings. Arrangements such as this are referred to as "co-generation" or "combined heat and power" and can achieve efficiencies of 80-90%. Another alternative is "integrated coal-gasification combined cycle" power plants which convert coal into a gaseous mixture before combustion in a gas turbine (Figure 3). Efficiencies of up to 45% can be achieved with this type of system. Natural gas can be used to generate electricity in many different ways. Natural gas power plants generating more than a couple of hundred megawatts (1 megawatt = 1 MW = 1 million watts) use the same technology as coal-fired power plants. Natural gas is burned to produce heat which boils water, creating steam which passes through a turbine to generate electricity. This type of power plant is rarely more than 37% efficient, releasing great amounts of excess energy (heat) into the environment. Slightly smaller natural gas power plants can use gas turbines to produce electricity. Gas turbines are similar to jet engines and can convert up to half the energy of the natural gas into electricity (50% efficient). For very small electrical loads, natural gas can be burned in a reciprocating engine (similar to an automobile engine), which turns a generator.

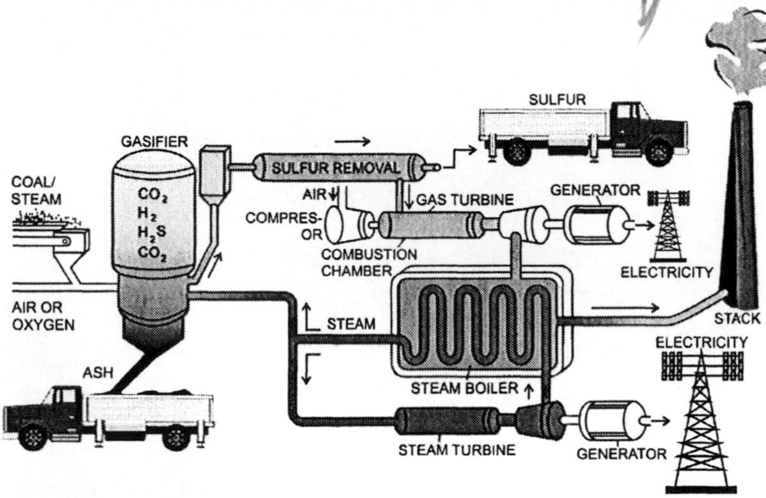

Figure 3. Integrated coal-gasification combined cycle (IGCC).
Source: Scientific American, September 1990.

Natural gas is a clean burning fuel; therefore it is a prime candidate for co-generation, also called combined heat and power. Co-generation power plants capture the excess heat given off during the production of electricity, and distribute it to local industries and buildings for process or space heating applications. Figure 4 is a diagram of a gas turbine (most often fuelled with natural gas) of the type used for co-generation power plants with size from about 500 W to 50 MW. These turbines are similar to jet engines used in aircraft. In this size range, gas turbines are more efficient than any other type of fossil fuel fired power plants, reaching electrical efficiencies of up to 45% and with the addition of waste heat recovery (co-generation), efficiencies of over 80%. When used for co-generation, the hot exhaust gases from the gas turbine are passed through a heat exchanger where the heat is transferred to water in pipes producing steam.

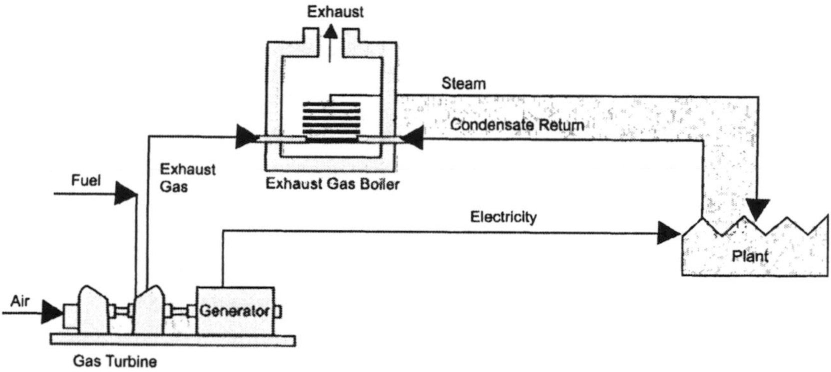

Figure 4. A gas turbine topping cycle
Source: http://www.iclei.org/efacts/cognfig2.gif

Co-generation requires a market for the excess heat; therefore such power plants are most often situated in urban areas, where more polluting coal-fired power plants might not be acceptable.

To take advantage of economies of scale, electrical energy is generated in large centralised facilities for distribution to consuming activities. The demand for electrical energy varies on a daily, weekly, and seasonal cycle. Since this form of energy cannot be conveniently stored, the installed generating capacity must match the peak demand and some of this capacity must be idle during periods of low demand. The more economic plants in the system, which may be fossil or nuclear facilities operating on a steam power cycle or hydroelectric plants, are usually operated as much as possible in a so-called base-loaded condition, while the older and less efficient plants and special gas-turbine installations are utilised only during periods of peak demand. The use of pumped storage can serve to flatten out the demand curve by using excess power produced during periods of low demand to pump water uphill where it can be used during later periods of high demand by recovering its potential energy. Transmission ties between electric utility systems in different regions of the country can be used to take advantage of load diversity since the timing of seasonal and daily peak demands varies depending on location.

Electric generating plants with an output of over 1000 MW are not uncommon and stations of up to 10,000 MW capacity are anticipated by the year 2000, perhaps involving an energy centre concept where the power source is integrated on the same site with industrial, agricultural, and/or desalination operations. Natural gas and low-sulphur residual oil may be used in steam-electric plants with minimal air pollution but these fuels are limited in their availability. The provision of control systems for CO_2 and NO, emissions from steam plants fired with coal or high sulphur oil will increase the cost of power generation.

Some promising alternatives for centralised power production that can utilise fossil resources are fuel cells and magnetohydrodynamic (MHD) generators.

Fuel Cells: This direct conversion device is not limited in efficiency by thermodynamic considerations and can convert chemical energy directly into electrical energy without the intermediate conversion to thermal and kinetic energy. Over-all efficiencies as high as 75% have been attained in special purpose applications. With hydrogen and oxygen fuel fed to electrodes submerged in a suitable electrolyte, this device produces 0.7 to 0.85 volts (dc)/cell and many cells must be connected in series to produce useful voltages for transmission. Development work is in progress on cells that could operate on gasified coal or other gaseous fuels with air as the oxidiser and a conceptual design has been completed for such a plant.

Air pollution and waste heat discharges would be reduced in a fuel cell power plant because of the improved efficiency of fuel utilisation. If coal were used as the source of a gaseous fuel, the impurities in the coal and particulates would have to be controlled in the gasification plant, but such control would be easier to provide in this operation than in a conventional power plant. In the course of the development of fuel cells, it is more likely that they will be applied first to smaller decentralised power systems.

Magnetohydrodynamics: MHD generators can utilise either a fossil or nuclear thermal energy source. In a fossil-fuelled system, hot combustion gases, seeded with potassium or caesium to make the gas conductive, are expanded at high velocity through a magnetic field. The dc current produced in the moving conductive gas is picked up at electrodes embedded in the walls of the gas channel in various geometries depending upon the particular type of generator. The advantage of this system is its high thermal efficiency of 50 to 60% when operated at a gas temperature in the 4000° to 5000°F range.

The environmental effects of MHD generation would be similar to those in any fossil-fuelled combustion system but would be mitigated because of the improved efficiency of conversion. The seed material in the gases could not be released in any case, for economic as well as environmental reasons, and must be recovered. It is anticipated that recovery of the other pollutants can be accomplished in the same operation.

Energy conversion systems currently utilised in the decentralised stationary power plants involve mainly combustion devices for space heat and industrial process heat applications. For economic reasons they are generally not as amenable to as high a level of emission control as larger centralised systems, save for conversion to cleaner fuels such as natural gas and perhaps methane or hydrogen produced from coal. These applications are also candidates for conversion to electrical energy thereby shifting the emission problem from decentralised plants to centralised power generating facility.

Decentralised electric power generating facilities of up to 5 MW output are sometimes installed in shopping centres and housing complexes. These now use diesel generators or gas turbines but could also use fuel cells when these are developed. Waste heat from these power plants is used for space healing and air-conditioning, and it is claimed that up to 85% of the energy in the fuel may be effectively utilised in these systems as compared with only about 40% in central station power plants.

Even in the age when air pollution was not such a concern as at present, coal was gradually replaced by oil and gas. The reason is that coal is not readily compatible with automatic combustion systems or with a pipeline transportation system. The economical disadvantages arising for these reasons were obvious.

The combustion of coal results in exhaust gases containing carbon dioxide (CO_2), carbon monoxide (CO), sulphur dioxide (SO_2), nitrous oxides (NO_x) and particulates. CO_2 and CO are greenhouse gases associated with global warming while SO_2 and NO_x contribute to acid rains. When burned in a relatively uncontrolled fashion, as has been the case in much of eastern Europe, coal can cause a lot of damage due to smog and acid rain. With modern technologies and strict controls it is possible to remove most of the CO, SO_2 and NO_x before they are emitted from a power plant, but removing the CO_2, while theoretically possible would be prohibitively expensive. Coal contains more carbon and less hydrogen than other fossil fuels such as oil and natural gas, and as such it gives off more CO_2 per unit of electricity produced than any other fuel. At the present time, coal is responsible for 30-40% of world CO_2 emissions from fossil fuels.

Acid gases (SO_2 and NO_x) can be "scrubbed" out of the exhaust stream before they are emitted from the smokestack. Flue gas scrubbers can be added to new or existing coal fired power plants. Such scrubbers generally add a limestone slurry to the exhaust which reacts with the SO_2 to form a compound which can be removed as solid waste. Although scrubbers can remove up to 97% of the SO_2 emissions from a power plant, they slightly decrease the efficiency of the combustion process, thus increasing CO_2 emissions and the costs of running the plant. Burning coal with a low sulphur content is another way to reduce acid gas emissions from any coal combustion. In North America, coal reserves in the eastern states and provinces tend to have high sulphur contents while those from the west are low in sulphur.

On the positive side, coal power plants have none of the radiation risks associated with nuclear power plants and the transportation of coal does not carry any large environmental risks like those associated with oil spills. When burned in power plants with state-of-the-art pollution control equipment, acid gas and particulate emissions from coal can be greatly reduced. In order to prevent environmental damage both in the industrialised and the developing worlds, it is essential that the industrialised countries of the world help to ensure that these technologies are employed worldwide.

Fossil fuel power plants generally have the most widespread effect on the environment, as the combustion process produces airborne pollutants that spread over a wide area. Fossil fuel power plants produce environmental problems including land and water use, air emissions, thermal releases, climatic and visual impacts from cooling towers, solid waste disposal, ash disposal (for coal), and noise. Due to the need for large amounts of steam, plants can have a great effect on water use. For example, a typical 500 MW coal-fired power plant uses 25×10^9 l/GW-year of water, which must be taken from a water source, and then cooled to return to the water source with as little environmental effect as possible. The biggest effect fossil fuel plants have overall is the emission of air pollutants, particularly SO_x, NO_x, CO, CO_2, and hydrocarbons. CO, CO_2 and hydrocarbons are the "greenhouse gases", which may be responsible for global warming. SO_x and NO_x can produce acid when released into the atmosphere, leading to the production of acid rain. Generally, air emissions are controlled by the use of scrubbers and precipitators located at the plant.

5.2 Hydro-electric Power Plants

Hydro-electric power plants convert the kinetic energy contained in falling water into electricity. The energy in flowing water is ultimately derived from the sun, and is therefore constantly being renewed. Energy contained in sunlight evaporates water from the oceans and deposits it on land in the form of rain. Differences in land elevation result in rainfall runoff, and allow some of the original solar energy to be captured as hydro-electric power.

Hydro power is currently the world's largest renewable source of electricity, accounting for 6% of worldwide energy supply or about 15% of the world's electricity. Traditionally thought of as a cheap and clean source of electricity, most large hydro-electric schemes being planned today are coming up against a great deal of opposition from environmental groups and native people.

The first recorded use of water power was a clock, built around 250 BC. Since that time, humans have used falling water to provide power for grain and saw mills, as well as a host of other applications. The first use of moving water to produce electricity was a waterwheel on the Fox river in Wisconsin in 1882, two years after Thomas Edison unveiled the incandescent light bulb. The first of many hydro-electric power plants at Niagara Falls was completed shortly thereafter. Hydro power continued to play a major role in the expansion of electrical service early in this century, both in North America and around the world. Contemporary Hydro-electric power plants generate anywhere from a few kW, enough for a single residence, to thousands of MW, power enough to supply a large city.

Early hydro-electric power plants were much more reliable and efficient than the fossil fuel fired plants of the day. This resulted in a proliferation of small to medium sized hydro-electric generating stations distributed wherever there was an adequate supply of moving water and a need for electricity. As electricity demand soared in the middle years of this century, and the efficiency of coal and oil fuelled power plants increased, small hydro plants fell out of favour. Most new hydro-electric development was focused on huge "mega-projects".

The majority of these power plants involved large dams that flooded vast areas of land to provide water storage and therefore a constant supply of electricity. In recent years, the environmental impacts of such large hydro projects are being identified as a cause for concern. It is becoming increasingly difficult for developers to build new dams because of opposition from environmentalists and people living on the land to be flooded. This is shown by the opposition to projects such as Great Whale (James Bay II) in Quebec and the Gabickovo-Nagymaros project on the Danube River in Czechoslovakia.

Hydro-electric power plants capture the energy released by water falling through a vertical distance, and transform this energy into useful electricity. In general, falling water is channelled through a turbine that converts the water's energy into mechanical power. The rotation of the water turbines is transferred to a generator that produces electricity. The amount of electricity which can be generated at a hydro-electric plant is dependant upon two factors. These factors are (1) the vertical distance through which the water falls, called the "head", and (2) the flow rate, measured as volume per unit time. The electricity produced is proportional to the product of the head and the rate of flow. The following is an equation that may be used to roughly determine the amount of electricity that can be generated by a potential hydro-electric power site:

$$\text{POWER (kW)} = 5.9 \times \text{FLOW} \times \text{HEAD}$$

In this equation, FLOW is measured in cubic meters per second and HEAD is measured in meters.

Based on the facts presented above, hydro-electric power plants can generally be divided into two categories. "High head" power plants are the most common and generally utilise a dam to store water at an increased elevation. The use of a dam to impound water also provides the capability of storing water during rainy periods and releasing it during dry periods. This results in the consistent and reliable production of electricity, able to meet demand. Heads for this type of power plant may be greater than 1000 m. Most large hydro-electric facilities are of the high head variety. High head plants with storage are very valuable to electric utilities because they can be quickly adjusted to meet the electrical demand on a distribution system.

"Low head" hydro-electric plants are power plants which generally utilise heads of only a few meters or less. Power plants of this type may utilise a low dam or weir to channel water, or no dam and simply use the "run of the river". Run of the river generating stations cannot store water, thus their electric output varies with seasonal flows of water in a river. A large volume of water must pass through a low head hydro plant's turbines in order to produce a useful amount of power. Hydro-electric facilities with a capacity of less than about 25 MW (1 MW = 1,000,000 Watts) are generally referred to as "small hydro", although hydro-electric technology is basically the same regardless of generating capacity.

"Pumped Storage" is another form of hydro-electric power. Pumped storage facilities use excess electrical system capacity, generally available at night, to pump water from one reservoir to another reservoir at a higher elevation. During periods of peak electrical demand, water from the higher reservoir is released through turbines to the lower reservoir, and electricity is produced. Although pumped storage sites are not net producers of electricity - it actually takes more electricity to pump the water up than is recovered when it is released - they are a valuable addition to electricity supply systems. Their value is in their ability to store electricity for use at a later time when peak demands are occurring. Storage is even more valuable if intermittent sources of electricity such as solar or wind are hooked into a system.

Another possible classification of hydropower plants is Micro-Scale, Small-Scale "Run-of-the-River" power plants. As their name implies, micro-hydroelectric plants are the smallest type of hydroelectric energy systems. They generate between one kilowatt and one megawatt of power. The main application for these hydro systems is in small, isolated villages in developing countries. They are ideal for powering smaller services such as the operation of processing machines.

Small-scale hydropower systems can supply up to 20 megawatts of energy. These systems are relatively inexpensive and reliable. They have the potential to provide electricity to rural areas in developing countries throughout the world. Small systems are especially important to countries that may not be able to afford the costs of importing fossil fuels such as petroleum from other countries.

"Run-of-the-River". In some areas of the world, the flow rate and elevation drops of the water are consistent enough that hydroelectric plants can be built directly in the river. The water passes through the plant without greatly changing the flow rate of the river. In many instances a dam is not required, and therefore the hydroelectric plant causes minimal environmental impact on its surroundings. However, one problem with run-of-the-river plants is the obstruction of fish and other aquatic animals.

Hydro-electric power plants have many environmental impacts, some of which are just beginning to be understood. These impacts, however, must be weighed against the environmental impacts of alternative sources of electricity. Until recently there was an almost universal belief that hydro power was a clean and environmentally safe method of producing electricity. Hydro-electric power plants do not emit any of the standard atmospheric pollutants such as carbon dioxide or sulphur dioxide given off by fossil fuel fired power plants. In this respect, hydro power is better than burning coal, oil or natural gas to produce electricity, as it does not contribute to environmental pollution or global warming. Similarly, hydro-electric power plants do not result in the risks of radioactive contamination associated with nuclear power plants. A few recent studies of large reservoirs created behind hydro dams have suggested that decaying vegetation, submerged by flooding, may give off quantities of greenhouse gases equivalent to those from other sources of electricity. If this turns out to be true, hydro-electric facilities such as the James Bay project in Quebec that flood large areas of land might be significant contributors to global warming. Run of the river hydro plants without dams and reservoirs would not be a source of these greenhouse gases.

The most obvious impact of hydro-electric dams is the flooding of vast areas of land, much of it previously forested or used for agriculture. The size of reservoirs created can be extremely large. The La Grande project in the James Bay region of Quebec has already submerged over 10,000 square kilometres of land; and if future plans are carried out, the eventual area of flooding in northern Quebec will be larger than the country of Switzerland. Reservoirs can be used for ensuring adequate water supplies, providing irrigation, and recreation; but in several cases they have flooded the homelands of native peoples, whose way of life has then been destroyed. Many rare ecosystems are also threatened by hydro-electric development.

Large dams and reservoirs can have other impacts on a watershed. Damming a river can alter the amount and quality of water in the river downstream of the dam, as well as preventing fish from migrating upstream to spawn. These impacts can be reduced by requiring minimum flows downstream of a dam, and by creating fish ladders that allow fish to move upstream past the dam. Silt, normally carried downstream to the lower reaches of a river, is trapped by a dam and deposited on the bed of the reservoir. This silt can slowly fill up a reservoir, decreasing the amount of water that can be stored and used for electrical generation. The river downstream of the dam is also deprived of silt, which fertilises the river's flood-plain during high water periods.

Bacteria present in decaying vegetation can also change mercury, present in rocks underlying a reservoir, into a form that is soluble in water. The mercury accumulates in the bodies of fish and poses a health hazard to those who depend on these fish for food. The water quality of many reservoirs also poses a health hazard due to new forms of bacteria that grow in many of the hydro rivers.

Therefore, run of the river type hydro plants generally have a smaller impact on the environment.

The theoretical size of the worldwide hydro power is about four times greater than that which has been exploited at this time. The actual amount of electricity which will ever be generated by hydro power will be much less than the theoretical potential. This is due to the environmental concerns outlined above, and economic constraints. Much of the remaining hydro potential in the world exists in the developing countries of Africa and Asia. Harnessing this resource would require billions of dollars, because hydro-electric facilities generally have very high construction costs. In the past, the World Bank has spent billions of foreign aid dollars on huge hydro-electric projects in the third world. Opposition to hydro power from environmentalists and native people, as well as new environmental assessments at the World Bank will restrict the amount of money spent on hydro-electric power construction in the developing countries of the world.

In North-America and Europe, a large percentage of hydro power potential has already been developed. Public opposition to large hydro schemes will probably result in very little new development of big dams and reservoirs. Small scale and low head hydro capacity will probably increase in the future as research on low head turbines, and standardised turbine production, lowers the costs of hydro-electric power at sites with low heads. New computerised control systems and improved turbines may allow more electricity to be generated from existing facilities in the future. Also, many small hydro electric sites were abandoned in the 1950s and 60s when the price of oil and coal was very low, and their environmental impacts unrealised. Increased fuel prices in the future could result in these facilities being refurbished.

Hydro-electric power has always been an important part of the world's electricity supply, providing reliable, cost effective electricity, and will continue to do so in the future. Hydro power has environmental impacts which are very different from those of fossil fuel power plants. The actual effects of dams and reservoirs on various ecosystems are only now becoming understood. The future of hydro-electric power will depend upon future demand for electricity, as well as how societies value the environmental impacts of hydro-electric power compared to the impacts of other sources of electricity.

5.3 Nuclear Power Plants

Nuclear fission is the splitting of an atom into two or more parts. When such an occurrence takes place, a very large amount of energy is released. This can occur very quickly as in an atomic bomb, or in a more controlled manner allowing the energy to be captured for useful purposes. Only a few naturally occurring substances are easily fissionable. These include uranium-235 and plutonium-239, two isotopes of uranium and plutonium. Isotopes are forms of the same chemical element that have the same number of protons in their nuclei, but a different number of neutrons.

Starting a fission reaction is accomplished by bombarding fissionable nuclei with neutrons. This causes the nuclei to fly apart, splitting into two fission products and emitting two or three neutrons of their own. These neutrons may break apart other nearby fissionable nuclei, starting a chain reaction, and resulting in the release of a great deal of energy in the form of radiation and heat. The major fragments of the split atoms are now different chemical elements, all highly radioactive. These fission products include such isotopes as iodine-131, caesium-137 and strontium 90.

The first large scale use of nuclear fission occurred on July 16, 1945, in New Mexico, with the test of the world's first atomic bomb. Following the Second World War, research was undertaken on how to use the power of the atom for "peaceful" purposes. In 1955, the US navy submarine "Nautilus" travelled over 62,000 miles, powered by a single lump of uranium the size of a golf ball. Shortly thereafter, electricity was produced in commercial amounts by reactors in both the US and the then Soviet Union; and Canada soon developed its own reactor design, the CANDU reactor. In the following years, nuclear reactors were envisioned as a clean and cheap source of electricity, capable of meeting vastly increased demand in the future. Miniature backyard reactors were also seen as possibilities for supplying heat to single family homes.

The set of activities required for producing nuclear power, from the mining and processing of uranium to its use in reactors and final disposal, is known as the nuclear fuel cycle. The mining of uranium is similar to the mining of many other ores; but miners must also be protected against radioactive dust and radon, a radioactive gas. Uranium ores occur naturally in many parts of the world but the uranium extracted from them must often be "enriched" before it can be used as fuel in a nuclear reactor. This is because naturally occurring uranium contains about 99.3% uranium-238, a non-fissionable isotope of uranium, and only 0.7% of the fissionable uranium-235. Uranium enrichment increases the proportion of uranium-235 in the mixture, enabling it to sustain a fission reaction. Such uranium fuel is placed in the core of a nuclear reactor, and the heat given off by the fission chain reaction is captured to produce electricity.

Like any other fuel, enriched uranium eventually becomes exhausted. This occurs after all the readily fissionable isotopes in the fuel have been used up. The fuel has now been changed into a mixture of fission products and other non-fissionable material such as uranium-238, which has been subjected to a massive bombardment by neutrons. As a result, spent fuel is a very hot and highly radioactive waste, which must be removed from a reactor and disposed. Some of the radioactive waste produced by fission reactors will remain highly radioactive for thousands of years, and is a potential source of the material required for the production of nuclear weapons. At the present time, there is no agreed upon method of permanently disposing such wastes, and they are piling up in temporary holding tanks. Plans are underway to bury these wastes deep underground in rock caverns; but to date no such facilities have been approved.

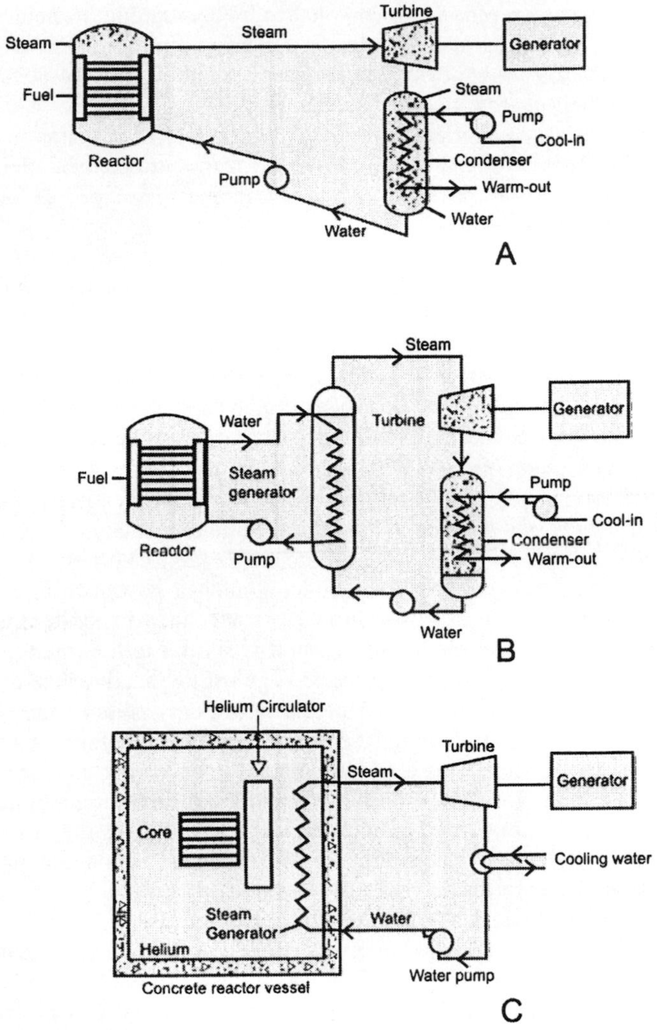

Figure 5. Four types of nuclear reactors for power generation by nuclear fission: A. Boiling water reactor; B. Pressured water reactor; C. High-temperature gas-cooled reactor.

Source: http://www.iclei.org/efacts/nucfis2.gif

Although there are many different types of fission reactor designs, the basic mechanism behind all of them is similar (Figure 5). Fissionable material as discussed above is placed in the "core" of a reactor. The rate of the fission chain reaction is controlled and "moderated", and the heat generated is converted into electricity. Control and moderation refer, respectively, to the manipulation of both the number and velocity of the neutrons present in the core. Control rods made of boron or other neutron absorbing materials control the number of neutrons present. Raising and lowering the control rods in the core can speed up or slow down the rate of the chain reaction. Similarly, regular ("light") or "heavy water" (water where the hydrogen contains the isotope deuterium which has one extra neutron) is used to control the speed of the neutrons and thus also the rate of the reaction. The majority of reactors in operation today are either "boiling water" or "pressurised water" reactors, using either normal or heavy water to both cool and moderate the fission reaction.

In boiling water reactors, the cooling water circulates through the core and boils, producing steam which is directly fed through a turbine to generate electricity. Pressurised water reactors use a separate circuit of cooling water under high pressure, and a heat exchanger to produce steam for a turbine and generator. In this type of system, the cooling water in the core is under such high pressure that it does not boil.

Heavy water is a much better moderator than light water, slowing electrons effectively without absorbing them. However, heavy water is relatively expensive to produce; and thus most reactors worldwide use light water as a moderator. The main commercially available heavy water reactor is the CANDU (CANadian Deuterium Uranium). The CANDU reactor circulates coolant through hundreds of separate fuel rods, which are surrounded by heavy water acting as a moderator. A separate heat exchanger and secondary light water circuit are used to generate steam and electricity. The use of heavy water allows reactors to use un-enriched uranium; whereas light water reactors require enriched uranium.

Gas-cooled reactors and "breeder" reactors are newer reactor designs which are not yet as widespread as the earlier generation of reactors. Various gas-cooled reactor designs have been built, with the common feature of high temperature gas used as a coolant. Breeder reactors use neutrons generated by a fission chain reaction to convert uranium-238 into plutonium-239, a fissionable material. Such reactors allow much more energy to be captured from the same initial amount of uranium; but like all reactor designs, they have their own safety and waste disposal problems which must be solved.

At the present time, about 430 nuclear reactors are connected to the world's electricity grids, supplying 16% of the world's electricity demand. The majority of these reactors are located in the industrialised countries of the world. This amount of electricity generation is far less than that which had been predicted back in the 1960s when nuclear power was in its infancy. The increasing cost of nuclear power plant construction is one reason why nuclear energy has not lived up to its potential; but the main reason is safety concerns. Nuclear power plant accidents such as those at Three Mile Island in Pennsylvania and Chernobyl in the former USSR have drastically increased public opposition to nuclear power. Recent worldwide concern over the threats of global warming and acid rain has, however, resulted in some renewed interest.

Nuclear reactors use the process of fission, or atom splitting, to release the energy from the nucleus of the fuel. Typically, ^{235}U is used as fuel in most nuclear power plants because it is a fissile material, one which will undergo fission upon encountering any neutron, especially a very slow one. The added neutron causes the nucleus to become unstable, and it splits into nuclear fragments.

Nuclear reactors use **enriched** uranium (3% uranium-235 and 97% uranium-238) as the fuel source. Since normal uranium found in the ground is only 0.7% ^{235}U and 99.3% ^{238}U, we put it through an enrichment process in order to increase this percentage to 3%. The fuel is placed in the **core** of the nuclear reactor. A chain reaction is initiated by bombarding the fuel with slow neutrons because slower neutrons with less thermal energy have approximately 1000 times greater chance of causing a fission reaction to occur than faster neutrons. Neutrons must be slowed down by water or graphite moderators to produce a chain reaction. The process repeats itself rapidly or slowly depending on the presence of control rods. Control rods are made of cadmium or boron which absorb neutrons to control or stop a chain reaction. Heat from the chain reaction and the resulting speed of the fission products, such as Kr and Ba in the last example, is absorbed by water in the reactor. Very fast neutrons, or thermal neutrons, are released too. If there is no moderator to slow them down, the chain reaction will stop by itself. US reactors use the cooling water as the moderator. If the coolant is lost or the reactor gets too hot and it boils away, the moderator is lost as well, and the reaction stops. Unfortunately, the Russian Chernobyl reactor was designed with a graphite moderator. When the coolant was lost the reactor got even hotter and caught on fire. Because water is both the moderator and the coolant in US reactors, an accident like Chernobyl cannot physically occur.

The main advantage of a **breeder reactor** is that it generates more nuclear fuel, ^{239}Pu, than it uses. It converts ^{238}U, a plentiful non-fissile, or stable, isotope into a fissile one, making this fuel source virtually inexhaustible. Supplies of ^{238}U will last for more than the next 40,000 years. There are also some disadvantages of breeder reactors. If plutonium escapes into the environment, it carries a high health risk due to its toxicity. Plutonium is also used to make atomic weapons. Though ^{235}U can also be used for weapons, it requires such an enormous amount of effort to purify it that it is not easily used. Breeder reactors also have the ability to melt down if problems occur. This problem has been solved recently by Argone National Laboratory through the development of a Fast Breeder Reactor. The nuclear reaction will stop automatically if the fuel temperature gets too high in this type of reactor. Unfortunately, the US congress has removed funding from this project which held a safe answer to our energy needs.

One obstacle to using nuclear power is that the nuclear wastes generated cannot just be thrown in a dumpster, it is radioactive! High-level radioactive wastes, the fission products in the spent fuel rods, will be dangerous for the next hundred or thousand years. Engineers have developed ways of storing this waste in hopes of protecting the environment. Spent fuel rods are first stored in large tanks or swimming pools on the site of the power plant to remove the heat left over from the reaction. Once they are no longer thermally hot, the spent fuel rods, usually in the form of small metal tubes, are encapsulated in ceramic or glass containers which can withstand radioactive decay. These small containers are then placed in stainless steel containers which are stored underground in large caves. Because the waste is all in solid form, nothing can leak from the inside. In order to prevent water from leaking in, materials are placed all around the waste which will absorb any ground water that may seep in. These "caves" are always contained within very stable geologic formations. This type of containment system is called a multiple barrier containment system.

Fortunately, very little high level waste is made per reactor per year. Unlike a coal plant which produces about 15 tons of carbon dioxide, 200 pounds of sulphur dioxide, and about 1000 tons of solid ash per *minute,* the high level waste from one *year* of nuclear power plant operation produces about 1.5 tons and would occupy a volume of about half a cubic yard, which could easily fit under your coffee table!

However, other things become radioactive in the process of operating a nuclear power plant. Objects like water and air filters for trapping radioactive material, rags, gloves, lab equipment, pipes, and mops are considered low-level radioactive waste. They have been used near or in the reactor and were exposed to neutrons. About 25% of all low-level waste comes from hospitals, research labs, and industry. Although the radioactivity in low-level waste is about a million times lower than that in high level waste, it occupies about 1000 times the volume of high-level waste. Because the radioactivity is so low, low-level waste is buried at about 20 feet underground in controlled areas and allowed to decay.

A major problem with radioactive waste is not the amount or even what to do with it. The real problem is the public's perception. Most people seem to agree that we need to do something with this waste, but no one wants it in their neighbourhood, no matter how safe the containment structure. Here is another instance where energy becomes perhaps a greater political issue than a scientific one.

One major event in the history of American nuclear reactors was the accident at the nuclear power plant, a PWR, at Three Mile Island in 1979. Many term the accident a "near meltdown", while others feel that this is a gross over-exaggeration. The cause of the accident was a failed valve, which allowed water to run out of the pressure vessel. Of course, with no moderator, the chain reaction stopped. However, the core was still hot and needed to be cooled to keep the fuel from melting and ruining the reactor. The engineers thought the valve was closed due to a faulty indicator on their instrument panel, but were able to determine the cause of the problem and close an auxiliary valve to keep the water from escaping. Had the water continued to run out for 30-60 more minutes, the loss of coolant may have caused a meltdown. A meltdown occurs when the fuel rods become so hot that they melt, allowing the radioactivity to escape into the reactor vessel. However, what many people don't realise is that the containment structure for the reactor is designed to keep all the radioactivity inside and filter it out of the inside atmosphere in the event of an accident. Containment structures are tested for susceptibility to tornadoes, earthquakes, airplanes flying into them (really), and explosives. In the case of Three Mile Island, the containment structure worked and very little radioactive material was released into the environment.

The world's most serious nuclear power plant accident occurred in 1986 when the plant at Chernobyl, Russia exploded. The Chernobyl reactor is an RMBK type reactor, which uses water as the coolant and graphite as the moderator with natural uranium. As a result of a poorly conducted test, the coolant ended up at a low level in the reactor vessel, which prompted the removal of some control rods. When the power increased back to normal levels, there was not enough time to replace them. Thus, the coolant was at a very low level and began to boil. Due to the reactor design, the graphite moderator was still intact, and the chain reaction continued. The high temperature and heat built up and caused two chemical explosions (like dynamite), **not** nuclear ones, which blew off part of the top of the reactor building. Note that there was not a sophisticated containment structure surrounding the reactor vessel like those in the United States. As a result, a large amount of the radioactivity that was once in the reactor core was dispersed to the surrounding areas as radioactive dust. The fires were eventually put out by dropping sand onto the reactor by helicopter.

Fission reactors are very complicated devices, capable of causing a great deal of harm both to humans and to the environment. The effects of nuclear reactors can be divided into those occurring from an accident and those which are a result of the normal operation of nuclear power plants. With any nuclear reactor, there is the possibility of a malfunction which could cause the chain reaction in the core to run out of control, resulting in very high temperatures and a core "meltdown". Meltdowns that breach reactor containment vessels could potentially release huge amounts of radiation into the surrounding environment, as seen by the accident at Chernobyl in 1986. Following a major accident, along with the initial radiation exposure, the land and water covering a large area around an accident site could become contaminated, and unfit for human habitation for thousands of years.

Human or animal exposure to very high levels of radiation can result in death, cancer or birth defects in future generations. Individual cells may be killed if exposed to high levels of radiation. If enough cells are killed, it may result in the death of the entire organism.

The "normal" operation of a nuclear power plant also results in the release of small amounts of radiation into the environment. Mining uranium releases radiation into the environment and results in huge piles of radioactive mine tailings. Processing the uranium into fuel for reactors can also result in low level radioactive contamination, as can reactor operation and fuel disposal. Several studies have claimed to discover higher levels of some cancers such as leukemia, and birth defects in those living near nuclear power plants; but more study is needed in this area.

Electricity generated by nuclear power results in almost none of the greenhouse and acid gas emissions associated with fossil fuel fired power plants. For this reason, supporters of nuclear power have called for a widespread increase in the number of nuclear plants worldwide in order to combat global warming and acid rain. However, nuclear power is becoming increasingly expensive. The recently completed power plant at Darlington, Ontario, cost over $13 billion. There exist many new efficient technologies which can drastically reduce our demand for electricity. Every dollar spent on nuclear power could displace up to seven times more carbon dioxide if it was spent on improving the energy efficiency of our electricity end use technologies.

Nuclear power has not fulfilled its early promise as a cheap, clean and unlimited source of electricity. Public concern over potential accidents, "acceptable" emissions of radiation, disposal of radioactive waste and the possibility of weapons proliferation have resulted in opposition to the construction of new power plants. In fact, no new nuclear reactors have been ordered in the United States since the partial core meltdown at Three Mile Island in 1979. In Europe, countries such as Sweden and Germany have passed laws calling for the phasing out of nuclear power. At the present time, worldwide use of electricity is so inefficient that it is cheaper to save energy through efficiency improvements than it is to build new nuclear power plants to supply more electricity. New designs such as breeder reactors may be more efficient; but they still have the same problems of radiation risk and waste disposal. For these reasons, barring any drastic technology improvements, nuclear power will probably continue to play a limited role in the world's energy picture for the foreseeable future.

5.4 Wind Energy Technology

We capture wind energy with sails or windmills. People have been using sails for 5,000 years and windmills for nearly 3000 years. We still use only those two methods to capture wind energy today.

We convert the movement of wind, which we cannot control, into movement that we can control. Wind pushes against sails and moves a vessel. Wind turns the vanes of a windmill, which turn an attached shaft. People attach different devices to the rotating shaft to do work. Windmills were first used to pump water for irrigation and later to grind grain. They are still used around the world for both purposes. Today, new kinds of windmills, called wind turbines, generate electricity. The vanes turn a generator, which produces electricity.

Wind turbines come in two basic types, horizontal and vertical axis. Despite their different appearances, the basic mechanics of the two systems are very similar. Wind passing over the blades is converted into mechanical power, which is fed through a transmission to an electrical generator. The transmission is used to keep the generator operating efficiently throughout a range of different wind speeds. The electricity generated can either be used directly, fed into a transmission grid or stored for later use.

Modern wind turbines come in a wide range of sizes, from small 100 watt units designed to provide power for single homes or cottages, to huge turbines with blade diameters over 50 m, generating over 1 MW (1 million watts) of electricity. The vast majority of wind turbines produced at the present time are horizontal axis turbines with three blades, 15-30 m in diameter, producing 50-350 kW of electricity (1kW = 1000 W). These turbines are often grouped together to form "wind farms" which provide power to an electrical grid. In Canada, where vast areas of land with moderate wind speeds exist, wind turbine development is concentrating on vertical axis machines which may work more efficiently than horizontal axis machines at lower wind speeds.

The location of wind turbines is a very important factor which influences the performance of the machines. In general, wind speeds increase with elevation. This is why most wind turbines are placed at the top of a tower. Limitations in the strength of affordable materials has limited most towers to heights of approximately 30 m. On wind farms, turbines are most often spaced at intervals of 5-15 times the blade diameter. This is necessary to avoid turbulence from one turbine affecting the wind flow at others.

Wind carries more power at higher speeds. Wind turbines will not work in winds below about 13 kilometres an hour. They work best where the wind speed averages 22 kilometres an hour or more.

Most places do not have strong enough winds, blowing often enough, for wind turbines to be practical. Winds blow strongest near coasts, in mountain passes and on prairies. These are usually the best places for wind turbines.

Some of the best windy places have many wind turbines. They are all connected to the same transmission line, which carries the electricity where it will be used. These collections of wind turbines are called wind farms. The most famous wind farm, in Altamont Pass, California, has 7500 turbines.

Most wind turbines look like airplane propellers mounted on towers. The propellers rotate on an axis that is horizontal to the ground. These turbines are called horizontal-axis turbines.

Some wind turbines have a vertical axis. One kind, the Darius, looks like an upside-down eggbeater. Another kind, the Savonius windmill, is made of two upright semi-cylinders. They are both called vertical-axis turbines.

Harnessing wind energy was one of man's earliest achievements. Small windmills pumped water in ancient Syria and sailing ships used windpower to first circumnavigate the globe. The modern use of wind turbines originated in the 17th Century where the Renaissance Dutch used wind power to recover hundreds of thousands of acres of land by draining the Rhine River delta.

The classic Dutch windmill design predominated for 300 years, pumping water, grinding grain and sawing wood until the multibladed American Farm Windmill was developed in the middle of the 19th century. These machines covered the continent, pumping water on every farm and in every town until rural electrification (and rust) brought about their demise in the middle of the 20th century.

Advances in the fields of aerodynamics and composite materials have made modern electric power generating wind turbines a reality. These machines range in size from a meter to a hundred meters in rotor diameter and from a hundred watts to a thousand kilowatts in power output. Wind turbines suitable for residential or village scale wind power range from 500 watts to 50 kilowatts. These machines fall into three categories:

- Utility interconnected wind turbines generate power which is synchronous with the grid and are used to reduce utility bills by displacing the utility power used in the household and by selling the excess power back to the electric company. These machines are economically attractive where there is a good wind resource and where the local power costs are in excess of 15 cents per kilowatt hour.
- Wind turbines for remote homes (off the grid) generate DC current for battery charging.
- Wind turbines for remote water pumping generate 3 phase AC current suitable for driving an electrical submersible pump directly.

Several types of wind power plants exist: remote, hybrid, and grid-connected. Remote systems are small, relatively cheap sources of energy. They are best suited for rural environments because they can be left unattended for long periods of time. Further, they can operate under harsh conditions, and thus have potential for powering extremely remote regions of the world.

Hybrid. The very nature of wind-powered generators makes them ideal to use in conjunction with other sources of energy. Wind and solar generators have been extremely successful as supplements to one another. The presence of the wind generator means that the other energy source does not have to be producing as much of the time.

Grid connected systems are already in wide use in areas that are already hooked up to a utility grid. Their main use is as a supplement to other forms of energy. This is important because average wind turbines only generate electricity about 25% of the time.

Because individual wind-powered systems by themselves do not produce a great deal of energy, so-called "wind farms" have been developed. These collections of many wind generators gathered in one place provide a source of relatively high energy output.

Advantages of wind energy:

- Once a wind device is installed, the only cost is the cost of maintaining the equipment. The energy to run it is free.
- Wind is continually renewed. It does not get used up and will always be available.
- Wind is available everywhere. Wind energy can be used around the world and far from electrical power lines.
- Using wind energy causes no polluting waste products. Once a windmill or turbine is built, it continues to work without damage to the environment.
- Wind machines are quite simple to set up and use. Small windmills and turbines can be used on farms or homes.
- Wind energy cannot be controlled by anyone. It is impossible for a company or a nation to ration or boycott wind energy for its own purposes.
- Electricity from many wind turbines can be combined to generate large amounts of electricity. It is much easier and faster to build a wind farm from many wind turbines than to build a power plant or hydro dam to generate the same amount of electricity.

- Disadvantages of wind energy:

- Wind energy is expensive. The direct cost of electricity from wind is usually several times higher than the cost of electricity from a central generating plant.
- Wind varies a great deal. It is hard to predict. Sometimes it does not blow at all.
- Because wind is not steady, electricity from wind is not reliable. To use wind energy for electricity, people must store electricity or have other ways to make up for the changeable supply. Batteries to store wind energy are expensive and difficult to use.
- Using wind energy causes some environmental impact. Building windmills, turbines and sailing vessels uses many resources and manufactured products. Each step causes some environmental damage.
- Wind farms take up large areas of land. They are noisy and easy to see.

5.5 Biomass Energy Technology

There are several methods of converting biomass into energy. These methods include burning, alcohol fermentation, pyrolysis, and anaerobic digestion.

Direct burning of biomass is the most straightforward method of energy production. Mankind has burned wood and other forms of biomass for thousands of years, to keep warm, to cook food, and eventually to forge weapons and other tools.

The energy released by direct combustion takes the form of heat, and can be used to directly influence the temperature of a small environment or to power steam-driven turbines to produce electricity. Unfortunately, the burning of biomass is the cause of a great deal of pollution and has contributed to the so-called "greenhouse effect" and global warming.

A relatively new field of research is the development of high energy crops specifically designed to be burned for power generation. Because at most only about 5% of a plant's mass is edible, the potential for large-scale biomass production is relatively great.

At the moment, however, growing large amounts of crops is still quite expensive. Thus, other methods of biomass energy production are being pursued with somewhat greater success. These methods include alcohol fermentation, anaerobic fermentation, and pyrolysis.

In alcohol fermentation, the starch in organic matter is converted to sugar by heating. This sugar is then fermented by yeast (as in the production of beer and wine). The resulting ethanol (also known as ethyl alcohol or grain alcohol) is distilled and then blended with another fuel. "Gasohol", the end product, has been used successfully in Brazil and the United States as an alternative to regular gasoline. The drawback to this method of biomass energy conversion is that the process itself requires the use of fossil fuels, and is therefore somewhat inefficient.

Anaerobic digestion converts biomass, especially waste products, into methane (a major component of natural gas) and carbon dioxide. The biomass is mixed with water and stored in an airtight tank. This form of biomass energy conversion is attractive because it converts human, animal, and agricultural waste into a gas that is readily used as an energy source. Although the process is quite costly, it is relatively efficient.

Pyrolysis involves the heating of biomass in the absence of oxygen. Biomass such as wood or agricultural waste is heated to around 1000 degrees Fahrenheit and allowed to decompose into gas and charcoal (carbon). A major advantage of pyrolysis is that carbon dioxide, one of the main drawbacks to most biomass energy conversion processes, is not produced. A disadvantage, however, is that the biomass must be heated to relatively high temperatures, a process that in and of itself requires significant amounts of energy.

Conversion processes of biomass to energy could be classified as: 1.Combustion; 2. Dry Chemical Processes; and 3. Aqueous Processes. Another classification contains: 1. Biological Conversion; 2. Thermal Conversion; 3.Chemical Conversion as presented in Figure 6.

Methanol, also known as wood alcohol, is a liquid fuel, which has a reasonably high energy density, and can be produced from coal, biomass or natural gas. Methanol is a very volatile fuel, which has been used in race cars for many years. Normal automobile engines can be converted to run on methanol. Natural gas can also be used, but methanol has the advantage of a liquid form for ease of handling and higher energy densities.

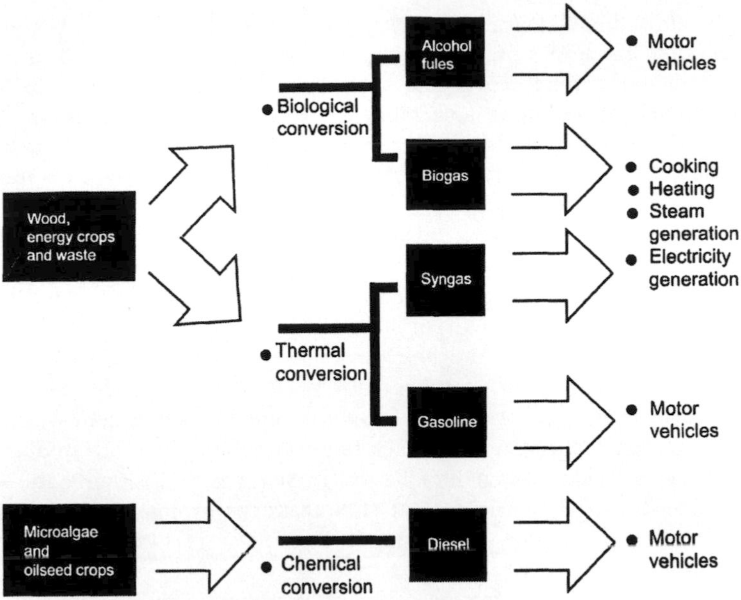

Figure 6. Pathways for the production of biofuels.
Source: http://www.iclei.org/efacts/altfig3.gif

When it is used in an internal combustion engine, or in a fuel cell, methanol burns very cleanly with few emissions of NO_x and HC. The main exhaust gases are CO_2 and water vapour. The use of methanol in vehicles will therefore improve urban air pollution, regardless of the source of the methanol. When methanol is produced by the thermo-chemical pyrolysis of biomass such as wood, it results in no net emissions of CO_2, because the CO_2 released was recently taken from the atmosphere during photosynthesis. Methanol, which has been produced from natural gas, produces even larger CO_2 emissions than those from natural gas vehicles. Methanol from coal vehicles, would produce twice as much CO_2 as their gasoline equivalents. Therefore, although methanol from coal or natural gas is an attractive option for countries with reserves of these fuels, there is no benefit in terms of greenhouse gases.

Ethanol is a liquid fuel that can be produced from a variety of sugar or grain crops, through the process of fermentation or distillation. Ethanol can either be blended with gasoline (gasohol) and burned in regular automobile, or used straight, in modified engines. In Brazil, three billion gallons of ethanol are produced each year from sugar cane, supplying a large percentage of that country's automotive fuel needs. The world's other major producer of ethanol is the United States, where ethanol from corn is blended with gasoline. Figure 7 presents the process flow diagram for conversion of cellulosic biomass to ethanol.

As with other biomass based fuels, ethanol is clean burning, resulting in low NO_x and HC emissions, and no net CO_2 emissions. Using corn or sugar cane for fuel could potentially conflict with the need to produce food. In fact, meeting 10% of the US's current automotive fuel demand with ethanol would require 40% of that country's corn harvest. Research is currently underway in an effort to develop enzymes which could help convert wood into ethanol. Large resources of wood products exist in many parts of the world, and fast growing trees can be grown on soils which are not suitable for agriculture. Overall, if large amounts of biomass are to be converted into ethanol, trade-offs will have to be made between food production, fuel production and wildlife habitat conservation.

There are several ways of converting different types of biomass into the equivalent of diesel fuel or gasoline. Oils produced by plants such as rapeseed (canola), sunflowers and soybeans can be extracted and refined into fuel which can be burned in diesel engines. Winter rapeseed is a promising crop for diesel fuel production, as it can be grown in the off-season. Research is also currently underway in an effort to develop fast growing, high oil yielding aquatic algae, which could be used to produce diesel fuel.

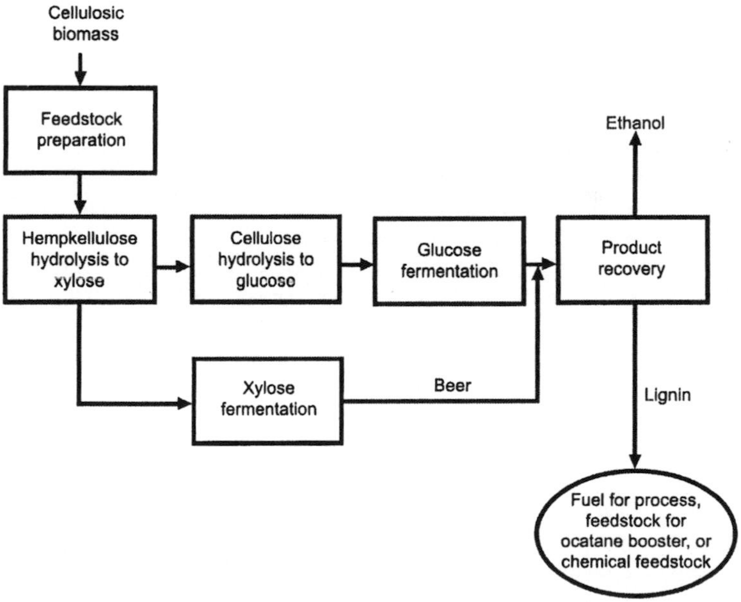

Figure 7. Process flow diagram for conversion of cellulosic biomass to ethanol.
Source: http://www.iclei.org/efacts/altfig1.gif

The technology also exists to allow the conversion of wood and municipal wastes into gasoline. Thermal pyrolysis and a series of catalytic reactions can convert the hydrocarbons in these materials into a gasoline like product. At the present time, gasoline produced from wood is significantly more expensive than that produced from petroleum. As world supplies of petroleum become more scarce in the next 50 years, gasoline from wood may become more attractive.

Another example of biomass use for energy production is the use of biogas in India. Biogas means social benefits for women and children. Woman and children are the big winners in India where every year 200,000 families turn away from the traditional fireplace and have a biogas plant installed to provide energy for cooking and lighting. A smoke-free and ash-free kitchen means women are no longer prone to lung and throat infections and can look forward to a longer life expectancy. In rural areas, where there is generally no electricity supply, the introduction of biogas has given women a sense of self-worth and time to engage in more activities outside the home.

Dung is no longer stored in the home but is fed directly into the biogas plant, along with toilet waste. As a result, standards of hygiene have improved, and the vegetable patch has gained a top quality fertiliser that guarantees a better crop.

More than 2 million biogas plants have been built in India so far. Almost 200,000 permanent jobs have been created for the male bread-winners of Indian families. With a potential market for 30 plants attached to households with three cattle or more, the social and environmental advantages of biogas are only just beginning to be explored.

Development of biogas plants in India addresses a number of problems: scarce firewood; indoor health problems with cooking on firewood or cow dung fire; loss of fertiliser from burning dung; gathering firewood that is time-consuming and a burden for many women; and lack of efficient and affordable light sources for studying during evening.

Main actors in this program are: local NGOs establishing teams of masons to construct the plants; national NGO networks providing training and technical support for local NGOs; Indian Ministry of Non-Conventional Energy Sources providing financial support for the investment; international donors supporting national NGOs; and national NGOs and research centres improving biogas plant design.

Technical development started in the 1950s with an initiative to develop village technologies. The formation of NGOs active in the field has greatly improved the success rate, while the support of government and external donors has been crucial in reaching the current level of dissemination.

This success can be repeated in other parts of the world where the right conditions are present, including: clear benefits for users; suitable climate conditions (enough water, high soil temperature); a functioning design made of locally available and affordable materials; involvement and training of users via

NGOs; government support; and long-term involvement of all partners. Based on the Indian experience, biogas plants have been successfully introduced in Nepal, Kenya, Tanzania, and other countries.

Principles that identify this solution as sustainable are: global environmental benefits (alternative to increased fossil fuel use for light and cooking); local environmental benefits (reduces deforestation) clear benefits for users; and supports sustainable social development (rural development, job creation, increased independence of external fuel inputs).

Advantages of biomass energy:

• Biomass is found around the world. Animal and crop wastes from farms and forests are abundant in many parts of the world.

• Biomass is often free or inexpensive. The wastes may be available free, and in some places, wood can be gathered without charge.

• Biomass is renewable. Crops and animal wastes are continually renewed. Wood from forests is renewable if people do not harvest more than the forest can grow back.

• The machines for creating and burning biomass fuels are simple and inexpensive. People around the world can use the vehicle and cooking fuels that come from biomass.

• Biomass makes solid, liquid and gaseous fuels. The solid fuels can be burned easily, although they may be inconvenient. Liquid and gaseous fuels burn cleanly. They are easy to store, handle and use.

Disadvantages of biomass energy:

Burning biomass releases carbon dioxide, which contributes to the warming of the atmosphere and possible climatic change. Burning also creates soot and other air pollutants.

• Overcollecting wood can destroy forests. Soils bared of trees erode easily and do not hold rainfall. Increased run-off can cause flooding downstream.

• When plant and animal wastes are used as fuel, they cannot be added to the soil as fertiliser. Soil without fertiliser can be depleted of nutrients and produce fewer crops.

• Biomass has less energy than a similar volume of fossil fuels.

• Biomass fuels can be more expensive than similar fossil fuels.

5.6 Ocean Energy Systems

Two-thirds of the earth's surface is covered by oceans. These bodies of water are vast reservoirs of renewable energy. In a four day period, the planet's oceans absorb an amount of thermal energy from the sun and kinetic energy from the wind equivalent to all the world's known oil reserves. Several technologies exist for harnessing these vast reserves of energy for useful purposes. The most promising are ocean thermal energy conversion (OTEC) and wave power plants.

OTEC power plants can be located either on-shore or at sea, with the generated electricity transmitted to shore by electrical cables, or used on site for the manufacture of electricity intensive products or fuels. For OTEC plants situated on shore to be economical, the floor of the ocean must drop off to great depths very quickly. This is because a large portion of the electricity generated by an OTEC system is used to pump the cold water up from the depths of the ocean. The longer the cold water pipe, the lower the net electrical output of the power plant.

There are three potential types of OTEC power plants, open-cycle, closed-cycle and hybrid systems. Open-cycle OTEC systems, illustrated in Figure 8a, exploit the fact that water boils at temperatures below its normal boiling point when it is under lower than normal pressures. Open-cycle systems convert warm surface waters into steam in a partial vacuum, and then use this steam to drive a turbine connected to an electrical generator. Cold water piped up from deep below the ocean's surface condenses the steam. Unlike the initial ocean water, the condensed steam desalinated (free of salt) and may be used for drinking or irrigation.

Closed-cycle OTEC systems, illustrated in Figure 8b, use warm surface waters passed through a heat exchanger to boil a working fluid, such as ammonia or a Chlorofluorocarbon, which has a low boiling point. The vapour given off is passed through a turbine/generator producing electricity. Cold deep ocean water is then used to condense the working fluid and it is returned to the heat exchanger to repeat the cycle. Hybrid OTEC systems produce both electricity, with a closed-cycle system, and fresh water, with an open-cycle system.

Unlike electrical generation from most other forms of renewable energy which varies with weather and time of day, such as solar and wind energy, OTEC power plants can produce electricity 24 hours per day, 365 days per year.

This capability makes OTEC an attractive alternative to conventional base load power plants powered by fossil fuels or nuclear fission. Fresh water production is just one of the potential beneficial by-products of OTEC. The cold deep ocean water can be used for aqua-culture (fish farming) as it is pathogen free and nutrient rich, or air-conditioning and refrigeration in nearby buildings.

Winds blowing across the surface of the world's oceans are converted into waves. The total amount of power released by waves breaking along the world's coastlines has been estimated to be 2-3 million megawatts, equivalent to the output of 3000 large power plants. Although this vast amount of energy is spread out along thousands of kilometres of coasts, in favourable locations, the energy density can average 65 MW per mile of coastline, an amount which can lead to economical wave generated electricity. Wave size is a factor of wind speed and "fetch", the distance over the ocean's surface which the wind travels. Favourable wind energy sites are generally western coastlines facing the open ocean such as those in North America and Northern Europe. Norway, Denmark, Japan and the United Kingdom are the world leaders in wave energy technologies.

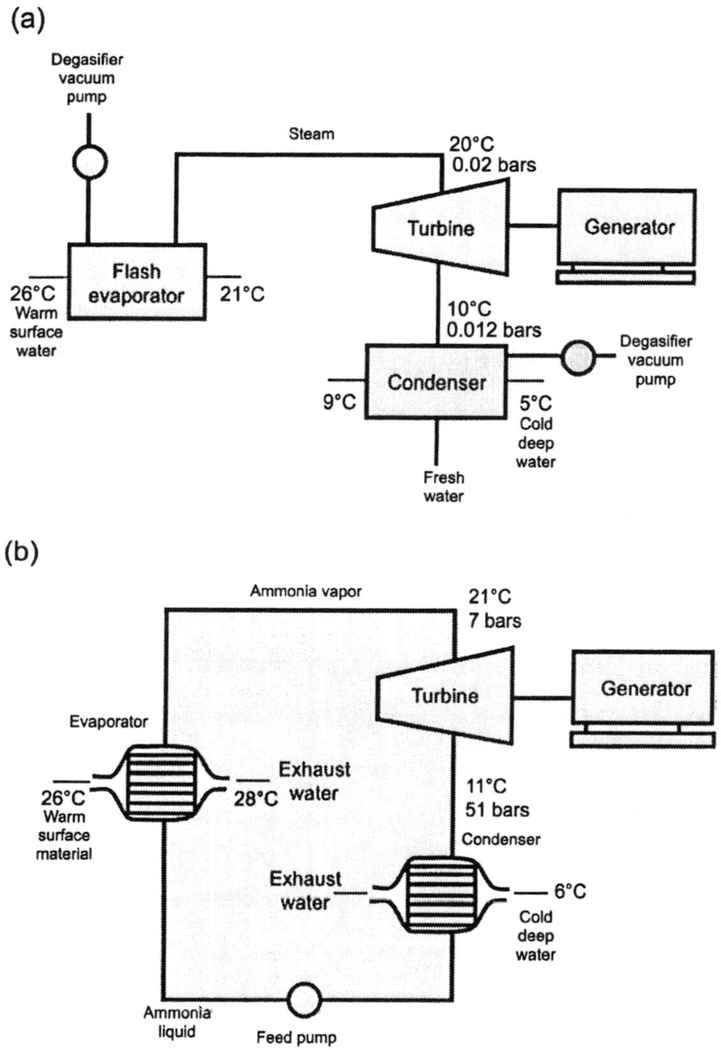

Figure 8. OTEC plants: a. Open-cycle OTEC plant; b. Closed-cycle OTEC plant.
Source: http://www.iclei.org/efacts/ocensys2.gif

Although a wide variety of devices have been constructed to capture wave energy, commercial electrical generation from wave power will be one of three general types:

- surface-followers using floats or pitching devices
- oscillating water columns
- surge or focusing devices.

Surface following devices use a mechanical linkage between two floating objects or between a floating and a fixed object to produce useful mechanical power. This mechanical power can either be connected directly to a generator or transferred to a working fluid, water or air, which drives a turbine generator.

One high efficiency pitching device which has been tested is called the "Salter Duck", so named because it was developed by Steven Salter at the University of Edinburgh. It looks like a series of floating ducks. These ducks pivot about a stiff shaft and this pivoting motion drives a hydraulic fluid to produce electricity. Test on the Salter ducks show that they are capable of capturing 80% of the energy carried by incoming waves.

Oscillating water columns (OWC) use the force of waves entering a fixed device to perform work or generate electricity. The simplest examples of these are navigational buoys where waves entering the anchored buoy compress air in a vertical pipe. This compressed air can be used to simply blow a whistle, or to drive a turbine generator producing electricity for a light. Japan has installed hundreds of OWC-powered navigational buoys since 1965 and is currently operating two small demonstration OWC power plants.

Focusing or surge devices are manmade barriers which channel and concentrate large waves into a small area. This focusing drastically increases the height of the waves, and these elevated waves are channelled into an elevated reservoir. This water then passes through hydro-electric turbines on its way back to sea level, thus generating electricity. A 350 kilowatt, grid-connected power plant has been operating on the North Sea coast of Norway since 1986. It uses a "Tapered channel" design to focus the waves.

One of the problems associated with wave power plants is that, during severe storms, the energy unleashed by breaking waves can be over 10 times that of the average for a coast, and wave energy plants must be built to withstand this sort of punishment. This adds a great deal to the cost of wave energy facilities. Although focusing devices are the most costly of the three types of wave power plants, their robust nature makes them less susceptible to damage by storms. The Norwegian Tapered Channel design has proven to be the most durable of any wave energy plants. This has led to two orders for commercial 1.5 megawatt power plants based on this design, one in Java, Indonesia and one on King Island located between Tasmania and the Australian mainland.

Wave energy power plants consume no fuel during their operation and as such have no emissions of harmful pollutants. But large scale wave energy facilities can have an impact on nearby coastal environments. Offshore wave energy facilities such as surface followers or OWCs would reduce the height of waves reaching the shore. This would change patterns of erosion and sedimentation. Focusing devices result in more erosion where the waves are concentrated and more sedimentation in adjacent areas. The effect that these changes in erosion and sedimentation could have on local ecosystems is variable and poorly understood.

Theoretical concepts for generating electricity from ocean currents and salinity gradients (differences in salt content) are being investigated. More research and development on these concepts is required before they will reach the stage of demonstration power plants.

The world's oceans represent an enormous and virtually untapped source of clean, non-polluting renewable energy. Technologies exist to exploit this resource but at the present time, high initial construction costs make electricity produced from these power plants more expensive than that from traditional sources. Technological breakthroughs, standardised plant designs, increased fossil fuel prices and/or increased world concern over environmental issues such as global warming will increase the pace at which ocean wave and ocean thermal energy conversion systems are utilised.

OTEC power plants have some negative impacts on the natural environment, but overall they are a relatively clean, non-polluting source of electricity when compared to conventional options such as fossil fuels or nuclear power. Cold water released at the ocean's surface will release trapped carbon dioxide, a greenhouse gas, but emissions are only about 4-7% of those from a fossil fuel power plant. Discharging the cold water at the oceans' surface could change local concentrations of nutrients and dissolved gases. However, this could be minimised by discharging the cold water at depths of greater than 50 m.

At the present time, despite the fact that OTEC systems have no fuel costs and can produce useful by-products, the high initial cost of building such power plants makes OTEC generated electricity more expensive than conventional alternatives. As such, OTEC systems at the present time are restricted to experimental and demonstration units. Island nations that currently rely on expensive, imported fossil fuels for electrical generation are the most promising market for OTEC. More experience in building OTEC power plants and standardised plant designs could bring OTEC costs down in the future. Heightened world concern over environmental issues such as global warming could also hasten the development of OTEC as a practical source of electricity.

5.7 Geothermal Energy Technology

To enhance efficiency of geothermal energy, binary cyclic power generation has been developed. This system is composed of two generation processes, one of which uses a gas turbine driven by flon or ammonia and the other a water vapour utilisation turbine.

Geothermal systems usually need both underground water and magma heat. However, there are few places where both coexist. Therefore some new systems have been investigated, for example, magma or heated rock systems which utilise artificially injected water to obtain hot steam.

High grade technologies will be applied first to identify suitable sites. LANDSAT, an artificial satellite, searches using infrared rays. Shallow resources (100-200 [m], 100-250°C) are likely to be found in this way, deeper resources being more difficult to identify. Magnetic research using, for example, Josephson's device which is very sensitive to magnetism, and other sophisticated instruments can be used. Another application of future technology is to effectively remove precipitate and chemical material attached to the vapour pipe lines.

Suitable sites for geothermal power plants are along volcanic zones where magma exists near to the earth's surface. These mountainous regions have fine landscapes and are often designated as National Parks, so that development is nearly impossible. Most of the suitable sites belong to such areas. The list of representative geothermal power plants is given in Table 12.

Table 12. Representative geothermal power plants (Ohta 1994)

Field	Country	Capacity 10^3kW
Cerro Prieto	Mexico	630
The Geysers	USA	1700
Kakkonda	Japan	55
Larderello	Italy	410
Namfjall	Iceland	3
Pauzhetsk	Russia	5.7
Wairakei	New Zealand	202

Geothermal energy can either be used directly as heat for a district heating system or industrial process, or, if the temperature is high enough, converted into electricity. Unlike other renewable sources of electricity, geothermal power is not intermittent. It provides a reliable source of electricity 24 hours a day. The technology required to extract geothermal energy depends upon the type of the geothermal reservoir and the end use. Technologies for producing electricity from the four types of geothermal resources outlined above will be looked at in detail. Using geothermal energy directly for heating involves the same heat extraction stages, but eliminates the need for a turbine and generator.

Hydrothermal reservoirs containing high temperature steam are the simplest source of geothermal electricity. Two holes or wells are drilled into the formation containing the steam. The steam is drawn out of one of the wells (the "production well") and allowed to pass through a standard turbine such as those used at thermal electricity generating stations (Figure 9). After passing through the turbine and thus turning a generator, the steam is condensed and returned to the rock formation through the second, "injection well". Returning the condensed liquid into the ground maintains a supply of geothermal fluids in the reservoir.

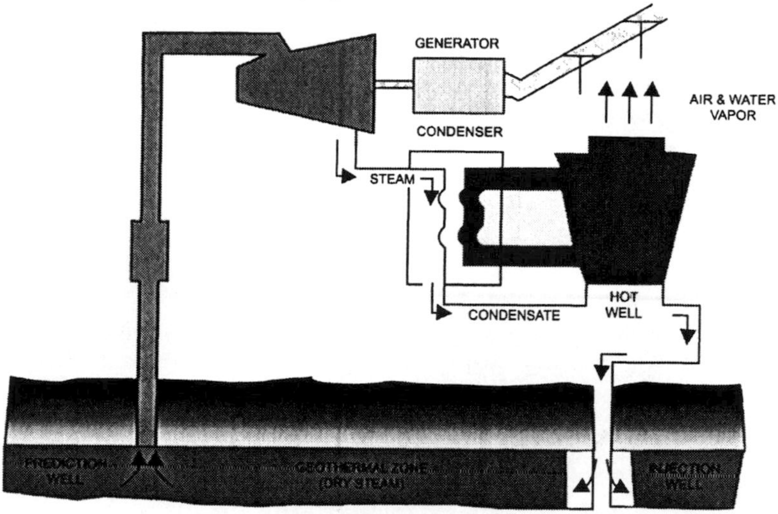

Figure 9. Schematic of a Geothermal Electricity Generating System for Vapour-Dominated Hydrothermal Resources.
Source: http://www.iclei.org/efacts/geofig2.gif

Hydrothermal and geopressurised reservoirs containing very hot water rather than steam are exploited in a similar fashion; but the hot water must first be "flashed" into steam as its pressure is reduced above the ground. Pumps are required to extract the water from hydrothermal reservoirs, while geopressurised systems often do not require a pump. Variations on the above technology include systems where steam is passed through two successive turbines, called a "double flash". The more expensive double flash systems capture more of the energy of the geothermal fluid and are therefore 10 to 20 percent more efficient than single flash plants.

Electricity production from lower temperature (Hot dry rock (HDR) geothermal reservoirs are tapped by drilling two long boreholes and then fracturing the rock at whatever depth it is hot enough to provide useful amounts of energy. Water is pumped down one hole and comes up the other at an elevated temperature. Most HDR resources provide water at moderate temperatures (200°C), suitable for heating or use in a binary cycle power plant. Magma, or molten rock geothermal resources are very high temperature sources of geothermal energy. Although there is currently no existing technology for recovering heat from magma, it is a source of large amounts of energy when the magma is at reasonable depths.

Although geothermal energy generally results in negligible greenhouse gas emissions, it is not without environmental impacts. The main environmental concern with geothermal energy is the result of natural contaminants dissolved in the water or brine extracted from the ground. Silica, sulphates, sulphides, carbonates, silicates and halides present in geothermal fluids present problems for both equipment and the environment. Hydrothermal and geopressurised water and brines are often very corrosive. This complicates the choice of materials for pipes, pumps and turbines. Dissolved compounds also tend to precipitate out of solution when these fluids are flashed into steam, clogging up the system.

Most geothermal power plants attempt to keep the working geothermal fluids within a closed system that returns them to the original reservoir after useful energy has been extracted. Despite this, many geothermal power plants release small amounts of these fluids into the surface environment. This is a result of having to vent steam that has reached excessive pressures, or mechanical breakdowns such as broken pipes. The major gaseous discharge from geothermal plants is hydrogen sulphide (H_2S), which smells like rotten eggs and can be toxic or fatal at high concentrations. The release of acidic geothermal fluids into surface water is also a concern, as it can damage aquatic ecosystems or contaminate drinking water supplies. Finally, locations with potential geothermal resources have often become tourist destinations due to attractions like hot springs and geysers. Producing energy from these resources can eliminate these naturally occurring features, hurting tourism and altering natural processes.

Geothermal energy represents a potentially huge source of reliable heat and electricity. The technology exists to exploit this resource in an environmentally acceptable manner, although only a few sites are cost effective at the present time. The best geothermal resources are not evenly distributed around the world; but more costly sources of geothermal energy such as HDR are widely available. The amount of geothermal energy utilised in the future will depend upon the cost and environmental concerns associated with traditional sources of energy, rather than the limits of the geothermal resource. As supplies of fossil fuels dwindle, or the impacts of global warming and acid rain become more severe, geothermal energy will become an attractive option for supplying heat and electricity in the future.

Geothermal energy is both renewable and non-renewable. In some places, deposits of steam or hot water lie underground. If they are brought to the surface they can be used up. This kind of geothermal energy is non-renewable.

In other places, hot magma is close to the surface. Water that is pumped down can be heated and brought back to the surface. The magma always remains hot. This resource cannot be used up and is renewable.

Advantages of geothermal energy:

- Geothermal energy can be inexpensive if it is used near the source.

• Geothermal energy releases no carbon dioxide and few pollutants compared to fossil fuels.

• Geothermal energy can provide a continuous energy source for a long time.

• Geothermal energy is free once the initial buildings and machinery are installed.

• Geothermal deposits are widespread around the world.

• Disadvantages of geothermal energy:

• It can be expensive to find areas of hot rock deep underground.

• Initial buildings and machinery can be expensive.

• The steam that comes from underground can contain air pollutants and other chemicals.

• The hot water and steam can run out.

5.8 Solar Energy Technology

One quite common application of renewable energy is passive solar heating for the home. A passive solar heating system collects energy from the sun and uses this energy to heat a space directly, such as a sun room, or to heat a fluid. If a fluid is heated, it is considered a source of thermal mass for the system, which can be used later to radiate the heat to the surroundings. The five main components of passive solar heating are the collector, absorber, storage mass, distribution system, and control system. In the case of a sunroom, the **collector** is the double layer of glass in thermal window panes that trap the heat in and reduce the amount of heat loss by convection. The **absorber** consists of several parts: surfaces of the walls, floors, and any water-filled containers inside the sunroom. The **storage mass**, or thermal mass, is the building material such as concrete, brick, and any water. Thermal mass usually has a high heat capacity to retain the heat absorbed during the daylight hours, and radiate it at night. One method of increasing the thermal mass of a house is to build the house partially underground. A **distribution system** of fans or vents should be installed to move the heat by natural convection. Control systems, or heat regulation devices such as movable insulation, roof overhangs, thermostatically controlled fans, and adjustable vents are used to control the temperature of specific rooms. Hot water heating systems may heat a primary fluid that will not freeze in the winter, and pump that fluid to a heat exchanger to heat water for use inside a building. Many innovative passive solar heating systems have been designed to optimise the efficiency of the passive solar home.

Another method of capturing the sun's energy is through the use of active solar systems, or **photovoltaic systems** (Figure 10). Photovoltaic systems use solar cells to directly produce electricity from solar radiation. The photovoltaic cell is made by using two semi-conducting materials that have different types of charge carriers, so when they are placed back-to-back a potential difference can be measured.

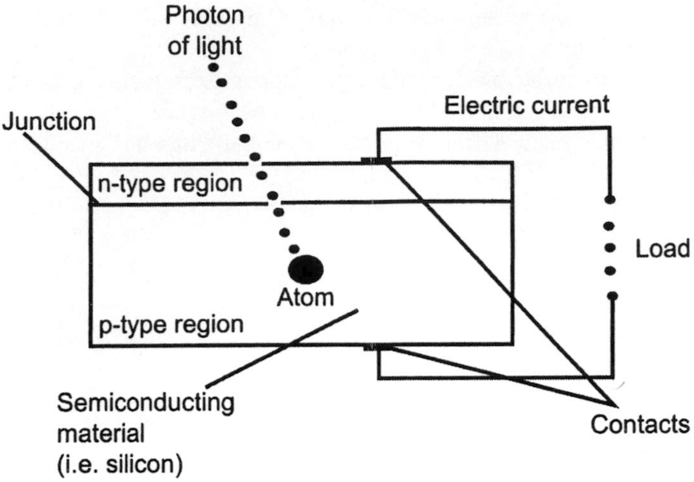

Figure 10. Photovoltaics: Electricity from the Sun.
Source: http://www.iclei.org/efacts/photov1.gif

The boundary between the two conductors is called a **depletion region**. If a photon, or "bundle" of electromagnetic energy, from the sun strikes an electron near the boundary between these elements, that electron moves to a higher energy level. The potential difference moves this free electron leaving an unoccupied space, or "hole". The entire process causes a charge separation. As the electron and the hole move across the photovoltaic cell and travel through the wire connected to what's being powered (a solar calculator for example), an electrical current in the circuit is produced.

This system is very cost effective in situations where electric power is not readily available and the power requirements are relatively low. It is roughly estimated that about 10,000 square miles of solar cells could produce enough energy for the entire nation! So, why haven't we converted our energy usage to active solar? 10,000 square miles of solar cells is a lot of solar cells! They would have to be built, a maintenance system would be required in order to maximise efficiency, the weather would have to be dependable, and it would be expensive. It has not been economical to develop this source because the cost of the cells is too high. Perhaps as the replacement of fossil fuels becomes essential, this technology may be better developed. Many homes and businesses use solar cells to reduce their electric bill. Solar cars have also been developed as a result of competitive races between major universities.

Solar ponds are also utilised to capture the sun's power. A solar pond uses the principles of energy transfer by convection to heat water to steam for heat production. The bottom of the pond is dark coloured in order to absorb the sun's rays. The pond is filled with saline water made with NaCl, $MgCl_2$, sodium carbonate, or sodium sulphate. A gradient is maintained at varying densities. The bottom is the most dense and is used as a **storage zone**. It is **convective** and can store a working temperature of up to 80-85°C. Above the bottom layer is a nonconvective zone, or **insulation zone**, with a density gradient which facilitates a temperature gradient as well. This layer functions as insulation. There is no convection in the gradient layer because even though the warm water would normally rise, the high salt concentration at lower levels does not allow the water to be light enough to float up as it warms. This prevents heat in the bottom from reaching the top of the pond. The top layer, or **surface zone**, is convective due to wind-induced mixing and daily heating and cooling. The hot brine, or salt water, on the bottom may be extracted and used for direct heating and low-temperature industrial uses like drying crops and agricultural shelter heating. The problem with solar ponds is that it is essential to have a controlled saline density gradient, which is quite difficult to maintain. Additionally, the pond must be kept free of dirt and other light-absorbing materials. Thus, for large scale operations, the difficulties are too great to rely upon solar ponds for efficient heat production.

Here is one possible system for converting the heat energy from the salt water to electricity. An organic fluid is heated and boiled as it is pumped through tubes in an evaporator. The hot brine is pumped from the bottom of the solar pond through the evaporator (where it transfers heat to the organic fluid), and returned to the pond. The organic fluid, which is now a vapour, has sufficient pressure to spin the turbine and generator. The vapour has transferred some of its kinetic energy to the turbine. The cooler vapour is pumped to the condenser where it is condensed to a liquid as it transfers energy to the cold water being pumped through the tubes of the condenser. The organic liquid is now pumped to the evaporator to continue the process. As the gradient layer diffuses as time passes, new freshwater and salt water can be pumped into the pond to maintain a sufficient gradient layer. Solar cells are thin wafers of silicon which, when exposed to sunlight, produce DC electric current. These devices, which were developed for the space program in the 1950s, have a maximum conversion efficiency of about 15%. When a number of solar cells are mounted on a surface and are wired together in series, they become a solar module, the building block of a solar photovoltaic system. The solar photovoltaic module's relatively high initial cost (about $5/watt) is offset by a very long life and very low maintenance requirements.

Suitable applications for solar photovoltaic systems almost always involves their use in remote locations (whether spacecraft or remote homes) because their 20 year power cost of about 20 cents per kWh is not competitive with current utility power costs.

Solar water heating is one of the most efficient and least expensive of the renewable energy technologies. These systems use the heat of the sun's rays to heat water for domestic use. Each system has two separate components:

- the collector which converts the sun's energy to heat
- an insulated storage tank to keep the water hot until ready for use.

The design of these systems varies according to the climate of the location of intended use. In tropical climates, these systems commonly employ thermal syphon pumping to circulate the hot water between the collector and the tank which must be placed above the collector. In colder climates, where freezing is a possibility, glycol is employed to transfer heat between the collector and the storage tank. A heat exchanger is used to keep the glycol from mixing with the domestic hot water.

Solar hot water systems give some of the best value compared to other solar energy technologies because of their relative low cost and high collector efficiency.

Electricity produced from photovoltaics has a far smaller impact on the environment than traditional methods of electrical generation. During their operation, PV cells use no fuel other than sunlight, give off no atmospheric or water pollutants and require no cooling water. Unlike fossil fuel (coal, oil, natural gas) fired power plants, photovoltaics do not contribute to global warming or acid rain. Similarly photovoltaics present no radioactive risks. The only negative environmental impacts associated with photovoltaics are potentially toxic chemicals used during their manufacture, and the amount of land used to produce electricity.

Manufacturing some types of PV cells, particularly gallium arsenide cells, may involve the production of some potentially toxic substances. These substances are generated in a centralised facility, and proper control of the manufacturing process, and proper disposal of any toxic wastes, should reduce the risks of any environmental contamination. Disposal of PV cells after their useful life is finished, generally 30 years, could present some waste disposal problems, but most of the toxic materials in any cells can probably be recycled.

The amount of land required to produce large amounts of electricity from photovoltaics has been identified as a concern by some people. The fact is, however, that if all the stages in electrical generation are taken into account, PV arrays use the same amount of land per unit of electricity as coal or nuclear power plants. Photovoltaics use land at the point of electrical generation, while coal and nuclear plants use land during mining, processing and electrical generation. When all these items are considered, the land use requirements of the three different options are remarkably similar. In fact, if only one percent of the land in the US was covered with solar cells, all their electrical needs could be met On top of this, PV arrays can be placed on roofs or on land with little other value such as deserts.

5.9 Tidal Power Generation

The technology required to convert tidal energy into electricity is very similar to the technology used in traditional hydroelectric power plants. The first requirement is a dam or "barrage" across a tidal bay or estuary. Building dams is an expensive process. Therefore, the best tidal sites are those where a bay has a narrow opening, thus reducing the length of dam which is required. At certain points along the dam, gates and turbines are installed. When there is an adequate difference in the elevation of the water on the different sides of the barrage, the gates are opened. This "hydrostatic head" that is created, causes water to flow through the turbines, turning an electric generator to produce electricity. The principle of the tidal power generation is presented in Figure 11. The barrage, or dam, holds back the water in the estuary as the tide falls. Then, gates are opened and the water rushes seaward through the turbine. Later, the rising tide will be held back by the barrage, then released to flow through another turbine into the river estuary.

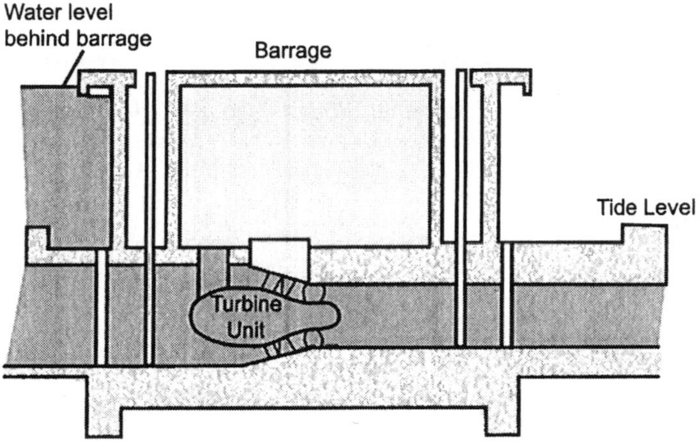

Figure 11. The principle of tidal power generation.
Source: http://www.iclei.org/efacts/tidalen2.gif

Electricity can be generated by water flowing both into and out of a bay. As there are two high and two low tides each day, electrical generation from tidal power plants is characterised by periods of maximum generation every twelve hours, with no electricity generation at the six hour mark in between. Alternatively, the turbines can be used as pumps to pump extra water into the basin behind the barrage during periods of low electricity demand. This water can then be released when demand on the system its greatest, thus allowing the tidal plant to function with some of the characteristics of a "pumped storage" hydroelectric facility.

The demand for electricity on an electrical grid varies with the time of day. The supply of electricity from a tidal power plant will never match the demand on a system. But tidal power, although variable, is reliable and predictable and can make a valuable contribution to an electrical system which has a variety of sources. Tidal electricity can be used to displace electricity which would otherwise be generated by fossil fuel (coal, oil, natural gas) fired power plants, thus reducing emissions of greenhouse and acid gasses.

Currently, although the technology required to harness tidal energy is well established, tidal power is expensive, and there is only one major tidal generating station in operation. This is a 240 megawatt (1 megawatt = 1 MW = 1 million watts) at the mouth of the La Rance river estuary on the northern coast of France (a large coal or nuclear power plant generates about 1000 MW of electricity). The La Rance generating station has been in operation since 1966 and has been a very reliable source of electricity for France. La Rance was supposed to be one of many tidal power plants in France, until their nuclear program was greatly expanded in the late 1960s. Elsewhere there is a 20 MW experimental facility at Annapolis Royal in Nova Scotia, and a 0.4 MW tidal power plant near Murmansk in Russia.

Studies have been undertaken to examine the potential of several other tidal power sites worldwide. It has been estimated that a barrage across the Severn River in western England could supply as much as 10% of the country's electricity needs (12 GW). Similarly, several sites in the Bay of Fundy, Cook Inlet in Alaska, and the White Sea in Russia have been found to have the potential to generate large amounts of electricity.

The late President C. de Gaulle (1890-1970) of France made up his mind to construct a tidal power station at the mouth of the river Ranee in 1961. The station, finished in 1966, is composed of 24 water turbines, each of which has a capacity of 10^4 [kW]; it generates 5.48×10^8 [kWh] in a year. The bank between the gulf of St. Malo and the artificial dam has a length of 300 [m], height of 12.3 [m], and a width of 20 [m]. Under this bank the 24 turbines are equipped to generate electric power when the high tide comes in and also when the water leaves the bay.

China has also constructed several tidal power stations on the coast facing the Po Hai bay. Their output is estimated to be 6000 [kW].

There are many suitable sites where the high tide occurs, especially in Canada, Northern Europe, and Northern Russia. However, the investment cost is so expensive that no government has undertaken the efforts except for President de Gaulle.

One of the main barriers to the increased use of tidal energy is the cost of building tidal generating stations. For example, it has been estimated that the construction of the proposed facility on the Severn River in England would have a construction cost of $15 billion. Operating and maintenance costs of tidal power plants are very low because the "fuel", sea-water, is free; but the overall cost of electricity generated is still very high.

The major factors in determining the cost effectiveness of a tidal power site are the size (length and height) of the barrage required, and the difference in height between high and low tide. These factors can be expressed in what is called a site's "Gibrat" ratio. The Gibrat ratio is the ratio of the length of the barrage in metres to the annual energy production in kilowatt hours (1 kilowatt hour = 1 KWH = 1000 watts used for 1 hour). The smaller the Gibrat site ratio, the more desirable the site. Examples of Gibrat ratios are La Rance at 0.36, Severn at 0.87 and Passamaquoddy in the Bay of Fundy at 0.92.

Tidal energy is a renewable source of electricity which does not result in the emission of gases responsible for global warming or acid rain associated with fossil fuel generated electricity. Use of tidal energy could also decrease the need for nuclear power, with its associated radiation risks. Changing tidal flows by damming a bay or estuary could, however, result in negative impacts on aquatic and shoreline ecosystems, as well as navigation and recreation.

The few studies that have been undertaken to date to identify the environmental impacts of a tidal power scheme have determined that each specific site is different and the impacts depend greatly upon local geography. Local tides changed only slightly due to the La Rance barrage, and the environmental impact has been negligible, but this may not be the case for all other sites. It has been estimated that in the Bay of Fundy, tidal power plants could decrease local tides by 15 cm. This does not seem like much when one considers that natural variations such as winds can change the level of the tides by several metres.

Very little is understood about how altering the tides can affect incredibly complex aquatic and shoreline ecosystems. Unfortunately, one of the only methods of increasing our knowledge about how tidal barrages affect ecosystems may be the study of the effects after such facilities have been built.

Chapter 5
Energy Economics

Understanding energy-economy coupling is crucial for designing energy systems compatible with sustainable economic growth. Different perspectives are leading to divergent views of this coupling. Therefore, means are needed for negotiating and integrating the different approaches. The greenhouse-gas debate provides an illustration. A central question concerns the development of energy systems compatible with both economic growth and management of the risk of climate change.

Much of the debate is focused on the links between economic growth, level of energy demands, development of the energy system to supply these demands, and technology and resource bases to support the energy system. The debate is often connected with alternative analytical approaches. The approaches are distinguished by their designs and uses of various models, as well as the emphasis on technological databases. The alternative philosophies may be labelled top-down macroeconomic and bottom-up engineering. The two approaches tend to disagree on the effects of energy-efficiency improvements on future levels of energy demands. The macroeconomic approach usually leads to fewer effects on compounded future energy demands than the systems engineering approach. An interesting question is whether it is possible to identify the causes of the disagreements as either different interpretations and uses of data or differences in methodology and modelling tools.

The two approaches differ considerably in their identification of the relevant system. The bottom-up or systems engineering approach builds on detailed analysis of technological options and potentials for technical changes in the energy system. The models are focused on energy flows. With the more sophisticated systems engineering models, the complex network of resources, technologies and final users may be mapped with the desired scope and detail. Alternative energy pathways can be explored from extraction to final use. Such models are ideal tools for investigating fundamental technological changes in the energy system, including consequences for emissions, investments and cash flows. Development of systems engineering models started in the 1970s.

In the top-down or macroeconomic approach, energy enters as a production factor. The interplay with other production factors to create economic growth is captured in production functions. The technical energy system is usually treated as a black-box that is characterised by transfer functions with elasticities describing tendencies to change the fuel mix. Price changes trigger fuel switches and alter the relation between the use of energy and other production factors, but the technologies responsible for these changes are not identified. Productivity improvements are usually specified by external parameters.

The macroeconomic models thus capture feedbacks between the energy system and the rest of the economy. They address the effects of changing prices on economic activity, including possible reallocation of resources that affect capital formation and economic growth. The macroeconomic models have one more important function, namely, its use helps us to avoid the *reductionist fallacy,* e.g. the belief that the components in the compounded energy demand will remain the same in the future. Conversely, by using the systems engineering models we avoid another fallacy, which may be called the *black-box fallacy,* e.g. the belief that observations of previous inputs and outputs exhaust all possible responses (i.e. possible internal states) of the energy system.

Fundamental technological changes in the energy system may involve considerable feedbacks to the rest of the economy. Conversely, evaluation of economic instruments to control the risk of climate change must include consideration of the technological response of the energy system. Linking a macroeconomic model and a systems engineering model will provide a tool for the required joint energy-economy analysis. It should also help us to avoid both the reductionist and the black-box fallacies. For linking, it is possible to use peer-reviewed models, which avoids repeating earlier work and provides needed initial quality assurance to the efforts.

1 Energy Supply and Demand

Energy is utilised in various forms by the demand sectors of the economy. Household and commercial consumers require thermal energy for comfort and for the preparation of food, and electrical energy for lighting and for the operation of electronic and motor-driven appliances that provide entertainment, communication, and labour-saving functions. Energy in mechanical form is needed for both public and private transportation. Industry has similar needs with added requirements involving thermal and chemical energy for materials processing, refining, and the manufacture of synthetic materials and consumer goods. The use of specific energy resources to satisfy these demands depends on their relative economics and convenience as well as on the systems that are available for conversion into the form of energy that is ultimately required.

About 8.4×109 [oet] (oil equivalent ton = 12.2×106 [kcal]) of energy are consumed each year in the world. For developed countries, the final consumption is distributed roughly as 31% for industry, 22% for transport, 31%

for residential, tertiary, and agriculture, 6.5% for non-energy uses (manufacturing of plastics et al.), and 9.5% for the energy industry. The above percentage for transport is not valid in North America where the share is more than 35%. Energy for transport is almost exclusively gasoline or light oil for automobiles in Europe and North America, but the use of electric trains is appreciable in Japan.

World energy consumption is projected to increase by 65 percent from 1996 to 2020 (see Table 13). Growth in energy demand has been severely hampered by the current international economic troubles. The curtailed demand for oil and natural gas resulting from the Asian economic recession and warmer than expected winters in North America and Europe in 1998 resulted in worldwide energy surpluses which have, in turn, helped drive oil prices to 20-year lows. Uncertain financial markets have made it difficult to secure financial backing for some projects. Exploration and development expenditures for oil and gas were sharply cut back in most parts of the world at the end of 1998. Russia's economic troubles have meant that investments that would have been used to expand the country's participation in international oil and natural gas markets have been tabled for the near future.

Table 13. World Total Energy Consumption by Region, 1990-2020 (Quadrillion Btu)

Region/ Country	History			Projections					Average Annual Percent Change, 1996-2020
	1990	1995	1996	2000	2005	2010	2015	2020	
Industrialised Countries									
North America	99.7	108.0	111.6	119.3	126.9	134.9	141.3	147.5	1.2
United States[a]	83.9	90.4	93.3	99.2	104.7	110.8	115.5	119.9	1.0
Canada	10.9	12.2	12.6	13.5	14.5	15.4	16.2	16.9	1.2
Mexico	4.9	5.5	5.6	6.5	7.7	8.6	9.6	10.7	2.7
Western Europe	60.0	62.3	64.0	67.6	71.3	74.6	77.9	81.5	1.0
United Kingdom	9.4	9.3	9.9	10.5	11.2	11.7	12.3	12.8	1.1
France	9.3	10.2	10.6	11.0	11.5	12.0	12.5	13.0	0.9
Germany	14.7	14.2	14.5	15.2	16.0	16.8	17.6	18.4	1.0
Italy	6.7	7.1	7.2	7.6	8.1	8.6	9.1	9.6	1.2
Netherlands	3.3	3.5	3.7	3.9	4.1	4.4	4.6	4.8	1.1
Other Western Europe	16.6	18.0	18.2	19.4	20.3	21.1	21.9	22.8	1.0
Industrialised	23.0	26.3	26.9	26.3	29.6	30.9	32.4	33.9	1.0

Asia									
Japan	18.1	20.8	21.4	20.4	23.3	24.4	25.6	26.7	0.9
Australasia	4.9	5.6	5.5	5.9	6.2	6.5	6.8	7.1	1.1
Total Industrialised	182.7	196.6	202.5	213.2	227.8	240.4	251.6	262.8	1.1
EE/FSU									
Former Soviet Union	58.5	40.8	39.8	38.4	41.8	44.7	47.8	51.1	1.0
Eastern Europe	15.2	12.4	12.6	13.5	15.1	16.3	17.5	18.7	1.7
Total EE/FSU	73.6	53.2	52.4	52.0	56.9	61.0	65.3	69.8	1.2
Developing Countries									
Developing Asia	51.4	71.8	74.5	84.5	106.1	127.6	151.0	177.9	3.7
China	27.0	36.4	37.1	43.6	55.0	67.6	81.8	98.3	4.1
India	7.7	11.1	11.5	14.1	17.5	20.8	24.2	28.2	3.8
South Korea	3.7	6.5	7.2	7.5	9.4	11.3	13.3	15.4	3.2
Other Asia	13.0	17.8	18.8	19.3	24.1	28.0	31.8	36.0	2.8
Middle East	13.1	16.4	17.3	20.1	23.5	27.0	30.6	34.7	2.9
Turkey	2.0	2.5	2.7	3.2	3.7	4.2	4.8	5.5	3.0
Africa	9.2	10.7	11.1	12.0	13.8	15.5	17.1	18.9	2.3
Central and South America	13.7	16.8	17.7	21.0	26.3	32.6	39.4	47.7	4.2
Brazil	5.4	6.4	6.8	7.1	8.7	10.6	12.7	15.2	3.4
Other Central/South America	8.3	10.4	10.9	13.9	17.7	22.0	26.7	32.4	4.7
Total Developing	87.4	115.7	120.6	137.6	169.6	202.8	238.2	279.2	3.6
Total World	343.8	365.6	375.5	402.7	454.3	504.2	555.1	611.8	2.1

[a]Includes the 50 States and the District of Columbia. U.S. Territories are included in Australasia.

Notes: EE/FSU = Eastern Europe/Former Soviet Union. Energy totals include net imports of coal coke and electricity generated from biomass in the United States. Totals may not equal sum of components due to independent rounding. The electricity portion of the national fuel consumption values consists of generation for domestic use plus an adjustment for electricity trade based on a fuel's share of total generation in the exporting country.

Sources: History: Energy Information Administration (EIA), International Energy Annual 1996, DOE/EIA-0219(96) (Washington, DC, February 1998). Projections: EIA, Annual Energy Outlook 1999, DOE/EIA-0383(99) (Washington, DC, December 1998), Table A1; and World Energy Projection System (1999).

Despite the current economic problems affecting the countries outside the industrialised world, energy consumption in the developing world (defined as developing Asia, Africa, the Middle East, and Central and South America) is expected to more than double over the next two decades, with highest growth rates expected in developing Asia and Central and South America. Indeed, energy use in the developing world is projected to surpass that of the industrialised world by 6 percent in 2020 - some 16 quadrillion Btu - whereas in 1996 energy consumption in the developing countries was about 40 percent lower than that in the industrialised countries (see Table 14).

Table 14. World Total Energy Consumption by Region and Fuel, 1990-2020, (Quadrillion Btu)

Region/ Country	History			Projections					Average Annual Percent Change, 1996-2020
	1990	1995	1996	2000	2005	2010	2015	2020	
Industrialised Countries									
North America									
Oil	40.4	41.8	43.2	47.0	49.8	53.5	56.3	59.1	1.3
Natural Gas	22.7	26.2	26.8	28.2	31.8	35.1	38.4	40.5	1.7
Coal	20.4	21.1	22.0	24.3	24.9	25.7	26.8	28.1	1.0
Nuclear	7.0	8.3	8.2	8.0	7.6	6.8	5.4	4.5	-2.5
Other	9.2	10.6	11.4	11.7	12.9	13.8	14.4	15.2	1.2
Total	99.7	108.0	111.6	119.3	126.9	134.9	141.3	147.5	1.2
Western Europe									
Oil	25.8	28.0	28.2	29.8	30.6	31.5	32.2	33.0	0.7
Natural Gas	9.9	12.2	13.7	15.7	18.4	20.8	23.8	27.1	2.9
Coal	12.5	9.1	9.1	8.4	7.8	7.3	6.9	6.4	-1.4
Nuclear	7.4	8.2	8.6	8.9	8.9	8.6	8.0	7.3	-0.7
Other	4.4	4.8	4.5	4.8	5.7	6.3	7.0	7.6	2.2
Total	60.0	62.3	64.0	67.6	71.3	74.6	77.9	81.5	1.0
Industrialised Asia									
Oil	12.5	14.1	14.3	13.9	14.4	15.2	15.9	16.7	0.7
Natural Gas	2.9	3.3	3.6	3.4	5.1	4.9	5.5	6.0	2.2
Coal	4.2	4.6	4.7	4.6	5.2	5.3	5.3	5.4	0.6
Nuclear	2.0	2.8	2.9	3.1	3.1	3.8	3.7	3.7	1.0
Other	1.4	1.4	1.4	1.3	1.8	1.8	1.9	2.0	1.6
Total	23.0	26.3	26.9	26.3	29.6	30.9	32.4	33.9	1.0

Total Industrialised									
Oil	78.7	83.9	85.7	90.7	94.7	100.2	104.5	108.9	1.0
Natural Gas	35.5	41.8	44.0	47.4	55.3	60.8	67.7	73.7	2.2
Coal	37.2	34.8	35.8	37.3	37.8	38.3	39.1	40.0	0.5
Nuclear	16.3	19.4	19.8	20.0	19.6	19.2	17.0	15.5	-1.0
Other	15.0	16.8	17.2	17.8	20.3	21.9	23.3	24.8	1.5
Total	182.7	196.6	202.5	213.1	227.8	240.4	251.6	262.8	1.1
EE/FSU									
Oil	21.0	12.4	12.0	12.5	12.7	13.4	13.9	14.4	0.8
Natural Gas	26.0	21.4	21.7	22.2	26.4	30.2	34.0	38.7	2.4
Coal	20.8	13.8	13.0	11.8	11.8	11.1	10.2	9.1	-1.5
Nuclear	2.9	2.5	2.8	2.8	2.9	3.0	3.1	2.7	-0.2
Other	2.8	3.0	2.9	2.7	3.1	3.4	4.1	4.9	2.3
Total	73.6	53.2	52.4	52.0	56.9	61.0	65.3	69.8	1.2
Developing Countries									
Developing Asia									
Oil	16.0	23.6	24.8	28.4	32.4	38.7	45.5	50.9	3.0
Natural Gas	3.0	5.1	5.7	6.8	13.1	18.1	24.8	31.9	7.4
Coal	28.1	38.0	38.7	43.0	51.5	60.3	68.9	82.4	3.2
Nuclear	0.9	1.2	1.3	1.5	2.1	2.6	3.0	3.2	3.8
Other	3.2	4.0	4.0	4.8	7.0	7.9	8.7	9.6	3.7
Total	51.4	71.8	74.5	84.5	106.1	127.6	151.0	177.9	3.7
Middle East									
Oil	8.1	9.8	10.1	10.9	13.7	15.7	17.9	20.5	3.0
Natural Gas	3.9	5.2	5.7	7.3	7.8	9.0	10.2	11.4	2.9
Coal	0.8	0.8	0.9	1.0	1.0	1.1	1.1	1.1	1.1
Nuclear	0.0	0.0	0.0	0.0	0.0	0.1	0.2	0.2	--
Other	0.4	0.5	0.6	0.9	1.0	1.1	1.3	1.5	4.0
Total	13.1	16.4	17.3	20.1	23.5	27.0	30.6	34.7	2.9
Africa									
Oil	4.2	4.8	5.0	5.5	6.2	7.3	8.4	9.7	2.8
Natural Gas	1.4	1.9	2.0	2.1	2.7	3.1	3.4	3.7	2.7
Coal	3.0	3.3	3.4	3.5	3.8	4.0	4.1	4.3	1.0
Nuclear	0.1	0.1	0.1	0.1	0.1	0.1	0.1	0.1	-0.2
Other	0.6	0.6	0.6	0.7	0.9	1.0	1.1	1.2	2.8
Total	9.2	10.7	11.1	12.0	13.8	15.5	17.1	18.9	2.3
Central and South America									
Oil	6.9	8.0	8.1	9.7	12.9	15.1	17.4	20.3	3.9
Natural Gas	2.1	2.9	3.1	4.3	6.0	9.6	13.5	18.1	7.6
Coal	0.7	0.8	1.0	1.1	1.2	1.2	1.3	1.4	1.4
Nuclear	0.1	0.1	0.1	0.1	0.2	0.2	0.2	0.1	1.3

Other	3.9	5.1	5.4	5.8	6.1	6.5	7.1	7.7	1.5
Total	13.7	16.8	17.7	21.0	26.3	32.6	39.4	47.7	4.2
Total Developing Countries									
Oil	35.2	46.2	48.1	54.5	65.2	76.8	89.2	101.3	3.2
Natural Gas	10.5	15.0	16.5	20.5	29.6	39.8	51.9	65.1	5.9
Coal	32.5	42.9	43.9	48.7	57.5	66.6	75.5	89.2	3.0
Nuclear	1.1	1.4	1.5	1.7	2.4	3.0	3.5	3.6	3.6
Other	8.1	10.2	10.6	12.2	14.9	16.5	18.2	20.0	2.7
Total	87.4	115.7	120.6	137.6	169.6	202.8	238.2	279.2	3.6
Total World									
Oil	134.9	142.5	145.7	157.7	172.7	190.4	207.5	224.6	1.8
Natural Gas	72.0	78.1	82.2	90.1	111.3	130.8	153.6	177.5	3.3
Coal	90.6	91.6	92.8	97.7	107.1	116.0	124.8	138.3	1.7
Nuclear	20.4	23.3	24.1	24.5	24.9	25.2	23.6	21.7	-0.4
Other	25.9	30.1	30.7	32.7	38.3	41.9	45.6	49.7	2.0
Total	343.8	365.6	375.5	402.7	454.3	504.2	555.1	611.8	2.1

[a]Includes the 50 States and the District of Columbia. US Territories are included in Australasia.

Notes: EE/FSU = Eastern Europe/Former Soviet Union. Energy totals include net imports of coal coke and electricity generated from biomass in the United States. Totals may not equal sum of components due to independent rounding. The electricity portion of the national fuel consumption values consists of generation for domestic use plus an adjustment for electricity trade based on a fuel's share of total generation in the exporting country.

Sources: History: Energy Information Administration (EIA), International Energy Annual 1996, DOE/EIA-0219(96) (Washington, DC, February 1998). Projections: EIA, Annual Energy Outlook 1999, DOE/EIA-0383(99) (Washington, DC, December 1998), Table A1; and World Energy Projection System (1999).

The projections for Eastern Europe and the former Soviet Union (EE/FSU) have been lowered during the last year. Less than a year ago, most forecasting sources were projecting positive growth for Russia's economy - the largest economy in the FSU - and accelerating recovery in the years to come; but at the end of 1998 it seemed likely that there would be negative economic growth in 1999 with no positive growth expected before 2001.

In the industrialised countries, a major issue for the development of energy markets appears to be the possible impact of the Kyoto Climate Change Protocol, which would require reductions or limits to the growth of carbon emissions between 2008 and 2012, resulting in a combined 4-percent reduction in emissions relative to 1990 levels. As of March 15, 1999, 83 countries had signed the Kyoto Protocol; however, none of the countries had ratified to the end of 1999. Should the Kyoto Protocol enter into force, it could have profound effects on the use of energy in the industrialised world. If the Protocol's emissions targets were achieved solely by reducing fossil energy use, consumption of fossil fuels in the industrialised countries would be reduced by between 30 and 60 quadrillion Btu - equivalent to between 15 and 30 million barrels of oil per day. It is more likely, however, that fuel-switching opportunities will be used and that a more modest reduction in total fossil fuel use will be required. Emissions trading and other offsets (such as reforestation) that may be allowed under the Protocol could further lower the need for fossil fuel reductions; however, the specific mechanisms for such offsets have not yet been established.

An offset that could provide an alternative to reducing fossil fuel consumption is the concept of "joint implementation" under the Kyoto Protocol. Joint implementation is a mechanism by which emissions reduction projects could be undertaken by private parties or governments outside their own countries. The Kyoto Protocol proposes two parallel mechanisms to implement the concept of joint implementation: Article 6, under which projects undertaken in a participated country could generate emissions reduction units transferable to another participated country; and Article 12, the "clean development mechanism", under which projects undertaken in a non-participated country could generate certified emissions reductions transferable to a participated country to meet its emissions target

By the middle of 1998, declining world oil prices caused renewed efforts to lower oil production under the sponsorship of the Organisation of Petroleum Exporting Countries (OPEC). In both March and June, OPEC and key non-OPEC producers Mexico and Norway agreed to restrict their crude oil sales, and there were indications from several other producers that they would cut back production. Their efforts were not supported by Iraq, which wanted to increase oil sales. As a result, oil production management efforts had only modest success. OPEC's share of world oil supply is projected to increase significantly over the forecast horizon, but competitive forces are expected to remain strong enough to forestall efforts to increase real oil prices substantially.

The given estimation, based on "business as usual" assumptions, projects that every energy source except nuclear power will grow over the 1996 to 2020 forecast period, although renewable energy sources are not expected to grow as fast over the next 24 years as they have in the past. Worldwide, oil remains the dominant source of energy throughout the projection horizon, as it has since 1970. Oil's key role in the transportation sector - where it does not currently have any serious competition from other energy sources - helps to sustain its position among fuel sources. Oil use in the electric power sector is projected to decline in relative terms, but the fast-paced growth of personal transportation, especially in the developing world, will absorb any losses in the electricity sector (see Table 15).

Table 15. World Oil Consumption by Region, 1990-2020 (Million Barrels per Day)

Region/ Country	History			Projections					Average Annual Percent Change, 1996-2020
	1990	1995	1996	2000	2005	2010	2015	2020	
Industrialised Countries									
North America	20.4	21.3	22.0	23.6	25.5	27.4	28.8	30.2	1.3
United States[a]	17.0	17.7	18.3	19.5	21.2	22.7	23.7	24.7	1.2
Canada	1.7	1.8	1.8	2.0	2.0	2.1	2.2	2.3	1.0
Mexico	1.7	1.9	1.9	2.0	2.3	2.6	2.9	3.3	2.4
Western Europe	12.5	13.5	13.7	14.4	14.8	15.3	15.6	16.0	0.7
United Kingdom	1.8	1.8	1.8	1.9	2.0	2.1	2.1	2.2	0.7
Francc	1.8	1.9	1.9	2.0	2.1	2.1	2.2	2.2	0.6
Germany	2.7	2.9	2.9	3.0	3.1	3.2	3.3	3.3	0.6
Italy	1.9	2.0	2.1	2.1	2.3	2.5	2.6	2.8	1.2
Netherlands	0.7	0.8	0.8	0.8	0.9	0.9	0.9	0.9	0.8
Other Western Europe	3.6	4.1	4.1	4.7	4.4	4.5	4.5	4.6	0.4
Industrialised Asia	6.2	7.0	7.1	6.8	7.1	7.5	7.9	8.3	0.7
Japan	5.1	5.7	5.9	5.6	5.7	6.0	6.3	6.6	0.5
Australasia	1.0	1.2	1.2	1.2	1.4	1.5	1.6	1.7	1.4
Total Industrialised	39.0	41.8	42.7	44.9	47.4	50.1	52.3	54.5	1.0
EE/FSU									
Former Soviet Union	8.4	4.6	4.4	4.4	4.5	4.7	4.9	5.2	0.7
Eastern Europe	1.6	1.3	1.3	1.6	1.6	1.7	1.7	1.7	1.0
Total EE/FSU	10.0	5.9	5.7	6.0	6.1	6.4	6.6	6.9	0.8
Developing Countries									
Developing Asia	7.6	11.3	11.9	13.6	15.5	18.5	21.8	24.3	3.0
China	2.3	3.3	3.5	4.6	5.0	6.4	8.1	8.8	3.8
India	1.2	1.6	1.7	1.9	2.6	3.1	3.5	4.1	3.8
South Korea	1.0	2.0	2.2	2.1	2.8	3.4	4.0	4.7	3.3
Other Asia	3.1	4.3	4.5	5.0	5.1	5.7	6.3	6.8	1.8
Middle East	3.9	4.7	4.8	5.2	6.5	7.5	8.5	9.8	3.0
Turkey	0.5	0.6	0.6	0.7	0.9	1.0	1.2	1.4	3.2

Africa	2.1	2.3	2.4	2.7	3.0	3.5	4.1	4.7	2.8
Central and South America	3.4	3.9	4.0	4.8	6.3	7.4	8.5	10.0	3.9
Brazil	1.3	1.5	1.5	1.6	1.9	2.3	2.8	3.4	3.4
Other Central/South America	2.1	2.4	2.5	3.2	4.5	5.1	5.8	6.6	4.2
Total Developing	17.0	22.2	23.1	26.2	31.4	37.0	42.9	48.7	3.2
Total World	66.0	69.9	71.5	77.1	84.8	93.5	101.8	110.1	1.8

[a]Includes the 50 States and the District of Columbia. US Territories are included in Australasia.

Notes: EE/FSU = Eastern Europe/Former Soviet Union. Totals may not equal sum of components due to independent rounding. The electricity portion of the national fuel consumption values consists of generation for domestic use plus an adjustment for electricity trade based on a fuel's share of total generation in the exporting country.

Sources: History: Energy Information Administration (EIA), International Energy Annual 1996, DOE/EIA-0219(96) (Washington, DC, February 1998). Projections: EIA, Annual Energy Outlook 1999, DOE/EIA-0383(99) (Washington, DC, December 1998), Table A21; and World Energy Projection System (1999).

Table 16. World Natural Gas Consumption by Region, 1990-2020 (Trillion Cubic Feet)

Region/ Country	History			Projections					Average Annual Percent Change, 1996-2020
	1990	1995	1996	2000	2005	2010	2015	2020	
Industrialised Countries									
North America	22.0	25.4	26.0	27.4	30.8	34.0	37.3	39.3	1.7
United States[a]	18.7	21.6	21.9	22.5	25.2	28.0	30.8	32.3	1.6
Canada	2.4	2.9	3.1	3.3	3.6	3.8	4.1	4.5	1.7
Mexico	0.9	1.0	1.0	1.5	2.0	2.1	2.3	2.5	3.8
Western Europe	10.1	12.4	13.8	15.8	18.5	20.9	23.8	27.1	2.9
United Kingdom	2.1	2.7	3.2	3.9	4.5	5.0	5.5	6.1	2.8
France	1.0	1.2	1.3	1.5	1.8	2.1	2.4	3.0	3.4
Germany	2.7	3.4	3.7	4.2	4.9	5.7	6.7	7.5	3.0
Italy	1.7	1.9	2.0	2.2	2.3	2.4	2.6	2.8	1.4
Netherlands	1.5	1.7	1.9	2.1	2.2	2.3	2.4	2.6	1.4
Other Western Europe	1.2	1.6	1.8	1.9	2.9	3.4	4.3	5.2	4.6
Industrialised	2.6	3.1	3.3	3.2	4.7	4.5	5.1	5.5	2.2

Asia									
Japan	1.9	2.2	2.4	2.1	3.6	3.4	3.9	4.4	2.5
Australasia	0.8	0.9	0.9	1.1	1.1	1.1	1.1	1.2	1.1
Total Industrialised	34.8	41.0	43.1	46.4	54.0	59.5	66.2	72.0	2.2
EE/FSU									
Former Soviet Union	25.0	20.6	20.7	20.6	23.9	26.5	29.4	33.0	2.0
Eastern Europe	3.1	2.7	2.9	3.5	4.7	6.2	7.5	8.9	4.8
Total EE/FSU	28.1	23.4	23.7	24.1	28.6	32.7	36.8	41.9	2.4
Developing Countries									
Developing Asia	3.0	4.7	5.3	6.2	12.0	16.5	22.6	28.9	7.3
China	0.5	0.6	0.7	1.3	2.9	4.3	7.0	9.5	11.7
India	0.4	0.6	0.7	1.2	1.9	2.8	3.8	5.0	8.6
South Korea	0.1	0.3	0.5	0.6	0.8	1.1	1.4	1.9	6.1
Other Asia	1.9	3.2	3.5	3.0	6.4	8.3	10.2	12.4	5.4
Middle East	3.7	5.0	5.4	7.0	7.4	8.6	9.7	10.9	2.9
Turkey	0.1	0.2	0.3	0.6	0.6	0.7	0.9	1.1	5.9
Africa	1.4	1.7	1.8	1.9	2.4	2.8	3.1	3.3	2.7
Central and South America	2.0	2.6	2.9	4.0	5.6	8.9	12.5	16.8	7.6
Brazil	0.1	0.2	0.2	0.3	1.0	1.7	2.6	3.5	12.5
Other Central/South America	1.9	2.4	2.7	3.7	4.6	7.2	10.0	13.4	6.9
Total Developing	10.1	14.0	15.4	19.1	27.5	36.8	47.8	59.9	5.8
Total World	73.0	78.3	82.2	89.6	110.1	129.0	150.9	173.8	3.2

[a]Includes the 50 States and the District of Columbia. US Territories are included in Australasia.

Notes: EE/FSU = Eastern Europe/Former Soviet Union. Totals may not equal sum of components due to independent rounding. The electricity portion of the national fuel consumption values consists of generation for domestic use plus an adjustment for electricity trade based on a fuel's share of total generation in the exporting country. To convert cubic feet to cubic meters, divide each number in the table by 35.315.

Sources: History: Energy Information Administration (EIA), International Energy Annual 1996, DOE/EIA-0219(96) (Washington, DC, February 1998). Projections: EIA, Annual Energy Outlook 1999, DOE/EIA-0383(99) (Washington, DC, December 1998), Table A13; and World Energy Projection System (1999).

Natural gas is expected to be the fastest-growing primary energy source from 1996 to 2020. Worldwide consumption of natural gas increases by 3.3 percent per year (on a Btu basis) over the 24-year projection period, nearly twice as fast as oil (1.8 percent per year) and coal (1.7 percent per year). Gas is increasingly the fuel of choice for new electric power generation, primarily because combined-cycle gas turbine plants tend to be less expensive to build and are more efficient than other means of power generation. It is also a fuel of choice for environmental reasons. Local air pollution can be lessened by shifting from coal to natural-gas-fired generation. On a Btu basis, carbon emissions from natural gas combustion are less than half those for coal. Within the next decade, natural gas use is expected to exceed coal consumption, with the margin growing ever larger in subsequent years (see Table 16).

Coal use worldwide is projected to increase by 2.4 billion short tons, from 5.2 to 7.6 billion short tons, between 1996 and 2020. Strongest growth in demand is projected for the developing world, where coal use increases by 3.0 percent per year over the next two decades. The worldwide increase in coal use is attributable mainly to increases in developing Asia – particularly, China and India. In the industrialised world, coal demand remains relatively flat through 2020, with average annual growth of 0.4 percent. Further, in Eastern Europe and the FSU (EE/FSU), coal consumption is projected to decline by 1.5 percent per year. There have been major declines in coal production and use in the EE/FSU since the social and political upheaval of the late 1980s and early 1990s. As the economies of the region recover, natural gas is expected to be used in place of those uses historically ascribed to coal (see Table 17).

Table 17. World Coal Consumption by Region, 1990-2020 (Million Short Tons)

Region/ Country	History			Projections					Average Annual Percent Change, 1996-2020
	1990	1995	1996	2000	2005	2010	2015	2020	
Industrialised Countries									
North America	957	1,013	1,056	1,166	1,196	1,236	1,296	1,366	1.1
United States[a]	896	941	983	1,092	1,120	1,156	1,211	1,275	1.1
Canada	55	59	60	58	57	57	61	67	0.5
Mexico	7	13	14	15	19	23	24	25	2.4
Western Europe	898	607	600	563	527	504	481	451	-1.2
United Kingdom	121	79	81	63	55	46	40	28	-4.3
France	36	26	26	20	14	8	7	6	-6.1
Germany	528	298	290	277	266	259	250	241	-0.8
Italy	25	20	19	19	20	19	19	17	-0.3
Netherlands	15	15	15	15	14	14	13	12	-1.0
Other Western Europe	173	170	170	169	158	158	152	148	-0.6
Industrialised	233	257	266	259	288	291	296	300	0.5

Asia									
Japan	125	140	144	135	163	166	170	172	0.7
Australasia	108	117	121	124	124	125	127	128	0.2
Total Industrialised	2,088	1,876	1,922	1,988	2,011	2,031	2,072	2,117	0.4
EE/FSU									
Former Soviet Union	848	508	472	399	395	388	368	339	-1.4
Eastern Europe	523	426	413	408	412	369	330	283	-1.6
Total EE/FSU	1,372	934	885	807	807	757	697	622	-1.5
Developing Countries									
Developing Asia	1,555	2,030	2,065	2,299	2,761	3,238	3,706	4,446	3.2
China	1,124	1,489	1,500	1,682	2,069	2,469	2,876	3,540	3.6
India	242	312	321	371	416	465	498	536	2.2
South Korea	42	51	58	62	65	77	86	90	1.9
Other Asia	148	178	186	183	210	228	247	280	1.7
Middle East	66	76	80	89	92	97	102	104	1.1
Turkey	60	67	72	79	80	88	91	93	1.1
Africa	152	172	174	183	198	208	215	222	1.0
Central and South America	30	32	40	45	47	50	52	57	1.4
Brazil	17	19	27	27	30	31	34	37	1.2
Other Central/South America	13	13	13	18	17	18	19	20	1.7
Total Developing	1,803	2,310	2,360	2,616	3,098	3,592	4,075	4,829	3.0
Total World	5,263	5,120	5,167	5,412	5,916	6,381	6,845	7,568	1.6

[a]Includes the 50 States and the District of Columbia. US Territories are included in Australasia.

Notes: EE/FSU = Eastern Europe/Former Soviet Union. Totals may not equal sum of components due to independent rounding. The electricity portion of the national fuel consumption values consists of generation for domestic use plus an adjustment for electricity trade based on a fuel's share of total generation in the exporting country. To convert short tons to metric tons, divide each number in the table by 1.102.

Sources: History: Energy Information Administration (EIA), International Energy Annual 1996, DOE/EIA-0219(96) (Washington, DC, February 1998). Projections: EIA, Annual Energy Outlook 1999, DOE/EIA-0383(99) (Washington, DC, December 1998), Table A16; and World Energy Projection System (1999).

Nuclear power is the only primary energy source projected to decline over the forecast period. After peaking at 2,390 billion kilowatt-hours worldwide in 2010, nuclear energy use is projected to decline to 2,068 billion kilowatt-hours in 2020. The worldwide decline is attributed to retirements of nuclear facilities in the industrialised world and in the FSU, where countries are operating older reactors and have other, more economical options for new generating capacity. In the developing world - especially developing Asia - increases in nuclear power generation still are planned in China, India, and South Korea. In addition, it is possible that ratification of the Kyoto Protocol could modify the outlook for nuclear power in the countries, where the operating lives of nuclear facilities could potentially be extended to constrain greenhouse gas emissions (see Table 18).

Table 18. World Nuclear Energy Consumption by Region, 1990-2020
(Billion Kilowatt-hours)

Region/ Country	History			Projections					Average Annual Percent Change, 1996-2020
	1990	1995	1996	2000	2005	2010	2015	2020	
Industrialised Countries									
North America	649	774	770	746	710	633	498	422	-2.5
United States[a]	577	673	675	659	630	554	419	359	-2.6
Canada	69	93	88	79	72	72	72	56	-1.9
Mexico	3	8	7	8	8	8	8	8	0.3
Western Europe	703	785	824	850	844	821	757	693	-0.7
United Kingdom	59	77	82	82	82	80	76	70	-0.6
France	298	358	376	400	401	409	411	395	0.2
Germany	145	146	154	159	151	132	106	106	-1.5
Italy	0	0	0	0	0	0	0	0	0.0
Netherlands	3	4	4	3	3	3	0	0	-100.0
Other Western Europe	198	200	208	207	207	198	165	122	-2.2
Industrialised Asia	192	277	283	299	305	368	363	358	1.0
Japan	192	277	283	299	305	368	363	358	1.0
Australasia	0	0	0	0	0	0	0	0	0.0
Total Industrialised	1,544	1,837	1,877	1,896	1,859	1,822	1,619	1,473	-1.0
EE/FSU									
Former Soviet Union	201	172	194	195	194	202	213	182	-0.3
Eastern Europe	54	57	60	60	73	70	68	61	0.1
Total EE/FSU	256	229	254	255	267	272	281	243	-0.2
Developing Countries									
Developing	88	117	128	149	205	258	296	312	3.8

Asia									
China	0	12	14	13	38	69	88	112	9.2
India	6	6	7	9	14	22	33	43	7.6
South Korea	50	64	70	92	100	107	116	106	1.7
Other Asia	32	34	37	35	53	59	60	51	1.4
Middle East	0	0	0	0	0	10	17	17	0.0
Turkey	0	0	0	0	0	0	6	6	0.0
Africa	8	11	12	11	11	11	11	11	-0.2
Central and South America	9	9	9	10	15	17	17	13	1.3
Brazil	2	2	2	3	8	9	9	9	5.7
Other Central/South America	7	7	7	7	7	8	8	4	-2.4
Total Developing	105	138	149	170	232	296	341	353	3.7
Total World	1,905	2,203	2,280	2,321	2,358	2,390	2,241	2,068	-0.4

[a]Includes the 50 States and the District of Columbia. US Territories are included in Australasia.

Notes: EE/FSU = Eastern Europe/Former Soviet Union. Totals may not equal sum of components due to independent rounding. The electricity portion of the national fuel consumption values consists of generation for domestic use plus an adjustment for electricity trade based on a fuel's share of total generation in the exporting country. Sources: History: Energy Information Administration (EIA), International Energy Annual 1996, DOE/EIA-0219(96) (Washington, DC, February 1998). Projections: EIA, Annual Energy Outlook 1999, DOE/EIA-0383(99) (Washington, DC, December 1998), Table A8; and World Energy Projection System (1999).

Hydroelectricity and other renewable resources maintain an 8-percent share of total energy consumption throughout the projection period. The growth of renewable resources is expected to be restrained somewhat by low fossil fuel prices, which discourage the development of renewable energy sources. As with nuclear power, ratification of the Kyoto Protocol could help renewable energy gain market share if the signatory countries used non-carbon-emitting energy sources to reduce their reliance on fossil fuels and consequently, reduce their greenhouse gas emissions. In Western Europe there is increasing activity in renewable installations, involving particularly wind-generated electricity. The German government announced in December 1998 that Germany's renewable energy use expanded by 30 percent between 1996 and 1997, to 5 billion kilowatt-hours; however, this still represents only about 1 percent of the nation's total electricity consumption (see Table 19).

Table 19. World Consumption of Hydroelectricity and Other Renewable Energy by Regions, 1990-2020 (Quadrillion Btu)

Region/ Country	History			Projections					Average Annual Percent Change, 1996-2020
	1990	1995	1996	2000	2005	2010	2015	2020	
Industrialised Countries									
North America	9.2	10.6	11.4	11.7	12.9	13.8	14.4	15.2	1.2
United States[a]	5.8	6.8	7.3	7.3	7.5	7.8	8.2	8.6	0.7
Canada	3.1	3.4	3.6	4.0	4.8	5.2	5.4	5.7	1.9
Mexico	0.3	0.4	0.4	0.5	0.6	0.7	0.8	0.9	3.2
Western Europe	4.4	4.8	4.5	4.8	5.7	6.3	7.0	7.6	2.2
United Kingdom	0.1	0.1	0.0	0.1	0.2	0.3	0.4	0.5	10.1
France	0.6	0.7	0.7	0.7	0.8	0.9	1.0	1.0	1.8
Germany	0.2	0.2	0.2	0.3	0.5	0.6	0.8	0.9	6.3
Italy	0.4	0.5	0.5	0.5	0.5	0.6	0.6	0.6	1.0
Netherlands	0.0	0.0	0.0	0.0	0.1	0.1	0.2	0.3	18.8
Other Western Europe	3.2	3.3	3.1	3.1	3.6	3.8	4.0	4.3	1.4
Industrialised Asia	1.4	1.4	1.4	1.3	1.8	1.8	1.9	2.0	1.6
Japan	1.0	0.9	0.9	0.8	1.2	1.1	1.2	1.2	1.4
Australasia	0.4	0.5	0.5	0.6	0.6	0.6	0.7	0.8	1.9
Total Industrialised	15.0	16.8	17.2	17.8	20.3	21.9	23.3	24.8	1.5
EE/FSU									
Former Soviet Union	2.4	2.5	2.2	2.1	2.3	2.4	2.6	2.9	1.1
Eastern Europe	0.4	0.6	0.6	0.6	0.7	1.0	1.5	2.0	4.9
Total EE/FSU	2.8	3.0	2.9	2.7	3.1	3.4	4.1	4.9	2.3
Developing Countries									
Developing Asia	3.2	4.0	4.0	4.8	7.0	7.9	8.7	9.6	3.7
China	1.3	1.9	1.9	2.2	3.8	4.2	4.4	4.5	3.7
India	0.7	0.7	0.7	1.2	1.4	1.6	2.1	2.6	5.3
South Korea	0.1	0.1	0.1	0.1	0.1	0.1	0.2	0.2	6.2
Other Asia	1.1	1.3	1.3	1.3	1.7	1.9	2.1	2.3	2.2
Middle East	0.4	0.5	0.6	0.9	1.0	1.1	1.3	1.5	4.0
Turkey	0.2	0.4	0.4	0.5	0.5	0.5	0.6	0.6	1.6
Africa	0.6	0.6	0.6	0.7	0.9	1.0	1.1	1.2	2.8
Central and South America	3.9	5.1	5.4	5.8	6.1	6.5	7.1	7.7	1.5
Brazil	2.2	2.7	2.8	2.8	3.0	3.0	3.2	3.3	0.7

Other Central/South America	1.7	2.4	2.6	2.9	3.1	3.5	3.9	4.4	2.3
Total Developing	8.1	10.2	10.6	12.2	14.9	16.5	18.2	20.0	2.7
Total World	25.9	30.1	30.7	32.7	38.3	41.9	45.6	49.7	2.0

[a]Includes the 50 States and the District of Columbia. US Territories are included in Australasia.

Notes: EE/FSU = Eastern Europe/Former Soviet Union. Totals may not equal sum of components due to independent rounding. The electricity portion of the national fuel consumption values consists of generation for domestic use plus an adjustment for electricity trade based on a fuel's share of total generation in the exporting country. US totals include net electricity imports, methanol, and liquid hydrogen.

Sources: History: Energy Information Administration (EIA), International Energy Annual 1996, DOE/EIA-0219(96) (Washington, DC, February 1998). Projections: EIA, Annual Energy Outlook 1999, DOE/EIA-0383(99) (Washington, DC, December 1998), Table A1; and World Energy Projection System (1999).

World net electricity consumption is expected to increase from 12 trillion kilowatt-hours in 1996 to 22 trillion kilowatt-hours in 2020. The economic troubles of Southeast Asia and Russia are expected to slow the growth in electricity demand over the next few years, but electricity demand in the developing countries still is projected to increase by a robust average of 4.4 percent per year, and the strongest long-term growth is projected for the developing countries of Asia, as well as Central and South America (see Table 20). Rapid population growth, along with greater industrialisation and more widespread household electrification, will increase electricity use in those regions. In the industrialised countries, annual growth in net electricity consumption is projected to average around 1.6 percent over the next two decades, primarily because of the continuing spread of electricity-using equipment.

Table 20. World Electricity Consumption by Region, 1990-2020 (Billion Kilowatt-hours)

Region/ Country	History			Projections					Average Annual Percent Change, 1996-2020
	1990	1995	1996	2000	2005	2010	2015	2020	
Industrialised Countries									
North America	3,255	3,759	3,859	4,004	4,329	4,671	5,028	5,359	1.4
United States[a]	2,713	3,163	3,243	3,333	3,585	3,843	4,113	4,345	1.2
Canada	435	462	473	506	536	577	616	657	1.4
Mexico	107	134	144	164	208	251	299	357	3.9
Western Europe	2,064	2,209	2,245	2,380	2,635	2,893	3,174	3,473	1.8
United Kingdom	286	301	305	318	351	381	412	445	1.6
France	324	365	378	402	440	483	527	570	1.7
Germany	485	473	473	483	539	598	662	727	1.8
Italy	222	247	248	278	320	364	413	466	2.7
Netherlands	71	82	85	94	105	117	130	144	2.2
Other Western Europe	675	742	756	804	879	950	1,030	1,121	1.7
Industrialised Asia	930	1,068	1,090	1,146	1,335	1,437	1,547	1,653	1.8
Japan	750	864	882	894	1,053	1,127	1,204	1,280	1.6
Australasia	180	204	207	251	281	310	343	373	2.5
Total Industrialised	6,248	7,037	7,194	7,529	8,298	9,001	9,749	10,485	1.6
EE/FSU									
Former Soviet Union	1,488	1,168	1,133	1,000	1,089	1,164	1,245	1,331	0.7
Eastern Europe	420	384	401	396	448	509	568	634	1.9
Total EE/FSU	1,908	1,552	1,535	1,396	1,536	1,673	1,813	1,965	1.0
Developing Countries									
Developing Asia	1,268	1,912	2,002	2,350	3,105	3,937	4,918	6,122	4.8
China	551	881	925	1,107	1,520	2,030	2,672	3,486	5.7
India	257	367	378	493	644	802	981	1,192	4.9
South Korea	95	162	181	190	237	285	335	387	3.2
Other Asia	365	501	519	560	704	819	930	1,056	3.0
Middle East	272	371	386	440	525	619	719	826	3.2
Turkey	51	76	85	128	179	262	327	452	7.2
Africa	285	320	332	371	454	544	637	746	3.4
Central and	449	575	604	735	950	1,182	1,421	1,728	4.5

South America									
Brazil	229	288	303	336	440	574	734	939	4.8
Other Central/South America	220	286	301	399	509	608	687	789	4.1
Total Developing	2,274	3,178	3,324	3,895	5,033	6,282	7,695	9,422	4.4
Total World	10,431	11,767	12,053	12,821	14,868	16,956	19,257	21,872	2.5

[a]Includes the 50 States and the District of Columbia. US Territories are included in Australasia.
Notes: EE/FSU = Eastern Europe/Former Soviet Union. Electricity consumption equals generation plus imports minus exports minus distribution losses.
Sources: History: Energy Information Administration (EIA), International Energy Annual 1996, DOE/EIA-0219(96) (Washington, DC, February 1998), Table 6.2. Projections: EIA, Annual Energy Outlook 1999, DOE/EIA-0383(99) (Washington, DC, December 1998), Table A8; and World Energy Projection System (1999).

2 Evaluation of Energy

Five types of energies were classified. Now we shall consider the quality of energy, and which energy has the highest quality. If energy A is relatively easier to convert to energy B but energy B is relatively harder to convert to energy A, then the quality of energy A is defined as being higher than that of B. The ranking of energy quality is also defined in a similar way.

This classification can be easily understood when considering the same type of energy, for example, the energy of a moving body has higher quality when it moves with higher velocity, heat with higher temperature has higher quality, light with higher frequency has higher quality, and so on. Similar concepts are applied to classify the five types of energies:

(1) Conversion between mechanical energy and electrical energy is achieved with very high efficiency. The turbine generator and the electromotor have nearly the same efficiency, therefore we cannot say which has the higher quality. However, the only electrical energy which exists in natural circumstance is lightning, while many mechanical energies exist. Therefore electromagnetic energy is ranked first, followed by mechanical energy.

(2) Photon energy can be produced by electric current, but this process requires heat with high temperature. Mechanical energy can hardly be converted to photon energy, but photons exert mechanical pressure upon the comets. However, this condition is not true in terrestrial circumstances and we may say that mechanical energy is still of higher ranking on earth. Moreover, photons can be converted very easily to heat. Photon energy is therefore, ranked third.

(3) Any kind of energy eventually becomes heat with low temperature and hence heat energy has the lowest ranking. The higher the temperature of heat, the higher the quality of energy.

(4) Insofar as chemical energy is concerned, it can be converted easily to heat, but is difficult to change to other kinds of energies and is therefore, ranked before heat.

The order of the energy quality ranking is thus: (1) Electromagnetic (2) Mechanical (3) Photon (4) Chemical (5) Heat.

Another scientific analysis of energy ranking is the concept of "availability" that was proposed by the late W. Thomson in 1851. His scientific investigation was continued by Z. Rant in Germany and developed as "die Exergie" (the exergy). This concept indicates that the available energy can be estimated by taking its circumstances into account. For example the availability of photon energy in space is much higher than that on earth.

3 Cost Evaluation

Primary energies are classified as (i) fossil fuels (coal, oil, natural gas, etc.), (ii) nuclear energy, and (iii) natural energy (solar energy, hydro power, wind power, etc.). The cost of primary energy is composed of the searching cost (*R*), the development cost (*D*), and the operation cost (*W*). The total cost (*T*) is given by

$$T = R + D = W .$$

We shall consider, first, the searching cost (Ohta 1994). If the total cost paid to search for the primary energy resource is R_0, and the total quantity of the resource reserve is Q_0, then the depreciation to the search investment is given by

$$R = (R_0 / Q_0) F(n) ,$$

where $F(n)$ is a function of the years *n* since the resource began producing. The unit of *R* is [$/t]. Even using modern, advanced technologies, it is very difficult and expensive to locate oil or gas fields. The chance of locating a big oil field with reserves of more than 10^8 [t] is less than 0.1%.

The investment R_0 must be depreciated with an interest ϵ per year. If the life time of the resource reserves is *n* years and the depreciation is paid equally every year of production, then

$$F(n) = (1+\varepsilon)^n [(1+\varepsilon)^n - 1] .$$

In the same way, we have for the depreciation of the development cost

$$D(n) = D_0 F(n) / Q_0 .$$

The operation cost W is composed of (1) personal expenses, (2) maintenance (repair, supply, etc.), (3) earnings (dividend, saving, etc., excluding interest), (4) taxes, (5) insurance, (6) preservation of safety, (7) public associations, and (8) other expenses.

The evaluation described above is the simplest way to estimate costs, and if the decrease of the reserved amount is taken into account, the factor Q_0 is replaced by $Q_0G(n)$:

$$Q_0C(n') = q\sum_{x=0}^{n'}(1-d)^x$$

where q is the annual output quantity of the n'-th production year since the oil field or the coal mine or gas field first commenced. If d, the annual decline rate of the output, is independent of n and $q = q_0$ is a constant, then we have

$$Q_0C(n') = (q_0/d)(1-d)^n .$$

Referring to equations given in this paragraph, we may conclude that the low cost of a primary energy is obtained under the conditions: (1) large Q_0, i.e., the most important factor is that the total quantity of reserves is large, (2) large n, i.e., the number of depreciation years is long, with small interest ϵ, (3) small d, i.e., the annual decline rate of output must be small, and (4) small W.

However, the actual price of the primary energy is usually decided by the policies of the exporting and importing countries. The theoretical cost conditions are much better in the Middle East than in other regions.

As an example of secondary energy we shall use electrical energy. However, the discussion described below can be generalised to any secondary product, such as city gas, oil refining, and so on.

If the price of the secondary energy that is produced from a facility with an output capacity of N [kW] is Ts [$/kWh], then we have

$$T_s = [IF(n)]/(8{,}760w) + 860P/(\eta q) + W/(8{,}760N),$$

where the first, the second, and the third terms of the right hand side of the given equation represent the plant depreciation cost, the fuel cost, and the operation cost, respectively. The newly introduced parameters are: I [$/kW], the construction cost of the plant per [kW], 8,760w is the operation hours in a year; P the price of the primary energy per 1 [t] and 860 indicates the kcal equivalent to 1 [kWh] (= 860 [kcal]); η, the conversion efficiency from heat energy (primary energy) to electrical energy (secondary energy), q [kcal/t], the heat energy density of the fuel.

Requiring a low price for T_s it is obvious that a small I, W and large w, q and N are necessary.

3.1 Costs of Transport

Practical and popularised energy transport schemes are classified roughly into (1) batch, (2) pipeline, and (3) utility power line.

The standard is taken as the pipeline transportation of oil. The cost estimation is not exact because it is different, case by case, depending upon time and place. Our new estimation states that the cost of electric power transport is reduced by 1/3, because the quality of electric power is 3 times that compared to oil, gas, and coal in caloric equivalence. The reason is that the conversion efficiency from the fuels to electric power is about 1/3.

The cost T of energy transport is evaluated as

$$T = D + W,$$

where D is depreciation cost of the energy transport facility (tanker, train, pipeline, utility power line etc.) and W is the operation cost.

(1) Transport of oil by pipeline. The depreciation cost is much higher than the operation cost, and the investment cost per unit distance is independent of the total distance, therefore the transport cost [$/(kJ-km)l is nearly constant. In order to compensate for the pressure drop, the flowing oil is pressurised at pumping stations. This cost is small compared to the investment costs.

(2) Gas transport by pipeline. This is about 1.8-2 times more costly compared to that of oil. The reason is simple: the transportable energy density is much smaller than that of oil, in spite of higher volumetric transporting speed.

(3) Batch type. The cheapest energy transport is due to batch type processing such as a tanker where the depreciation cost is also overwhelming. Transportation fees increase with distance, while the operational cost does not increase so sharply compared to the fee.

(4) LNG tanker. Investment cost per transportable calorie of a LNG tanker is much higher than that of an oil tanker because (i) the transportable energy is less, and (ii) the associated heat-insulating equipment is more costly.

(5) Coal transport. The reason that the cost of coal transport by conventional railway is high is due to the tariff, imposed by railway companies.

(6) Utility power line. Energy transport by utility power line is most costly. This is due to the costs of facility depreciation and operation being comparatively high.

3.2 Political Cost

The economic superiority of fossil fuels and nuclear energy have been demonstrated in the above section. For this reason, more than 88% of the primary energy in the world in recent years has been generated from fossil fuels. However, the exhaust gases from combusted fossil fuels have accumulated to an extent where serious damage is being done to the global environment. The exhaust gases can be classified into the three kinds. The first group is composed of water vapour (H_2O), carbon dioxide (CO_2), and nitrogen dioxide (NO_2). These are not naturally injurious, and their emission control is impossible. Water vapour recycles in three days at most. Carbon dioxide is quite harmless, but contributes to the greenhouse effect (GHE) that locks heat within the atmosphere by preventing the escape of thermic rays from the earth. The accumulated amount is estimated at *ca.* 750×109 [cet] (carbon equivalent ton - one [cet] is equivalent to 11/3 [t] of CO_2), and the global temperature is increasing. The century-long global warming is to be about 0.5°C for the period from 1900 to 1990.

We shall now mention the global damage due to the global temperature rise. Firstly, by unusual change of weather affects agricultural products and, secondly the surface level of the sea has risen. Assuming that the average depth of the seas in the world is 3,795 [m], the coefficient of volume expansion is 2×10^{-4}/°C, and the sectional areas of the seas are constant, then we can assume an approximate sea level rise of about 80 [cm/°C]. In addition, the ice mountains on the Antarctic continent will melt and the surface level of the sea will rise up an additional 30-40 [cm/°C]. Thus most of the coastal industrial and metropolitan zones will sink down below the seawater. The resulting damage is too huge to estimate.

The origins of global warming are energy utilisation (57%), CFCs (flons) (17%), agriculture (14%), and land development (9%). Energy utilisation implies the emission of exhaust gas which is almostly entirely CO_2.

The second and third groups have both directly and indirectly harmful effects (e.g., disease of the respiratory organs and acid rain). However, these groups are subject to control in industrial countries, but are not yet controlled in developing countries.

It is expected that advanced technology will be more widely available to all countries in the near future, so that gas belonging to the second and third groups will no longer appear. The biggest problem then is how to control CO_2.

What are the real costs of energy? Despite the fact that many people believe that we in the non-communist world live in a "free market", there are two main areas where the market does not adequately account for the costs of energy use. These are the environmental degradation caused by the use of many types of energy, and government subsidies to various forms of energy. When some of the costs of energy use are placed on society rather than the individual consumer, it tends to result in increased energy use. The principle that polluters should pay for the damage they cause is becoming more widely accepted. Applying this principle to energy use would drastically affect the choices made by energy consumers. In addition, the type of energy we use has direct impacts on other economic factors such as local employment.

In "capitalist" countries such as those in North America, Western Europe and the rest of the non-communist world, the price of goods is generally determined by the "free market". Traditional economic theory says that prices are determined by market forces such as supply and demand. This holds true for many of the commodities traded on open markets; but, because energy is so important to the economy of every country, governments have often intervened in energy markets. Many different methods have been used to influence the energy use and energy choices of consumers. These include direct subsidies, such as tax breaks and research and development funding to specific energy sectors, and military spending.

In many countries, oil and other fossil fuels such as coal and natural gas have historically been seen as the backbone of industrial economy. For this reason, governments have directly subsidised the exploration, extraction and processing of these fuels through research and development money, tax credits and regulated prices. These costs are not included in the calculations in comparing the relative costs of different sources of electricity. Such direct subsidies, therefore, influence both our choice of energy supply and the market price of different sources of energy.

Governments also subsidise energy prices in more indirect ways. In 1989, it was estimated that the United States' military spent between $15 and $54 billion safeguarding oil supplies in the Middle East. The Gulf War in 1991 cost at least an additional $30 billion on top of the regular yearly expense. The most conservative estimate of military spending represents a government subsidy of $23.50 per barrel of oil imported into the US. This is a significant amount, approximately equal to the market price of a barrel of crude oil. If the cost of safeguarding oil supplies was paid for by oil consumers, gasoline prices at the pumps would be much higher.

Another area in which governments indirectly subsidise a specific type of energy is nuclear power. In most countries, operators of nuclear power plants are not liable for the full costs of any accidents. This means that nuclear operators do not require expensive insurance policies to cover the risks of an accident. Electricity produced by nuclear power is therefore cheaper for consumers than it would be if the insurance costs were internalised, and the risks of a nuclear accident are transferred to those living near the nuclear plants.

All energy use has some negative impact on the environment. Burning fossil fuels such as coal and oil produces emissions of greenhouse and acid gases which result in environmental pollution and global warming respectively. Fossil fuels are also responsible for urban air pollution (smog) and its associated health hazards. Nuclear power plants expose the environment to low levels of radiation during many stages of the nuclear fuel cycle, and also impose the risk of a major accident such as Chernobyl. Even renewable technologies using energy from the sun have some negative impacts on the environment. Hydro-electric dams, for example, can flood vast areas of land and damage aquatic ecosystems. In general, however, renewables such as solar and wind energy have a smaller impact on the environment than fossil fuels and nuclear power.

When the use of a commodity, gasoline for example, imposes a burden on society that is not covered by its stated price, this burden is called an externality. The costs of externalities are borne by parties who were not part of the transaction. In the case of gasoline, the damage caused by acid rain and global warming, and the health costs of urban air pollution, are not considered in the price when an automobile owner purchases his/her gasoline. This neglect of environmental externalities results in what has been referred to as the "tragedy of the commons", first used to describe overgrazing on public lands. Imperfect markets tend to distort the choices of consumers, leading to over-consumption and misuse of items such as clean air and water that are very difficult to assign a dollar value to, and are perceived as public goods, free for anybody to exploit.

It is interesting to note that the progress of human civilisation can be charted in terms of the internalisation of costs formerly left as externalities. In prehistoric times, the cost of raw materials was internalised in the price of goods by rules of private property and land ownership. Slowly, other costs have become internalised, such as labour, with the elimination of serfdom or slavery. Similarly, in some countries the costs of education, child care, health care and work-place safety are internalised through government regulations and taxation. There is a proposal in Europe to include the costs of global warming in energy prices, through a tax on carbon dioxide emissions. This may represent the next step in the progress of civilisation towards the internalisation of all costs.

One of the main reasons that externalities such as health problems and environmental damage have not been included in energy prices is that it is very hard to put a dollar value on such commodities. How much is clean air or water worth? If asked this question, it is likely that everybody would have a different answer. Actual damage to other commercial goods is a little bit easier to quantify. For example, it has been estimated that acid rain causes annual damages of $197 billion to commercial forests worldwide. In order to internalise the external cost of energy, some consensus must be reached on the value of such externalities.

Global warming is a growing concern worldwide. At this time it is virtually impossible to accurately calculate the monetary value of changes to the earth's climate. It is, however, possible to roughly calculate the amount of tax, which, if applied to fossil fuel use, could result in the stabilisation of carbon dioxide (CO_2) emissions. It has been estimated that such stabilisation could be achieved if world governments got together and imposed a tax on all fuels that emit CO_2 (coal, oil, natural gas) equivalent to $24 per barrel of oil. This so-called "carbon tax" has been discussed, especially in Europe; but it faces a great deal of resistance from energy intensive industries, and oil producers.

One final economic impact of energy use that is exceedingly difficult to quantify is employment. There is no doubt that different sources of energy create different numbers of jobs. The economic impact of job creation is very complicated and beyond the scope of this book. It will suffice to say that the local employment benefits of various energy sources has rarely been considered in our energy supply decisions.

It is very difficult to put a value on the external costs of energy use. Our failure to do so, and continuing government subsidies to certain energy sectors, influence the amount and type of energy used by consumers. While these distortions may benefit certain energy suppliers and consumers, they generally result in negative impacts on the environment and the economy as a whole. As the world becomes more aware of continuing environmental degradation, making polluters pay the full cost of their damage will become more common. Creating a true "free market" by internalising the external costs of energy use, and removing unequal subsidies, would go a long way towards reducing the negative impacts of energy use.

3.3 External Cost

According to Griffin & Steele (1986), external costs exist when "the private calculation of benefits or costs differs from society's valuation of benefits or costs". Pollution represents an external cost because damages associated with it are borne by society as a whole and are not reflected in market transactions.

Many analysts have attempted to quantify societal costs of pollution and other externalities associated with fossil fuel combustion, and some regulatory bodies have even attempted to crudely incorporate externality costs into investment decisions (Cohen et al. 1990, Hashem & Haites 1993). Efforts to incorporate externalities have generally been confined to the regulated sectors of the energy system (electricity, and to a lesser extent, natural gas).

Unfortunately, estimates of externality costs are often based on quite different assumptions, making comparisons difficult. Uncertainties in such estimates are large, and can even span orders of magnitude.

Exploitation of any energy source generates externalities, defined as societal costs that are not reflected in market transactions. A comprehensive analysis of external costs must treat each and every stage in the process, which makes any such calculation inherently difficult.

Figure 12 (Holdren 1981) presents insults, pathways, stresses, and costs. Insults are humankind's physical and chemical intrusions into the natural world. Pathways are those mechanisms by which insults are converted to stresses. Stresses, defined as changes in ambient conditions (social, political, or environmental), then lead directly to societal costs.

While it is often possible to quantify the size of the insult, the pathways may be so numerous or complicated that only the crudest approximations are possible. Even if it is possible to confidently predict stresses from a given insult, translating those stresses into societal costs is problematic.

***Insults** to Physical and Human Environment*
- Resources Used (land, water, energy)
- Material Effluents (NO_x, SO_2, CO_2)
- Non-Material Effluents (noise, radiation)
- Other Physical Transformations (dredging)
- Socio-political Influences (politics, employment)

***Pathways** (Convert Insults to Stresses)*
- Media (air, water, ice, soil, rock, biota)
- Processes (evaporation, diffusion, conduction)

***Stresses** (Physical or Social Consequences of Insults)*
- Altered ambient conditions (temperature, humidity, concentrations, EM fields)
- Altered physical or social processes

***Environmental and Social Costs** of Insults*
- Magnitudes of Consequences
- Temporal Distribution of Harm
- Spatial Distribution of Harm
- Coincidence of Risks and Benefits
- Scaling (linear or non-linear)
- Resistance to Remedy
- Irreversibility
- Visibility of Harm
- Quality of Evidence of Harm

Figure 12. Insults, pathways, stresses, and environmental costs

In general, external costs can be crudely characterised by equation:

$$\textit{Externality Cost} = \textit{Size of Insult} \times \textit{Value of Environmental Damage per unit of insult},$$

where *Externality Cost* = total external cost to society, in dollars; *Size of Insult* is expressed in physical units (lbs emitted or hectares degraded); and *Value of Environmental Damage* (VED) is expressed in dollars per physical unit of insult.

Externality costs must be normalised to some common unit of service for consistent comparison. This unit is *delivered* kWh, which includes transmission and distribution losses. For direct fuel consumption, the unit of service is MMBtu.

Consistent comparisons require that environmental insults from both energy efficiency and supply technologies must be included in externality assessments. Emissions from supply technologies are both direct (from the combustion of fossil fuels) and indirect (from the construction of the equipment and the extraction, processing, and the transport of the fuel).

Emissions from efficiency technologies are generally only of the indirect type. On balance, increasing the efficiency of end-use reduces emissions and other externalities.

Direct and indirect emissions for fossil fuels are calculated by DeLuchi et al. (1987b), Unnasch et al. (1989), Fritsche et al. (1989), Meridian Corp. (1989), and San Martin (1989). For a complete treatment of both direct and indirect emissions of carbon dioxide, NO_x and SO_2 associated with the latest fossil-fired co-generation and district heating technologies, see Krause et al. (1994a). The net emissions from co-generation vary by co-generation fuel, co-generation technology, and boiler fuel, and are rarely analysed.

Indirect emissions for nuclear power are calculated by Meridian Corp. (1989), San Martin (1989), and Fritsche et al. (1989), while emissions and other environmental insults for nuclear are calculated by Ottinger et al. (1990) and Krause et al. (1994b). Meridian Corp. (1989), and San Martin (1989) also show indirect emissions for renewable power sources.

Feist (1988) investigates eleven different insulating materials and wall compositions that are widely used in the FRG. He finds, based on process analyses for the manufacture and installation of alternative insulating systems by Marmé & Seeberger (1982), that for wall insulation thicknesses now typically applied in retrofits or new buildings in Europe (5-15 cm), indirect primary energy consumption can be neglected, since it amounts to less than five percent of the direct primary energy savings associated with installing the insulation. An analysis of efficiency technologies in the American context (Anderson 1987) came to a similar conclusion.

There are two basic approaches to calculating the value of incremental emissions reductions: "direct damage estimation" and "cost of abatement". Direct damage estimation involves calculating damages that can be definitively linked to emissions of a particular pollutant, in dollar terms (Hohmeyer 1988, Ottinger et al. 1990). For instance, Cavanagh et al. (1982) monetise and tally the human health and environmental effects due to coal consumption in new power plants. These effects include premature human deaths, increased health costs, potential famine induced by global warming, and other effects. Direct estimation is extremely difficult, even when there are relatively few pathways. Some of the most important effects are impossible to quantify, while others depend on pathways that we do not fully understand.

Cost of abatement approaches typically use the cost of pollution controls imposed by regulatory decisions as a proxy for the true externality costs imposed by a pollutant (Chernick & Caverhill 1989, Marcus 1989). This approach (sometimes called "revealed preferences") assumes that regulators' choices embody society's preferences for pollution control, that the marginal costs of mitigation are known, and that these marginal mitigation costs are incurred solely to reduce emissions of a single pollutant (i.e., that there are no other benefits to a pollution reduction investment).

If society's preferences are changing rapidly, abatement cost calculations may be misleading, because society's previous preferences for pollution control may not accurately represent its present preferences. If mitigation measures have multiple or incommensurate benefits, revealed preference calculations become difficult. For instance, the cost of an energy conservation measure cannot be used to estimate the true value of mitigating SO_2 emissions, since the conservation measure avoids power plants, reduces fuel use, and eliminates other pollutants (Krause & Koomey 1989). In contrast, the cost of flue-gas desulfurisation equipment or the price premium of low-sulphur oil over high-sulphur oil can be used without modification in abatement cost analysis, because the cost of these mitigation measures is incurred solely to reduce sulphur emissions.

Holdren (1980) identifies pitfalls in calculating total societal costs associated with energy technologies, which affect both direct estimation and cost of abatement approaches. These include: 1) inconsistent boundaries; 2) confusing average and marginal effects; 3) illusory precision; 4) environmental stochasticity; 5) "confusing things that are countable with things that count".

1) Inconsistent boundaries: boundaries must be drawn consistently to ensure that comparisons between estimates of external costs are fair. This principle implies that the service delivered by competing resources be identical, that all relevant stages of each resource be included in the comparison, and that geographic boundaries be drawn to include all external effects.

2) Average versus marginal comparisons: Hohmeyer (1988) calculates costs of externalities from the existing power supply mix in West Germany. While this calculation is useful to show total societal costs from power production, it will almost certainly be misleading to use these embedded externality costs per kWh to calculate the cost of externalities from either *new* power plants or from *marginal existing capacity*, both of which may have characteristics quite different from average existing plants.

3) Illusory precision: there are often large uncertainties in specifying the size of insults, in translating insults through pathways to stresses, in converting stresses to consequences, and in valuing consequences. To ignore such uncertainty by specifying single point estimates to many significant figures can be quite misleading, since it creates the illusion that the estimates are certain. To avoid misunderstandings, externality cost estimates should be assigned appropriate error bounds. Such uncertainty creates a quandary for regulators, since most regulatory determinations *must* be in terms of point estimates. Analysts can best serve regulators by making the uncertainties explicit and understandable.

4) Stochasticity: Environmental and social systems are often characterised by *stochasticity*, or probabilistic variability about some mean value. The most interesting and important interactions between human societies and the natural

world occur when one or both of these systems are far from their respective mean values. Overzealous averaging of important parameters may disguise damages that occur only under extreme conditions. For instance, calculations of damages from ambient air pollutant concentrations may yield vastly different results depending on how the concentrations are averaged over time. Damages may not be linearly related to pollutant concentration, and may only occur if concentrations exceed some threshold value. Calculating damages based on the annual average pollutant concentration might be misleading for these reasons. Daily or hourly averages sorted by concentration would give a more accurate picture.

5) "What's countable versus what counts": Analysts often focus on those things that are amenable to quantitative treatment. Yet the probabilities, consequences, and risk-adjusted expected costs of many important external effects (like nuclear sabotage, nuclear proliferation, or global warming) may be difficult or impossible to quantify, and may also be irreversible once the damages are incurred. Since the "facts" are uncertain or non-existent, and may not become certain before decisions need to be made, such costs can only be valued through the political process. In that circumstance, it is especially crucial that analysts' value judgements be made explicit.

There are huge uncertainties in assessing externality costs related to greenhouse gas emissions, and the exact values of these costs are probably unknowable. In spite of such uncertainties, it is clear that all emissions that contribute to global warming should be treated similarly. Carbon, which is the most important contributor to the global warming problem, is by no means the only one. Radiatively active trace gases like methane (CH_4), nitrous oxide (N_2O), and chlorofluorocarbons (CFCs) should all be assigned the same externality cost per unit of global warming contribution. The appendices in Krause et al. (1989) explain how to convert concentrations of the other gases into *equivalent* CO_2 *concentrations*, which can then be used to assign these gases externality costs (once the appropriate cost for CO_2 has been determined). Others have also derived "warming factors" that can be used to achieve the same result (e.g., Unnasch et al. (1989) and DeLuchi et al. (1987a)).

An important consideration for policymakers in this area is that "getting prices right" is not the end of the story. Many market failures affecting energy use will still remain after external costs are incorporated (Fisher & Rothkopf 1989, Koomey 1990b, Levine et al. 1994, Sanstad et al. 1993). They are amenable to a variety of non-price policies, including efficiency standards, and incentive, information, and research & development programs.

Estimates of the consequences of technological choices (including, but not limited to, estimates of externality costs) will always be inaccurate because many effects are spread geographically and chronologically, and the causal links are extremely complicated. As in all areas of life, externality policy must be made in the face of imperfect information. We can make action easier by looking for common ground and by undertaking policies that have multiple benefits. We must be prepared to experiment, to change course in response to new information, and to learn from our mistakes. To not incorporate externalities in prices is to implicitly assign a value of zero, a number that is demonstrably wrong.

4 The Economics of Energy

A sustainable energy future is compatible with strong economic growth. Moreover, pursuit of a sustainable energy path facilitates the realisation of sustainable socio-economic growth over the longer-term.

Investment in the energy sector accounts for 15 to 20% of all fixed capital investment in the world economy. Meeting energy-sector investment needs is particularly a problem in developing countries, where the capacity to finance investments is a major factor limiting growth.

While future capital requirements for energy are huge and are expected to continue to increase, the challenge of meeting capital needs for energy is not inherently so daunting as was thought to be the case just a few years ago. Moreover, pursuing a sustainable development strategy would reduce the magnitude of the energy investment challenge. However, particular attention would have to be given to how capital resources are allocated, since the smaller-scale, clean, and innovative energy supply investments and the energy efficiency investments needed under a sustainable development strategy are discriminated against in existing capital markets.

Under a sustainable development strategy, energy pricing reform would be given high priority. This would make energy-sector investments more attractive to prospective investors, easing the capital crisis conditions that now exist in many developing countries and giving developing countries considerable power in capital markets relating to energy. The capital challenge is not so much the unavailability of the needed capital as it is the risks perceived in energy market investments by would-be investors.

For a number of years capital markets have grown faster than total GDP, and this trend is unlikely to change. The formation of domestic capital markets in developing countries would be encouraged under a sustainable development strategy, so as to expand capital availability by mobilising domestic savings for productive investments. At present the domestic savings rate averages about 24% of GDP in developing countries compared to 21% in OECD countries.

Also, policies aimed at driving down capital costs would be pursued under sustainable development conditions. Already, increasingly competitive conditions in global energy markets have led to sharp declines in specific capital costs in recent years. For example, turnkey plant costs for 250 MWe coal steam-electric plants fell from US$1355-US$1720/kW in 1992 to US$985-US$1265/kW in 1995, while those for 250 MWe natural gas combined cycle plants fell from US$615-US$720/kW to US$480-US$535/kW in this period.

Reductions in capital costs over time would be characteristic of sustainable development scenarios because many of the technologies that are best-suited for meeting sustainable development objectives are small, modular, and very good candidates for cost-cutting via organisational learning after they are launched in the market.

Although a shift to renewables and other energy technologies suitable for use in the pursuit of sustainable development objectives sometimes will lead to higher specific capital costs for energy-producing equipment compared to conventional fossil energy supplies, this is not always the case. For example, grid-connected combined heat and power systems located near users typically lead to savings of capital as well as fuel. Also, providing electricity via stand-alone renewable energy systems for applications such as lighting to households remote from utility grids, is less costly than extending central grids to these low-demand users. Installing distributed grid-connected power sources (e.g., photovoltaic and fuel cell systems) reduces investment needs by reducing distribution capacity requirements to meet peak loads. Finally, the overall need for new energy supply capacity would be less for sustainable development than for business-as-usual development, because of the emphasis given to efficient use of energy. At present, less capital is often required in all countries to save a given amount of energy (by employing more energy-efficient technologies) than to expand the energy generating capacity by an equivalent amount.

Finally it should be noted that higher specific capital costs are not inherently problematic, since savings in fuel and other operating costs can offset higher up front costs. Properly functioning capital markets make it practically feasible to evaluate alternative energy technologies on a lifecycle-cost rather than a first-cost basis.

In energy futures compatible with sustainable development objectives there would be a diversification of energy supplies to the extent that oil would compete with synthetic fluid fuels (derived from natural gas, biomass, and coal, sometimes in conjunction with fuel decarbonisation and sequestration of the separated CO_2). To the extent that these alternatives are based on the use of domestic feedstocks, they would not require as much foreign exchange as oil imports. This would be advantageous for the many countries with balance of payment problems, releasing foreign exchange for other developmental needs.

Energy prices are also distorted when they fail to include external costs such as environmental costs associated with energy production and use. Environmental costs include the human health impacts of air pollution, land degradation, acidification of soils and waters, and climate change. When market prices do not fully take into account the external costs, the advantages of cleaner energy options are not reflected adequately in the marketplace. With policies designed so that energy prices reflect the true and full costs of energy, sustainable energy options will be much more viable.

Externalities can be internalised by taxes on emissions, by fines for damages, or through regulations designed to limit emissions and damages. A great deal of global experience has been accumulated in recent decades with many approaches. Internalising externalities is not straightforward, however. There is no consensus concerning the economic values to assign to environmental damages, or even on the methodologies for estimating such damages. Not only do different analysts and stakeholders tend to assign different values to the same damages, but many values are inherently difficult to quantify in monetary terms. The difficulties in framing appropriate policies for controlling externalities are compounded by the fact that policy changes have to take into account the impacts of new policies on a variety of stakeholders that might be adversely effected by the new policies (e.g., the impacts of higher energy prices from taxation on low-income consumers and impacts on the competitiveness of industries that are regulated or taxed).

There are two notable trends in formulating policies to deal with externalities. One is to emphasise the role of markets in finding the least costly approaches to achieving a particular objective, once that objective has been decided upon in the political process. For pollutants that have regional or global impacts, governments might choose, for example, to set a ceiling for, or a cap on, total emissions per year. It is then economically efficient to allow market forces to work out the least-cost solution to achieve the emissions objective. In early 1997 a group of more than 2000 economists, including six Nobel Laureates, called upon the nations of the world to co-operate in addressing the challenge of climate change by using market-based instruments such as the levying of carbon taxes or the auctioning of CO_2 emissions permits that can be traded internationally, using the revenues generated from such policies to reduce government budget deficits or to lower existing taxes. They argued that such policies could be effective in slowing climate change without harming living standards and could in fact improve economic productivity in the long run.

Another recent trend has involved the use of regulations or alternative incentives to force major, rather than incremental, technological change in the pursuit of sustainable development objectives. One notable example is a regulation in the state of California requiring that, by 2003, 10% of new cars sold in the state be characterised by zero air pollution emissions - a regulation that is helping to speed up the development of electric drive vehicles. A non-regulatory example of forcing major technological change is the Partnership for a New Generation of Vehicles, a collaboration between the United States government and United States automakers to develop, in a period of a decade, production-ready prototypes of automobiles that would be three times as fuel-efficient as today's cars, while meeting all air pollution and safety standards and costing no more than conventional cars.

Policies that could speed up the rate of introduction of inherently clean and safe energy technologies should have considerable appeal in developing countries, where environmental problems are often severe both because population densities are high (e.g., 13,000; 50,000; and 95,000 per km^2 in

Mexico City, Lagos, and Hong Kong, respectively, compared to 4000 and 6000 per km^2 in London and New York), and because rapid growth in demand can quickly erode incremental improvements on conventional energy technologies to reduce pollutant emissions. To the extent such policies can be successful, they would lead to major environmental improvements while providing ancillary benefits. Whereas making incremental environmental improvements in existing technologies typically leads to increased costs for the energy services provided, a major technological innovation typically improves multiple attributes of a product or process simultaneously, often including cost reductions once the new technology becomes well established in the market. The prospect of gaining multiple benefits reduces the importance of gaining precision in the valuation of externalities. Moreover, successful introduction of inherently clean and safe technologies would also reduce the need for large regulatory bureaucracies that would otherwise be engaged in continually tightening regulations that mandate incremental improvements.

The rapid growth in the demand for energy services in developing countries provides a favourable theatre for such innovations. Moreover, if developing countries are successful in bringing about the needed economic reforms in the energy sector (so that decisions regarding energy technology can be decoupled from the securing of financing for energy investments) they would have a great deal of market power in encouraging the introduction of inherently clean and safe technologies through regulations or purchases by state-owned enterprises or utilities. Under such conditions, energy vendors from the industrialised world would be eager to compete in these developing country markets via various kinds of industrial collaborations, including international joint ventures, because these markets account for most energy demand growth worldwide.

To the extent that the introduction of new inherently clean technologies in developing countries leads initially to higher costs for the energy services provided, ways should be found for industrialised and developing countries to work together to share the financial risks of "buying down" the costs of new technologies in exchange for the future shared benefits that would arise from successfully commercialised products.

Chapter 6
Energy Planning and Policy

1 Energy Planning

Energy planning is a general term that is applied to a variety of issues. It addresses designing energy supply and utilisation in new buildings as well as municipal planning of district heat supply and the structure of heating systems. In national energy planning the focus is on political targets like diversification of energy sources or environmental targets like reducing acidification of soil and lakes. International bodies like the World Energy Council (WEC), the International Energy Agency (IEA) or the Intergovernmental Panel on Climate Change (IPCC) investigate the future of our energy system on a multinational or even global level. Many research institutions and scientists focus their research on the long-term future of the global energy system.

Depending on the scope of the problem and the decision makers involved the targets of such investigations differ. Industrial bodies and energy utilities strive for strategies with minimum costs. In this case other objectives, like environmental or social aspects, are viewed as constraints. As an example, fuel use in a power plant can be constrained due to site-specific regulatory emission limits. Three types of problems are addressed by industrial or utility decision makers:

- long-term planning (supporting decision makers; planning periods of 15 to 20 years), especially for investment decisions,
- medium-term planning for one or two years, generally addressing resource allocation, contract and plant management and
- short-term operation planning for the day or week, deciding on plant schedules and unit commitment.

National or international bodies, politicians and scientific investigators focus directly on political, social and environmental aspects of the problem. Such investigations generally emphasise the longer term, focusing on 20 to 50 years, while medium-term analyses in this field have a time frame of some 5 to 10 years. Recently, the issue of global warming with the very long time constants involved, has triggered a multitude of energy related studies with a time horizon up to 2100 or even beyond. Such investigations are not directly targeted towards investment or operation decisions, they rather supply a foundation for long term policy decisions, legal acts and international treaties and provide a basis to focus later R&D funds on specific problems.

In energy modelling a wide variety of models have been employed. Three types have found most widespread use:

1. Simulation models that mimic technical features of the modelled system. Their results are directly determined by the input. Such models are useful to evaluate fully defined systems with no degrees of freedom. Open questions have to be investigated by the user prior to model application. They are used for technology-oriented analyses, e.g., to determine the size of the heating system and the degree of insulation for different housing types.

2. Econometric models expanding past behaviour into the future. Econometric estimates of time series supply the basis for models explaining one variable, e.g., energy use, by some driving forces, like income, prices, etc. Such models are mainly used for demand evaluations and investigating consumer responsiveness to prices.

3. Economy models viewing the energy sector as part of the overall economy. Various types of such models exist, like General Equilibrium models or neo-classical growth models. Their common feature is that the energy system is viewed from outside, with the main focus on the interrelations with the rest of the economy. Their main use is in the evaluation of energy policies with respect to the consequences on the economy or vice versa.

4. Optimisation models deriving optimal investment strategies or operation plans for specific utilities or municipalities. Used in national energy planning or international investigations for analysing the future of an energy system, such models derive the optimal strategies assuming optimal behaviour of all acting agents under the given constraints.

Among the optimisation models, the most commonly used approach is linear programming (LP). LP models have found widespread application in refinery scheduling, national energy planning and technology-related long-term energy research. There is a growing tendency to base municipal energy plans on formalised modelling tools, mostly also LP models.

Modelling the actual system of an electric utility requires greater detail in formulating technical properties and relations; it does not allow full linearisation of all relations. Mixed Integer Programming (MIP) offers the possibility to improve the formulations of pure linear (LP) models: it allows to include yes or no (0-1) decisions and nonconvex relations in a model. Unit commitment problems, with decisions on the start-up or shut-down of thermal units, and expansion planning, deciding on which type and size of power plant to build, involve discrete decisions that are most commonly modelled with MIP techniques. Alternative modelling approaches include dynamic programming, which gives fast solutions on 0-1 decision problems with low complexity. Smooth non-linear optimisation problems are often solved using Lagrange relaxation methods. Recently modern techniques like genetic algorithms, simulated annealing, etc., are penetrating the decision support market in the energy utility sector. For more complex problems combinations of modelling approaches are applied to solve the problem in a hierarchical or iterative manner.

The accuracy of depicting the system, the choice of modelling technique and decision variables all depend on the type of system, the time horizon and the questions asked.

Energy-related decision support systems generally fall under two categories:

- Systems applied by specialists (in industrial, institutional or scientific environments), where the evaluated results are presented to the decision maker. This type of decision support is generally applied if high-ranking persons are involved or if the decisions have far-reaching consequences.
- Systems continuously used for short to medium-term planning. Such systems are mostly applied by the decision makers themselves. As an example, scheduling and resource planning for the production of an electric utility is decided by the load dispatcher, who is also using the decision support software.

Clearly the two types of users and the two types of decision makers call for different types of decision support systems. The most important requirement to decision support systems for high-ranking decision makers is flexibility in order to answer any upcoming question. Strategic investigations often call for changes in existing models. The requirements on the man-machine-interface (MMI) are moderate, because the system is applied by specialists with specific interest in the issue. The decision makers, who are usually not applying the DSS themselves, require relevant strategic information of the what-is-when type. They need to understand the implications of certain decisions and the interrelations of the components in the system investigated. Generally, decisions with far-reaching consequences are not taken according to the solutions proposed by a model. They are evaluated on the basis of model results, but incorporating the specific experience, skills and judgement of the persons involved.

Decision support systems of the second type, like scheduling the operation of power plants and energy exchange contracts for a utility, which are applied by the load dispatcher with some special training, have quite different requirements: they must be linked to the data base of the utility in order to always reflect the current situation; they have to be of high quality (error-free) and give defined results under all circumstances; and the man-machine-interface (MMI) must be easy to operate and understand and cover all possible manipulations including transfer of the results to any consecutive process. In operation planning, the decision maker (load dispatcher) analyses the proposed solution in view of his experiences and objectives and either accepts it or disagrees with one or more of the decisions involved. As a consequence, the DSS has to have the flexibility to start from the last solution proposed and incorporate additional constraints or other settings given by the load dispatcher. Most DSS of that sort also offer the option to just simulate a solution defined completely by the operator of the power system.

A major problem faced by load dispatchers of energy utilities are uncertainties in basic parameters influencing the decision process. Uncertainties in short-term decision problems usually concern the demand given by the load curve over the day or the week and the uncertainties in the supplies from some energy sources (e.g. inflow into a water reservoir, water freight of rivers). In countries like Austria this concerns hydro-power generation, which is highly dependent on rainfalls in the water catchment areas. Various types of forecasting systems can expand the range of fairly exact results to a period of up to 8 hours. Forecasts exceeding this time frame tend to be of a more speculative nature. Consequently, another requirement of on-line decision support systems is the ability to start a new model run at any point in time from the current situation, revising the plans in operation according to any changes in forecast data. Also forced-outages of power-plants can lead to new emergency plans.

In any case, maintaining the consistency of the data base and the model are of utmost importance in continuous model application. Changes in exogenous conditions, internal structure or objectives of the system should be continuously monitored.

2 Energy Policies

2.1 Electricity Market Competition

Throughout the world governments are promoting competitive electricity markets. In particular, there is a move away from administrative price setting by government institutions to market price setting through the introduction of competition. Today this is often focused on competition in generation. However, competition among final electricity suppliers and distributors to provide effective consumer choice is a further step that governments are likely to pursue as experience with market reform grows.

The basic objective of all efforts to reform electricity markets is to improve the economic efficiency of a secure electricity supply, and to pass through the benefits to consumers through lower prices. Other objectives, however, remain very important. As electricity markets are changed, some of these policy objectives constrain the range of available choices for the new market structure. The most important examples are the policy objectives to maintain security of fuel supply, system reliability, and environmental performance.

The single most important influence of competition on electricity supply systems will be the greater emphasis on cost efficiency by utilities. This is one of the fundamental benefits competition is intended to promote. Competitive markets provide incentives, in a way that no other approach can, to reduce costs and increase productivity.

Electricity market competition is expected to:

- concentrate efforts by plant owners to reduce expenditure on generation and to maximise returns;
- re-orient decision making to incorporate private rather than public costs and benefits;
- lead to more transparent and effective pricing, to better reflect costs.

Utilities will seek new methods and technologies to ensure that they are able to provide secure and clean electricity at the lowest possible cost in comparison with their competitors. A recent International Energy Agency (IEA) study identifies specific utility strategies to minimise costs in generation. Utilities have always pursued cost-effective operation through "technical" approaches related to improvements in plant investments, operations and maintenance, and fuel efficiency. The ultimate scope for further cost reductions in specific utilities from competition will depend on how successful, or not, regulators and governments were at maximising commercial efficiency under the former monopoly supply conditions.

Utility responses to the introduction of competition are not restricted to improvements in generation plant and operations, although these areas are fundamental. Business practices in general will become more oriented towards profitability. As monopoly supply rights disappear, marketing will grow in importance. Marketing and pricing will increasingly be tailored to user needs in all respects: avoidance or tolerance of supply interruptions, seasonal or daily variations in demand, power quality, related services such as customer system maintenance, green pricing, and other areas.

An important change in the framework for power development under competitive markets will be the clearer separation of commercial and government decision-making. Under non-competitive supply systems, governments had available a number of mechanisms to pursue public policy objectives without any easily identifiable public or private expense. The essential arrangement was to assign the responsibility for executing policies to utilities, which, through state ownership, regulation, or in a "co-operative" spirit, bore the costs. These expenses could be passed on quietly and diffusely to electricity ratepayers.

The list of such policy objectives pursued through electricity utilities is long and extends well beyond energy-related policies. Among others, it includes support for domestic coal mining, support for domestic power equipment suppliers, regional development, consumer protection, rural electrification, employment, environmental objectives, and promotion of energy security. Seemingly every type of generation technology/fuel combination has been promoted or discouraged in one country or another in support of various policy objectives. Governments followed this approach because they felt that least-cost development of electricity supply might not have resulted in the same business choices.

In markets where electricity supply becomes open to competition, individual investment and operational decisions will no longer incorporate non-economic requirements unless they are made explicit by government action. Investment decisions will also reflect commercial reality more closely in, for example, projected investment costs or fuel price escalation rates. Policy costs previously borne by monopoly utilities will be made transparent by the arrival of competition. This forces governments to either make their policies and policy instruments transparent or to abandon them. Governments must establish a democratic consensus for policies affecting electricity markets and demonstrate that they are best pursued through the electricity sector rather than through other areas of the economy.

In particular, government support for specific generation sources must become open. The cost of support policies will become apparent and brought to the attention of consumers. For example, in the United Kingdom and Spain, competition in electricity supply has highlighted the cost of policies to support domestic coal mining. In the Netherlands and other countries, support for renewable electricity production has been a particular issue. In Germany, support for combined heat and power systems was extensively debated during their reform of the electricity market.

There is no fundamental incompatibility between competitive markets and the pursuit of government policy objectives of any kind, as the long experience of OECD governments shows. Countless social, economic, defence, and other policies have been implemented through mechanisms that allow markets to function while still taking into account public objectives. The essential requirement is to translate policy decisions into constraints and costs that markets can assimilate. For example, environmental policies can be implemented as technical limits on emissions of pollutants or tradable pollution permits. Owners of industrial and power plants must then pay for pollution control equipment or permits, thus incorporating the cost of the policy measures in their commercial decisions.

There are numerous market-compatible policies and measures that may be used to implement public policy choices. For example, governments can require non-competitive parts of the electricity supply system to bear the costs of some policies. Charges on the use of the network can include such a policy-related component. Taxes, investment support, special-purpose markets, and government research and development are potential measures.

2.2 Energy Conservation

Energy conservation is an integral part of energy policies around the world. Governments, industries, and end users must all work together and contribute to conserving energy in order for it to be successful. Energy is essential in everything from illuminating light bulbs at night to casting steel in a mill. Presently, approximately 90% of this energy is provided by the combustion of fossil fuels, quantities of which are limited. Though supplies, especially of natural gas, are larger than previously thought, depletion of these fossil fuels will eventually be inevitable. Furthermore, petroleum, which powers almost 100% of our transportation sectors, is concentrated in the unstable region of the Middle East where war is frequent. Since the Middle East supplies 42% of the world oil supply, an incident like the Persian Gulf War of 1990 can suddenly cut off much of the needed supply, leaving whole nations dry. Such dependence on fossil fuels promote the drive for energy conservation. By conserving energy, the limited supplies of fossil fuels will be used more effectively and countries like Japan, Korea and Taiwan that do not own natural resources of their own can reduce their dependence on foreign imports.

Increasing the efficiencies of appliances, automobiles, furnaces, boilers, turbines, electric power plants all lead to reduction in the amount of fuel being burned, essentially conserving energy. This is an economic incentive for industries and commercial sectors since costs can be dramatically reduced and efficiencies increased, resulting in a leaner and meaner operation with more competitive edge.

However, the main driving force for energy conservation may be due to pollution and environmental degradation. Energy conservation cannot be discussed without discussing the environment as well.

Energy conservation may seem like a straightforward concept, yet there are numerous definitions and ways it could be applied. One way to proceed with energy conservation is to conserve all forms of energy, regardless of the type of energy (fossil fuel combustion, nuclear, solar, etc.). Technology development is important but just as important is the co-operation by citizens of the world to make an effort to conserve energy. An effective campaign to conserve energy may be just as effective as a development of new technology. The second possibility is to concentrate on the conservation of non-renewable forms of energy such as oil, coal, and natural gas. Only a finite supply of these fossil fuels exist and once they are depleted, there is no choice but to look towards alternative energy sources to power the planet Thus, development of renewable energies such as wind, photovoltaic, and geothermal power will conserve the precious supply of non-renewable fossil fuels.

Furthermore, conservation of environmentally degrading forms of energy is an important consideration. Presently, 90% of our planet's air pollution problem arises from the burning of fossil fuels, killing animals, natural habitats, and even people. Combustion of coal, petroleum, and to a lesser extent, natural gas all contribute to the degradation of our atmosphere, resulting in such phenomenon's as acid rain and photochemical smog. Nuclear power plants, which are becoming an indispensable part of many countries' electricity generation capacity, have the potential of experiencing accidents and resulting in disaster such as Chernobyl's.

Even dams, built to provide hydroelectricity, disrupt normal flows of rivers and destroy natural habitats of many fish and animals that live in the area. Continuing to degrade the environment only means the devastation of our planet and death of humankind.

However, all of this initiative about energy conservation will not come cheap. Implementation of policies and regulations, enforcement of these policies, research and development of new technologies, and retrofitting old, existing systems will come with a hefty price tag. Therefore, energy conservation must be considered in a way so as not to impede economic growth. On the other hand, energy conservation policies may actually create numerous jobs and vitalise the economy.

Energy conservation is also a touchy issue politically when considered in an economic sense among nations. Many of the undeveloped or actively developing countries see energy conservation as a threat to their economic growth from the economic superpowers of Europe, USA, and Japan. Some believe that the industrialised nations are hindering the less developed nations from achieving the same kind of success, by limiting energy consumption that is essential for economic growth.

All of these considerations must be made simultaneously, which makes decision making and implementation most difficult.

2.3 Energy Policies at the Local, National and Global Levels

Many of the technologies needed for an energy revolution are virtually ready to go. But the pace of change will be heavily influenced by the ability of societies to overcome the policy barriers that remain. Most of the rules of the present energy economy were created decades ago, when the central issue was how to expand fossil fuel use rapidly. The industries that have grown up under the influence of those policies will lobby fiercely to retain them.

The needed policy changes number in the hundreds, but most fall into one of four categories: reducing subsidies for fossil fuels and raising taxes on them to reflect environmental costs, redirecting research and development spending to focus on critical new energy technologies, accelerating investment in the new devices, and channelling international energy assistance to developing countries. Many of the measures will require recasting the role of government, which in the past has been more centrally involved in the energy sector than in almost any other part of the civilian economy. In most areas, greater reliance on the market and less direct government involvement are called for, although in a number of cases governments will need to set the rules, focusing on ways to ensure that environmental costs are considered when economic decisions are made.

Energy price reform is a prerequisite to the development of a sustainable energy system. Governments routinely provide heavy subsidies to traditional energy sources, keeping prices artificially low and encouraging waste. In 1991, direct fossil fuel subsidies totalled some $220 billion a year worldwide, according to World Bank estimates, equivalent to 20-25% of the value of all fossil fuels sold. China and the formerly centrally planned economies of Europe accounted for three quarters of those subsidies, though the situation is changing rapidly in both areas. At the same time, most developing countries continue long-standing policies that keep energy prices low. World Bank economists estimate that gradually removing such subsidies worldwide would cut carbon emissions in 2010 to 7% below the projected level.

In industrial market countries, smaller but still pernicious subsidies exist, though instead of being direct price supports, they generally take the form of tax policies, government loan guarantees, and assured markets. In the United States, energy industries received federal subsidies worth more than $36 billion in 1989 (the most recent data available), with the fossil fuel and nuclear industries reaping nearly 60% and 30%, respectively, of the total. Other countries also lavish financial breaks for particular energy sources, from nuclear power in the United Kingdom to coal in Germany and hydropower in Quebec, Canada.

Governments have begun to remove some of these subsidies, occasionally with spectacular results. In the United Kingdom, for instance, gradual withdrawal of subsidies to coal - which were channelled through the government-owned utility company before it was broken up - resulted in a 20% decline in coal use between 1990 and 1993, with further erosion expected in the next few years. Similarly, China has begun to reduce its sizeable coal subsidies.

The next step in energy price reform is to ensure that fossil fuel prices reflect their full environmental costs. One of the best ways to incorporate these into day-to-day economic decisions is to levy energy taxes that are high enough so that the environmental cost is roughly embodied in the price consumers pay. Wuppertal Institute in Germany proposes gradually increasing taxes on fossil fuels, pushing prices up by 5-7% a year until eventually oil costs more than $100 per barrel. Such a tax would encourage individuals and companies to choose fuels based on their contribution to global warming. Renewable energy sources that do not contribute to the buildup of carbon dioxide would not be taxed at all.

Environmental costs can be internalised in energy decision making in a variety of other ways. Many environmental laws, for example, force energy users to pay the cost of meeting a pollution standard; in the United States, federal, state, and local governments have taken the additional step of setting a pollution cap for a region and then allowing companies to buy and sell pollution permits. In some cases this has effectively created a market for clean energy and encouraged companies to invest in an array of new energy options. Although these caps sometime create regional inequities, they are an effective spur for new energy technologies. The caps will need to be gradually reduced over time, however, if they are to have continuing positive effects. In addition, costs can be internalised through the electric utility planning process by requiring that they be weighed when different power options are evaluated by utility economists.

The second major area for reform is the energy research and development (R&D) programs of governments. Nuclear energy and fossil fuels have traditionally dominated the portfolios of government research efforts. In fact, the

23 member governments of the International Energy Agency spent 85% of their $115-billion energy research budgets on nuclear energy and fossil fuels between 1978 and 1991, and less than 6 and 9%, respectively, on energy-efficiency and renewable energy technologies. In most countries, energy R&D budgets continue to reflect priorities of the recent past, not those of the future.

By the mid-nineties, the tilt toward nuclear power and fossil fuels remained, though spending on efficiency and renewables had begun to rise. In the United States, for example, government-funded R&D in efficiency and renewables climbed 72 and 67%, respectively, between 1991 and 1994, with additional increases proposed in President Clinton's 1995 budget In the past, R&D funds were wasted on large, premature demonstration projects, but most governments now seem to recognise that smaller efforts to advance key technologies and cost-shared commercialisation efforts with private companies are more effective. Planners would do well to examine the experience with solar photovoltaics and fuel cells, where government R&D efforts - much of it channelled through military R&D - took key technologies to the threshold of widespread commercial use.

The third priority for energy reformers is to spur the expansion of commercial markets for technologies such as efficient electric motors, wind turbines, fuel cells, and a host of other innovations. Creating large markets will encourage companies to scale up production and reduce the costs of these manufactured devices. Technologies such as fuel cells, compact fluorescent bulbs, wind turbines, and photovoltaics are still in the early stages of what is likely to be an extended period of cost reduction. Total production of wind turbines, for example - from all companies combined - was less than 2000 units a year in the early nineties, while the largest manufacturer of fuel cells recently built a facility capable of producing just 200 intermediate-sized cells per year. Some of the most rapid cost gains are likely to come in photovoltaics, which have dropped 33% in price for each doubling of cumulative production since 1975. The faster these markets grow in the future, the more economical the technologies will become.

The key goal for policymakers is to catalyse market-driven, multiyear purchases, so that manufacturers can scale up production. A government strategy to promote continuing development of new technologies can rely either on direct purchasing programs or on partnerships with private industry. These could range from large purchases of solar generators for use on military bases or government buildings to utility demand-side management programs that use corporate capital as leverage to expand the market for energy-efficient lighting, refrigerators, or furnaces.

The government of Japan has aggressively pursued this approach with other technologies in the past, and is now using it to generate a large market for fuel cells and photovoltaics over the next decade. Several European governments are doing the same for photovoltaics. At the same time, a group of US utilities is arranging bulk purchases of solar cells, albeit on a scale that, according to many in the industry, is not large enough to make a significant difference. In addition, some US companies are working with the government to build a series of large solar thermal power plants on a former nuclear test site in the Nevada desert.

The final key to reform lies in developing countries, where most of the increased demand for energy over the next three decades is expected. Turning the energy market toward new technologies there is critical. Rather than spending billions of dollars on infrastructure that is increasingly obsolete, developing countries can follow a sustainable energy strategy from the start. To do this, however, the large energy assistance programs that earlier pushed them down the fossil fuel path need to be redirected.

The multilateral development banks play the largest role. Although these agencies provide no more than 10 percent of the roughly $60 billion invested in developing countries' energy sectors each year, they often supply the "seal of approval" that private banks are looking for. Nearly four fifths of the $57 billion the World Bank has loaned for energy projects since 1948 has been for power supply; less than 1% of the $67 billion lent for energy projects by all the development banks in the eighties went to improving end-use energy efficiency.

Some changes have begun at the World Bank. In recent years, for example, the organisation has increased its support for natural gas, apparently at the expense of electric power projects. Late in 1991, the Bank formed an alternative energy unit in its Asian section to encourage investments in energy efficiency and renewable energy technologies. And the following year the Bank's directors approved a new policy for the electric power sector, intended to promote energy efficiency. Still, there is little evidence so far that this is having much effect on actual lending patterns; during the first half of 1993, only 2 of the 46 electricity loans being considered were consistent with the new policy.

Funding for these kinds of projects is also being provided by the Global Environment Facility (GEF), a fund that was set up in 1990 under the auspices of the World Bank, the United Nations Development Programme, and the United Nations Environment Programme to fund projects that are not yet fully justifiable in local economic terms but that have global environmental benefits. So far, the GEF has financed several dozen energy efficiency and renewable energy projects under its mandate to support programs that reduce greenhouse gas emissions. Included were a rooftop photovoltaics project in Zimbabwe, a project for extracting energy from sugarcane residues in Mauritius, and efficient lighting in Mexico.

Although some of the GEF energy projects are worthwhile, the effects have been limited so far. The total funding available to GEF - $2 billion for the three years starting in mid-1994, of which 40-50% can be energy-related - is far too little to reform energy development. In fact, the multilateral development banks lend 18 times as much each year for traditional energy projects. Moreover, by including energy-efficient lighting, for instance, in its portfolio, GEF gives the false impression that these projects are not economical on their own and should only be pursued for their global environmental benefits - perhaps undermining their economic legitimacy in the eyes of government planners. The institution's potential impact will only be felt if its projects begin to influence the broader energy loan portfolios of the development banks themselves - a point that GEF appears to be addressing in its next round of loans.

GEF's limitations also expose a glaring weakness of the United Nations: the only central UN energy agency is the International Atomic Energy Agency which promotes the export of nuclear power to developing nations in addition to monitoring nuclear proliferation. This one-dimensional organisation has been criticised by the World Bank itself for providing poor advice to developing countries. In response, a growing number of critics argue for a broader approach by the international community.

To be effective, government planners will need to be flexible, abandoning programs that do not work and fine-tuning those that do. And they will need to find ways to harness the power of the market more efficiently, reducing the need for government micromanagement of the energy system.

The road ahead will not be without obstacles and detours. The investments required for achieving a sustainable energy system are sizeable, the economic forces to be overcome well organised, and the challenges to human ingenuity enormous. Still, when economic historians look back on the mid-nineties, they may well decide that the world had already embarked on a major energy transition by then - just as, with hindsight, we can say the same about the 1890s. Today, as then, economic, environmental, and social pressures have made the old system unsustainable and obsolete, and the process of change is quietly gathering momentum. Slowly, people and governments are rising to one of the most fundamental challenges humanity has ever faced: passing on to our children a natural environment that has not been substantially degraded by our short-term needs.

Chapter 7
Energy and Society

1 Energy and Social Development

Sustainable energy paths do exist and can be taken for the 21st century. This is not going to be an easy task but there is no other alternative choice, since the current trends are not sustainable. The current approach to energy, widely used by industrialised countries and for the industrialisation of developing countries, has permitted growth and development. Still, it cannot be considered an overwhelming success. It has failed in two major areas: satisfying human needs and avoiding negative environmental impacts. It has often failed to satisfy some basic features of sustainability such as equity, public health, economic efficiency, long term viability and peace.

The direct linkages between energy and major global issues can be identified in at least three main areas:

- Human development (poverty, women, population, health)
- Environmental sustainability (climate change, acidification, land degradation, waste, competitive use of land for food and energy)
- Economic and geostrategic issues (investment, foreign exchange impacts, R&D, fossil fuel reserves, energy imports, nuclear proliferation)

As far as human development is concerned, first of all, energy plays a key role in the fight against poverty. The world's population has more than doubled in the past 45 years. From 2.52 billion people in 1950, it has mushroomed to 5.72 billion in mid-1995, 4.55 billion of whom live in less developed regions. Poverty and energy are inextricably intertwined, resulting in a vicious circle in which some 2 billion people do not have or have limited access to basic energy services. In addition, the poor devote a larger amount of their limited assets and of their time for these energy services, while the quality of these services is often low. This has considerable consequences directly to the standard of living as it aggravates the economic hardship endured by poor households. They are less likely to make the investments that are necessary to use more efficient fuels.

"Poverty is the world's deadliest disease" according to the World Health Organisation. The growing economic gap becomes literally a matter of life or death for millions who pay the price of inequity. The poor use the biggest part of their energy for basic services such as cooking, heating or lighting. It has been proved that there is a strong correlation between indoor pollution generated by the use of traditional fuels in many developing countries and the incidence of respiratory illness or other serious diseases. These serious consequences on health seem to concern in particular children (respiratory infections) and women (chronic lung disease in non-smoking women). Moreover, indirect impacts from lack of fuel for proper cooking and boiling water are likely to be significant although very difficult to document.

Women directly concerned by and involved in the energy services are very often victims of energy scarcity and related environmental degradation that is accompanied by a decline in life support systems. In the Least Developed Countries (LDC), women are at the same time principal users of energy resources, producers of traditional biomass fuels and "human energy" services, victims of the energy provision system. Conventional approach to energy has intensified gender disparity in these regions. Coupled with economic degradation, it has deteriorated even more their living conditions. Energy certainly contributes to the fact that poverty has a woman's face: of 1.3 billion in poverty, 70% are women, according to UNDP's Human Development Report 1995.

As far as environmental sustainability is concerned, during the past five years there has been increasingly convincing evidence and arguments concerning the impact of human activity on climate. Scientific reports from the Intergovernmental Panel on Climate Change (IPCC) have spurred governments to sign the United Nations Framework Convention on Climate Change (UNFCCC). According to the IPCC reports continued increase in greenhouse gas concentrations will lead to significant climate change with serious impacts both to natural and human systems. Climate change is an energy-related problem because current energy systems are based on the combustion of fossil fuels that account for 78% of the world's primary energy. Industrialised countries account for about 60% of current carbon dioxide emissions. They are also responsible for most of the historical accumulated emissions (about 80%). Although they operate at much lower absolute levels, the emissions of developing countries are growing more rapidly than in the industrialised ones.

Nuclear power, sometimes proposed as an "ecological" solution to energy, appears far from introducing an environmentally sustainable alternative. Chernobyl demonstrated that large-scale toxic releases to the atmosphere can have extensive transboundary impacts for which practically no country is prepared. Thousands of people have already died from fatal cancers and more are estimated to be seriously affected by thyroid tumours and other serious diseases related to radiation worldwide. Radioactive waste is steadily accumulating, as nobody has resolved the problem until now. Nuclear power is also closely linked to the problem of nuclear proliferation and the related threat to peace.

Last but not least, energy is directly or indirectly linked to economic and geostrategic issues. The present level of investment in the energy related sector i.e., US$450 billion per year is likely to increase to approximately $1,000 billion by the year 2020, if the current trends continue. The search for new sources of finance has led to a drive of privatisation in the energy sector to attract private capital. At the same time, besides the impression of a trend towards deregulation and liberalisation, important subsidies still exist on a variety of energy sources and in particular on the production and consumption of fossil fuel and of nuclear energy.

Moreover, increased reliance on fossil fuel and on geopolitically unstable regions such as the Middle East, have been proven several times during this second half of this century to lead to growing stress and tension as well as serious problems, especially for oil importing developing countries.

The current approach to energy - basically putting the accent on centralised energy supply of fossil fuels to the detriment of energy efficiency, decentralised/integrated resource planning and renewable energy sources - has failed to address adequately many of the serious problems that human kind is facing at this end of the century. If energy is viewed as a means of contributing to the sustainable development of the world, business-as-usual energy patterns have to be abandoned leaving the space for new approaches to energy.

If the vision of sustainable development has at the centre of concerns the welfare of human beings, and their inalienable right to development so as to equitably meet the needs of present generations without compromising the future ones, then sustainable energy should become an instrument for peace. Sustainable energy strategies are those which include in their top priorities the urgent need to break the vicious circle of rising disparities between the industrialised countries and those striving to find their own path of development.

Sustainable energy strategies also reduce at the long term dependence on oil imports, reducing potential areas of conflict and friction, and eliminating progressively the high risks related to nuclear energy and nuclear waste.

If the vision is clear and the conceptual barriers are gone, then the solutions already exist. There is no need to wait for technological or other miracles before starting to work on how to operationalise sustainable energy. Energy efficiency and renewable energy constitute the basic elements, with considerable margin for development both in developing and industrialised countries.

Meeting the requirements and the needs of sustainable energy paths in developing countries will make it necessary to support institutional and endogenous capacity building, to encourage technological "leap-frogging", to create financial incentives for investment in clean technologies. It will also call for better balance between public and private funding dedicated to conventional energy and to sustainable energy projects and policies.

Centralised energy management should be complemented by decentralised, locally adapted, sustainable energy solutions. Experiences all around the globe advocate in favour of decentralised, community-based energy management. In many cases, in particular in remote and rural areas, local energy policies are much more efficient than centrally imposed solutions. Empowering people locally implies raising awareness and responsibility, finding sustainable solutions, building local capacity, creating community-based financial mechanisms and transferring the necessary technology. Such policies are consistent with avoiding waste and respecting the environment.

Meeting the requirements and the needs of sustainable energy paths in industrialised countries will require changing above all the mind-set, the way of thinking about energy. This new mind-set should include introducing integrated approaches to sustainable energy and fostering the linkages between energy and other global issues. In the effort to eliminate existing market and non-market barriers, a global partnership is needed in order to involve actors from all levels of decision making and from all parts of the civil society and the private sector.

If peace, development and environment are interdependent and indivisible, energy is certainly one of the basic constituting elements of this complex interdependence and a sine qua non condition for a sustainable future.

2 Energy and Human Health

The energy-health nexus arises from the fact that, without proper control, the production and use of energy can be accompanied by adverse impacts on the environment, and ultimately on human health. Indeed, as shown in Table 21 the amount and type of energy use is itself a useful general indicator of the potential for a number of important environmental health risks. It shows that across many energy sectors, there are profound influences on environmental parameters due to human activities.

Fundamental to an evaluation of the environmental and health impact of energy is the concept of fuel (or flow) cycle; that is, the chain of activities that extend from energy source extraction, through processing, transport, and storage, to the end use. In such a fuel cycle, the ultimate demand and consumption of energy comes at the end of the cycle.

In cases such as the gathering of agricultural wastes for fuel in a Bangladeshi village, the spatial domain and time period over which the fuel cycle operates is short. What is gathered today is burned nearby tomorrow. At the other end of the spectrum, however, are the large-scale fuel cycles for conventional energy, which link activities occurring over many parts of the globe extending over months, years, or even centuries in the case of waste disposal.

Table 21. Human Impact on the Global Environment: Portion Attributed to Energy

			Share of human disruption caused by:			
Affected quantity	**Natural baseline**	**Human disruption index***	**Industrial energy**	**Traditional energy**	**Agriculture**	**Manufacturing other**
Lead flow	25,000 tons/year	15	63% fossil-fuel burning including additives	small	Small	37% metal processing, manufacturing, refuse burning
Oil flow to oceans	500,000 tons/year	10	60% oil harvesting, processing, transport	small	Small	40% disposal of oil wastes
Cadmium flow	1,000 tons/year	8	13% fossil-fuel burning	5% burning traditional fuels	12% agricultural burning	70% metal processing, manufacturing, refuse burning
SO_2 flow	50 million tons/year	1.4	85% fossil-fuel burning	0.5% burning traditional fuels	1% agricultural burning	13% smelting, refuse burning
Methane stock	800 parts per billion	1.1	18% fossil-fuel harvesting and processing	5% burning traditional fuels	65% rice paddies, domestic animals, land clearing	12% landfills
Mercury flow	25,000 tons/year	0.7	20% fossil-fuel burning	1% burning traditional fuels	2% agricultural burning	77% metal processing, manufacturing, refuse burning
Nitrous oxide flow	10 million tons/year	0.4	12% fossil-fuel burning	8% burning traditional fuels	80% fertiliser, land clearing, aquifer disruption	small
Particle flow	500 million tons/year	0.25	35% fossil-fuel burning	10% burning traditional fuels	40% agricultural burning, wheat handling	15% smelting, non-agricultural land clearing, refuse burning
CO_2 flow	280 parts per million	0.25	75% fossil-fuel burning	3% net deforestation for fuelwood	15% net deforestation for land clearing	7% net deforestation for lumber, cement manufacturing

* Human disruption index is defined as the ratio of human-generated flow to the natural (baseline) flow

Source: Holdren, 1990.

In each case, however, full understanding of the impacts of energy use is achieved only by tracing the fuel cycle from end-use of the fuel cycle to its source (origin) so as to examine impacts at every stage. Conceptually, evaluation is done by assuming that, for example, a litre of petrol burned in a vehicle not only causes local air pollution, but also adds incrementally to the impacts associated with petroleum recovery, transport, processing, and storage at various sites before the fuel is ultimately consumed.

Many stages of the major world fuel cycles have important direct environmental health implications. Broadly these can be categorised as follows:

- human exposures to chemical or radioactive pollution from routine operations;
- accidents and diseases in work related to the fuel-cycle;
- shifts in disease-vector distributions from hydropower development;
- physical injury or pollutant contamination from major accidents.

The ingenious use of inanimate energy has stimulated and financed enormous advances in public health and medicine. An abundance of cheap energy, mainly from the fossil fuels, allowed the emergence of industrial and technological society. In such societies, although most of the energy surplus has gone into machines and structures, some of it has been allocated to improving the health and working conditions of labourers, allowing them to be more productive when coupled to machines; part has been used to improve the health and longevity of consumers, so that consumption could keep pace with growth in productive ability; and part has been devoted to mass education, so that the range of desire and ability in the society would expand to meet the needs of industrial growth.

The greatest advances in medicine and public health have been made within the past 350 years (starting with William Harvey's famous essay in 1628 and the introduction of quinine into Europe in 1632), mainly within those countries that led the way in the application of inanimate energy to industrial processes - England, Germany, Austria, France and the United States. Since 1650, a map of significant events in the history of medicine and public health would have been also a map of high-energy society, in which per capita energy use was substantially above the world average and drawing away from it.

The growth of high-energy society, however bad its consequences for certain groups of labourers, especially the children and women economically drafted into mines and textile mills, brought great improvements in general health conditions. Through the early years of the 19th century it was common for persons to sleep in their clothes and highly uncommon to take baths. Under such conditions, contagion could spread easily. Even in hospitals it was common to find two or more patients, related only by disease, sharing a bed.

As affluence, generated largely by energy "profits" from the use of sailing ships, falling water and firewood, began to spread through the world, this scene changed. People could afford to heat more than one room of the house, and even to install bathtubs. The introduction of cheap soap and cheap textiles for clothing probably advanced public health more than any single subsequent breakthrough in knowledge of disease vectors, with the possible exception of treatment of drinking water and wastewater.

In the 20th century, petroleum products and electricity used in farm machines, trucks, trains and processing plants, as well as in the production of fertiliser, pesticides and herbicides, revolutionised the food supply system. At the same time, the buildup of a chemical arsenal against microscopic forms of disease has shifted the balance of mortality causes away from the diseases that struck all age groups, that were epidemic mainly amongst the aged, and that were not contagious. The great advances in chemotherapy, as well as in mechanical means of prolonging life, could have been made only in a society with surplus energy to spend in research, development and specialised education. One of the striking differences between low- and high-energy societies is in the associated levels of health-care delivery.

The development of high-energy society, however, has brought new problems. The direct environmental impacts of intensive energy use have been given much attention, and significant steps have been taken to ameliorate air and water pollution and to preserve selected areas in a quasi-natural state. Public concern has concentrated on birds killed by oil spills, fields destroyed by strip mining, people who choked on petrochemical smog, fish killed by pesticides, caribou fenced in by pipelines, the danger of nuclear reactor meltdowns, and on the somatic hazards of lead, mercury and ionising radiation in the atmosphere. However, each has either a known preventive or remedial treatment; none reflects a risk of killing millions of people or of lowering their standard of living permanently.

It seems clear that indirect or hidden impacts of energy use may be much more dangerous to mankind than tanker spills or strip mining.

Man does not live by bread alone; nevertheless, it is a basic requirement. Many people in low-energy societies (where per capita daily energy supply from inanimate sources is less than 50,000 kcal) are underfed and/or poorly fed because their diet is deficient in protein. Both the calorie and protein deficiencies of low-energy societies largely result from the growth of high-energy society. The medical and public health technologies of high-energy society have been exported to low-energy societies, greatly reducing their death rates, especially among the young, and thus causing their populations to grow and to press against available food supplies. Attempts to export agricultural technology have been far less successful (the Green Revolution notwithstanding), and there is a real prospect of mass starvation in one or more parts of the world. Furthermore, high-energy society has drained protein from the regions where it is needed, by trading for it the trappings, but not the substance, of industrialisation which is energy. The United States, which produces far more protein than it needs, also imports fish and meat, much of which is fed to animals.

Many people in high-energy society are overfed and/or poorly fed in relation to the exercise they get. Overfeeding in high-energy society is possible because mechanised agriculture and the entire food delivery system are highly subsidised by the fossil fuels. It has been calculated that more than eight units of fossil fuel energy are consumed for every unit of food energy on an table high-energy society. Even countries that do not grow enough food to feed themselves may eat well if their goods and services can be produced with cheap energy and traded for food.

Basic to the food problem of any country is population growth. Some countries may subsidise their food supplies by use of cheap (in man hours) inanimate energy that replaces field workers and supports elaborate transport, processing and storage facilities in their food systems. Ultimately, they will encounter limits to the energy subsidy and to land productivity. Then, if the number of people to be fed keeps growing, the amount of food supplied per capita will decrease. Many countries, however, already have insufficient energy to subsidise food production for their populations, have limits of arable land, and must keep as many workers in the fields as possible because of unemployment and inadequate welfare systems. In such countries population growth has a more immediate impact on food sufficiency than in the high-energy countries. Unfortunately, it is precisely in the low-energy countries where the highest rates of population growth are found.

Economic "miracles" do not seem to offer much hope of the "demographic transition", i.e., the transition from a high population growth rate in the early stage of economic development to a low or zero rate in the mature stage. The fast economic growth of Mexico in the 1940s and 1950s, as of Brazil in the 1950s and 1960s, once a cause for optimism, has faltered as neither food production nor the work force is growing as fast as the general population. One result is a rising flood of illegal migrants from Mexico to the United States.

The food preservation and distribution system in North America has been remarkably effective in spreading some of the benefits of cheap fossil fuel throughout the society. It has facilitated a geographic and institutional structuring of the economy that has promoted enormous increases in non-agricultural production of goods and services (by greatly decreasing the human labour component in agriculture and allowing a wide range of food to be available almost everywhere in all seasons). However, the same food system has encouraged dietary habits that may carry some serious health risks to an increasingly sedentary population. That life expectancy for adults in the United States has increased only slightly during the decades when life expectancy at birth has increased substantially strongly suggests that high-energy lifestyle (especially lack of exercise), diet, environment or some combination of these three factors has a countereffect on the medical and public health advances of the past half century.

Health effects of nuclear power will come from both planned and accidental additions of ionising radiation to the human environment. The carcinogenic and mutagenic effects of man-induced ionisation, the greatest part of which is released by machines under the control of medical personnel, and probably will continue to be even if nuclear power grows to be man's principal source of electricity, do not differ greatly from those of some industrial and agricultural chemicals' now being studied intensively.

It is a high-energy society that needs nuclear power, and can afford to develop and apply thousands of drugs and food additives, as well as agricultural and industrial chemicals. The health impacts of some of these substances are becoming known and some potentially catastrophic. If thalidomide, for example, had been a delayed genotoxin, whose effects showed up only in several generations, and produced a much more common birth defect than phocomelia (seal limbs), such as cleft palate, for example, its impact on the human species would have been even more disastrous. On the other hand, enormous benefits have accrued already to high-energy society from the use of radiation, drugs, food additives and agricultural chemicals. Consequently, it is argued by many that we must risk using them without being able to know the long-term effects; others contend we should be certain of the harmlessness of a new substance before it is used, or at least first attempt to weigh its known advantages or benefits against its possible disadvantages or costs.

It is high-energy society for which crude oil, petroleum products and natural gas are transported across the ocean and for which oil and gas wells are drilled in coastal wetlands and on continental shelves. Drilling, extraction and transport in the oceanic and coastal environments inevitably causes incidences of pollution.

The intensive use of inanimate energy in industrialised or high-energy society has subsidised research, development, higher education and food production, and has brought about changes in nutrition and lifestyle that have led to great advances in public health and medicine. The emergence of high-energy society, however, has brought with it a new set of health problems, within which the effects of measurable pollution may be more easily dealt with than some of the indirect consequences of high energy use.

High-energy society is critically dependent on geologic energy resources that are being depleted rapidly, the most important of which are crude oil and natural gas. Much of the remaining reserves are not controlled by the industrialised nations. Technological solutions are sought while the international politics of energy grows more intense.

Low-energy society needs food, the basic energy resource. Population growth is relentless and petroleum, the basis of economic development, grows more costly. The health problems of low-energy society stem from nutritive lacks and contagion and strike hardest at the young, while those of high-energy society come from nutritive excesses and environmental pollution and strike hardest at the elderly.

3 Energy Legislation

International co-operation and legislation is essential for economic progress, social development and a better quality of life. Security of energy supply, efficient management and use of energy resources and environmental improvement require co-ordinated international action. There is no broader forum for promoting sustainable development in the energy sector than the Energy Charter Conference, which brings together more than 50 countries from East and West. The Energy Charter Conference is an independent International Organisation. It meets periodically to manage the Energy Charter process and to set the policy.

It defines activities such as:

- how to increase private energy investment
- how to improve conditions for energy transit.

The Energy Charter Secretariat, established in Brussels in 1996, supports the Energy Charter Conference and assumes specific functions on the Conference's behalf, such as facilitating transit conciliation.

The European Energy Charter idea was launched in 1990 at the meeting of the European Council in Dublin, the European Commission is asked to develop a proposal for the creation of a European Energy Charter. The European Energy Charter was opened for signature in 1991.

It is a political declaration of international energy co-operation based on market economy, mutual assistance and non-discrimination. The Energy Charter Treaty was signed in 1994.

This is the legally binding "backbone" of the commitments set out in the Charter. It will create an open energy market between its Contracting Parties. The Energy Charter Secretariat was established in 1996 in Brussels, to serve the Energy Charter Conference. It acts as a facilitator and supports the implementation of the Treaty, including negotiations that advance the Energy Charter process. In 1998 the Energy Charter Treaty was entered into force and the Trade Amendment was adopted.

The mission of the European Energy Charter and the Energy Charter Treaty is to ensure this co-operation, within the framework of a market economy - and based on mutual assistance and confidence. To meet the global economy's rapidly increasing energy demand over the coming 20 years, new and diverse sources of energy supply are needed. The Energy Charter Treaty creates, through a legal regime, the conditions for market economy and strikes an appropriate balance between governments' necessary regulatory intervention and energy companies' freedom to go about their business.

The Energy Charter Treaty is an instrument of international law. With 50 signatory countries it is also a political fact. The Energy Charter process is open to all countries committed to the principles of an open, non-discriminatory energy market. The Energy Charter Treaty will ensure an open, competitive and profitable energy market for the benefit of energy companies, investors and energy consumers. The goal of the Energy Charter Treaty is to promote a new model for long-term energy co-operation - based on the principles of market economy, mutual assistance and non-discrimination.

The Treaty is recognised as the primary binding legal instrument for tomorrow's open and competitive energy markets. Its importance is acknowledged both by governments and the international business community. The Energy Charter Treaty, which was opened for signature in 1994, entered into force on 16 April 1998.

The Treaty is developed out of the European Energy Charter (1991), a political declaration of intention of 53 governments and the European Communities. Charter Signatories extend from North America, across Europe to Central Asia, Japan and Australia. The Charter was created to promote energy co-operation and to assist structural reforms in the Countries in Transition in Central and Eastern Europe and the Newly Independent States.

The Energy Charter Treaty is the legal tool which will help the global economy meet its evolving energy requirements into the 21st Century. Global energy consumption is expected to increase by more than 50% between 1998 and 2020. Annual energy investment requirements may total 3 to 4% of world GDP. To meet the future energy demand, more diverse and secure sources of energy need to be developed. A major responsibility for supply rests on the oil and gas reserves in Russia, Central Asia and other Countries in Transition. Hydrocarbons produced there need long-distance pipelines to reach consumer markets. Therefore, secure and uninterrupted transit is vital. A reliable international partnership between countries will avoid uncertainties such as arbitrary political intervention. Through the implementation of the Treaty, and the Protocol on Energy Efficiency and Related Environmental Aspects, countries commit themselves to minimising harmful environmental impacts of the Energy Cycle, in an economically efficient manner.

The Energy Charter Treaty will ensure an open, competitive and profitable energy market for the benefit of energy companies, investors and energy consumers. The Treaty covers all activities in the Energy Cycle from exploration and extraction to production, refining, transit, distribution, sale and efficient use. All forms of energy are included: oil, gas, coal, renewables, etc. The Treaty will create the conditions for mutually profitable business relations between energy companies/investors, consumers and producers. Transit service providers stand to profit from substantial long-term revenues.

All Treaty governments support five principles relevant for business:

- legal protection for foreign energy investment
- application of GATT/ WTO rules to trade in energy products and materials and energy related equipment
- secure transit of energy and energy products (including a legally binding conciliation procedure for disputes over any matter arising from transit)

- dispute settlement through international arbitration/conciliation or trade panels
- minimising harmful environmental impacts and encouraging energy efficiency.

Main points of the Energy Charter Treaty:

- Secure energy investment
- Facilitating trade
- Freedom of transit
- Effective dispute settlement for investment
- Promoting sustainable development and energy efficiency.

Treaty Participants are committed to creating stable, equitable favourable and transparent conditions for energy investments. Non-discrimination is the key principle. All foreign investments established in a host country are entitled to Most Favoured Nation Treatment or National Treatment, whichever is best in a given situation.

The contractual obligations between an investor and a host country must be respected. According to the Treaty's dispute resolution provisions, a company or government can take a host government to international arbitration for a breach of a contractual obligation.

Investors have the right to employ key personnel of their choice, regardless of their nationality, provided they have local working and residence papers. The investor is guaranteed non-discriminatory treatment and compensation in the event of expropriation, natural disaster or armed conflict.

Host governments will allow foreign companies to transfer after-tax profits to any other country, without delay and in a freely convertible currency. The Treaty balances this with provisions for protection of creditor's rights, securities and the satisfaction of judgements.

Under the Treaty, GATT/WTO rules apply to all trade in energy materials and products where a non-WTO member is involved. For signatories /Contracting Parties that are not yet WTO members, the Treaty is an important step toward their WTO accession.

The 1998 Trade Amendment updates the Treaty's trade regime to WTO rules and extends it to trade in energy-related equipment. It also introduces the option to move from best endeavours to a legally binding commitment on customs duties. Under the Amendment a major part of the WTO rules on trade in goods becomes applicable, in particular, reinforcing transparency requirements and the non-discrimination principle.

For disputes on trade and Trade Related Investment Measures, where a non-WTO member is involved, the Treaty provides a consultation and panel system that follows the WTO model but is lighter in structure.

Safe, stable and uninterrupted transit of energy and energy products from producer to consumer markets requires close multilateral co-operation between all countries linked in any transit chain. The Treaty is the first international agreement that establishes an elaborated multilateral transit framework for oil and gas pipelines and electricity grids. It contains a commitment to non-discrimination for use of facilities and transit conditions. Governments shall facilitate transit without imposing any unreasonable delay, restrictions or charges.

In the event of a dispute over matters arising from transit, governments must not interrupt or reduce existing transit flows prior to the conclusion of a specific conciliation procedure. Under this procedure, a conciliator, appointed by the Secretary-General of the Energy Charter Secretariat, is to seek agreement of the Parties concerned, and may, if no quick agreement can be reached, impose an interim tariff.

The Treaty provides for international dispute settlement procedures that can be used between governments or investors. Investors and governments have the right to choose the form of international arbitration that best suits their needs. Investors can look to dispute resolution under the arbitration rules of the United Nations Commission on International Trade Law (UNCITRAL), The Stockholm Chamber of Commerce or through the Washington-based International Centre for Settlement of Investment Disputes (ICSID).

The Encrgy Charter Treaty promotes internationally acknowledged standards for sustainable development such as the "polluter pays" principle and the practice of transparent environmental impact assessment. The importance of energy efficiency is also recognised as the crucial tool to achieve environmental objectives.

Treaty Participants, among other things, agree to:

- Co-operate to attain the Energy Charter's sustainable development objectives and to follow international environmental standards.
- Promote public awareness of the environmental impact of energy production.
- Exchange Research and Development information on technologies, practices and processes, which minimise harmful environmental impact and promote energy efficiency.
- Share information on environmentally sound and economically efficient energy policies, practices and technologies.

The Treaty is supported by a Protocol on Energy Efficiency and Related Environmental Aspects, which commits all Protocol Parties to develop the principles of energy efficiency and sustainable development. The Protocol is a specific legal instrument which promotes international co-operation and encourages the integration of energy efficiency into countries' energy policies.

4 Energy Education

Energy is a prerequisite of a modern standard of living. The demand for energy by developing nations continues to escalate as aid becomes increasingly energy-related. Meanwhile the production and use of energy is acknowledged as a major cause of environmental damage such as air pollution, acid rain, deforestation, and climate change.

The decisions and activities of engineers are often intimately connected with the choice of energy systems and their far reaching effects on society and the environment. Yet there is little or no explicit "sustainable energy education" - that is, education about the role that the production and use energy plays in modern society, including the related technical aspects - in most undergraduate engineering courses.

Environmental education has often been seen as the preserve of biologists, geologists and other "earth" sciences. There has been confusion as to how environmental principles relate to other disciplines and/or whether environmental education ought to be a discipline in its own right.

Environmental education theory differentiates strongly between education *about* the environment (e.g., teaching environmental facts and concepts), education *through* the environment (e.g., experiential learning through nature) and education *for* the environment (e.g., actively engaging students in the resolution of environmental problems).

It is education for the environment that is seen by many environmental education theorists as the most effective way to make a genuine contribution to environmental well-being since it combines social critique with political and practical action.

The roots of engineering can be traced to its conception as a solely military activity of the first patriarchal city-states, e.g., the Roman Empire. The term "civil" engineering was coined only in the eighteenth century to distinguish it from the more typical military pursuits of engineers. The first engineering schools, such as West Point in the USA, were military academies.

In many ways engineering both created, and was created by, the Industrial Revolution. At the beginning of the Industrial Revolution fossil fuels began to be mined in vast quantities. Engineering as a profession was made possible by the growth of large corporations. In 1816 the engineering profession scarcely existed in America but between 1880-1920 increased by almost 2000 percent. Engineering is by far the largest of the new professions to have emerged from that period. The engineer is thus the original "organisation man".

Most engineers work for very large bureaucracies; they are not independent self-employed professionals in the sense that are doctors or lawyers. The essence of the engineer's dilemma lies in bureaucracy, not capitalism, and in the conflict between an assumed professional independence and ethics and bureaucratic loyalty. Furthermore, studies have shown that those who choose engineering as a profession are less likely than most to have an interest in social structure or the complexities of social relations. Engineering education does little to increase student's awareness of these phenomena.

Yet historical precedents exist for engineering having an enormous beneficial effect on society. For example civil engineering (and town planning) played a major role in improving public health via the provision of basic sanitation services, i.e., running water, sewer systems, rubbish collection. These innovations, it has been argued, had more to do with eliminating highly contagious disease such as tuberculosis than the discovery of a vaccine cure by medical science. But the role of engineers is rarely acknowledged.

Once lauded as the harbingers of sought after modern conveniences and comfort, in recent years engineers and engineering have come to be seen as contributing to degradation of the environment and to unsustainable development. Given the centrality of energy to modern society, engineers have an important role to play in creating a sustainable future. In the process the profession could reclaim its positive image.

In recent years there has been growing awareness by engineers of environmental issues and the profession's role in addressing them. But energy issues remain largely unaddressed. A vision of a sustainable energy future needs to be developed on the part of engineers and their educators as well as society and industry.

Energy use and production is an obvious and important nexus between environment issues and engineering training. Energy education is a subset, albeit an important one, of both.

There is now a fair body of research and interest in environmental issues in engineering education, but few which refer specifically to energy education.

Energy education should be a fundamental part of engineering education and ongoing training because energy is a fundamental part of the decision making of virtually all engineering these days and to quality of life. Energy education is virtually absent from general engineering education. Engineers might get some input regarding energy issues as it related to their particular specialisation but the social, political and environmental context were rarely addressed. Nowadays, energy education such as it is, ignores "demand side" issues (i.e., conservation/energy efficiency) as non-technical and therefore not engineering tasks.

The overall aims of energy education in engineering should be the awareness of the significance of energy to society, environment and engineering activities, that is energy education in context; ability to critically appraise how energy is currently used and produced and to develop alternatives and understanding of "demand" and "supply" issues as complementary elements of the energy "equation".

The major barrier cited to energy education in engineering training is a lack of appreciation of energy issues on the part of educators and industry. Academics lack expertise in energy issues, particularly on non-technical issues (e.g., demand management, social and environmental impacts, political perspectives). Other barriers are the influence of established (fossil fuel-based) industries on the setting of tertiary engineering curricula and an inappropriately high focus on technical content in the curriculum at the expense of social, environmental and management issues.

Approaches to energy education in engineering training should include:

- integrating energy education across the engineering curriculum
- developing a highly practical, "hands on" energy education experience for students
- the use of guest lecturers from industry and interest groups
- tranships in a variety of energy-related companies
- researching educators with teaching materials
- tertiary institutions to incorporate energy efficiency, renewable energy and the principles of sustainable development in their own buildings, grounds and operations as a living example to students.

There are positive signs that the engineering profession and educators have begun to acknowledge engineering's key role in the protection of the Earth. Environmental Engineering degrees have been developed within several universities while many engineering courses now include a required subject on "Engineering and Society" (a sort of catchall for the impacts of technology, this subject normally includes some coverage of environmental impacts).

Sustainable energy issues emerge from this overview as one of the major absences in current engineering education. Given the historical and cultural backdrop of our society and the engineering profession, it is not surprising. The engineering curriculum has been embedded in assumptions which bound the engineering profession as a whole: acceptance of intensive energy use and fossil fuel-based energy production; of engineering's symbiotic relationship with "big industry", and a utilitarian view of the natural world.

But there are signs of hope. More "sustainable energy" courses are available than three years ago.

Ultimately it could be that a shift within society - not just engineering education or tertiary campuses - will be needed. What role can individual engineers hope to play in securing a sustainable energy future in light of the fact that technology, after all, may be just "tinkering" with respect to the real problems?

- population and consumption
- that as employees of "big industry" individual engineers have little influence
- that technical skills are only a fraction of what engineers need to know to be effective change agent's
- that engineering education is still not preparing them to deal with non-technical issues.

Chapter 8
Energy and the Global Environment

In recent years, the principal international energy issues have shifted from supply interruptions and their implications for energy security and price stability to the impact of energy production and consumption on regional and global environments. Frequently, regional and global environmental goals are in conflict. For example, nuclear or hydropower energy projects may be opposed within a given country, while on a global scale they lessen emissions of carbon dioxide - the principal greenhouse gas. Although the focus of this analysis is on global environmental issues such as climate change, it should be understood that local environmental concerns and political decisions based on them may affect the ability of the world community to meet global environmental goals. In the coming decades, global environmental issues and their policy implications could significantly affect patterns of energy use.

The challenges of energy use and environmental quality facing the industrialised countries differ from those for the developing world. The industrialised countries have predicated their economic development on the availability of relatively low-cost fossil fuels. Accordingly, the infrastructure has been built to accommodate private vehicle travel and single-family dwelling units with relatively large amounts of space per person, especially in North America. Given the amount of capital investment in place, policies that modify underlying sources of energy inputs and end-use patterns will require time for turnover of existing capital stock if potentially large economic displacements are to be avoided. The principal challenge then, to the industrialised countries, is to implement policies that protect the global environment while allowing for flexible adjustment of their energy systems.

The developing world, while seeking to grow economically, is confronted with the environmental lessons learned in the process of the economic growth achieved by the industrialised countries. Within developing countries, much of the infrastructure that would support an industrialised economy is not yet in place. This presents an advantage in terms of identifying development paths that will allow greater scope for alternative energy sources and patterns of end-use consumption as new capital stock is put in place. On the other hand, developing economies are not likely to adopt policies that encourage alternative patterns of energy production and consumption if there is the perception that such policies are more costly and undermine near-term growth objectives.

Several environmental issues could be considered as global in the context of energy-environment interactions: acid rain, global warming, greenhouse gases, oil spills and radioactive wastes.

1 Acid Rain

Acid rain is a term that is used to describe a variety of processes which might more accurately be referred to as acidic deposition. Natural rainfall is slightly acidic due to dissolved carbon dioxide, picked up in the atmosphere. Organisms and ecosystems all over the planet have adapted to the slightly acidic nature of normal rain, and thus it poses no environmental problems. It is an increase in the acidity of rain, caused by human activities such as the combustion of fossil fuels that has turned acid rain into a problem. Highly acidic rain can damage or destroy aquatic life, forests, crops and buildings, as well as posing a threat to human health.

The actual term "acid rain" was first used over one hundred years ago by British chemist Robert Angus Smith. At that time, he realised that smoke and fumes from human activities could change the acidity of precipitation. Despite this awareness, acid rain was not considered an environmental concern until the 1950s. Around this time, increased levels of acidity were discovered in lakes in both Canada and Scandinavia. At first, this was looked at as simply an interesting situation, rather than a problem. Since that time, much research has gone into identifying the sources of acid rain and the damage that it causes. As research continued, the situation reached crisis proportions in the late 1970s. By this time, thousands of lakes in Canada and Scandinavia had been declared dead, devoid of life, while emissions of acid gasses continued to increase.

As mentioned earlier, the term acid rain is used to describe a variety of different types of acidic deposition. These include "wet" deposition such as rain, snow and fog, as well as "dry" deposition in the form of acidic gases and dust. The term acid rain is only used to describe deposition that is more acidic than normal. Acidity is measured on the pH scale, a scale that runs from 0 to 14, neutral water has a pH of 7. On the scale, pH levels below 7 represent acidic solutions, while those above 7 are alkaline. Each decrease of one number on the pH scale represents a tenfold increase in acidity. For example, rain with a pH of 4 is ten times more acidic than rain with a pH of 5.

Normal rain is slightly acidic, with a pH of around 5.5. This acidity is a result of naturally occurring carbon dioxide (CO_2), which dissolves into water vapour in the atmosphere. Human activities such as the use of fossil fuels for energy can result in the release of sulphur dioxide (SO_2), and nitrous oxides (NO_x) into the atmosphere. These gases can travel for thousands of kilometres before coming back down to earth in the form of dry particles or acid precipitation. In the atmosphere, SO_2 and NO_x react with water vapour to form weak solutions of nitric and sulphuric acid. In some regions of New York State, rain with a pH of 2.6 has been measured.

Over 90% of the SO_2 and NO_x present in the atmosphere over eastern North America is a result of human activities. The major sources of sulphur emissions are coal (and to a lesser extent, oil) burning electric power plants, and industries such as ore smelting. Together, these two industries account for over 70% of the sulphur emissions in North America. About 40% of NO_x emissions come from the transportation sector, (cars, trucks, planes etc.). The rest are emitted from fossil fuel fired power plants and other combustion processes. Once emitted into the atmosphere, acid gases can travel for thousands of kilometres before being deposited back on to the ground. In fact, about half of the acid rain that falls on Canada originated from United States sources. A similar situation exists in Scandinavia where Sweden, Norway and Finland are exposed to acid rain from Great Britain and other northern European countries.

Acid rain has a wide variety of environmental and health impacts. The magnitude of these impacts is very dependant upon the type of bedrock and soil in a specific region. Regions where the bedrock and/or soil contain carbonates such as limestone and dolomite are less susceptible to damage by acid rain than areas with igneous bedrock. This is because the carbonate material acts to neutralise the acidity of the precipitation. Carbonates act as a "buffer"; they tend to keep both surface and groundwater at a constant pH. The amount of damage to aquatic and terrestrial ecosystems is therefore dependant upon both the amount of acid deposition, and the type of soil and bedrock.

Soils, surface waters such as lakes and rivers, and forests can all be damaged by acid rain. The actual interactions between aquatic organisms (such as fish, crustaceans, insects and amphibians) and changes in water chemistry are extremely complex. Acidification can hinder the ability of aquatic organisms to reproduce. This is especially true for fish and amphibians that spawn in streams or shallow bays in the early spring. Large influxes of runoff from melting (acid) snow can drastically depress the pH in these areas for short periods in the spring. This "acid shock" can kill the eggs of many species. Many species of frogs and salamanders, for example, can't reproduce when the acidity of their breeding habitat goes below a pH of 5.

In addition to reproductive failures, acidification can reduce the amount of calcium available to vertebrates such as fish, as well as increasing the concentration of toxic heavy metals in surface waters. Both of the above can result in deformed bone structures, and poor growth in fish. The decline of any one member of a food chain impacts on many other species. Birds such as loons and osprey, which eat fish, can't survive without their main source of food. Similarly many mammals depend upon aquatic organisms such as crustaceans for their food. Acidification can eventually result in a "dead" lake. Such lakes exhibit very clear water, because there are no aquatic organisms such as plankton to colour the water.

The affects of acid rain on terrestrial (land based) plants and animals are also both complex and potentially devastating. Soils can be damaged by the removal of needed nutrients and the dissolving of toxic heavy metals from the soil. Metals such as aluminium can get into the roots of plants and prevent the uptake of other important nutrients. Forests in areas with sensitive soils can be severely affected by acidification. Acid rain can damage the foliage of trees (leaves etc.), and retard their growth.

Acid rain can also result in human health concerns and damage to buildings. Acid rain can aggravate respiratory ailments such as bronchitis and asthma. Humans may also be affected by drinking water that contains higher levels of toxic metals, which have been dissolved from soils and pipes by the increased acidity of drinking water supplies. Construction materials such as limestone, marble and sandstone can also be damaged by acid rain, resulting in eroded buildings and monuments.

In North America, and in some European nations, public concern over the effects of acid rain has been transformed (after a lot of controversy and fighting) into laws (such as the recent Clean Air Act in the United States), restricting the amount of SO_2 and NO_x that can be released by electric utilities and industries. The result has been a slight decrease in annual acidic deposition in some areas. There is also evidence that when acid deposition is reduced ecosystems can recover. Many of the lakes near Inco's nickel smelter in Sudbury have drastically improved as local levels of acid deposition have decreased over the last twenty years. In the future, it will be very important for the industrialised world to lend the developing world its technology and experience, in order to make sure that the same acid rain problems do not occur as these countries consume more energy during the process of industrialisation.

2 Global Warming

In June 1992, many nations from around the world signed a "Climate Change Convention", pledging to adopt policies that would limit their emissions of "greenhouse gases". This convention was a response to a growing consensus among atmospheric scientists that certain gases released into the atmosphere by human activities would cause the planet's surface to warm. Records show that the earth's surface air temperatures have increased by about 0.5°C in the last 85 years.

However, during the past 1000 years, temperatures have naturally fluctuated by about 1 degree so this rise is not necessarily a result of the greenhouse effect.

The latest computer models predict that global temperatures could rise 2-5 degrees Celsius by the middle of the next century if current trends persist. Global warming could result in sea level rises, changes to patterns of precipitation, increased variability in the weather and a variety of other consequences. The production and human use of energy contributes 60% of the human impact on global warming. Other activities which increase the level of greenhouse gases in the atmosphere are the use of chemicals such as chlorofluorocarbons (15%), agriculture (12%), land-use modifications (9%), and other human activities (4%). At the present time, the rate of worldwide greenhouse gas emissions is increasing every year. In order to minimise the magnitude of future warming these emissions must begin to decrease. Reducing the consumption of fossil fuels such as coal, oil and natural gas, especially in the industrialised world, is the single most important factor in controlling global warming.

Although it has only been in the news for the past decade or so, the "greenhouse effect" is a natural phenomenon and is responsible for keeping the earth's climate warm enough to sustain life. Naturally occurring greenhouse gases such as carbon dioxide (CO_2), water vapour and methane (CH_4), trap some of the radiation that is reflected by the earth. These gases, which make up only a very small fraction of the earth's atmosphere act as an insulating blanket for the earth. Without them, the planet's surface temperatures would be about 33°C colder on average than they are today.

Evidence from air bubbles trapped deep within glacial ice shows a close correlation between levels of CO_2 and CH_4 in the atmosphere and global temperatures. Over the past 160,000 years, the concentration of CO_2, the most important greenhouse gas, has varied between levels of 180 to 300 parts per million by volume (ppmv). During this time, there have been temperature swings of up to 10 degrees, resulting in several ice ages separated by warmer, inter-glacial periods. It is felt that these changes in CO_2 concentration, and similarly those of methane, were initiated by climatic changes caused by periodic changes in the earth's orbit, variations in the sun's output, or periods of intense volcanic activity. The changes in CO_2 and CH_4 concentrations occurred as the biosphere and oceans adapted to the initial climate change and the alteration in the incoming solar radiation. These gases then enhanced the change which had already started, acting as a "positive feedback" mechanism.

It can be seen that temperature variations and changes in greenhouse gas concentrations are part of the planet's natural cycles. In the past, temperatures and concentrations of greenhouse gases have changed slowly over periods of thousands of years. This slow rate of change allowed life on earth the time to adapt to the new conditions. In the past 150 years human activities such as the consumption of fossil fuels have drastically increased atmospheric concentrations of CO_2 and other greenhouse gases. The concentration of CO_2 is now 350 ppmv compared to a pre-industrial level of 280 ppmv. When included in calculations, the other greenhouse gases bring the figure up to a level equivalent to a CO_2 concentration of 425 ppmv and rising. This represents a concentration of greenhouse gases far higher than anything the earth has experienced over the past 160,000 years. Both the absolute level and rate of greenhouse gas build-up caused by human activities are without precedent in human history. It is quite possible that the rate of climate change caused by this build-up will be too great to allow for various ecosystems to adapt.

Increased levels of greenhouse gases in the atmosphere should lead to warmer temperatures on the earth's surface. There is little disagreement among atmospheric scientists on this fact. There is disagreement on the magnitude and rate of any warming. This is because predicting the amount of warming is complicated by thousands of factors that can influence both weather over the short term and long term climates. Some of these factors operate independently of the greenhouse effect, while others are "feedbacks" which are influenced by climatic changes. An example of a climate/weather control mechanism which is largely unaffected by global warming is the amount of particulate matter in the atmosphere. Very small particles of dust, called aerosols, are released into the atmosphere by natural processes such as volcanoes, as well as human activities such as the combustion of wood or coal. These small particles reflect incoming solar radiation, thus having a cooling effect on the earth's temperature. The cold weather experienced over much of North America in the summer of 1992 was blamed on the volcanic eruption of Mount Pinatubo in the Philippines, which released a great amount of dust into the atmosphere.

Several positive and negative feedback mechanisms have also been identified that have the potential to greatly influence future temperatures and make prediction difficult. Methane trapped in frozen permafrost could be released by warmer arctic climates causing even more warming. This would be a "positive feedback" which would act to reinforce any initial warming. Change in cloud cover is one potential feedback mechanism, but there is disagreement whether this would be a positive or negative factor. A warming of the atmosphere would result in the increased evaporation of sea water, creating more cloud cover over the planet. Clouds are composed of water vapour, a greenhouse gas that traps outgoing heat, but clouds also reflect incoming solar radiation, thus acting to offset the warming. The overall effects of the cloud feedback mechanism are therefore difficult to estimate. The ocean-atmosphere coupling is also an important system to understand, in estimating how the greenhouse gases might dissipate over the centuries.

These are just a couple of examples which illustrate the difficulty of predicting the warming that the earth will experience as a result of increased atmospheric concentrations of greenhouse gases. Several different computer models have been developed in an effort to make climate predictions. These "Global Circulation Models" (GCMs) are enormous computer programs which break the earth's atmosphere up into a three dimensional grid. The models then attempt to take into account the thousands of interactions between these sectors and determine future climates.

GCMs have been created by the Canadian Climate Centre, The Goddard Institute for Space Studies, the Geophysical Fluid Dynamics Laboratory and the National Centre for Atmospheric Research in the United States and the United Kingdom Meteorological Office among others. Depending upon assumptions of future population growth, energy use and the various feedback mechanisms, these models predict a global mean temperature change of between 1.5 and 4°C by the end of the next century.

A global mean temperature increase of 1.5-4 degrees would not be distributed evenly around the planet Temperatures at the poles would increase more than those near the equator and winter temperatures would rise more than those in the summer. These temperature increases could destroy many fragile arctic ecosystems, as plants and animals can not adapt quickly enough to keep pace with such a fast rate of warming.

To some people, a winter warming of 10 degrees in Canada might not seem like a problem. It is not the absolute magnitude of the warming which is a problem, so much as the rate of the warming. A global mean temperature rise of 1.5-4 degrees in the next century would have widespread and complex impacts on the world's already strained ecosystems many of which are very difficult to predict. All the climate models agree that an increase in the global mean temperature will result in increases in both evaporation and precipitation. The precipitation would not increase everywhere however, in some places such as the interior areas of continents it would actually decrease. This could mean that formerly fertile agricultural areas such as the Great Plains of North America could become desertified and barren.

The rate of temperature increase predicted by the models would force ecosystems to migrate north at rates of 100-200 km per decade in order to survive. Natural rates of forest migration are on the order of 20-50 km per century. It is likely therefore that the southern margins of existing ecosystems would experience the dieback of existing forests. Some types of plants and animals are able to migrate more quickly than others and this could also cause problems. Insect pests are likely to migrate faster than their predators, thereby causing more insect infestations further damaging threatened ecosystems.

Water expands as it warms, and the thermal expansion of the world's oceans combined with the melting of glacial ice masses as a result of a global mean temperature increase could result in a sea-level rise of 0.5-1.0 m. Such a sea level rise would displace hundreds of millions of people worldwide who live near existing coastlines, as well as reducing agricultural production in these areas. Some countries such as Bangladesh and the Maldive Islands would be virtually wiped off the map. Coastal wetlands, which play important ecological roles and provide homes for large numbers of species, would also be destroyed.

3 Greenhouse Gases

A build-up of certain gases in the earth's atmosphere threatens to significantly increase the planet's temperature in the next century. These "greenhouse" gases which are a result of human activities, referred to as "anthropogenic"; contribute to global warming by trapping heat within the earth's atmosphere rather than allowing it to radiate out into space. The most important greenhouse gas is carbon dioxide (CO_2) which is responsible for about two thirds of the potential warming to date; but methane (CH_4), chlorofluorocarbons (CFCs), nitrous oxide (N_2O) and several other gases trap more heat per molecule than CO_2 and are becoming increasingly important. There is a great deal of uncertainty regarding the magnitude of the potential change, but the best global climate models are predicting a planetary warming of 1.5-4°C by the end of the 21st century.

The "business as usual" scenario estimates the build-up of greenhouse gases that will occur without significant policy changes in the industrialised world. This diagram also shows the "global warming potentials" of each of these gases. It can be seen that various CFCs can trap over 10,000 times more heat per molecule than CO_2. Therefore, although atmospheric concentrations of CFCs are much lower than those of CO_2, these molecules are a very important component of the global warming threat. Each of these greenhouse gases has various sources and "sinks" which affect their concentration in the atmosphere. The sinks that remove the gases from the atmosphere are generally natural processes that have a limited capacity. Therefore in order to reduce potential warming, the sources of greenhouse gases, which are a result of human activities, must be controlled.

Carbon Dioxide. Prior to the industrial revolution in the 18th century, the earth's atmosphere was made up of 280 parts per million by volume (ppmv) CO_2. Since that time, the combustion of fossil fuels (coal, oil and natural gas), land-use changes such as deforestation and the production of cement have increased that concentration to 355 ppmv. Currently, fossil fuel combustion is responsible for 80% of the world's annual anthropogenic emissions of CO_2, deforestation 17% and cement production 3%. In 1992, these emissions totalled 27.3 Gigatonnes (1 Gt = 1 billion tonnes) of CO_2. This is equivalent to 3.5 ppmv in the earth's atmosphere, but the build-up of CO_2 in the earth's atmosphere is presently only occurring at a rate of 1.8 ppmv/year (14.0 Gt CO_2/year)due to several natural carbon dioxide sinks which work to remove the gas from the planet's atmosphere.

The two major natural sinks for CO_2 are the oceans and "terrestrial biomass" (land based plants). Oceans absorb CO_2 from the atmosphere because the concentration of CO_2 in the atmosphere is greater than that in the oceans. This difference in "partial pressure" of CO_2 results in the gas being absorbed into the world's oceans. The amount of CO_2 which can be taken up by the oceans in a given year is a function of wind speed, air and water temperatures and concentration gradients and is therefore difficult to determine accurately.

Similarly, the absolute amount of CO_2 that the oceans will be able to absorb is currently a matter of debate. The best estimates of the ocean sink are that the oceans are absorbing 7.4 Gt CO_2/year (0.9 ppmv/year).

Terrestrial biomass has turned out to be a larger CO_2 sink than scientists had previously imagined. Forests, grasslands and other land based plants are currently absorbing an estimated 5.5 Gt CO_2/year (0.7 ppmv/year). The reason for this increased sink is that increased levels of atmospheric CO_2 have acted to 'fertilise' plant matter, causing increased growth. The regeneration of forests on abandoned farmland in the northern hemisphere may also be contributing to the capacity of this sink. Slowing the build-up of CO_2 in the earth's atmosphere can be accomplished by consuming fewer fossil fuels, stopping deforestation and planting trees. With the population of the planet ever increasing, and many previously under-developed countries industrialising their economies, demand for energy in the future will inevitably increase. Energy efficiency and renewable sources of energy such as solar, wind, wave and tidal power are possible means of preventing increased CO_2 emissions from fossil fuels in the future. Slowing deforestation and planting trees will increase the planet's terrestrial biomass sink, also slowing CO_2 build-up in the atmosphere.

Methane (CH_4) is the second most important greenhouse gas, responsible for about 15% of the greenhouse gas build-up in the atmosphere to date. Molecule for molecule, methane traps about 27 times more heat than CO_2. Methane is thus referred to as having a "global warming potential" of 27. Current atmospheric concentrations of methane are 1.72 ppmv (which is about double its pre-industrial concentration of 0.8 ppmv). Recent evidence indicates that the concentration of atmospheric methane gas, which was increasing by 1.1% per year in the 1970s, and 0.6% per year in the 1980s, has now levelled off, perhaps because of much tighter controls on methane wastage in Russia and Eastern Europe.

Anthropogenic sources of atmospheric methane include; the coal, petroleum and natural gas industries (coal mining, natural gas transportation etc. 28%), rice paddies (17%), domestic animals such as cows (from digestion and wastes 29%), domestic sewage treatment (6%), landfills (9%) and biomass burning (11%). There are also several natural sources of methane such as wetlands, digestion of biomass by termites and the oceans. Methane is naturally removed from the atmosphere by hydroxyl (OH) ions in the troposphere (the lower part of the earth's atmosphere), and absorption into soils.

These natural sources and sinks balanced each other to keep the atmospheric concentration of CH_4 relatively stable in pre-industrial times. Reducing our fossil fuel use, new methods of cultivating rice, reducing the number of domestic animals and capturing CH_4 before it is released by landfills are all ways in which anthropogenic emissions of methane could be reduced.

In the frozen tundra and beneath the oceans on the continental shelves in the northern hemisphere are vast reserves of methane, which have been trapped for thousands of years. If the earth were to experience significant warming, from the greenhouse effect, it is possible that some of this frozen methane could melt and enter the atmosphere. This extra methane would cause even more warming and the cycle would continue. This is known as positive feedback. The total reservoir of frozen methane is large enough that it has the potential to cause more warming than the combustion of the all the world's fossil fuel resources.

Chlorofluorocarbons or CFCs are a family of compounds composed of large relatively stable molecules that have been used in aerosol sprays, refrigeration units (refrigerators, freezers, air conditioners), blowing agents for foam products and cleaning solvents. More famous for depleting the planet's protective ozone layer, CFCs also contribute to the greenhouse effect. Once in the atmosphere, CFCs stay there for a long time because they are artificial and are broken down very slowly by natural processes. Various CFCs have very high global warming potentials, with the maximum being a compound known as CFC-12, which retains 10,000 times more heat per molecule than CO_2. Current atmospheric concentrations of CFCs are in the range of 1.3 ppbv (parts per billion volume) and are estimated to increase by about 65% by the middle of the next century.

About 8% of the potential greenhouse warming to date has been caused by CFCs but this percentage is bound to increase in the future due to the long life of CFCs in the atmosphere. Most industrialised countries in the world have agreed in the "Montreal Protocol" to phase out the most common CFCs, CFC-11, CFC-12 and CFC-13 by the year 2000. Future concentrations of CFCs in the atmosphere will be determined by how "industrialising" countries that have not signed the Montreal protocol deal with their needs for refrigerants etc. Many CFC substitutes such as HCFCs and HFCs also have high global warming potentials, ranging from 300 to 5000. In the future, these chemicals could also be an important factor in the greenhouse effect.

Nitrous oxide (N_3O) is another important and long-lived greenhouse gas, responsible for about 3% of the potential warming to date. Currently, the atmospheric concentration of N_3O is 310 ppbv, which is about 10% greater than it was before the industrial revolution and is increasing at a rate of 0.25% per year. N_3O has a global warming potential of about 150.

Biomass burning, the combustion of fossil fuels (especially in vehicles), the production of adipic acid (used in making nylon) and nitrogen fertilisers are the main anthropogenic sources of N_3O.

Nitrous oxide in the atmosphere is broken down by sunlight, and some is removed by soils. N_3O concentrations in the atmosphere can be stabilised by reduced fossil fuel use, preventing the burning of tropical forests and by reducing our dependence on nitrogen based chemical fertilisers.

The concentrations, global warming potentials, sources and sinks of the major greenhouse gases are fairly well understood. Methods of reducing the world's anthropogenic emissions of these gases are available but in some cases may be more expensive than continuing with "business as usual". The magnitude of the potential global warming caused by the build-up of these gases and the impacts of such a warming have not been accurately determined. The world has two choices, to act now to reduce our emissions of greenhouse gases, despite the uncertainty, or to wait until the warming and its effects are proven. This is a political decision that may have profound impacts on the future of the planet

4 Oil Spills

Of all the different ways in which the industrialised world uses energy that can damage the natural environment, the most vivid for many people may be oil spills. On a seemingly regular basis, our newspapers and television screens are filled with pictures of listing tankers spilling crude oil (also known as petroleum), and oil soaked sea birds in various stages of death. While these oil spills may be the most publicised (the Exxon Valdez for example), accidental spills from tankers account for only about 20% of the crude oil discharged into the world's oceans each year. The remaining 80% is largely a result of routine oil tanker operations such as emptying ballast tanks. There are possible methods of reducing the amount of crude oil released into our oceans each year, but as long as vast amounts of oil are routinely transported by sea, there will be some amount of unavoidable spillage.

Many people assume that only those oil spills that occur near coastlines cause any damage. These spills do of course, have the largest immediate and economic impacts but although the world's oceans are large, no oil can be spilled without harming local ecosystems. Air and ocean currents can also transport pollutants for thousands of kilometres; therefore oil spills affect more than just isolated locations.

When crude oil is spilled into a marine environment it eventually breaks down into several different components, each of which have their own eventual fates and cause their own problems for the environment. In many spills involving tankers or offshore oil wells, some of the oil spilled initially catches fire. When crude oil burns, the combustion results in atmospheric emissions of gasses which contribute to global warming (CO_2) and acid rain (SO_2, NO_x), as well as large quantities of toxic ash. The toxic ash is made up of microscopic particles which can travel for hundreds of kilometres. Humans inhaling these particles may experience allergic reactions which result in sore throats and breathing problems.

The less dense (lighter) components of the spilled oil are more volatile and eventually evaporate into the atmosphere. This petroleum then reacts with sunlight and oxygen to form greenhouse and acid gasses similar to those from the combustion of oil. The negative impacts of oil that burns or evaporates is more diffuse (spread out) than that of oil which ends up on shore but still causes appreciable damage to the natural environment.

A few hours after being spilled the heavier portions of crude oil forms a sticky oil and water mixture called "mousse" and may either wash up on shore or sink to the bottom of the body of water in which it was spilled. This oil mixes with sediments on the ocean floor and turns into a thick tar-like mass which can destroy the habitat of many bottom dwelling organisms. These tar-like clumps can also drift with tides and currents, eventually washing up on beaches far away from the spill. If a spill occurs near a coastline, beached oil can leak into fresh groundwater reservoirs that often extend under beaches, contaminating local wells.

Finally, some oil from any spill is degraded into simpler substances by either sunlight or bacteria. In the presence of sunlight and oxygen, some of the oil will break down into simpler non-petroleum substances (this process is known as photo-oxidation), which may be less harmful to sea life than the original oil. Similarly, many species of bacteria are able to decompose and degrade oil. The amount of oil from any spill that is degraded depends upon air and water temperatures (higher temperatures cause chemical reactions to occur at a faster rate), the presence of suitable bacteria and the exact composition of the oil.

An oil spill that occurs near a coastline will always impact more living organisms than one that occurs in the open ocean. This is simply because coastal areas are home to many more concentrated and diversified populations of marine life than the open ocean. Nevertheless, all oil spills have an impact on marine organisms, and oil from open ocean spills can end up contaminating beaches hundreds of miles away. Oil spills can harm marine life in three different ways, by poisoning after ingestion, by direct contact and by destroying habitats.

The negative effects of ingesting toxic levels of oil are poorly understood for many specific organisms, especially micro-organisms such as plankton, bottom dwelling organisms and larval fish. The effects on larger creatures such as fish and marine mammals are much more fully documented. Fish ingest large amounts of oil through their gills. If this does not kill them directly, it can inhibit their ability to reproduce or result in offspring that are deformed. Especially vulnerable are slow moving shellfish such as clams, oysters and mussels. These creatures can't escape from an oil slick.

Marine mammals and birds which have been in direct contact with oil slicks often ingest a great deal of oil while attempting to clean themselves. Carnivorous animals and birds that end up eating the carcasses of other oiled creatures also end up ingesting potentially toxic amounts of oil. Ingesting oil can destroy an animal's internal organs (such as the liver) and interferes with the reproductive process. The famous "Exxon Valdez" oil spill in Alaska's Prince William Sound resulted in the deaths of 15,000 otters, predominantly as a result of ingesting oil.

Birds and marine mammals can also be killed by direct exposure to oil. Oil can clog a bird's feathers making it impossible for the bird to fly, and so heavy they may simply sink rather than float. Oil also eliminates the ability of a bird's feathers to keep it warm. In colder climates, many oiled birds die of hypothermia (drastically lowered body temperatures). Similarly, mammals in cold waters can also die of hypothermia as their fur loses its insulating ability once it has been covered in oil. The "Torrey Canyon" oil spill in 1967 left about 10,000 bird corpses on beaches in England, but it is estimated that 90% of the birds killed drown and sink to the bottom of the ocean before they can wash up on a beach.

Finally, when tar-like clumps of oil sink to the bottom, they can destroy living conditions for "benthic" (bottom dwelling) organisms, as well as ruining spawning sites for many types of fish and shellfish.

Once an oil spill has occurred there are several methods by which the damage caused can be limited and the oil cleaned up. The four most common methods include containment and recovery, dispersal, bio-remediation and burning.

Containment and recovery is usually the first measure used to attempt to clean up after an oil spill. Long, floating plastic or rubber barriers called booms are placed around the floating oil slick. These act as fences to contain the oil and prevent it from spreading or moving towards a shoreline. Once contained some of the oil can be removed by various types of "skimmers". Vacuum skimmers work well in calm water and are used to suck the oil out of the water and into storage tanks. In choppy waters floating disk and rope skimmers can be passed through the oil. The oil sticks to these skimmers and is scraped off later. Sorbent materials such as talc, straw and sawdust can also be added to the oil slick and then removed when they have soaked up some of the oil. Sorbent removal can work in choppy or fast moving water but this method is slow and expensive.

Chemical dispersants can be used to break up the oil slick into millions of small globs of oil. These small particles are more easily dispersed and carried out to sea than a coherent slick. Rather than removing the oil, dispersants tend to spread the effects of the oil spill out over many different ecosystems. Enhancing the biological degradation of oil spills by adding microbes and fertilisers to the affected areas is another method of cleaning up oil spills. This process works best when the oil has washed up on shore rather than in deep water situations and was used with some effectiveness after the Exxon Valdez spill. Burning is a seldom used option for cleaning up oil spills which like dispersal just spreads the pollution out rather than removing it from the natural environment.

As long as many countries in the industrialised world are dependent upon imported oil for a large part of their energy needs, accidental oil spills causing damage to marine ecosystems will occur. Double hulled tankers and better tanker crew training could reduce the frequency of these spills, and ever evolving methods of cleaning up oil spills could reduce the severity of their impacts but the only sure way to eliminate oil spills would be to eliminate the need to transport oil by ship.

5 Radioactive Wastes

Initially developed for use in weapons, in the past 30 years nuclear fission has been harnessed to produce electricity. In many ways these nuclear power plants can be seen as a "clean" source of electricity because they do not emit the atmospheric pollutants given off by fossil fuel fired power plants. The nuclear industry has also spawned many different technologies used in medical procedures and industrial applications. Although the benefits from the nuclear industry are great they are not without their risks, for any use of nuclear energy produces some waste that is radioactive.

Radioactive waste differs from chemical waste in its unique property of emitting radioactive ionisation. This ionisation comes in the form of Alpha particles, nuclei of Helium-4 with 2 protons and 2 neutrons and a +2 charge, Beta particles (electrons with a -1 charge), and Gamma Rays, electromagnetic radiation similar to X-rays which has shorter wavelengths and is more penetrating. These radioisotopes can strip electrons from atoms or split molecules into pieces and can be very harmful to living creatures. Beta and gamma radiation are the most dangerous to living creatures. The damage to living tissue caused by radiation depends on which parts of an organism are exposed and the intensity and duration of the radiation.

Radioactive waste is also different from chemical waste in that it cannot be changed with a chemical reaction to form a non-radioactive product. No matter how it is treated or with what it is mixed, it still emits radiation until it naturally decays. The rate of decay of a radioactive isotope is called its half-life, the time in which half the initial amount of atoms present takes to decay (Figure 1). The half-life for different isotopes can range from several minutes to millions of years. For example, the half-life of Uranium-238 is 3.5 billion years, the half-life for Carbon-14 is 5730 years, and the half-life of radon-222 is 3.82 days. The purpose in understanding the theory behind half-life is to realise that radioactive waste stays radioactive until all the atoms have decayed.

Low level waste comes from both nuclear power plants and the nuclear medicine industry. This waste includes such things as protective clothing used in power plants, contaminated reactor water, X-ray equipment, and smoke alarms. About 99% of the low level waste comes from nuclear reactors in the form of fuel-related and non-fuel related substances. Fuel-related wastes are those that contain water contaminated by fission products that have leaked from the fuel rods. Non-fuel or activation products are objects other than fuel that have become radioactive due to bombardment by stray neutrons. A good example of an activation product is the nuclear reactor itself that becomes radioactive after a few decades of operation. Low level wastes release smaller amounts of radiation and have a shorter half life than high level wastes.

The disposal of low level waste is generally done in two stages. At first, the low level waste is kept on site where it is packaged in sealed containers and is left to stand for the majority of its half-life. After most of the radiation has decayed it is then packaged into tighter, water-proof caskets and is buried in landfill sites. Ontario Hydro utilises a different measure, by placing the sealed barrels in a specially designed building with internal drainage, fire extinguishers and radioactive monitoring equipment. This system is one of the better designs in the world as it keeps a careful eye on the waste instead of putting it "out of sight, out of mind".

Preventing materials from becoming radioactive is the best way of decreasing the amount of low level waste that needs to be disposed. Another method is to divide the low level wastes into categories that are founded on the half-life of the radioisotopes. In this way, materials with lower half lives will be separated from longer ones which would then be stored with high level waste.

Mill tailings constitute the largest amount of radioactive waste, by volume. Mill tailings are created when the Uranium ore obtained in mining is crushed and sifted to extract the Uranium. Of the ore mined only about 1% is actual Uranium, while the rest of the rock (which is still slightly radioactive) is discarded. In the past and in some parts of the world today, the discarded ore has been left in huge piles to freely react with the environment. These piles are low level in their radiation, yet have radionuclides that have a very long half-life. The radionuclides released are thorium, radium and radon.

High level nuclear waste consists of spent nuclear fuel, reprocessed materials, and transuranic materials (heavier than natural isotopes of Uranium, i.e., Plutonium). The spent fuel rods contain about 94% irradiated Uranium, 1% plutonium isotopes and 5% various other isotopes. High level waste is unique due to a very long half life and a high emission of radiation.

At the moment, high level wastes are stored on site at nuclear power plants. Originally designed for the short term, this on-site storage consists of lead lined concrete pools of water. The water cools the spent fuel rods and controls the release of gamma radiation. Metal grids infused with Boron separate the fuel rods and prevent fission by absorbing free neutrons. The nuclear industry feels that this method of storage is safe for up to 1000 years, but considering that high level radiation has a half life longer than this, some method is thus needed for permanent storage.

Any method of permanent storage would have to prevent the waste from getting into the hydrological (water) cycle, and it would also have to be placed in a geologically stable area where events like earthquakes and volcanos would not disturb the storage site. At present, two alternatives are to bury containers of nuclear waste in natural salt formations where there is no presence of water, or in deep (1000 m) disposal vaults in granitic rock.

Abandoned ideas for long term storage of high level waste include ejecting the waste into outer space. This was terminated due to great economic expense in addition to the potential dangers of a launching accident. Another idea for waste storage was to bury it in the Antarctic Ice Sheet, but this was cancelled due to the instability of the area, and the fact that it would make the area uninhabitable.

At present there is no actual site for the long term storage of nuclear waste. Considering that nuclear waste has been accumulating for decades, it is no wonder that there is some public opposition to nuclear energy. If nuclear power is to continue to play a major role in the world's production of electricity, more research must be done into finding a permanent method to safely dispose of nuclear waste.

7 Future Global Aspects of Energy

Present human activities are unsustainable, and current energy demand and supply patterns are contributing to this problem. Based on an analysis of the important linkages between energy, social, environmental, economic and security issues, it could be concluded that the world's present energy systems and trends are not compatible with reaching the social and environmental goals and objectives emanating from UNCED and other United Nations global conferences of the 1990s, nor those of the environment-related conventions. Major changes in the energy service delivery system are required to meet these objectives.

It will not be easy to bring about a fundamental reorientation from strategies that focus only on conventional supply expansion to those that emphasise energy services through a combination of energy end-use efficiency improvements, increased use of renewable sources of energy, and a new generation of fossil-fuel-using technologies. Discussions about energy demand still focus on how to increase supplies of energy rather than on the more important question of how to obtain the required energy services. Shifting the existing supply paradigm to a focus on energy services will require fundamental readjustments of public polices to promote and adopt sustainable energy options.

Fortunately, a number of feasible technology options are available or could become available in the near term to meet energy service demands in a sustainable manner. Considerable benefits in social, environmental, economic and security terms would arise from moving towards a sustainable energy future. Thus, new energy systems that are compatible with sustainable development goals are conceivable, feasible and beneficial.

Energy systems have changed dramatically during the course of history - from the use of wood as the dominant fuel in the early 1800s, to coal in the early 1900s, to the current predominance of oil and natural gas. These changes, which took place over several decades, were driven by resource availability, technology developments, and prices.

Today, in contrast to the prevailing assumption in the 1970s, shortages of oil and natural gas are not imminent. In fact, the ratios of reserves to production have been growing steadily. In addition, the world has vast coal resources. So, a transition to a new sustainable energy system will not be driven by either limitations of reserves or resource scarcity, for a long time to come.

Another significant change is the importance of the present environmental situation, locally, regionally, and globally, and the recognition of opportunities to address social concerns through actions related to energy. Concerns in these areas create a new and different set of drivers for change in the energy sector.

Moreover, shifting patterns of demand are creating new opportunities. Historically, most energy technology development has taken place in the industrialised countries, where economic growth has been strong, and rapidly growing markets provided a good context for innovation in energy-intensive processes. Today these conditions have changed radically. The energy-intensive industries are facing stagnation or experiencing slow growth in the markets of industrialised countries, while growth in the demand for energy and material-intensive products in many developing countries is rapid. Growth in the industrialised countries is now primarily in service and knowledge-intensive industries that use little materials or energy. The shift in growth patterns provides new opportunities for developing countries to become leaders of innovation for the development of new energy-efficient and clean production and end-use technologies.

The first step in designing energy systems consistent with the goal of sustainable development is recognition that the measures to advance sustainable development will have to be shaped in the context of current global trends that are operating through, or in conjunction with, strong constraints on traditional actors. This is the topic of the next section.

Major trends in the overall political and economic environment in which the new global energy system will evolve include globalisation, the information revolution, marketisation, the changing role of governments, governments' fiscal austerity, and popular participation in public sector decision-making.

Globalisation: As markets become globalised, trade barriers between countries arc becoming increasingly difficult to erect or maintain. Out-sourcing, the procurement of inputs (materials and services) from distant and foreign sources, is becoming common practice. New technology is diffusing globally, at rates faster than ever before.

Information revolution: Worldwide access to information is rapidly improving through the use of modern information technology, including the Internet Thus, there are new pathways for providing bases for information and dissemination of new technology and know-how. This expansion will facilitate increased awareness of sustainable energy options and deployment of new systems.

Marketisation: Since the end of the Cold War and the collapse of planned economies in central and eastern Europe, significant changes have occurred and continue to occur in the structures of many economies. The questions of what, how, and how much to produce, which in some countries had been a preoccupation of central authorities and bureaucracies, are now being decided by market mechanisms. The allocation of manpower, materials, and financial resources as well as the selection of products and production technologies increasingly is a function of market conditions. The process of marketisation is not restricted to the borders of countries; it is extending beyond national frontiers to regions and the whole world.

Changing role of government: Government functions are increasingly moving towards rule-making and monitoring the application and observance of the rules. Thus, the role of governments is changing drastically towards becoming the caretaker of the rules and regulations that ensure that markets can work efficiently. Governments also have crucial responsibilities that cannot be left to the market - to provide leadership in ensuring that people living in poverty and women have access to modern energy services; to work for the empowerment of communities and regions and strengthen their self-reliance; and to protect the environment.

Governments' fiscal austerity: In most countries, governments currently have budget deficit problems. As a result, only limited government finance is available for infrastructure investments. This affects the role of governments as investors in energy and in research and development, and as Official Development Assistance (ODA) donors. Public fiscal constraints also indicate that measures to implement new energy systems must not create fiscal burdens on public treasuries. Fortunately, as will be discussed below, technological advancement and the development of new policy instruments are resulting in the availability of innovative measures that are not costly to governments.

Popular participation in public sector decision-making: Perhaps the most encouraging development facilitating the emergence of sustainable energy systems is the democratisation that is sweeping the world. Growing awareness and concern about development and environmental issues is beginning to affect elections and consumption patterns. Throughout the world local groups and networks are becoming more involved in the decision-making processes and are having impacts on the formulation of public policies. The challenge of ensuring sustainability is being taken up by public interest groups instead of being left to governments and their bureaucracies alone. Women's groups, with their natural propensity for concern for the next generation, are getting involved in ensuring that sustainable development stays on the agenda.

New public policies are needed to promote energy strategies compatible with the sustainable development objectives set forth in the major United Nations conferences and conventions, in light of current global trends and constraints - energy policies that emphasise energy services, promote efficient markets, promote universal access to modern energy services, include external social costs in energy market decisions, accelerate the development and market penetration of sustainable energy technologies, promote indigenous capacity building, and encourage broad participation of stakeholders in energy decision-making.

Emphasise energy services: People want the services that energy provides, not fuel or electricity. Energy policies should be framed so as not to promote the expansion of energy supplies or consumption levels but instead encourage the provision of energy services in the most cost-effective ways that are compatible with sustainable development objectives. Emphasis on energy services in energy policy-making would facilitate the realisation of energy futures characterised by relatively low levels of energy demand. In such futures sustainability goals are more easily met than in high energy demand futures.

Promote efficient markets: The ongoing trends toward privatisation and increased competition can be helpful in meeting sustainable development objectives. Privatisation is bringing needed additional resources to the energy sector that increasingly fiscally constrained governments can no longer provide.

Price reforms and the increasing roles of market forces and competition are leading to a much greater efficiency in the allocation of resources. Reformed markets will also increase countries' technological choices by freeing them of the need to meet energy needs with the "technology/financing package deals" that have taken place in many developing countries in recent years. Governments have many roles to play in bringing about more efficient energy markets.

Governments can establish and maintain a level playing field among alternative supply and end-use technologies in providing energy services. Reforms needed to accomplish this include elimination of permanent subsidies to particular energy technologies, the pricing of energy to reflect its full cost, measures that improve the flow of information to market decision-makers, and measures that improve the access to capital for technology investments that are discriminated against in current capital markets (e.g., investments in energy end-use efficiency improvement and distributed power generation). Governments can also be helpful in accelerating the development of domestic capital markets (e.g., via establishing pension funds, insurance funds). And governments can create a policy environment that will build private investor confidence, facilitate the formation of joint ventures, promote equity participation by foreign interests, and promote competition among providers of energy services. The needed policy environment would include, inter alia, clear ownership rules, litigation procedures, protection of intellectual property rights, and the introduction of transparent accounting and auditing. Such conditions have been or are being created in many countries.

Despite the importance of efficient markets, many of the goals of sustainable development cannot be met simply by making markets more efficient.

Promote universal access to modern energy services: While the growing emphasis on market mechanisms in the energy sector will lead to more efficient allocation of resources, market forces alone will not address concerns about equity. Governments have a responsibility to shape the rules that will guide market forces in ways that will promote universal access to modern energy services, giving emphasis to those consumers, e.g., in rural households and low-income households, whom free markets are likely to exclude or serve inadequately.

Include external social costs in energy market decisions: Free markets do not take into account adverse local, regional, and global environmental and safety impacts of energy production and use. Under a sustainable development strategy governments would internalise such "externalities" through imposition of taxes, fees, and/or regulations. Such public policies would encourage the market to choose technologies that are inherently clean and safe.

Accelerate the development and market penetration of sustainable energy technologies. Private firms generally tend to under-invest in research and development, because they cannot avoid the appropriation by free riders of some of the economic benefits of such investments. This traditionally has been the main justification for public-sector support for research and development; under a sustainable development paradigm, government support for research and development would emphasise technologies that are compatible with sustainability objectives. In light of the seriousness of the multiple challenges facing the energy system, and the wealth of near-term opportunities for alleviating these problems with new technologies, this research and development support should be increased substantially above current levels. Moreover, the significant public benefits that would arise from the successful commercialisation of energy technologies that are compatible with sustainability objectives justifies public sector support, not only for research and development, but also for accelerating the commercialisation of such technologies that are commercially ready. There are many opportunities for co-operation between industrialised and developing countries in these energy innovation-related activities and for developing countries to leapfrog to a development path that is sustainable.

Promote indigenous capacity building: Developing countries cannot leapfrog to a sustainable path for energy without a strong indigenous capacity to create, design, market, build, and manage the needed energy technologies. Developing countries also need a strong indigenous capacity for technology assessment to better inform the energy planning process about opportunities for meeting sustainability objectives with alternative technologies. Capacity-building can be accomplished in various ways, but international joint ventures and other international industrial partnerships can make important contributions to capacity building that warrant particular emphasis in light of ongoing trends towards globalisation and marketisation, particularly if the developing country participants in such collaborations have strong basic skills.

Encourage broad participation of stakeholders in energy decision-making: Evolution of the energy system in ways to make it compatible with sustainable development objectives would be greatly facilitated if there were broad consensus among stakeholders about the needed changes in the energy system. New mechanisms are needed to promote consensus building among industrial, environmental, and consumer stakeholders (both those without and with adequate purchasing power) and to facilitate inputs of these different stakeholders to energy decision-making.

Concerted efforts are needed at national and international levels involving governments, multilateral institutions, private sector investors, civil society and the energy industries to promote a sustainable energy path and to use energy as an effective instrument for sustainable human development. A number of encouraging developments along these lines are underway.

Growing awareness about development and environment issues throughout the world is beginning to have impacts on consumption patterns and political decisions. This increasing awareness is demonstrated by the emergence of local and regional groups that are committed to environmental and clean energy issues. In addition, many countries have adopted policies and programmes that clearly work towards a more sustainable energy future.

A number of international developments in this area are also encouraging. For example, the Framework Convention on Climate Change (FCCC) has entered into force and has been ratified by 164 countries (June 1996). The Global Environment Facility (GEF), as the financial mechanism for the FCCC, devotes a significant fraction of its resources to renewable energy and energy efficiency to reduce greenhouse gas emissions. Multilateral organisations including the United Nations Development Programme, the regional development banks and the World Bank are increasing their sustainable energy efforts. A report of the Secretary-General to the Commission on Sustainable Development (CSD) has detailed the special role of energy in meeting the challenges of sustainable development, reviewed the energy activities of the United Nations system, and recommended areas for future activities by the United Nations system (United Nations, 1997). The countries in the Americas have initiated a process of Hemispheric Energy Co-operation, which has strong mandates to advance efficiency, the use of renewable sources of energy, and rural electrification (Santa Cruz Declaration, 1996). Many developing countries, including China, India, and Brazil, as well as several industrialised countries, have launched sustainable energy programs. Recently, more than one hundred nations, including ten represented by Heads of State and ten represented by Heads of Government, and another forty by energy or environment ministers, participated in the World Solar Summit in Zimbabwe and expressed their commitment to solar energy.

Internationally, no one organisation is responsible for energy. Within the United Nations system there are numerous agencies that support diverse activities in both conventional and renewable energy. The World Energy Council, representing world energy industries, has called on various occasions for new partnerships between government, the private sector and consumers to facilitate the changes required to move the world to a path of sustainable development. Many other non-governmental organisations, primarily motivated by environmental and social concerns, have advanced similar propositions.

The ability to move towards a sustainable energy future depends on building coalitions around common development, economic, technological and energy service interests that are part of a sustainable approach to energy. No new international institutions need be established. Rather, a framework through which sustainable energy strategies are promoted and interested parties convened, could be developed to address common interests. A mechanism that encourages better dialogue among governments, the private sector, and non-governmental organisations on the mobilisation of investment funds, technology transfer, management, and training is needed.

In contrast to the past, most future investments in energy systems are likely to be in developing countries. It is of considerable economic and environmental interest to developing countries that new technological opportunities become available to them. If they were to have these opportunities, they would be able to leapfrog to the new generation of cleaner energy technologies, without having to retrace the unsustainable path that the industrialised countries have followed.

This sets the stage for development co-operation. It can contribute to implementing sustainable energy futures and thereby work towards poverty reduction, job creation, the advancement of women and protection of the environment. Key elements in this regard will be human capacity building, the formulation of legal and institutional frameworks supportive of these developments, the demonstration of key new technologies, and national action programmes for sustainable energy.

The international community has dealt with aspects of social, economic and sustainable development through UNCED and the United Nations global conferences of the 1990s. They have identified targets and goals and formulated international agreements, platforms of action, declarations and resolutions adopting these commitments. Energy issues must be squarely dealt with if these commitments are to be fulfilled, and the leadership must come from governments. Within an appropriate framework, energy companies, both privately and publicly owned, investors and civil society can all contribute and support each other to meet the goals of sustainable development. A public sector-led reorientation to promote and adopt sustainable energy is essential to meet the commitments of the global conferences.

Energy can become an instrument of sustainable development. While accomplishing this will not be easily achieved in light of the major changes needed, a continuation of present trends cannot be sustained.

Glossary of Energy Terms

-A-

Absorption Coefficient - In reference to solar energy conversion devices, the degree to which a substance will absorb solar energy. In a solar photovoltaic device, the factor by which photons are absorbed as they travel a unit distance through a material.

Absorption Cooling - A process in which cooling of an interior space is accomplished by the evaporation of a volatile fluid, which is then absorbed in a strong solution, then desorbed under pressure by a heat source, and then recondensed at a temperature high enough that the heat of condensation can be rejected to a exterior space.

Absorptivity - In a solar thermal system, the ratio of solar energy striking the absorber that is absorbed by the absorber to that of solar energy striking a black body (perfect absorber) at the same temperature. The absorptivity of a material is numerically equal to its emissivity.

Accumulator - A component of a heat pump that stores liquid and keeps it from flooding the compressor. The accumulator takes the strain off the compressor and improves the reliability of the system.

Acid Rain - Also called "acid precipitation" or "acid deposition", acid rain is precipitation containing harmful amounts of nitric and sulphuric acids formed primarily by nitrogen oxides and sulphur oxides released into the atmosphere when fossil fuels are burned. It can be wet precipitation (rain, snow, or fog) or dry precipitation (absorbed gaseous and particulate matter, aerosol particles, or dust). Acid rain has a pH below 5.6. Normal rain has a pH of about 5.6, which is slightly acidic. (The pH value is a measure of acidity or alkalinity, ranging from 0 to 14. A pH measurement of 7 is regarded as neutral. Measurements below 7 indicate increased acidity, and those above 7 indicate increased alkalinity.)

Active Cooling - The use of mechanical heat pipes or pumps to transport heat by circulating heat transfer fluids.

Active Power - The power (in Watts) used by a device to produce useful work. Also called input power.

Active Solar Heating Systems - A solar water or space-heating system that use pumps or fans to circulate the heat-transfer fluid from the solar collectors to a storage tank subsystem.

Adiabatic - Without loss or gain of heat to a system. An adiabatic change is a change in volume and pressure of a parcel of gas without an exchange of heat between the parcel and its surroundings. In reference to a steam turbine, the adiabatic efficiency is the ratio of the work done per pound of steam, to the heat energy released and theoretically capable of transformation into mechanical work during the adiabatic expansion of a unit weight of steam.

Air Collector - In solar heating systems, a type of solar collector in which air is heated in the collector.

Air Conditioner - A device for conditioning air in an interior space. A Room Air Conditioner is a unit designed for installation in the wall or window of a room to deliver conditioned air without ducts. A Unitary Air Conditioner is composed of one or more assemblies that usually include an evaporator or cooling coil, a compressor and condenser combination, and possibly a heating apparatus. A Central Air Conditioner is designed to provide conditioned air from a central unit to a whole house with fans and ducts.

Air Diffuser - An air distribution outlet, typically located in the ceiling, which mixes conditioned air with room air.

Air Pollution Control - The use of devices to limit or prevent the release of pollution into the atmosphere.

Air Quality Standards - The prescribed level of pollutants allowed in outside or indoor air as established by legislation.

Air Register - The component of a combustion device that regulates the amount of air entering the combustion chamber.

Airlock Entry - A building architectural element (vestibule) with two airtight doors that reduces the amount of air infiltration and exfiltration when the exterior most door is opened.

Air-Source Heat Pump - A type of heat pump that transfers heat from outdoor air to indoor air during the heating season, and works in reverse during the cooling season.

Air-to-Water Heat Pump - A type of heat pump that transfers heat in outdoor air to water for space or water heating.

Albedo - The ratio of light reflected by a surface to the light falling on it.

Alcohol - A group of organic compounds composed of carbon, hydrogen, and oxygen; a series of molecules composed of a hydrocarbon plus a hydroxyl group; includes methanol, ethanol, isopropyl alcohol and others.

Alternating Current - An electric current that reverses its direction at regularly recurring intervals, usually 50 or 60 times per second.

Alternative Fuels - A popular term for "non-conventional" transportation fuels derived from natural gas (propane, compressed natural gas, methanol, etc.) or biomass materials (ethanol, methanol).

Alternator - A generator producing alternating current by the rotation of its rotor, and which is powered by a primary mover.

Ampere - A unit of measure for an electrical current; the amount of current that flows in a circuit at an electromotive force of one Volt and at a resistance of one Ohm. Abbreviated as amp.

Amp-Hours - A measure of the flow of current (in amperes) over one hour.

Anaerobic Digestion - The complex process by which organic matter is decomposed by anaerobic bacteria. The decomposition process produces a gaseous by-product often called "biogas" primarily composed of methane, carbon dioxide, and hydrogen sulphide.

Angstrom Unit - A unit of length named for A.J. Angstome, a Swedish spectroscopist, used in measuring electromagnetic radiation equal to 0.000,000,01 centimeters.

Anhydrous Ethanol - One hundred percent alcohol; neat ethanol.

Annual Solar Savings - The annual solar savings of a solar building is the energy savings attributable to a solar feature relative to the energy requirements of a non-solar building.

Anode - The positive pole or electrode of an electrolytic cell, vacuum tube, etc. (see also sacrificial anode).

Anthracite (coal) - A hard, dense type of coal, that is hard to break, clean to handle, difficult to ignite, and that burns with an intense flame and with the virtual absence of smoke because it contains a high percentage of fixed carbon and a low percentage of volatile matter.

Anthropogenic - Referring to alterations in the environment due to the presence or activities of humans.

Apparent Day - A solar day; an interval between successive transits of the sun's centre across an observer's meridian; the time thus measured is not equal to clock time.

Apparent Power (kVA) - This is the voltage-ampere requirement of a device designed to convert electric energy to a non-electrical form.

Appliance - A device for converting one form of energy or fuel into useful energy or work.

Aquifer - A subsurface rock unit from which water can be produced.

Argon - A colorless, odorless inert gas sometimes used in the spaces between the panes in energy efficient windows. This gas is used because it will transfer less heat than air. Therefore, it provides additional protection against conduction and convection of heat over conventional double -pane windows.

Array (Solar) - Any number of solar photovoltaic modules or solar thermal collectors or reflectors connected together to provide electrical or thermal energy.

Ash - The non-combustible residue of a combusted substance composed primarily of alkali and metal oxides.

Asynchronous Generator - A type of electric generator that produces alternating current that matches an existing power source.

Atmospheric Pressure - The pressure of the air at sea level; one standard atmosphere at zero degrees centigrade is equal to 14.695 pounds per square inch (1.033 kilograms per square centimeter).

Atrium - An interior court to which rooms open.

Audit (Energy) - The process of determining energy consumption, by various techniques, of a building or facility.

Automatic (or Remote) Meter Reading System - A system that records the consumption of electricity, gas, water, etc., and sends the data to a central data accumulation device.

Automatic Damper - A device that cuts off the flow of hot or cold air to or from a room as controlled by a thermostat.

Autonomous system - A stand-alone PV system that has no back-up generating source. May or may not include storage batteries. Most battery systems are designed for a certain minimum "days of autonomy" - which means that the batteries can supply sufficient power with no sunlight to charge the batteries. This varies from 3-5 days in the sunbelt, to 5 to 10 days elsewhere.

Auxiliary Energy or System - Energy required to operate mechanical components of an energy system, or a source of energy or energy supply system to back-up another.

Availability - Describes the reliability of power plants. It refers to the number of hours that a power plant is available to produce power divided by the total hours in a set time period, usually a year.

Average Cost - The total cost of production divided by the total quantity produced.

Average Demand - The demand on, or the power output of, an electrical system or any of its parts over an interval of time, as determined by the total number of kilowatt-hours divided by the units of time in the interval.

Average Wind Speed (or Velocity) - The mean wind speed over a specified period of time.

Avoided Costs - The incremental costs of energy and/or capacity, except for the purchase from a qualifying facility, a utility would incur itself in the generation of the energy or its purchase from another source.

Awning - An architectural element for shading windows and wall surfaces placed on the exterior of a building; can be fixed or movable.

Axial Fans - Fans in which the direction of the flow of the air from inlet to outlet remains unchanged; includes propeller, tubaxial, and vaneaxial type fans.

Axial Flow Compressor - A type of air compressor in which air is compressed in a series of stages as it flows axially through a decreasing tubular area.

Axial Flow Turbine - A turbine in which the flow of a steam or gas is essentially parallel to the rotor axis.

Azimuth (Solar) - The angle between true south and the point on the horizon directly below the sun.

-B-

Backup Energy System - A reserve appliance; for example, a standby generator for a home or commercial building.

Bacteria - Single-celled organisms, free-living or parasitic, that break down the wastes and bodies of dead organisms, making their components available for reuse by other organisms.

Balance of System - In a solar energy system, refers to all components other than the collector. In terms of costs, it includes design costs, land, site preparation, system installation, support structures, power conditioning, operation and maintenance costs, indirect storage, and related costs.

Balance Point - An outdoor temperature, usually 20 to 45 degrees Fahrenheit, at which a heat pump's output equals the heating demand. Below the balance point, supplementary heat is needed.

Baling - A means of reducing the volume of a material by compaction into a bale.

Ballast - A device used to control the voltage in a fluorescent lamp.

Band Gap Energy - The amount of energy (in electron volts) required to frcc an outer shell electron from its orbit about the nucleus to a free state, and thus promote it from the valence to the conduction level.

Barrel (petroleum) - 42 U.S. gallons (306 pounds of oil, or 5.78 million Btu).

Basal Metabolism - The amount of heat given off by a person at rest in a comfortable environment; approximately 50 Btu per hour (Btu/h).

Base Power - Power generated by a utility unit that operates at a very high capacity factor.

Baseboard Radiator - A type of radiant heating system where the radiator is located along an exterior wall where the wall meets the floor.

Baseload Capacity - The power output of a power plant that can be continuously produced.

Baseload Demand - The minimum demand experienced by a power plant.

Baseload Power Plant - A power plant that is normally operated to generate a base load, and that usually operates at a constant load; examples include coal fired and nuclear fuelled power plants.

Batch Process - A process for carrying out a reaction in which the reactants are fed in discrete and successive charges.

Batt/Blanket - A flexible roll or strip of insulating material in widths suited to standard spacings of building structural members (studs and joists). They are made from glass or rock wool fibers. Blankets are continuous rolls. Batts are pre-cut to four or eight foot lengths.

Battery - An energy storage device composed of one or more electrolyte cells.

Battery Energy Storage - Energy storage using electrochemical batteries. The three main applications for battery energy storage systems include spinning reserve at generating stations, load leveling at substations, and peak shaving on the customer side of the meter.

Beam Radiation - Solar radiation that is not scattered by dust or water droplets.

Binary Cycle Geothermal Plants - Binary cycle systems can be used with liquids at temperatures less than 350°F (177°C). In these systems, the hot geothermal liquid vaporizes a secondary working fluid, which then drives a turbine.

Biochemical Oxygen Demand - The weight of oxygen taken up mainly as a result of the oxidation of the constituents of a sample of water by biological action; expressed as the number of parts per million of oxygen taken up by the sample from water originally saturated with air, usually over a period of five days at 20 degrees centigrade. A standard means of estimating the degree of contamination of water.

Bioconversion - The conversion of one form of energy into another by the action of plants or microorganisms. The conversion of biomass to ethanol, methanol, or methane.

Bioenergy - The conversion of the complex carbohydrates in organic material into energy.

Biogas - A combustible gas created by anaerobic decomposition of organic material, composed primarily of methane, carbon dioxide, and hydrogen sulphide.

Biogasification or biomethanization - The process of decomposing biomass with anaerobic bacteria to produce biogas.

Biomass - Organic nonfossil material of biological origin constituting a renewable energy source.

Biomass Energy - Energy produced by the conversion of biomass directly to heat or to a liquid or gas that can be converted to energy.

Biomass Fuel - Biomass converted directly to energy or converted to liquid or gaseous fuels such as ethanol, methanol, methane, and hydrogen.

Biophotolysis - The action of light on a biological system that results in the dissociation of a substrate, usually water, to produce hydrogen.

Biota - The flora and fauna of a region.

Black Liquor - A by-product of the paper production process that can be used as a source of energy.

Blackbody - An ideal substance that absorbs all radiation falling on it, and reflecting nothing.

Bleached Board - A wood product used for printed and graphically enhanced card stock, books, and packaging such as food cartons, microwave trays, beverages, candy, cosmetics, pharmaceuticals, and consumer electronic items. Pollutants, such as dioxins and furans, can result from processes that use chlorine in the manufacture of bleached board.

Blocking diode - A diode used to restrict or block reverse current from flowing backward through a module. Alternatively, diode connected in series to a PV string; it protects its modules from a reverse power flow and, thus, against the risk of thermal destruction of solar cells.

Boiler - A vessel or tank where heat produced from the combustion of fuels such as natural gas, fuel oil, or coal is used to generate hot water or steam for applications ranging from building space heating to electric power production or industrial process heat.

Boiler Rating - The heating capacity of a steam boiler; expressed in Btu per hour (Btu/h), or horsepower, or pounds of steam per hour.

Bone (Oven) Dry - In reference to solid biomass fuels, such as wood, having zero moisture content.

Bone Dry Unit - A quantity of (solid) biomass fuel equal to 2400 pounds bone dry.

Booster Pump - A pump for circulating the heat transfer fluid in a hydronic heating system.

Boot - In heating and cooling system distribution ductwork, the transformation pieces connecting horizontal round leaders to vertical rectangular stacks.

Boron - The chemical element commonly used as the dopant in solar photovoltaic device or cell material.

Bottled Gas - A generic term for liquefied and pressurised gas, ordinarily butane, propane, or a mixture of the two, contained in a cylinder for domestic use.

Bottoming-cycle - A means to increase the thermal efficiency of a steam electric generating system by converting some waste heat from the condenser into electricity. The heat engine in a bottoming cycle would be a condensing turbine similar in principle to a steam turbine but operating with a different working fluid at a much lower temperature and pressure.

Brayton Cycle - A thermodynamic cycle using constant pressure, heat addition and rejection, representing the idealized behaviour of the working fluid in a gas turbine type heat engine.

Brine - Water saturated or strongly impregnated with salt.

British Thermal Unit (Btu) - The amount of heat required to raise the temperature of one pound of water one degree Fahrenheit; equal to 252 calories. The most basic energy measurement unit of all fuels, defined as the amount of heat required to raise the temperature of one pound of water one degree Fahrenheit.

Building Energy Ratio - The space-conditioning load of a building.

Building Heat-Loss Factor - A measure of the heating requirements of a building expressed in Btu per degree-day.

Bulb Turbine - A type of hydro turbine in which the entire generator is mounted inside the water passageway as an integral unit with the turbine. These installations can offer significant reductions in the size of the powerhouse.

Bulk Density - The weight of a material per unit of volume compared to the weight of the same volume of water.

Burner Capacity - The maximum heat output (in Btu per hour) released by a burner with a stable flame and satisfactory combustion.

Burning Point - The temperature at which a material ignites.

Bus (electrical) - An electrical conductor that serves as a common connection for two or more electrical circuits; may be in the form of rigid bars or stranded conductors or cables.

Busbar - The power conduit of an electric power plant; the starting point of the electric transmission system.

Busbar Cost - The cost per kilowatt-hour to produce electricity, including the cost of capital, debt service, operation and maintenance, and fuel. The power plant "bus" or "busbar" is that point beyond the generator but prior to the voltage transformation point in the plant switchyard.

Bypass - An alternative path. In a heating duct or pipe, an alternative path for the flow of the heat transfer fluid from one point to another, as determined by the opening or closing of control valves both in the primary line and the bypass line.

Bypass diode - A diode connected across one or more solar cells in a photovoltaic module such that the diode will conduct if the cell(s) become reverse biased. Alternatively, diode connected anti-parallel across a part of the solar cells of a PV module. It protects these solar cells from thermal destruction in case of total or partial shading, broken cells, or cell string failures of individual solar cells while other cells are exposed to full light.

-C-

Cage - The component of an electric motor composed of solid bars (of usually copper or aluminium) arranged in a circle and connected to continuous rings at each end. This cage fits inside the stator in an induction motor in channels between laminations, thin flat discs of steel in a ring configuration.

Calorie - The amount of heat required to raise the temperature of a unit of water, at or near the temperature of maximum density, one degree Celsius (or Centigrade [C]); expressed as a "small calorie" (the amount of heat required to raise the temperature of 1 gram of water one degree C), or as a "large calorie" or "kilogram calorie" (the amount of heat required to raise one kilogram [1000 grams] of water one degree C); capitalization of the word calorie indicates a kilogram-calorie.

Calorific Value - The heat liberated by the combustion of a unit quantity of a fuel under specific conditions; measured in calories.

Candela - A unit of luminous intensity; the magnitude to the candela is such that the luminance of the total radiator, at the temperature of solidification of platinum, is 60 candelas per square centimeter.

Candle Power - The illuminating power of a standard candle employed as a unit for determining the illuminating quality of an illuminant.

Capability - The maximum load that a generating unit, power plant, or other electrical apparatus can carry under specified conditions for a given period of time, without exceeding its approved limits of temperature and stress.

Capability Margin - The difference between net electrical system capability and system maximum load requirements (peak load); the margin of capability available to provide for scheduled maintenance, emergency outages, system operating requirements and unforeseen loads.

Capacitance - A measure of the electrical charge of a capacitor consisting of two plates separated by an insulating material.

Capacitor - An electrical device that adjusts the leading current of an applied alternating current to balance the lag of the circuit to provide a high power factor.

Capacity - The load that a power generation unit or other electrical apparatus or heating unit is rated by the manufacture to be able to meet or supply.

Capacity (Condensing Unit) - The refrigerating effect in Btu/h produced by the difference in total enthalpy between a refrigerant liquid leaving the unit and the total enthalpy of the refrigerant vapour entering it. Generally measured in tons or Btu/h.

Capacity (Effective, of a motor) - The maximum load that a motor is capable of supplying.

Capacity (Heating, of a material) - The amount of heat energy needed to raise the temperature of a given mass of a substance by one degree Celsius. The heat required to raise the temperature of 1 kg of water by 1 degree Celsius is 4186 Joules.

Capacity Factor - The ratio of the average load on (or power output of) a generating unit or system to the capacity rating of the unit or system over a specified period of time.

Capacity Release or Capacity Reallocation - A term used under FERC Order 636, referring to the relinquishment of the right to use space in an interstate natural gas pipeline.

Capacity, Gross - The full-load continuous rating of a generator, prime mover, or other electric equipment under specified conditions as designated by the manufacturer. It is usually indicated on a nameplate attached to the equipment.

Capital Costs - The amount of money needed to purchase equipment, buildings, tools, and other manufactured goods that can be used in production.

Carbon Dioxide - A colorless, odorless noncombustible gas with the formula CO_2 that is present in the atmosphere. It is formed by the combustion of carbon and carbon compounds (such as fossil fuels and biomass), by respiration, which is a slow combustion in animals and plants, and by the gradual oxidation of organic matter in the soil.

Carbon Monoxide - A colorless, odorless but poisonous combustible gas with the formula CO. Carbon monoxide is produced in the incomplete combustion of carbon and carbon compounds such as fossil fuels (i.e., coal, petroleum) and their products (e.g., liquefied petroleum gas, gasoline), and biomass.

Carbon Zinc Cell Battery - A cell produces electric energy by the galvanic oxidation of carbon; commonly used in household appliances.

Carnot Cycle - An ideal heat engine (conceived by Sadi Carnot) in which the sequence of operations forming the working cycle consists of isothermal expansion, adiabatic expansion, isothermal compression, and adiabatic compression back to its initial state.

Catalytic Converter - An air pollution control device that removes organic contaminants by oxidizing them into carbon dioxide and water through a chemical reaction using a catalysis, which is a substance that increases (or decreases) the rate of a chemical reaction without being changed itself; required in all automobiles sold in the United States and EC, and used in some types of heating appliances.

Cathedral Ceiling/Roof - A type of ceiling and roof assembly that has no attic.

Cathode - The negative pole or electrode of an electrolytic cell, vacuum tube, etc., where electrons enter (current leaves) the system; the opposite of an anode.

Cathode Disconnect Ballast - An electromagnetic ballast that disconnects a lamp's electrode heating circuit once it has started; often called "low frequency electronic" ballasts.

Cathodic Protection - A method of preventing oxidation of the exposed metal in structures by imposing between the structure and the ground a small electrical voltage.

Caulking - A material used to seal areas of potential air leakage into or out of a building envelope.

Ceiling - The downward facing structural element that is directly opposite the floor.

Ceiling Fan - A mechanical device used for air circulation and to provide cooling.

Cell - A component of a electrochemical battery. A "primary" cell consists of two dissimilar elements, known as "electrodes", immersed in a liquid or paste known as the "electrolyte". A direct current of 1-1.5 volts will be produced by this cell. A "secondary" cell or accumulator is a similar design but is made useful by passing a direct current of correct strength through it in a certain direction. Each of these cells will produce 2 volts; a 12 volt car battery contains six cells.

Cell barrier - A very thin region of static electric charge along the interface of the positive and negative layers in a photovoltaic cell. The barrier inhibits the movement of electrons from one layer to the other, so that higher-energy electrons from one side diffuse preferentially through it in one direction, creating a current and thus a voltage across the cell. Also called depletion zone, cell junction, or space charge.

Cell junction - The area of immediate contact between two layers (positive and negative) of a photovoltaic cell. The junction lies at the centre of the cell barrier or depletion zone.

Cellulase - An enzyme complex, produced by fungi and bacteria, capable of decomposing cellulose into small fragments, primarily glucose.

Cellulose Insulation - A type of insulation composed of waste newspaper, cardboard, or other forms of waste paper.

Central Heating System - A system where heat is supplied to areas of a building from a single appliance through a network of ducts or pipes.

Central Power Plant - A large power plant that generates power for distribution to multiple customers.

Central Receiver Solar Power Plants - Also known as "power towers", these use fields of two-axis tracking mirrors known as heliostats. Each heliostat is individually positioned by a computer control system to reflect the sun's rays to a tower-mounted thermal receiver. The effect of many heliostats reflecting to a common point creates the combined energy of thousands of suns, which produces high-temperature thermal energy. In the receiver, molten nitrate salts absorb the heat energy. The hot salt is then used to boil water to steam, which is sent to a conventional steam turbine-generator to produce electricity.

Cetane Number - A measure of a fuel's (liquid) ease of self-ignition.

Char - A by-product of low-temperature carbonization of a solid fuel.

Charcoal - A material formed from the incomplete combustion or destructive distillation (carbonization) of organic material in a kiln or retort, and having a high energy density, being nearly pure carbon. (If produced from coal, it is coke.) Used for cooking, the manufacture of gunpowder and steel (notably in Brazil), as an absorbent and decolorizing agent, and in sugar refining and solvent recovery.

Charge Carrier - A free and mobile conduction electron or hole in a semiconductor.

Charge controller - An electronic device which regulates the voltage applied to the battery system from the PV array. Essential for ensuring that batteries obtain maximum state of charge and longest life.

Chemical Energy - The energy liberated in a chemical reaction, as in the combustion of fuels.

Chemical Vapour Deposition (CVD) - A method of depositing thin semiconductor films used to make certain types of solar photovoltaic devices. With this method, a substrate is exposed to one or more vaporised compounds, one or more of which contain desirable constituents. A chemical reaction is initiated, at or near the substrate surface, to produce the desired material that will condense on the substrate.

Chiller - A device for removing heat from a gas or liquid stream for air conditioning/cooling.

Chimney - A masonry or metal stack that creates a draft to bring air to a fire and to carry the gaseous byproducts of combustion safely away.

Chlorofluorocarbon (CFC) - A family of chemicals composed primarily of carbon, hydrogen, chlorine, and fluorine whose principal applications are as refrigerants and industrial cleansers and whose principal drawback is the tendency to destroy the Earth's protective ozone layer.

Circuit - A device, or system of devices, that allows electrical current to flow through it and allows voltage to occur across positive and negative terminals.

Circuit Breaker - A device used to interrupt or break an electrical circuit when an overload condition exists; usually installed in the positive circuit; used to protect electrical equipment.

Circuit Lag - As time increases from zero at the terminals of an inductor, the voltage comes to a particular value on the sine function curve ahead of the current. The voltage reaches its negative peak exactly 90 degrees before the current reaches its negative peak thus the current lags behind by 90 degrees.

Circulating Fluidized Bed - A type of furnace or reactor in which the emission of sulphur compounds is lowered by the addition of crushed limestone in the fluidized bed thus obviating the need for much of the expensive stack gas clean-up equipment. The particles are collected and recirculated, after passing through a conventional bed, and cooled by boiler internals.

Clerestory - A window located high in a wall near the eaves that allows daylight into a building interior, and may be used for ventilation and solar heat gain.

Climate Change (Greenhouse Effect) - The increasing mean global surface temperature of the Earth caused by gases in the atmosphere (including carbon dioxide, methane, nitrous oxide, ozone, and chlorofluorocarbons). The greenhouse effect allows solar radiation to penetrate the Earth's atmosphere but absorbs the infrared radiation returning to space.

Close Coupled - An energy system in which the fuel production equipment is in close proximity, or connected to, the fuel using equipment.

Closed Cycle - A system in which a working fluid is used over and over without introduction of new fluid, as in a hydronic heating system or mechanical refrigeration system.

Closed Loop Biomass - As defined by the Comprehensive National Energy Act of 1992 (or the Energy Policy Act; EPAct) - any organic matter from a plant which is planted for the exclusive purpose of being used to produce energy. This does not include wood or agricultural wastes or standing timber.

Codes - Legal documents that regulate construction to protect the health, safety, and welfare of people. Codes establish minimum standards but do not guarantee efficiency or quality.

Coefficient of Heat Transmission (U-Value) - A value that describes the ability of a material to conduct heat. The number of Btu that flow through 1 square foot of material, in one hour. It is the reciprocal of the R-Value (U-Value = 1/R-Value).

Coefficient of Performance (COP) - A ratio of the work or useful energy output of a system versus the amount of work or energy inputted into the system as determined by using the same energy equivalents for energy in and out. Is used as a measure of the steady state performance or energy efficiency of heating, cooling, and refrigeration appliances. The COP is equal to the Energy Efficiency Ratio (EER) divided by 3.412. The higher the COP, the more efficient the device.

Coefficient of Utilisation (CU) - A term used for lighting appliances; the ratio of lumens received on a flat surface to the light output, in lumens, from a lamp; used to evaluate the effectiveness of luminaries in delivering light.

Cogeneration - The generation of electricity or shaft power by an energy conversion system and the concurrent use of rejected thermal energy from the conversion system as an auxiliary energy source.

Cogenerator - A class of energy producer that produces both heat and electricity from a single fuel.

Coil - As a component of a heating or cooling appliance, rows of tubing or pipe with fins attached through which a heat transfer fluid is circulated and to deliver heat or cooling energy to a building.

Coincidence Factor - The ratio of the coincident, maximum demand of two or more loads to the sum of their noncoincident maximum demand for a given period; the reciprocal of the diversity factor, and is always less than or equal to one.

Coincident Demand - The demand of a consumer of electricity at the time of a power supplier's peak system demand.

Collector - The component of a solar energy heating system that collects solar radiation, and that contains components to absorb solar radiation and transfer the heat to a heat transfer fluid (air or liquid).

Collector Efficiency - The ratio of solar radiation captured and transferred to the collector (heat transfer) fluid.

Collector Fluid - The fluid, liquid (water or water/antifreeze solution) or air, used to absorb solar energy and transfer it for direct use, indirect heating of interior air or domestic water, and/or to a heat storage medium.

Collector Tilt - The angle that a solar collector is positioned from horizontal.

Color Rendering or Rendition - A measure of the ability of a light source to show colors, based on a color rendering index.

Combined-Cycle Power Plant - A power plant that uses two thermodynamic cycles to achieve higher overall system efficiency; e.g., the heat from a gas-fired combustion turbine is used to generate steam for heating or to operate a steam turbine to generate additional electricity.

Combustion - The process of burning; the oxidation of a material by applying heat, which unites oxygen with a material or fuel.

Combustion Air - Air that provides the necessary oxygen for complete, clean combustion and maximum heating value.

Combustion Chamber - Any wholly or partially enclosed space in which combustion takes place.

Combustion Gases - The gaseous byproducts of the combustion of a fuel.

Combustion Power Plant - A power plant that generates power by combusting a fuel.

Combustion Turbine - A turbine that generates power from the combustion of a fuel.

Comfort Zone - A frequently used room or area that is maintained at a more comfortable level than the rest of the house; also known as a "warm room".

Compact Fluorescent - A smaller version of standard fluorescent lamps which can directly replace standard incandescent lights. These lights consist of a gas filled tube, and a magnetic or electronic ballast.

Complete Mix Digester - A type of anaerobic digester that has a mechanical mixing system and where temperature and volume are controlled to maximise the anaerobic digestion process for biological waste treatment, methane production, and odor control.

Composting - The process of degrading organic material (biomass) by microorganisms in aerobic conditions.

Compressed Natural Gas (CNG) - Natural gas (methane) that has been compressed to a higher pressure gaseous state by a compressor; used in CNG vehicles.

Compressor - A device used to compress air for mechanical or electrical power production, and in air conditioners, heat pumps, and refrigerators to pressurize the refrigerant and enabling it to flow through the system.

Concentrator - A reflective or refractive device that focuses incident insolation onto an area smaller than the reflective or refractive surface, resulting in increased insolation at the point of focus.

Condensate - The liquid resulting when water vapour contacts a cool surface; also the liquid resulting when a vaporised working fluid (such as a refrigerant) is cooled or depressurized.

Condenser Coil - The device in an air conditioner or heat pump through which the refrigerant is circulated and releases heat to the surroundings when a fan blows outside air over the coils. This will return the hot vapour that entered the coil into a hot liquid upon exiting the coil.

Condensing Unit - The component of a central air conditioner that is designed to remove heat absorbed by the refrigerant and transfer it outside the conditioned space.

Conditioned Space - The interior space of a building that is heated or cooled.

Conduction - The transfer of heat through a material by the transfer of kinetic energy from particle to particle; the flow of heat between two materials of different temperatures that are in direct physical contact.

Conductivity (Thermal) - This is a positive constant, k, that is a property of a substance and is used in the calculation of heat transfer rates for materials. It is the amount of heat that flows through a specified area and thickness of a material over a specified period of time when there is a temperature difference of one degree between the surfaces of the material.

Conductor - The material through which electricity is transmitted, such as an electrical wire, or transmission or distribution line.

Conduit - A tubular material used to encase and protect one or more electrical conductors.

Connected Load - The sum of the ratings of the electricity consuming apparatus connected to a generating system.

Connection Charge - An amount paid by a customer for being connected to an electricity supplier's transmission and distribution system.

Conservation - To reduce or avoid the consumption of a resource or commodity.

Constant-Speed Wind Turbines - Wind turbines that operate at a constant rotor revolutions per minute (RPM) and are optimised for energy capture at a given rotor diameter at a particular speed in the wind power curve.

Consumption Charge - The part of an energy utility's charge based on actual energy consumed by the customer; the product of the kilowatt-hour rate and the total kilowatt-hours consumed.

Contact Resistance - The resistance between metallic contacts and the semiconductor.

Continuous Fermentation - A steady-state fermentation process.

Contrast - The difference between the brightness of an object compared to that of its immediate background.

Convection - Motion in a fluid or plastic material due to some parts being buoyant because of their higher temperature. Convection is a means of transferring heat through mass flow rather than through simple thermal conduction.

Conventional Fuel - The fossil fuels - coal, oil, and natural gas.

Conventional Heat Pump - This type of heat pump is known as an air-to-air system.

Conversion Efficiency - The amount of energy produced as a percentage of the amount of energy consumed.

Converter - A device for transforming the quality and quantity of electrical energy; also an inverter.

Cooling Capacity - The quantity of heat that a cooling appliance is capable of removing from a room in one hour.

Cooling Degree Day - A value used to estimate interior air cooling requirements (load) calculated as the number of degrees per day (over a specified period) that the daily average temperature is above 65 degrees Fahrenheit (or some other, specified base temperature). The daily average temperature is the mean of the maximum and minimum temperatures recorded for a specific location for a 24 hour period.

Cooling Tower - A structure used to cool power plant water; water is pumped to the top of the tubular tower and sprayed out into the centre, and is cooled by evaporation as it falls, and then is either recycled within the plant or is discharged.

Coproducts - The potentially useful byproducts of ethanol fermentation process.

Cord (of Wood) - A stack of wood 4 feet by 4 feet by 8 feet

Cost-of-Service - The total number of dollars required to return to a utility all of its costs for supplying a service. These costs include operating and maintenance expenses, cost of fuels, taxes (including income taxes), depreciation, debt cost, and a return on the utility's investment.

Coulomb - A unit for the quantity of electricity transported in 1 second by a current of 1 ampere.

Counterflow Heat Exchanger - A heat exchanger in which two fluids flow in opposite directions for transfer heat energy from one to the other.

Creosote - A liquid by-product of wood combustion (or distillation) that condenses on the internal surfaces of vents and chimneys, which if not removed regularly, can corrode the surfaces and fuel a chimney fire.

Critical Compression Pressure - The highest possible pressure in a fuel-air mixture before spontaneous ignition occurs.

Cubic Foot (of Natural Gas) - A unit of volume equal to 1 cubic foot at a pressure base of 14.73 pounds standard per square inch absolute and a temperature base of 60 degrees Fahrenheit.

Cull Wood - Wood logs, chips, or wood products that are burned.

Current (Electrical) - The flow of electrical energy (electricity) in a conductor, measured in amperes.

Current at maximum power (Imp) - The current at which maximum power is available from a module.

Customer Charge - An amount to be paid for energy periodically by a customer without regard to demand or energy consumption.

Cut-In-Speed - The lowest wind speed at which a wind turbine begins producing usable power.

Cut-Out-Speed - The highest wind speed at which a wind turbine stops producing power.

Cycle - In alternating current, the current goes from zero potential or voltage to a maximum in one direction, back to zero, and then to a maximum potential or voltage in the other direction. The number of complete cycles per second determines the current frequency.

Cycle life - Number of discharge-charge cycles that a battery can tolerate under specified conditions before it fails to meet specified criteria as to performance (e.g., capacity decreases to 80-percent of the nominal capacity).

Cycling Losses - The loss of heat as the water circulates through a water heater tank and inlet and outlet pipes.

Cyclone Burner - A furnace/combustion chamber in which finely ground fuel is blown in spirals in the combustion chamber to maximise combustion efficiency.

-D-

Dam - A structure for impeding and controlling the flow of water in a water course, and which increases the water elevation to create the hydraulic head. The reservoir creates, in effect, stored energy.

Damper - A movable plate used to control air flow; in a wood stove or fireplace, used to control the amount and direction of air going to the fire.

Darrius (Wind) Machine - A type of vertical-axis wind machine that has long, thin blades in the shape of loops connected to the top and bottom of the axle; often called an "eggbeater windmill."

Daylighting - The use of direct, diffuse, or reflected sunlight to provide supplemental lighting for building interiors.

Dc to dc converter - Electronic circuit to convert dc voltages (e.g., PV module voltage) into other levels (e.g., load voltage). Can be part of a maximum power point tracker (MPPT).

Decentralised (Energy) System - Energy systems supply individual, or small-groups, of energy loads.

Declination - The angular position of the sun at solar noon with respect to the plane of the equator.

Declining Block Rate - An electricity supplier rate structure in which the per unit price of electricity decreases as the amount of energy increases. Normally only available to very large consumers.

Decommissioning - The process of removing a power plant, apparatus, equipment, building, or facility from operation.

Decomposition - The process of breaking down organic material; reduction of the net energy level and change in physical and chemical composition of organic material.

De-energize(d) - To disconnect a transmission and/or distribution line; a power line that is not carrying a current; to open a circuit.

Deep Discharge - Discharging a battery to 20 percent or less of its full charge capacity.

Degree Day - A unit for measuring the extent that the outdoor daily average temperature (the mean of the maximum and minimum daily dry-bulb temperatures) falls below (in the case of heating, see Heating Degree Day), or falls above (in the case of cooling, see Cooling Degree Day) an assumed base temperature, normally taken as 65 degrees Fahrenheit, unless otherwise stated. One degree day is counted for each degree below (for heating) or above (in the case of cooling) the base, for each calendar day on which the temperature goes below or above the base.

Degree Hour - The product of 1 hour, and usually the number of degrees Fahrenheit the hourly mean temperature is above a base point (usually 65 degrees Fahrenheit); used in roughly estimating or measuring the cooling load in cases where processes heat, heat from building occupants, and humidity are relatively unimportant compared to the dry-bulb temperature.

Dehumidifier - A device that cools air by removing moisture from it.

Dekatherm (Dth) - An energy measurement which equals 10 therms, or 1 million etus (MMBtu's).

Demand - The rate at which electricity is delivered to or by a system, part of a system, or piece of equipment expressed in kilowatts, kilovoltamperes, or other suitable unit, at a given instant or averaged over a specified period of time.

Demand (Tankless) Water Heater - A type of water heater that has no storage tank thus eliminating storage tank standby losses. Cold water travels through a pipe into the unit, and either a gas burner or an electric element heats the water only when needed.

Demand Charge - A charge for the maximum rate at which energy is used during peak hours of a billing period. That part of a utility service charged for on the basis of the possible demand as distinguished from the energy actually consumed.

Demand(ed) Factor - The ratio of the maximum demand on an electricity generating and distribution system to the total connected load on the system; usually expressed as a percentage.

Demand-Side Management (DSM) - The process of managing the consumption of energy, generally to optimise available and planned generation resources.

Demand-Side Resource - A resource that reduces the demand for energy by implementing one or more demand-side measures.

Dendrite - A slender threadlike spike of pure crystalline material, such as silicon.

Dendritic Web Technique - A method for making sheets of polycrystalline silicon in which silicon dendrites are slowly withdrawn from a melt of silicon whereupon a web of silicon forms between the dendrites and solidifies as it rises from the melt and cools.

Dependable Capacity - The load-carrying ability of an electric power plant during a specific time interval and period when related to the characteristics of the load to be/being supplied; determined by capability, operating power factor, and the portion of the load the station is to supply.

Desiccation - The process of removing moisture; involves evaporation.

Design Cooling Load - The amount of conditioned air to be supplied by a cooling system; usually the maximum amount to be delivered based on a specified number of cooling degree days or design temperature.

Design Heating Load - The amount of heated air, or heating capacity, to be supplied by a heating system; usually the maximum amount to be delivered based on a specified number of heating degree days or design outside temperature.

Design Life - Period of time a system or appliance (or component of) is expected to function at its nominal or design capacity without major repair.

Design Temperature - The temperature that a system is designed to maintain (inside) or operate against (outside) under the most extreme conditions.

Design Voltage - The nominal voltage for which a conductor or electrical appliance is designed; the reference voltage for identification and not necessarily the precise voltage at which it operates.

Dessicant Cooling - To condition/cool air by dessication.

Desuperheater - An energy saving device in a heat pump that, during the cooling cycle, recycles some of the waste heat from the house to heat domestic water.

Dewpoint - The temperature to which air must be cooled, at constant pressure and water vapour content, in order for saturation or condensation to occur; the temperature at which the saturation pressure is the same as the existing vapour pressure; also called saturation point.

Difference of Potential - The difference in electrical pressure (voltage) between any two points in an electrical system or between any point in an electrical system and the earth.

Differential Thermostat - A type of automatic thermostat (used on solar heating systems) that responds to temperature differences (between collectors and the storage components) so as to regulate the functioning of appliances (to switch transfer fluid pumps on and off).

Diffuse insolation - Sunlight received indirectly as a result of scattering due to clouds, fog, haze, dust, or other obstructions in the atmosphere. Opposite of direct insolation.

Diffuse Solar Radiation - Sunlight scattered by atmospheric particles and gases so that it arrives at the earth's surface from all directions and can not be focused.

Diffusion - The movement of individual molecules through a material; permeation of water vapour through a material.

Diffusion Length - The mean distance a free electron or hole moves before recombining with another hole or electron.

Digester (Anaerobic) - A device in which organic material is biochemically decomposed (digested) by anaerobic bacteria to treat the material and/or to produce biogas.

Dimmer - A light control device that allows light levels to be manually adjusted. A dimmer can save energy by reducing the amount of power delivered to the light while consuming very little themselves.

Diode - An electronic device that allows current to flow in one direction only.

Dioxins - A classification of chlorine-containing compounds that are considered extremely toxic carcinogenic agents. Toxic effects include anorexia, hepatotoxicity, chloracne, vascular lesions, and gastric ulcers. Dioxins are byproducts in the manufacture of some chemicals. Causes of dioxin production in combustion begin with chlorine compounds in fuel, inadequate supply of combustion air, too low refractory temperatures, and improper mixing of fuel and air.

Dip Tube - A tube inside a domestic water heater that distributes the cold water from the cold water supply line into the lower area of the water heater where heating occurs.

Direct Access - The ability of an electric power consumer to purchase electricity from a supplier of their choice without being physically inhibited by the owner of the electric distribution and transmission system to which the consumer is connected to.

Direct Beam Radiation - Solar radiation that arrives in a straight line from the sun.

Direct Current - A type of electricity transmission and distribution by which electricity flows in one direction through the conductor; usually relatively low voltage and high current; typically abbreviated as dc.

Direct Vent Heater - A type of combustion heating system in which combustion air is drawn directly from outside and the products of combustion are vented directly outside. These features are beneficial in tight, energy-efficient homes because they will not depressurize a home and cause air infiltration, and backdrafting of other combustion appliances.

Direct Water Heater - A type of water heater in which heated water is stored within the tank. Hot water is released from the top of the tank when a hot water faucet is turned. This water is replaced with cold water that flows into the tank and down to just above the bottom plate under which are the burners.

Direct-Gain - The process by which sunlight directly enters a building through the windows and is absorbed and stored in massive floors or walls.

Discharge rate - The rate, usually expressed in amperes or time, at which electrical current is taken from the battery.

Discount Rate - The interest rate at which the Federal Reserve System stands ready to lend reserves to commercial banks. The rate is proposed by the 12 Federal Reserve banks and determined with the approval of the Board of Governors.

Displacement Power - A source of power (electricity) that can displace power from another source so that source's power can be transmitted to more distant loads.

Distributed Generation - A popular term for localized or on-site power generation.

Distributed systems - Systems that are installed at or near the location where the electricity is used, as opposed to central systems that supply electricity to grids. A residential photovoltaic system is a distributed system.

Distribution - The process of distributing electricity; usually defines that portion of an electrical utility's power lines between a utility's power pole and transformer and a customer's point of connection/meter.

Distribution Line - One or more circuits of a distribution system on the same line or poles or supporting structures usually operating at a lower voltage relative to the transmission line.

District Heating - A heating system in which steam or hot water for space heating or hot water is piped from a central boiler plant or electric power/heating plant to a cluster of buildings.

Diversity Factor - The ratio of the sum of the noncoincidental maximum demands of two or more loads to their coincidental maximum demands for the same period.

DOD – "Depth of Discharge", from 100-percent state of charge (SOC), in a battery or battery system.

Domestic Hot Water - Water heated for residential washing, bathing, etc.

Donor - In a solar photovoltaic device, an n-type dopant, such as phosphorus, that puts an additional electron into an energy level very near the conduction band; this electron is easily exited into the conduction band where it increases the electrical conductivity over that of an undoped semiconductor.

Dopant - A chemical element (impurity) added in small amounts to an otherwise pure semiconductor material to modify the electrical properties of the material. An n-dopant introduces more electrons. A p-dopant creates electron vacancies (holes).

Doping - The addition of dopants to a semiconductor.

Double Wall Heat Exchanger - A heat exchanger in a solar water heating system that has two distinct walls between the heat transfer fluid and the domestic water, to ensure that there is no mixing of the two.

Double-Pane or Glazed Window - A type of window having two layers (panes or glazing) of glass separated by an air space. Each layer of glass and surrounding air space reradiates and traps some of the heat that passes through thereby increasing the windows resistance to heat loss (R-value).

Downwind Wind Turbine - A horizontal axis wind turbine in which the rotor is downwind of the tower.

Draft - A column of burning combustion gases that are so hot and strong that the heat is lost up the chimney before it can be transferred to the house. A draft brings air to the fire to help keep it burning.

Draft Diverter - A door-like device located at the mouth of a fireplace chimney flue for controlling the direction and flow of the draft in the fireplace as well as the amount of oxygen that the fire receives.

Draft Hood - A device built into or installed above a combustion appliance to assure the escape of combustion byproducts, to prevent backdrafting of the appliance, or to neutralise the effects of the stack action of the chimney or vent on the operation of the appliance.

Drainback (Solar) Systems - A closed-loop solar heating system in which the heat transfer fluid in the collector loop drains into a tank or reservoir whenever the booster pump stops to protect the collector loop from freezing.

Draindown (Solar) Systems - An open-loop solar heating system in which the heat transfer fluid from the collector loop and the piping drain into a drain whenever freezing conditions occur.

Dry Bulb Temperature - The temperature of the air as measured by a standard thermometer.

Dry Steam Geothermal Plants - Conventional turbine generators are used with the dry steam resources. The steam is used directly, eliminating the need for boilers and boiler fuel that characterises other steam-power-generating technologies. This technology is limited because dry-steam hydrothermal resources are extremely rare. The Geysers, in California, is the nation's only dry steam field.

Dual Duct System - An air conditioning system that has two ducts, one is heated and the other is cooled, so that air of the correct temperature is provided by mixing varying amounts of air from each duct.

Duty Cycle - The duration and periodicity of the operation of a device.

Dynamic Head - The pressure equivalent of the velocity of a fluid.

Dynamo - A machine for converting mechanical energy into electrical energy by magneto-electric induction; may be used as a motor.

Dynamometer - An apparatus for measuring force or power, especially the power developed by a motor.

Dyne - The absolute centimeter-gram-second unit of force; that force that will impart to a free mass of one gram an acceleration of one centimeter per second per second.

-E-

Earth Berm - A mound of dirt next to exterior walls to provide wind protection and insulation.

Earth Cooling Tube - A long, underground metal or plastic pipe through which air is drawn. As air travels through the pipe it gives up some of its heat to the soil, and enters the house as cooler air.

Earth Sheltered Houses - Houses that have earth berms around exterior walls.

Earth-Coupled Ground Source (Geothermal) Heat Pump - A type of heat pump that uses sealed horizontal or vertical pipes, buried in the ground, as heat exchangers through which a fluid is circulated to transfer heat.

Earth-Ship - A registered trademark name for houses built with tires, aluminium cans, and earth.

Easement - An incorporated right, liberty, privilege, or use of another entity's property, distinct from ownership, without profit or compensation; a right-of-way.

Eccentric - A device for converting continuous circular motion into reciprocating rectilinear motion.

Economizer - A heat exchanger for recovering heat from flue gases for heating water or air.

Effective Capacity - The maximum load that a device is capable of carrying.

Efficiency - Under the First Law of Thermodynamics, efficiency is the ratio of work or energy output to work or energy input, and cannot exceed 100 percent. Efficiency under the Second Law of Thermodynamics is determined by the ratio of the theoretical minimum energy that is required to accomplish a task relative to the energy actually consumed to accomplish the task. Generally, the measured efficiency of a device, as defined by the First Law, will be higher than that defined by the Second Law.

Efficiency (Appliance) Ratings - A measure of the efficiency of an appliance's energy efficiency.

Elasticity of Demand - The ratio of the percentage change in the quantity of a good or service demanded to the percentage change in the price.

Electric Circuit - The path followed by electrons from a generation source, through an electrical system, and returning to the source.

Electric Energy - The amount of work accomplished by electrical power, usually measured in kilowatt-hours (kWh). One kWh is 1000 Watts and is equal to 3413 Btu.

Electric Furnace - An air heater in which air is blown over electric resistance heating coils.

Electric Power Plant - A facility or piece of equipment that produces electricity.

Electric Power Transmission - The transmission of electricity through power lines.

Electric Rate - The unit price and quantity to which it applies as specified in a rate schedule or contract.

Electric Rate Schedule - A statement of the electric rate(s), terms, and conditions for electricity sale or supply.

Electric Resistance Heating - A type of heating system where heat, resulting when electric current flows through an "element" or conductor, such as Nichrome, which has a high resistance, is radiated to a room.

Electric System - The physically connected generation, transmission, and distribution facilities and components operated as a unit.

Electric System Loss(es) - The total amount of electric energy loss in an electric system between the generation source and points of delivery.

Electric Utility - A corporation, person, agency, authority or other legal entity that owns and/or operates facilities for the generation, transmission, distribution or sale of electricity primarily for use by the public.

Electric Utility Sector - Those privately or publicly owned establishments that generate, transmit, distribute, or sell electricity.

Electric Vehicles - A battery-powered electrically driven vehicle.

Electrical Charge - A condition that results from an imbalance between the number of protons and the number of electrons in a substance.

Electrical grid - An integrated system of electricity distribution, usually covering a large area. As in "off the grid".

Electricity Generation - The process of producing electricity by transforming other forms or sources of energy into electrical energy; measured in kilowatt-hours.

Electrochemical Cell - A device containing two conducting electrodes, one positive and the other negative, made of dissimilar materials (usually metals) that are immersed in a chemical solution (electrolyte) that transmits positive ions from the negative to the positive electrode and thus forms an electrical charge. One or more cells constitute a battery.

Electrode - A conductor that is brought in conducting contact with a ground.

Electrodeposition - Electrolytic process in which a metal is deposited at the cathode from a solution of its ions.

Electrolysis - A chemical change in a substance that results from the passage of an electric current through an electrolyte. The production of commercial hydrogen by separating the elements of water, hydrogen, and oxygen, by charging the water with an electrical current.

Electrolyte - A nonmetallic (liquid or solid) conductor that carries current by the movement of ions (instead of electrons) with the liberation of matter at the electrodes of an electrochemical cell.

Electromagnetic Energy - Energy generated from an electromagnetic field produced by an electric current flowing through a superconducting wire kept at a specific low temperature.

Electromagnetic Field (EMF) - The electrical and magnetic fields created by the presence or flow of electricity in an electrical conductor or electricity consuming appliance or motor.

Electromotive Force - The amount of energy derived from an electrical source per unit quantity of electricity passing through the source.

Electron - An elementary particle of an atom with a negative electrical charge and a mass of 1/1837 of a proton; electrons surround the positively charged nucleus of an atom and determine the chemical properties of an atom.

Electron Volt - The amount of kinetic energy gained by an electron when accelerated through an electric potential difference of 1 Volt; equivalent to 1.603×10^{-12}; a unit of energy or work; abbreviated as eV.

Electronic Ballast - A device that uses electronic components to regulate the voltage of fluorescent lamps.

Electrostatic Precipitator - A device used to remove particulate matter from the waste gasses of a combustion power plant.

Emission Factor - A measure of the average amount of a specified pollutant or material emitted for a specific type of fuel or process.

Emission - The release or discharge of a substance into the environment; generally refers to the release of gases or particulates into the air.

End Use - The purpose for which useful energy or work is consumed.

Endothermic - A heat absorbing reaction or a reaction that requires heat.

Energize(d) - To send electricity through a electricity transmission and distribution network; a conductor or power line that is carrying current.

Energy - The capability of doing work; different forms of energy can be converted to other forms, but the total amount of energy remains the same.

Energy Audit - A survey that shows how much energy you use in your house or apartment. It will help you find ways to use less energy.

Energy Charge - That part of an electricity bill that is based on the amount of electrical energy consumed or supplied.

Energy Contribution Potential - Recombination occurring in the emitter region of a photovoltaic cell.

Energy Crops - Crops grown specifically for their fuel value. These include food crops such as corn and sugarcane, and nonfood crops such as poplar trees and switchgrass. Currently, two energy crops are under development: short-rotation woody crops, which are fast-growing hardwood trees harvested in 5 to 8 years; and herbaceous energy crops, such as perennial grasses, which are harvested annually after taking 2 to 3 years to reach full productivity.

Energy density - The ratio of energy available from a battery to its volume (Wh/1) or mass (Wh/kg), "watts to weight" ratio.

Energy Efficiency Ratio (EER) - The measure of the instantaneous energy efficiency of room air conditioners; the cooling capacity in Btu/hr divided by the watts of power consumed at a specific outdoor temperature (usually 95 degrees Fahrenheit).

Energy End-Use Sectors - Major energy consuming sectors of the economy. The Commercial Sector includes commercial buildings and private companies. The Industrial Sector includes manufacturers and processors. The Residential Sector includes private homes. The Transportation Sector includes automobiles, trucks, rail, ships, and aircraft.

Energy Factor (EF) - The measure of overall efficiency for a variety of appliances. For water heaters, the energy factor is based on three factors: 1) the recovery efficiency, or how efficiently the heat from the energy source is transferred to the water; 2) standby losses, or the percentage of heat lost per hour from the stored water compared to the content of the water; and 3) cycling losses. For dishwashers, the energy factor is defined as the number of cycles per kWh of input power. For clothes washers, the energy factor is defined as the cubic foot capacity per kWh of input power per cycle. For clothes dryers, the energy factor is defined as the number of pounds of clothes dried per kWh of power consumed.

Energy Intensity - The relative extent that energy is required for a process.

Energy Storage - The process of storing, or converting energy from one form to another, for later use; storage devices and systems include batteries, conventional and pumped storage hydroelectric, flywheels, compressed gas, and thermal mass.

Enthalpy - A thermodynamic property of a substance, defined as the sum of its internal energy plus the pressure of the substance times its volume, divided by the mechanical equivalent of heat. The total heat content of air; the sum of the enthalpies of dry air and water vapour, per unit weight of dry air; measured in Btu per pound (or calories per kilogram).

Entrained Bed Gasifier - A gasifier in which the feedstock (fuel) is suspended by the movement of gas to move it through the gasifier.

Entropy - A measure of the unavailable or unusable energy in a system; energy that cannot be converted to another form.

Epitaxial Growth - In reference to solar photovoltaic devices, the growth of one crystal on the surface of another crystal. The growth of the deposited crystal is oriented by the lattice structure of the original crystal.

Equinox - The two times of the year when the sun crosses the equator and night and day are of equal length; usually occurs on March 21 (spring equinox) and September 23 (fall equinox).

Erg - A unit of work done by the force of one dyne acting through a distance of one centimeter.

Ethanol - Ethyl alcohol (C_2H_5OH) - A colorless liquid that is the product of fermentation used in alcoholic beverages, industrial processes, and as a fuel additive. Also known as grain alcohol.

Evacuated Tube - In a solar thermal collector, an absorber tube, which is contained in an evacuated glass cylinder, through which collector fluids flows.

Evaporation - The conversion of a liquid to a vapour (gas), usually by means of heat.

Evaporative Cooling - The physical process by which a liquid or solid is transformed into the gaseous state. For this process a mechanical device uses the outside air's heat to evaporate water that is held by pads inside the cooler. The heat is drawn out of the air through this process and the cooled air is blown into the home by the cooler's fan.

Evaporator Coil - The inner coil in a heat pump that, during the cooling mode, absorbs heat from the inside air and boils the liquid refrigerant to a vapour, which cools the house.

Excitation - The power required to energize the magnetic field of a generator.

Exothermic - A reaction or process that produces heat; a combustion reaction.

External Combustion Engine - An engine in which fuel is burned (or heat is applied) to the outside of a cylinder; a Stirling engine.

Externalities - Benefits or costs, generated as a by-product of an economic activity, that do not accrue to the parties involved in the activity. Environmental externalities are benefits or costs that manifest themselves through changes in the physical or biological environment.

-F-

Fan - A device that moves and/or circulates air and provides ventilation for a room or a building.

Farad - A unit of electrical capacitance; the capacitance of a capacitor between the plates of which there appears a difference of 1 Volt when it is charged by one coulomb of electricity.

Feather - In a wind energy conversion system, to pitch the turbine blades so as to reduce their lift capacity as a method of shutting down the turbine during high wind speeds.

Feeder - A power line for supplying electricity within a specified area.

Feedstock - A raw material that can be converted to one or more products.

Fenestration - The arrangement, proportion, and design of windows in a building.

Fermentation - The decomposition of organic material to alcohol, methane, etc., by organisms, such as yeast or bacteria, usually in the absence of oxygen.

Fiberglass Insulation - A type of insulation, composed of small diameter pink, yellow, or white glass fibers, formed into blankets or batts, or used in loose-fill and blown-in applications.

Filament - A coil of tungsten wire suspended in a vacuum or inert gas-filled bulb. When heated by electricity the tungsten "filament" glows.

Fill Factor - The ratio of a photovoltaic cell's actual power to its power if both current and voltage were at their maxima. A key characteristic in evaluating cell performance.

Filter (air) - A device that removes contaminants, by mechanical filtration, from the fresh air stream before the air enters the living space. Filters can be installed as part of a heating/cooling system through which air flows for the purpose of removing particulates before or after the air enters the mechanical components.

Fin - A thin sheet of material (metal) of a heat exchanger that conducts heat to a fluid.

Fire-Rating - The ability of a building construction assembly (partition, wall, floor, etc.) to resist the passage of fire. The rating is expressed in hours.

Firewall - A wall to prevent the spread of fire; usually made of non-combustible material.

Firing Rate - The amount of BTUs/hour or kWs produced by a heating system from the burning of a fuel.

First Law of Thermodynamics - States that energy cannot be created or destroyed, but only changed from one form to another. First Law efficiency measures the fraction of energy supplied to a device or process that it delivers in its output. Also called the law of conservation of energy.

Flame Spread Classification - A measure of the surface burning characteristics of a material.

Flame Spread Rating - A measure of the relative flame spread, and smoke development, from a material being tested. The flame spread rating is a single number comparing the flame spread of a material with red oak, arbitrarily given the number 100 and asbestos cement board with a flame spread of 0. Building codes require a maximum flame spread of 25 for insulation installed in exposed locations.

Flashing - Metal, usually galvanized sheet metal, used to provide protection against infiltration of precipitation into a roof or exterior wall; usually placed around roof penetrations such as chimneys.

Flashpoint - The minimum temperature at which sufficient vapour is released by a liquid or solid (fuel) to form a flammable vapour-air mixture at atmospheric pressure.

Flash-Steam Geothermal Plants - When the temperature of the hydrothermal liquids is over 350°F (177°C), flash-steam technology is generally employed. In these systems, most of the liquid is flashed to steam. The steam is separated from the remaining liquid and used to drive a turbine generator. While the water is returned to the geothermal reservoir, the economics of most hydrothermal flash plants are improved by using a dual-flash cycle, which separates the steam at two different pressures. The dual-flash cycle produces 20% to 30% more power than a single-flash system at the same fluid flow.

Flat Plate Pumped - A medium-temperature solar thermal collector that typically consists of a metal frame, glazing, absorbers (usually metal), and insulation and that uses a pump liquid as the heat-transfer medium - predominant use is in water heating applications.

Flat Roof - A slightly sloped roof, usually with a tar and gravel cover. Most commercial buildings use this kind of roof.

Flat-Black Paint - Nonglossy paint with a relatively high absorptance.

Flat-Plate Solar Photovoltaic Module - An arrangement of photovoltaic cells or material mounted on a rigid flat surface with the cells exposed freely to incoming sunlight.

Flat-Plate Solar Thermal/Heating Collectors - Large, flat boxes with glass covers and dark-coloured metal plates inside that absorb and transfer solar energy to a heat transfer fluid.

Float charge - Float charge is the voltage required to counteract the self-discharge of the battery at a certain temperature.

Float life - Number of years that a battery can keep its stated capacity when it is kept at float charge (see float charge).

Float-Zone Process - In reference to solar photovoltaic cell manufacture, a method of growing a large-size, high-quality crystal whereby coils heat a polycrystalline ingot placed atop a single-crystal seed. As the coils are slowly raised the molten interface beneath the coils becomes a single crystal.

Flow Condition - In reference to solar thermal collectors, the condition where the heat transfer fluid is flowing through the collector loop under normal operating conditions.

Flow Control - The laws, regulations, and economic incentives or disincentives used by waste managers to direct waste generated in a specific geographic area to a designated landfill, recycling, or waste-to-energy facility.

Flow Restrictor - A water and energy conserving device that limits the amount of water that a faucet or shower head can deliver.

Flue - The structure (in a residential heating appliance, industrial furnace, or power plant) into which combustion gases flow and are contained until they are emitted to the atmosphere.

Flue Gas - The gas resulting from the combustion of a fuel that is emitted to the flue.

Fluffing - The practice of installing blow-in, loose-fill insulation at a lower density than is recommended to meet a specified R-Value.

Fluidized Bed Combustion (FBC) - A type of furnace or reactor in which fuel particles are combusted while suspended in a stream of hot gas.

Fluorescent Light - The conversion of electric power to visible light by using an electric charge to excite gaseous atoms in a glass tube. These atoms emit ultraviolet radiation that is absorbed by a phosphor coating on the walls of the lamp tube. The phosphor coating produces visible light.

Fly Ash - The fine particulate matter entrained in the flue gases of a combustion power plant.

Flywheel Effect - The damping of interior temperature fluctuations by massive construction.

Foam (Insulation) - A high R-value insulation product usually made from urethane that can be injected into wall cavities, or sprayed onto roofs or floors, where it expands and sets quickly.

Foam Board - A plastic foam insulation product, pressed or extruded into board-like forms, used as sheathing and insulation for interior basement or crawl space walls or beneath a basement slab; can also be used for exterior applications inside or outside foundations, crawl spaces, and slab-on-grade foundation walls.

Foot Candle - A unit of illuminance; equal to one lumen per square foot.

Foot Pound - The amount of work done in raising one pound one foot.

Force - The push or pull that alters the motion of a moving body or moves a stationary body; the unit of force is the dyne or poundal; force is equal to mass times velocity divided by time.

Forced Ventilation - A type of building ventilation system that uses fans or blowers to provide fresh air to rooms when the forces of air pressure and gravity are not enough to circulate air through a building.

Fossil Fuels - Fuels formed in the ground from the remains of dead plants and animals. It takes millions of years to form fossil fuels. Oil, natural gas, and coal are fossil fuels.

Fractional Horse Power Motor - An electric motor rated at less than one horse power (hp).

Francis Turbine - A type of hydropower turbine that contains a runner that has water passages through it formed by curved vanes or blades. As the water passes through the runner and over the curved surfaces, it causes rotation of the runner. The rotational motion is transmitted by a shaft to a generator.

Freon - A registered trademark for a cholorfluorocarbon (CFC) gas that is highly stable and that has been historically used as a refrigerant.

Fresnel Lens - An optical device for concentrating light that is made of concentric rings that are faced at different angles so that light falling on any ring is focused to the same point.

Friction Head - The energy lost from the movement of a fluid in a conduit (pipe) due to the disturbances created by the contact of the moving fluid with the surfaces of the conduit, or the additional pressure that a pump must provide to overcome the resistance to fluid flow created by or in a conduit.

Fuel - Any material that can be burned to make energy.

Fuel Cell - An electrochemical device that converts chemical energy directly into electricity.

Fuel Efficiency - The ratio of heat produced by a fuel for doing work to the available heat in the fuel.

Fuel Oil - Any liquid petroleum product burned for the generation of heat in a furnace or firebox, or for the generation of power in an engine.

Fuel Rate - The amount of fuel necessary to generate one kilowatt-hour of electricity.

Fuelwood - Wood and wood products, possibly including coppices, scrubs, branches, etc., bought or gathered, and used by direct combustion.

Full Sun - The amount of power density in sunlight received at the earth's surface at noon on a clear day (about 1000 Watts/square meter).

Fumarole - A vent from which steam or gases issue; a geyser or spring that emits gases.

Fungi - Plant-like organisms with cells with distinct nuclei surrounded by nuclear membranes, incapable of photosynthesis. Fungi are decomposers of waste organisms and exist as yeast, mold, or mildew.

Furling - The process of forcing, either manually or automatically, a wind turbine's blades out of the direction of the wind in order to stop the blades from turning.

Furnace (Residential) - A combustion heating appliance in which heat is captured from the burning of a fuel for distribution, comprised mainly of a combustion chamber and heat exchanger.

-G-

Gas Turbine - A type of turbine in which combusted, pressurised gas is directed against a series of blades connected to a shaft, which forces the shaft to turn to produce mechanical energy.

Gasification - The process in which a solid fuel is converted into a gas; also known as pyrolitic distillation or pyrolysis. Production of a clean fuel gas makes a wide variety of power options available.

Gasifier - A device for converting a solid fuel to a gaseous fuel.

Gasket/Seal - A seal used to prevent the leakage of fluids, and also maintain the pressure in an enclosure.

Gasoline - A refined petroleum product suitable for use as a fuel in internal combustion engines.

Gauss - The unit of magnetic field intensity equal to 1 dyne per unit pole.

Generation (Electricity) - The process of producing electric energy from other forms of energy; also, the amount of electric energy produced, expressed in watthours (Wh).

Generator - A device for converting mechanical energy to electrical energy.

Geopressured - A type of geothermal resource occurring in deep basins in which the fluid is under very high pressure.

Geopressurized Brines - These brines are hot (300ºF to 400ºF) (149ºC to 204ºC) pressurised waters that contain dissolved methane and lie at depths of 10,000 ft (3048 m) to more than 20,000 ft (6096 m) below the earth's surface. At least three types of energy could be obtained - thermal energy from high-temperature fluids; hydraulic energy from the high pressure; and chemical energy from burning the dissolved methane gas.

Geothermal Energy - Energy produced by the internal heat of the earth; geothermal heat sources include - hydrothermal convective systems; pressurised water reservoirs; hot dry rocks; manual gradients; and magma. Geothermal energy can be used directly for heating or to produce electric power.

Geothermal Heat Pump - A type of heat pump that uses the ground, ground water, or ponds as a heat source and heat sink, rather than outside air. Ground or water temperatures are more constant and are warmer in winter and cooler in summer than air temperatures. Geothermal heat pumps operate more efficiently than "conventional" or "air source" heat pumps.

Geothermal Plant - A plant in which a turbine is driven either from hot water or by natural steam that derives its energy from heat found in rocks or fluids at various depths beneath the surface of the earth. The fluids are extracted by drilling and/or pumping.

Geothermal Power Station - An electricity generating facility that uses geothermal energy.

Geyser - A special type of thermal spring that periodically ejects water with great force.

Giga - One billion.

Gigawatt (GW) - A unit of power equal to 1 billion Watts; 1 million kilowatts, or 1,000 megawatts.

Gin Pole - A pole used to assist in raising a tower.

Glare - The discomfort or interference with visual perception when viewing a bright object against a dark background.

Glauber's Salt - A salt, sodium sulphate decahydrate, that melts at 90 degrees Fahrenheit; a component of eutectic salts that can be used for storing heat.

Glazing - A term used for the transparent or translucent material in a window. This material (i.e., glass, plastic films, coated glass) is used for admitting solar energy and light through windows.

Global Insolation (or Solar Radiation) - The total diffuse and direct insolation on a horizontal surface, averaged over a specified period of time.

Global Warming - A popular term used to describe the increase in average global temperatures due to the greenhouse effect.

Governor - A device used to regulate motor speed, or, in a wind energy conversion system, to control the rotational speed of the rotor.

Grain Alcohol - Ethanol.

Green Power - A popular term for energy produced from renewable energy resources.

Green Pricing and Marketing - To price and sell green power/electricity higher than that produced from fossil or nuclear power plants, supposedly because some buyers are willing to pay a premium for green power.

Greenhouse Effect - A popular term used to describe the heating effect due to the trapping of long wave (length) radiation by greenhouse gases produced from natural and human sources.

Greenhouse Gases - Those gases, such as water vapour, carbon dioxide, tropospheric ozone, methane, and low level ozone that are transparent to solar radiation, but opaque to long wave radiation, and which contribute to the greenhouse effect.

Greenwood - Freshly cut, unseasoned, wood.

Greywater - Waste water from a household source other than a toilet This water can be used for landscape irrigation depending upon the source of the greywater.

Grid - A common term referring to an electricity transmission and distribution system.

Gross Calorific Value - The heat produced by combusting a specific quantity and volume of fuel in an oxygen-bomb colorimeter under specific conditions.

Gross Generation - The total amount of electricity produced by a power plant.

Ground - A device used to protect the user of any electrical system or appliance from shock.

Ground Reflection - Solar radiation reflected from the ground onto a solar collector.

Groundwater - Water occurring in the subsurface zone where all spaces are filled with water under pressure greater than that of the atmosphere.

-H-

Harmonic(s) - A sinusoidal quantity having a frequency that is an integral multiple of the frequency of a periodic quantity to which it is related.

Head - A unit of pressure for a fluid, commonly used in water pumping and hydro power to express height a pump must lift water, or the distance water falls. Total head accounts for friction head losses, etc.

Heat - A form of thermal energy resulting from combustion, chemical reaction, friction, or movement of electricity. As a thermodynamic condition, heat, at a constant pressure, is equal to internal or intrinsic energy plus pressure times volume.

Heat Balance - Energy output from a system that equals energy input.

Heat Content - The amount of heat in a quantity of matter at a specific temperature and pressure.

Heat Engine - A device that produces mechanical energy directly from two heat reservoirs of different temperatures. A machine that converts thermal energy to mechanical energy, such as a steam engine or turbine.

Heat Exchanger - A device used to transfer heat from a fluid (liquid or gas) to another fluid where the two fluids are physically separated.

Heat Gain - The amount of heat introduced to a space from all heat producing sources, such as building occupants, lights, appliances, and from the environment, mainly solar energy.

Heat Loss - The heat that flows from the building interior, through the building envelope to the outside environment.

Heat Pipe - A device that transfers heat by the continuous evaporation and condensation of an internal fluid.

Heat Pump - An electricity powered device that extracts available heat from one area (the heat source) and transfers it to another (the heat sink) to either heat or cool an interior space or to extract heat energy from a fluid.

Heat Pump Water Heaters - A water heater that uses electricity to move heat from one place to another instead of generating heat directly.

Heat Rate - The ratio of fuel energy input as heat per unit of net work output; a measure of a power plant thermal efficiency, generally expressed as Btu per net kilowatt-hour.

Heat Recovery Ventilator - A device that captures the heat from the exhaust air from a building and transfers it to the supply/fresh fresh air entering the building to preheat the air and increase overall heating efficiency.

Heat Register - The grilled opening into a room by which the amount of warm air from a furnace can be directed or controlled; may include a damper.

Heat Sink - A structure or media that absorbs heat.

Heat Source - A structure or media from which heat can be absorbed or extracted.

Heat Storage - A device or media that absorbs heat for storage for later use.

Heat Storage Capacity - The amount of heat that a material can absorb and store.

Heat Transfer - The flow of heat from one area to another by conduction, convection, and/or radiation. Heat flows naturally from a warmer to a cooler material or space.

Heat Transmission Coefficient - Any coefficient used to calculate heat transmission by conduction, convection, or radiation through materials or structures.

Heating Capacity (Also specific heat) - The quantity of heat necessary to raise the temperature of a specific mass of a substance by one degree.

Heating Degree Day(s) (HDD) - The number of degrees per day that the daily average temperature (the mean of the maximum and minimum recorded temperatures) is below a base temperature, usually 65 degrees Fahrenheit, unless otherwise specified; used to determine indoor space heating requirements and heating system sizing. Total HDD is the cumulative total for the year/heating season. The higher the HDD for a location, the colder the daily average temperature(s).

Heating Fuel Units - Standardised weights or volumes for heating fuels.

Heating Fuels - Any gaseous, liquid, or solid fuel used for indoor space heating.

Heating Load - The rate of heat flow required to maintain a specific indoor temperature; usually measured in Btu per hour.

Heating Season - The coldest months of the year; months where average daily temperatures fall below 65 degrees Fahrenheit creating demand for indoor space heating.

Heating Value - The amount of heat produced from the complete combustion of a unit of fuel. The higher (or gross) heating value is that when all products of combustion are cooled to the pre-combustion temperature, water vapour formed during combustion is condensed, and necessary corrections have been made. Lower (or net) heating value is obtained by subtracting from the gross heating value the latent heat of vaporisation of the water vapour formed by the combustion of the hydrogen in the fuel.

Heating, Ventilation, and Air-Conditioning (HVAC) System - All the components of the appliance used to condition interior air of a building.

Heliochemical Process - The utilisation of solar energy through photosynthesis.

Heliodon - A device used to simulate the angle of the sun for assessing shading potentials of building structures or landscape features.

Heliostat - A device that tracks the movement of the sun; used to orient solar concentrating systems.

Heliothermal - Any process that uses solar radiation to produce useful heat.

Heliothermometer - An instrument for measuring solar radiation.

Heliotropic - Any device (or plant) that follows the sun's apparent movement across the sky.

Hemispherical Bowl Technology - A solar energy concentrating technology that uses a linear receiver that tracks the focal area of a reflector or array of reflectors.

Hertz - A measure of the number of cycles or wavelengths of electrical energy per second.

Heterojunction - A region of electrical contact between two different materials.

Higher Heating Value (HHV) - The maximum heating value of a fuel sample, which includes the calorific value of the fuel (bone dry) and the latent heat of vaporisation of the water in the fuel

High-Temperature Collector - A solar thermal collector designed to operate at a temperature of 180 degrees Fahrenheit or higher.

Hole - The vacancy where an electron would normally exist in a solid; behaves like a positively charged particle.

Horizontal-Axis Wind Turbines - Turbines in which the axis of the rotor's rotation is parallel to the wind stream and the ground.

Horsepower (hp) - A unit of rate of operation. Electrical hp - a measure of time rate of mechanical energy output; usually applied to electric motors as the maximum output; 1 electrical hp is equal to 0.746 kilowatts or 2545 Btu per hour. Shaft hp - a measure of the actual mechanical energy per unit time delivered to a turning shaft; 1 shaft Hp is equal to 1 electrical Hp or 550 foot pounds per second. Boiler Hp - a measure to the maximum rate to heat output of a steam generator; 1 boiler Hp is equal to 33,480 Btu per hour steam output.

Horsepower Hour (hph) - One horsepower provided over one hour; equal to 0.745 kilowatt-hour or 2545 Btu.

Hot Air Furnace - A heating unit where heat is distributed by means of convection or fans.

Hub Height - The height above the ground that a horizontal axis wind turbine's hub is located.

Humidity - A measure of the moisture content of air; may be expressed as absolute, mixing ratio, saturation deficit, relative, or specific.

Hybrid Renewable Energy System - A renewable energy system that includes two different types of renewable energy technologies that produce the same type of energy; for e.g., a wind turbine and a solar photovoltaic array combined to meet a power demand.

Hydraulic Fracturing - Fracturing of rock at depth with fluid pressure. Hydraulic fracturing at depth may be accomplished by pumping water into a well at very high pressures. Under natural conditions, vapour pressure may rise high enough to cause fracturing in a process known as hydrothermal brecciation.

Hydroelectric Power Plant - A power plant that produces electricity by the force of water falling through a hydro turbine that spins a generator.

Hydrogen - A chemical element that can be used as a fuel since it has a very high energy content.

Hydrothermal fluids - These fluids can be either water or steam trapped in fractured or porous rocks; they are found from several hundred feet to several miles below the Earth's surface. The temperatures vary from about 90°F to 680°F (32°C to 360°C) but roughly 2/3 range in temperature from 150°F to 250°F (65.5°C to 121.1°C). The latter are the easiest to access and, therefore, the only forms being used commercially.

-I-

Ignition Point - The minimum temperature at which combustion of a solid or fluid can occur.

Illuminance - A measure of the amount of light incident on a surface; measured in foot-candles or Lux.

Impulse Turbine - A turbine that is driven by high velocity jets of water or steam from a nozzle directed to vanes or buckets attached to a wheel. (A pelton wheel is an impulse hydro turbine).

Incandescent - These lights use an electrically heated filament to produce light in a vacuum or inert gas-filled bulb.

Incident Solar Radiation - The amount of solar radiation striking a surface per unit of time and area.

Indirect Solar Gain System - A passive solar heating system in which the sun warms a heat storage element, and the heat is distributed to the interior space by convection, conduction, and radiation.

Indirect Water Heater - A type of water heater that circulates water through a heat exchanger in a boiler. The heated water then flows into an insulated storage tank.

Induction - The production of an electric current in a conductor by the variation of a magnetic field in its vicinity.

Induction Generator - A device that converts the mechanical energy of rotation into electricity based on electromagnetic induction. An electric voltage (electromotive force) is induced in a conducting loop (or coil) when there is a change in the number of magnetic field lines (or magnetic flux) passing through the loop. When the loop is closed by connecting the ends through an external load, the induced voltage will cause an electric current to flow through the loop and load. Thus rotational energy is converted into electrical energy.

Industrial Process Heat - The thermal energy used in an industrial process.

Inert Gas - A gas that does not react with other substances; e.g., argon or krypton; sealed between two sheets of glazing to decrease the U-value (increase the R-Value) of windows.

Infrared Radiation - Electromagnetic radiation whose wavelengths lie in the range from 0.75 micrometer to 1000 micrometers; invisible long wavelength radiation (heat) capable of producing a thermal or photovoltaic effect, though less effective than visible light.

Insolation - The solar power density incident on a surface of stated area and orientation, usually expressed as Watts per square meter or Btu per square foot per hour.

Installed Capacity - The total capacity of electrical generation devices in a power station or system.

Instantaneous Efficiency (of a Solar Collector) - The amount of energy absorbed (or converted) by a solar collector (or photovoltaic cell or module) over a 15 minute period.

Insulation - Materials that prevent or slow down the movement of heat.

Integrated Collector/Storage (ICS) Solar Systems - ICS solar systems are also called "batch" or "breadbox" water heaters. They combine the collector and storage tank in one unit. The sun shining into the collector strikes the storage tank directly, heating the water. The large thermal mass of the water, plus methods to reduce heat loss through the tank, prevent the stored water from freezing.

Integrated Heating Systems - A type of heating appliance that performs more than one function, for example space and water heating.

Interconnection - A connection or link between power systems that enables them to draw on each other's reserve capacity in time of need.

Intermittent Generators - Power plants, whose output depends on a factor(s) that cannot be controlled by the power generator because they utilise intermittent resources such as solar energy or the wind.

Internal Collector Storage (ICS) - A solar thermal collector in which incident solar radiation is absorbed by the storage medium.

Internal Combustion Electric Power Plant - The generation of electric power by a heat engine which converts part of the heat generated by combustion of the fuel into mechanical motion to operate an electric generator.

Internal Gain - The heat produced by sources of heat in a building (occupants, appliances, lighting, etc.).

Internal Mass - Materials with high thermal energy storage capacity contained in or part of a building's walls, floors, or freestanding elements.

Internal Rate of Return - A widely used rate of return for performing economic analysis. This method solves for the interest rate that equates the equivalent worth of an alternative's cash receipts or savings to the equivalent worth of cash expenditures, including investments. The resultant interest rate is termed the internal rate of return (IRR).

Interruptible Load - Energy loads that can be shut off or disconnected at the supplier's discretion or as determined by a contractual agreement between the supplier and the customer.

Intrinsic Layer - A layer of semiconductor material (as used in a solar photovoltaic device) whose properties are essentially those of the pure, undoped, material.

Inverter - A device that converts direct current electricity (from for example a solar photovoltaic module or array) to alternating current for use directly to operate appliances or to supply power to a electricity grid.

Ion - An electrically charged atom or group of atoms that has lost or gained electrons; a loss makes the resulting particle positively charged; a gain makes the particle negatively charged.

Ionizer - A device that removes airborne particles from breathable air. Negative ions are produced and give up their negative charge to the particles. These new negative particles are then attracted to the positive particles surrounding them. This accumulation process continues until the particles become heavy enough to fall to the ground.

Irradiance - The direct, diffuse, and reflected solar radiation that strikes a surface.

-J-

Jacket - The enclosure on a water heater, furnace, or boiler.

Joist - A structural, load-carrying building member with an open web system that supports floors and roofs utilising wood or specific steels and is designed as a simple span member.

Joule - A metric unit of energy or work; the energy produced by a force of one Newton operating through a distance of one meter; 1 Joule per second equals 1 Watt or 0.737 foot-pounds; 1 Btu equals 1055 Joules.

Joule's Law - The rate of heat production by a steady current in any part of an electrical circuit that is proportional to the resistance and to the square of the current, or, the internal energy of an ideal gas depends only on its temperature.

Junction - A region of transition between semiconductor layers, such as a p/n junction, which goes from a region that has a high concentration of acceptors (p-type) to one that has a high concentration of donors (n-type).

-K-

Kaplan Turbine - A type of turbine that that has two blades whose pitch is adjustable. The turbine may have gates to control the angle of the fluid flow into the blades.

Kerosene - A type of heating fuel derived by refining crude oil that has a boiling range at atmospheric pressure from 400 degrees to 550 degrees F.

Kilovolt-Ampere (kVa) - A unit of apparent power, equal to 1000 volt-amperes; the mathematical product of the volts and amperes in an electrical circuit.

Kilowatt (kW) - A standard unit of electrical power equal to one thousand watts, or to the energy consumption at a rate of 1000 Joules per second.

Kilowatt-hour - A unit or measure of electricity supply or consumption of 1000 Watts over the period of one hour; equivalent to 3412 Btu.

Kinetic Energy - Energy available as a result of motion that varies directly in proportion to an object's mass and the square of its velocity.

-L-

Lamp - A light source composed of a metal base, a glass tube filled with an inert gas or a vapour, and base pins to attach to a fixture.

Langley - A unit or measure of solar radiation; 1 calorie per square meter or 3.69 Btu per square foot.

Latent Cooling Load - The load created by moisture in the air, including from outside air infiltration and that from indoor sources such as occupants, plants, cooking, showering, etc.

Latent Heat - The change in heat content that occurs with a change in phase and without change in temperature.

Latent Heat of Vaporisation - The quantity of heat produced to change a unit weight of a liquid to vapour with no change in temperature.

Lattice - The regular periodic arrangement of atoms or molecules in a crystal of semiconductor material.

Law(s) of Thermodynamics - The first law states that energy can not be created or destroyed; the second law states that when a free exchange of heat occurs between two materials, the heat always moves from the warmer to the cooler material.

Lead Acid Battery - An electrochemical battery that uses lead and lead oxide for electrodes and sulphuric acid for the electrolyte.

Leading Edge - In reference to a wind energy conversion system, the area of a turbine blade surface that first comes into contact with the wind.

Lethe - A measure of air purity that is equal to one complete air change (in an interior space).

Levelized Life Cycle Cost - A total life cycle cost divided into equal amounts.

Lift - The force that pulls a wind turbine blade, as opposed to drag.

Light Quality - A description of how well people in a lighted space can see to do visual tasks and how visually comfortable they feel in that space.

Light Trapping - The trapping of light inside a semiconductor material by refracting and reflecting the light at critical angles; trapped light will travel further in the material, greatly increasing the probability of absorption and hence of producing charge carriers.

Light-Induced Defects - Defects, such as dangling bonds, induced in an amorphous silicon semiconductor upon initial exposure to light.

Line Loss (or Drop) - Electrical energy lost due to inherent inefficiencies in an electrical transmission and distribution system under specific conditions.

Liquid Collector - A medium-temperature solar thermal collector, employed predominantly in water heating, which uses pumped liquid as the heat-transfer medium.

Liquid-Based Solar Heating System - A solar heating system that uses a liquid as the heat transfer fluid.

Liquid-To-Air Heat Exchanger - A heat exchanger that transfers the heat contained in a liquid heat transfer fluid to air.

Lithium-Sulphur Battery - A battery that uses lithium in the negative electrode and a metal sulphide in the positive electrode, and the electrolyte is molten salt; can store large amounts of energy per unit weight.

Live Steam - Steam available directly from a boiler under full pressure.

Load - The demand on an energy producing system; the energy consumption or requirement of a piece or group of equipment.

Load Factor - The ratio of average energy demand (load) to maximum demand (peak load) during a specific period.

Load Forecast - An estimate of power demand at some future period.

Load Leveling - The deferment of certain loads to limit electrical power demand, or the production of energy during off-peak periods for storage and use during peak demand periods.

Load Management - To influence the demand on a power source.

Load Profile or Shape - A curve on a chart showing power (kW) supplied (on the horizontal axis) plotted against time of occurrence (on the vertical axis) to illustrate the variance in a load in a specified time period.

Load Shedding - Turning off or disconnecting loads to limit peak demand.

Load Shifting - A load management objective that moves loads from on-peak periods to off-peak periods.

Local Solar Time - A system of astronomical time in which the sun crosses the true north-south meridian at 12 noon, and which differs from local time according to longitude, time zone, and equation of time.

Log Law - In reference to a wind energy conversion system, the wind speed profile in which wind speeds increase with the logarithmic of the height of the wind turbine above the ground.

Long Ton - A unit that equals 20 long hundredweight or 2240 pounds. Used mainly in England.

Long-Wave Radiation - Infrared or radiant heat.

Loose Fill Insulation - Insulation made from rockwool fibers, fiberglass, cellulose fiber, vermiculite or perlite minerals, and composed of loose fibers or granules can be applied by pouring directly from the bag or with a blower.

Loss of Load Probability (LOLP) - A measure of the probability that a system demand will exceed capacity during a given period; often expressed as the estimated number of days over a long period, frequently 10 years or the life of the system.

Losses (Energy) - A general term applied to the energy that is converted to a form that can not be effectively used (lost) during the operation of an energy producing, conducting, or consuming system.

Low Btu Gas - A fuel gas with a heating value between 90 and 200 Btu per cubic foot.

Low-Flow Solar Water Heating Systems - The flow rate in these systems is 1/8 to 1/5 the rate of most solar water heating systems. The low-flow systems take advantage of stratification in the storage tank and theoretically allows for the use of smaller diameter piping to and from the collector and a smaller pump.

Low-Temperature Collectors - Metallic or nonmetallic solar thermal collectors that generally operate at temperatures below 110 degrees Fahrenheit and use pumped liquid or air as the heat transfer medium. They usually contain no glazing and no insulation, and they are often made of plastic or rubber, although some are made of metal.

Lumen - An empirical measure of the quantity of light. It is based upon the spectral sensitivity of the photosensors in the human eye under high (daytime) light levels. Photometrically it is the luminous flux emitted with a solid angle (1 steradian) by a point source having a uniform luminous intensity of 1 candela.

Luminaire - A complete lighting unit consisting of a lamp(s), housing, and connection to the power circuit.

Luminance - The physical measure of the subjective sensation of brightness; measured in lumens.

Lux - The unit of illuminance equivalent to 1lumen per square meter.

-M-

Masonry Stove - A type of heating appliance similar to a fireplace, but much more efficient and clean burning. They are made of masonry and have long channels through which combustion gases give up their heat to the heavy mass of the stove, which releases the heat slowly into a room. Often called Russian or Finnish fireplaces.

Mass Burner - A relatively large one-chamber combustion system used to incinerate municipal solid waste under conditions of excess air; it is built on site and consumes fuel without prior processing or sorting.

MCF - An abbreviation for one thousand cubic feet of natural gas with a heat content of 1,000,000 Btus, or 10 therms.

Mean Power Output (of a Wind Turbine) - The average power output of a wind energy conversion system at a given mean wind speed based on a Raleigh frequency distribution.

Mean Wind Speed - The arithmetic wind speed over a specified time period and height above the ground.

Mechanical Systems - Those elements of building used to control the interior climate.

Medium Btu Gas - Fuel gas with a heating value of between 200 and 300 Btu per cubic foot.

Medium Pressure - For valves and fittings, implies that they are suitable for working pressures between 125 to 175 pounds per square inch.

Medium-Temperature Collectors - Solar thermal collectors designed to operate in the temperature range of 140 degrees to 180 degrees Fahrenheit, but that can also operate at a temperature as low as 110 degrees Fahrenheit. The collector typically consists of a metal frame, metal absorption panels with integral flow channels (attached tubing for liquid collectors or integral ducting for air collectors), and glazing and insulation on the sides and back.

Megawatt - One thousand kilowatts, or 1 million watts; standard measure of electric power plant generating capacity.

Megawatt-hour - One thousand kilowatt-hours or 1 million watthours.

Methane - A colourless, odourless, tasteless gas composed of one molecule of Carbon and four of hydrogen, which is highly flammable. It is the main constituent of "natural gas" that is formed naturally by methanogenic, anaerobic bacteria or can be manufactured, and which is used as a fuel and for manufacturing chemicals.

Methanol (CH_3OH; Methyl alcohol or wood alcohol) - A clear, colourless, very mobile liquid that is flammable and poisonous; used as a fuel and fuel additive, and to produce chemicals.

Microclimate - The local climate of specific place or habitat, as influenced by landscape features.

Micrometer - One millionth of a meter (10^{-6} m).

Mill - A common utility monetary measure equal to one-thousandth of a dollar or a tenth of a cent.

Minority Carrier - A current carrier, either an electron or a hole, that is in the minority in a specific layer of a semiconductor material; the diffusion of minority carriers under the action of the cell junction voltage is the current in a photovoltaic device.

Minority Carrier Lifetime - The average time a minority carrier exists before recombination.

Mixing Valve - A valve operated by a thermostat that can be installed in solar water heating systems to mix cold water with water from the collector loop to maintain a safe water temperature.

Modified Degree-Day Method - A method used to estimate building heating loads by assuming that heat loss and gain is proportional to the equivalent heat-loss coefficient for the building envelope.

Modular Burner - A relatively small two-chamber combustion system used to incinerate municipal solid waste without prior processing or sorting; usually fabricated at a factory and delivered to the incineration site.

Module - The smallest self-contained, environmentally protected structure housing interconnected photovoltaic cells and providing a single dc electrical output; also called a panel.

Moisture Content - The water content of a substance (a solid fuel) as measured under specified conditions being the Dry Basis, which equals the weight of the wet sample minus the weight of a (bone) dry sample divided by the weight of the dry sample times 100 (to get percent); Wet Basis, which is equal to the weight of the wet sample minus the weight of the dry sample divided by the weight of the wet sample times 100.

Moisture Control - The process of controlling indoor moisture levels and condensation.

Monoculture - The planting, cultivation, and harvesting of a single species of crop in a specified area.

Monolithic - Fabricated as a single structure.

Motor - A machine supplied with external energy that is converted into force and/or motion.

Motor Speed - The number of revolutions that the motor turns in a given time period (i.e. revolutions per minute, rpm).

Movable Insulation - A device that reduces heat loss at night and during cloudy periods and heat gain during the day in warm weather. A movable insulator could be an insulative shade, shutter panel, or curtain.

Multijunction Device - A high-efficiency photovoltaic device containing two or more cell junctions, each of which is optimised for a particular part of the solar spectrum.

Municipal Solid Waste (MSW) - Waste material from households and businesses in a community that is not regulated as hazardous.

-N-

Natural Cooling - Space cooling achieved by shading, natural (unassisted, as opposed to forced) ventilation, conduction control, radiation, and evaporation; also called passive cooling.

Natural Draft - Draft that is caused by temperature differences in the air.

Natural Gas - A hydrocarbon gas obtained from underground sources, often in association with petroleum and coal deposits. It generally contains a high percentage of methane, varying amounts of ethane, and inert gases; used as a heating fuel.

Natural Gas Steam Reforming Production - A two step process where in the first step natural gas is exposed to a high-temperature steam to produce hydrogen, carbon monoxide, and carbon dioxide. The second step is to convert the carbon monoxide with steam to produce additional hydrogen and carbon dioxide.

Natural Ventilation - Ventilation that is created by the differences in the distribution of air pressures around a building. Air moves from areas of high pressure to areas of low pressure with gravity and wind pressure affecting the airflow. The placement and control of doors and windows alters natural ventilation patterns.

Net (Lower) Heating Value (NHV) - The potential energy available in a fuel as received, taking into account the energy loss in evaporating and superheating the water in the fuel. Equal to the higher heating value minus 1050 W where W is the weight of the water formed from the hydrogen in the fuel, and 1050 is the latent heat of vaporisation of water, in Btu, at 77 degrees Fahrenheit.

Net Energy Production (or Balance) - The amount of useful energy produced by a system less the amount of energy required to produce the fuel.

Net Generation - Equal to gross generation less electricity consumption of a power plant.

Net Metering - The practice of using a single meter to measure consumption and generation of electricity by a small generation facility (such as a house with a wind or solar photovoltaic system). The net energy produced or consumed is purchased from or sold to the generator, respectively, at the same price.

Net Photovoltaic Cell Shipment - The difference between photovoltaic cell shipments and photovoltaic cell purchases.

Net Photovoltaic Module Shipment - The difference between photovoltaic module shipments and photovoltaic module purchases.

Net Present Value - The value of a personal portfolio, product, or investment after depreciation and interest on debt capital are subtracted from operating income. It can also be thought of as the equivalent worth of all cash flows relative to a base point called the present.

Nitrogen Dioxide - This compound of nitrogen and oxygen is formed by the oxidation of nitric oxide (NO) which is produced by the combustion of solid fuels.

Nitrogen Oxides (NO_x) - The products of all combustion processes formed by the combination of nitrogen and oxygen.

Nominal Capacity - The approximate energy producing capacity of a power plant, under specified conditions, usually during periods of highest load.

Nominal Price - The price paid for goods or services at the time of a transaction; a price that has not been adjusted to account for inflation.

Non-renewable Fuels - Fuels that cannot be easily made or "renewed", such as oil, natural gas, and coal.

Non-Utility Generator/Power Producer - A class of power generator that is not a regulated utility and that has generating plants for the purpose of supplying electric power required in the conduct of their industrial and commercial operations.

Normal Recovery Capacity - A characteristic applied to domestic water heaters that is the amount of gallons raised 100 degrees Fahrenheit per hour (or minute) under a specified thermal efficiency.

N-Type Semiconductor - A semiconductor produced by doping an intrinsic semiconductor with an electron-donor impurity (e.g., phosphorous in silicon).

Nuclear Energy - Energy that comes from splitting atoms of radioactive materials, such as uranium, and which produces radioactive wastes.

-O-

Occupancy Sensor - An optical, ultrasonic, or infrared sensor that turns room lights on when they detect a person's presence and off after the space is vacated.

Occupied Space - The space within a building or structure that is normally occupied by people, and that may be conditioned (heated, cooled and/or ventilated).

Ocean Energy Systems - Energy conversion technologies that harness the energy in tides, waves, and thermal gradients in the oceans.

Ocean Thermal Energy Conversion (OTEC) - The process or technologies for producing energy by harnessing the temperature differences (thermal gradients) between ocean surface waters and that of ocean depths. Warm surface water is pumped through an evaporator containing a working fluid in a closed Rankine-cycle system. The vaporised fluid drives a turbine/generator. Cold water from deep below the surface is used to condense the working fluid. Open-Cycle OTEC technologies use ocean water itself as the working fluid. Closed-Cycle OTEC systems circulate a working fluid in a closed loop.

Off-Peak - The period of low energy demand, as opposed to maximum, or peak, demand.

Ohms - A measure of the electrical resistance of a material equal to the resistance of a circuit in which the potential difference of 1 volt produces a current of 1 ampere.

Ohm's Law - In a given electrical circuit, the amount of current in amperes (i) is equal to the pressure in volts (V) divided by the resistance, in ohms (R).

Oil (fuel) - A product of crude oil that is used for space heating, diesel engines, and electrical generation.

One Sun - The maximum value of natural solar insolation.

One-Axis Tracking - A system capable of rotating about one axis.

On-Peak Energy - Energy supplied during periods of relatively high system demands as specified by the supplier.

On-Site Generation - Generation of energy at the location where all or most of it will be used.

Open Access - The ability to send or wheel electric power to a customer over a transmission and distribution system that is not owned by the generator (seller) of the power.

Open-Circuit Voltage - The maximum possible voltage across a photovoltaic cell; the voltage across the cell in sunlight when no current is flowing.

Open-Loop System - A heating system, such as a solar water heater or geothermal heat pump, in which the working fluid is heated and used directly; in an open-loop solar system, the domestic water is circulated in the collector loop.

Operating Cycle - The processes that a work input/output system undergoes and in which the initial and final states are identical.

Outage - A discontinuance of electric power supply.

Outgassing - The process by which materials expel or release gasses.

Outside Air - Air that is taken from the outdoors.

Outside Coil - The heat-transfer (exchanger) component of a heat pump, located outdoors, from which heat is collected in the heating mode, or expelled in the cooling mode.

Overhang - A building element that shades windows, walls, and doors from direct solar radiation and protects these elements from precipitation.

Overload - To exceed the design capacity of a device.

Oxygenates - Gasoline fuel additives such as ethanol, ETBE, or MTBE that add extra oxygen to gasoline to reduce carbon monoxide pollution produced by vehicles.

Ozone - Three-atom oxygen compound (O_3) found in two layers of the Earth's atmosphere. One layer of beneficial ozone occurs at 7 to 18 miles above the surface and shields the Earth from ultraviolet light. Several holes in this protective layer have been documented by scientists. Ozone also concentrates at the surface as a result of reactions between byproducts of fossil fuel combustion and sunlight, having harmful health effects.

-P-

P/N - A semiconductor (photovoltaic) device structure in which the junction is formed between a p-type layer and an n-type layer.

Packing Factor - The ratio of solar collector array area to actual land area.

Pane (Window) - The area of glass that fits in the window frame.

Panel (Solar) - A term generally applied to individual solar collectors, and typically to solar photovoltaic collectors or modules.

Panel Radiator - A mainly flat surface for transmitting radiant energy.

Panemone - A drag-type wind machine that can react to wind from any direction.

Parabolic Dish - A solar energy conversion device that has a bowl shaped dish covered with a highly reflective surface that tracks the sun and concentrates sunlight on a fixed absorber, thereby achieving high temperatures, for process heating or to operate a heat (Stirling) engine to produce power or electricity.

Parabolic Trough - A high-temperature (above 180 degrees Fahrenheit) solar thermal concentrator with the capacity for tracking the sun using one axis of rotation.

Parallel - A configuration of an electrical circuit in which the voltage is the same across the terminals. The positive reference direction for each resistor current is down through the resistor with the same voltage across each resistor.

Parallel Connection - A way of joining photovoltaic cells or modules by connecting positive leads together and negative leads together; such a configuration increases the current, but not the voltage.

Passive Solar (Building) Design - A building design that uses structural elements of a building to heat and cool a building, without the use of mechanical equipment, which requires careful consideration of the local climate and solar energy resource, building orientation, and landscape features, to name a few. The principal elements include proper building orientation, proper window sizing and placement and design of window overhangs to reduce summer heat gain and ensure winter heat gain, and proper sizing of thermal energy storage mass (for example a Trombe wall or masonry tiles). The heat is distributed primarily by natural convection and radiation, though fans can also be used to circulate room air or ensure proper ventilation.

Passive Solar Heater - A solar water or space-heating system in which solar energy is collected, and/or moved by natural convection without using pumps or fans. Passive systems are typically integral collector/storage (ICS; or batch collectors) or thermosyphon systems. The major advantage of these systems is that they do not use controls, pumps, sensors, or other mechanical parts, so little or no maintenance is required over the lifetime of the system.

Passive Solar Home - A house built using passive solar design techniques.

Passive Solar - A system in which solar energy alone is used for the transfer of thermal energy. Pumps, blowers, or other heat transfer devices that use energy other than solar are not used.

Passive/Natural Cooling - To allow or augment the natural movement of cooler air from exterior, shaded areas of a building through or around a building.

Payback - The amount of time required for positive cash flows to equal the total investment costs.

Peak Clipping/Shaving - The process of implementing measures to reduce peak power demands on a system.

Peak Demand/Load - The maximum energy demand or load in a specified time period.

Peak Power - Power generated by a utility unit that operates at a very low capacity factor; generally used to meet short-lived and variable high demand periods.

Peak Shifting - The process of moving existing loads to off-peak periods.

Peak Watt - A unit used to rate the performance of a solar photovoltaic (PV) cells, modules, or arrays; the maximum nominal output of a PV device, in Watts (Wp) under standardised test conditions, usually 1000 Watts per square meter of sunlight with other conditions, such as temperature specified.

Peak Wind Speed - The maximum instantaneous wind speed (or velocity) that occurs within a specific period of time or interval.

Peaking Capacity - Power generation equipment or system capacity to meet peak power demands.

Peaking Hydropower - A hydropower plant that is operated at maximum allowable capacity for part of the day and is either shut down for the remainder of the time or operated at minimal capacity level.

Performance Ratings - Solar collector thermal performance ratings based on collector efficiencies, usually expressed in Btu per hour for solar collectors under standard test or operating conditions for solar radiation intensity, inlet working fluid temperatures, and ambient temperatures.

Perimeter Heating - A term applied to warm-air heating systems that deliver heated air to rooms by means of registers or baseboards located along exterior walls.

Permeance - A unit of measurement for the ability of a material to retard the diffusion of water vapour at 73.4°F (23°C). A perm, short for permeance, is the number of grains of water vapour that pass through a square foot of material per hour at a differential vapour pressure equal to one inch of mercury.

Phase - Alternating current is carried by conductors and a ground to residential, commercial, or industrial consumers. The waveform of the phase power appears as a single continuous sine wave at the system frequency whose amplitude is the rated voltage of the power.

Phase Change - The process of changing from one physical state (solid, liquid, or gas) to another, with a necessary or coincidental input or release of energy.

Phase-Change Material - A material that can be used to store thermal energy as latent heat. Various types of materials have been and are being investigated such as inorganic salts, eutectic compounds, and paraffins, for a variety of applications, including solar energy storage (solar energy heats and melts the material during the day and at night it releases the stored heat and reverts to a solid state).

Photobiological Hydrogen Production - A hydrogen production process that uses algae. Under certain conditions, the pigments in certain types of algae absorb solar energy. An enzyme in the cell acts as a catalyst to split water molecules. Some of the bacteria produces hydrogen after they grow on a substrate.

Photocurrent - An electric current induced by radiant energy.

Photoelectric Cell - A device for measuring light intensity that works by converting light falling on, or reach it, to electricity, and then measuring the current; used in photometers.

Photoelectrochemical Cell - A type of photovoltaic device in which the electricity induced in the cell is used immediately within the cell to produce a chemical, such as hydrogen, which can then be withdrawn for use.

Photoelectrolysis Hydrogen Production - The production of hydrogen using a photoelectrochemical cell.

Photogalvanic Processes - The production of electrical current from light.

Photon - A particle of light that acts as an individual unit of energy.

Photovoltaic (Conversion) Efficiency - The ratio of the electric power produced by a photovoltaic device to the power of the sunlight incident on the device.

Photovoltaic (PV) array - An interconnected system of PV modules that function as a single electricity-producing unit. The modules are assembled as a discrete structure, with common support or mounting. In smaller systems, an array can consist of a single module.

Photovoltaic (PV) cell - The smallest semiconductor element within a PV module to perform the immediate conversion of light into electrical energy (dc voltage and current).

Photovoltaic (PV) conversion efficiency - The ratio of the electric power produced by a photovoltaic device to the power of the sunlight incident on the device.

Photovoltaic (PV) generator - The total of all PV strings of a PV power supply system, which are electrically interconnected.

Photovoltaic (PV) module - The smallest environmentally protected, essentially planar assembly of solar cells and ancillary parts, such as interconnections, terminals, [and protective devices such as diodes] intended to generate dc power under unconcentrated sunlight. The structural (load carrying) member of a module can either be the top layer (superstrate) or the back layer (substrate).

Photovoltaic (PV) panel - often used interchangeably with PV module (especially in one-module systems), but more accurately used to refer to a physically connected collection of modules (i.e., a laminate string of modules used to achieve a required voltage and current).

Photovoltaic (PV) peak watt - Maximum "rated" output of a cell, module, or system. Typical rating conditions are 0.645 watts per square inch (1000 watts per square meter) of sunlight, 68°F (20°C) ambient air temperature and 6.2×10^{-3} mi/s (1 m/s) wind speed.

Photovoltaic (PV) system - A complete set of components for converting sunlight into electricity by the photovoltaic process, including the array and balance of system components.

Photovoltaic-Thermal (PV/T) Systems - A solar energy system that produces electricity with a PV module, and collects thermal energy from the module for heating. Physical Vapour Deposition - A method of depositing thin semiconductor (photovoltaic) films. With this method, physical processes, such as thermal evaporation or bombardment of ions, are used to deposit elemental semiconductor material on a substrate.

P-I-N - A semiconductor (photovoltaic) device structure that layers an intrinsic semiconductor between a p-type semiconductor and an n-type semiconductor; this structure is most often used with amorphous silicon PV devices.

Pitch Control - A method of controlling a wind turbine's speed by varying the orientation, or pitch, of the blades, and thereby altering its aerodynamics and efficiency.

Plenum - The space between a hanging ceiling and the floor above or roof; usually contains HVAC ducts, electrical wiring, fire suppression system piping, etc.

Plug Flow Digester - A type of anaerobic digester that has a horizontal tank in which a constant volume of material is added and forces material in the tank to move through the tank and be digested.

Point-Contact Cell - A high efficiency silicon photovoltaic concentrator cell that employs light trapping techniques and point-diffused contacts on the rear surface for current collection.

Pollution - Any substances in water, soil, or air that degrade the natural quality of the environment, offend the senses of sight, taste, and smell, and/or cause a health hazard. The usefulness of a natural resource is usually impaired by the presence of pollutants and contaminants.

Polycrystalline - A semiconductor (photovoltaic) material composed of variously oriented, small, individual crystals.

Porous Media - A solid that contains pores; normally, it refers to interconnected pores that can transmit the flow of fluids.

Potable Water - Water that is suitable for drinking, as defined by local health officials.

Potential Energy - Energy available due to position.

Pound of Steam - One pound of water in vapour phase; is NOT steam pressure, which is expressed as pounds per square inch (psi).

Pound Per Square Inch Absolute (psia) - A unit of pressure [hydraulic (liquid) or pneumatic (gas)] that does not include atmospheric pressure.

Power - Energy that is capable or available for doing work; the time rate at which work is performed, measured in horsepower, Watts, or Btu per hour. Electric power is the product of electric current and electromotive force.

Power (Output) Curve - A plot of a wind energy conversion device's power output versus wind speed.

Power (Solar) Tower - A term used to describe solar thermal, central receiver, power systems, where an array of reflectors focus sunlight onto a central receiver and absorber mounted on a tower.

Power Coefficient - The ratio of power produced by a wind energy conversion device to the power in a reference area of the free windstream.

Power Conditioning - The process of modifying the characteristics of electrical power (for e.g., inverting dc to ac).

Power Density - The amount of power per unit area of a free windstream.

Power Factor (PF) - The ratio of actual power being used in a circuit, expressed in watts or kilowatts, to the power that is apparently being drawn from a power source, expressed in volt-amperes or kilovolt-amperes.

Power Transmission Line - An electrical conductor/cable that carries electricity from a generator to other locations for distribution.

Preheater (Solar) - A solar heating system that preheats water or air that is then heated more by another heating appliance.

Present Value - The amount of money required to secure a specified cash flow at a future date at a specified return.

Pressure Drop - The loss in static pressure of a fluid (liquid or gas) in a system due to friction from obstructions in pipes, from valves, fittings, regulators, burners, etc, or by a breech or rupture of the system. Pressurization Testing - A technique used by energy auditors, using a blower door, to locate areas of air infiltration by exaggerating the defects in the building shell. This test only measures air infiltration at the time of the test. It does not take into account changes in atmospheric pressure, weather, wind velocity, or any activities the occupants conduct that may affect air infiltration rates over a period of time.

Primary Air - The air that is supplied to the combustion chamber of a furnace.

Prime Mover - Any machine capable of producing power to do work.

Process Heat - Thermal energy that is used in agricultural and industrial operations.

Producer Gas - Low or medium Btu content gas, composed mainly of carbon monoxide, nitrogen(2), and hydrogen(2) made by the gasification of wood or coal.

Products of Combustion - The elements and compounds that result from the combustion of a fuel.

Projected Area - The net south-facing glazing area projected on a vertical plane. Also, the solid area covered at any instant by a wind turbine's blades from the perspective of the direction of the windstream (as opposed to the swept area).

Propane - A hydrocarbon gas, C_3H_8, occurring in crude oil, natural gas, and refinery cracking gas. It is used as a fuel, a solvent, and a refrigerant. Propane liquefies under pressure and is the major component of liquefied petroleum gas (LPG).

Propeller (Hydro) Turbine - A turbine that has a runner with attached blades similar to a propeller used to drive a ship. As water passes over the curved propeller blades, it causes rotation of the shaft.

Proximate Analysis - A commonly used analysis for reporting fuel properties; may be on a dry (moisture free) basis, as “fired”, or on an ash and moisture free basis. Fractions usually reported include - volatile matter, fixed carbon, moisture, ash, and heating value (higher heating value).

Psi - Pounds of pressure per square inch.

Psia - Pounds/force per square inch absolute.

Psig - Pounds/force per square inch gauge.

Psychrometer - An instrument for measuring relative humidity by means of wet and dry-bulb temperatures.

Psychrometrics - The analysis of atmospheric conditions, particularly moisture in the air.

P-Type Semiconductor - A semiconductor in which holes carry the current; produced by doping an intrinsic semiconductor with an electron acceptor impurity (e.g., boron in silicon).

Pulpwood - Roundwood, whole-tree chips, or wood residues.

Pulse-Width-Modulated (PWM) Wave Inverter - A type of power inverter that produce a high quality (nearly sinusoidal) voltage, at minimum current harmonics.

Pumped Storage Facility - A type of power generating facility that pumps water to a storage reservoir during off-peak periods, and uses the stored water (by allowing it to fall through a hydro turbine) to generate power during peak periods. The pumping energy is typically supplied by lower cost base power capacity, and the peaking power capacity is of greater value, even though there is a net loss of power in the process.

PV - Abbreviation for photovoltaic(s).

Pyranometer - A device used to measure total incident solar radiation (direct beam, diffuse, and reflected radiation) per unit time per unit area.

Pyrheliometer - A device that measures the intensity of direct beam solar radiation.

Pyrolysis - The transformation on a compound or material into one or more substances by heat alone (without oxidation). Often called destructive distillation. Pyrolysis of biomass is the thermal degradation of the material in the absence of reacting gases, and occurs prior to or simultaneously with gasification reactions in a gasifier. Pyrolysis products consist of gases, liquids, and char generally. The liquid fraction of pyrolisized biomass consists of an insoluble viscous tar, and pyroligneous acids (acetic acid, methanol, acetone, esters, aldehydes, and furfural). The distribution of pyrolysis products varies depending on the feedstock composition, heating rate, temperature, and pressure.

-Q-

Quadrillion Btu - Equivalent to 10 to the 15th power Btu.

-R-

Radiant Barrier - A thin, reflective foil sheet that exhibits low radiant energy transmission and under certain conditions can block radiant heat transfer; installed in attics to reduce heat flow through a roof assembly into the living space.

Radiant Ceiling Panels - Ceiling panels that contain electric resistance heating elements embedded within them to provide radiant heat to a room.

Radiant Energy - Energy that transmits away from its source in all directions.

Radiant Floor - A type of radiant heating system where the building floor contains channels or tubes through which hot fluids such as air or water are circulated. The whole floor is evenly heated. Thus, the room heats from the bottom up. Radiant floor heating eliminates the draft and dust problems associated with forced air heating systems.

Radiant Heating System - A heating system where heat is supplied (radiated) into a room by means of heated surfaces, such as electric resistance elements, hot water (hydronic) radiators, etc.

Radiation - The transfer of heat through matter or space by means of electromagnetic waves.

Radiative Cooling - The process of cooling by which a heat absorbing media absorbs heat from one source and radiates the heat away.

Radiator - A room heat delivery (or exchanger) component of a hydronic (hot water or steam) heating system; hot water or steam is delivered to it by natural convection or by a pump from a boiler.

Radiator Vent - A device that releases pressure within a radiator when the pressure inside exceeds the operating limits of the vent.

Radioactive Waste - Materials left over from making nuclear energy. Radioactive waste can harm living organisms if it is not stored safely.

Radon - A naturally occurring radioactive gas found in nearly all types of soil, rock, and water. It can migrate into most buildings. Studies have linked high concentrations of radon to lung cancer.

Rafter - A construction element used for ceiling support.

Rankine Cycle - The thermodynamic cycle that is an ideal standard for comparing performance of heat-engines, steam power plants, steam turbines, and heat pump systems that use a condensable vapour as the working fluid; efficiency is measured as work done divided by sensible heat supplied.

Rate Schedule - A mechanism used by electric utilities to determine prices for electricity; typically defines rates according to amounts of power demanded/consumed during specific time periods.

Rated Life - The length of time that a product or appliance is expected to meet a certain level of performance under nominal operating conditions; in a luminaire, the period after which the lumen depreciation and lamp failure is at 70% of its initial value.

Rated Power - The power output of a device under specific or nominal operating conditions.

Rayleigh Frequency Distribution - A mathematical representation of the frequency or ratio that specific wind speeds occur within a specified time interval.

Reactive Power - The electrical power that oscillates between the magnetic field of an inductor and the electrical field of a capacitor. Reactive power is never converted to non-electrical power. Calculated as the square root of the difference between the square of the kilovolt-amperes and the square of the kilowatts. Expressed as reactive volt-amperes.

Real Price - The unit price of a good or service estimated from some base year in order to provide a consistent means of comparison.

Receiver - The component of a central receiver solar thermal system where reflected solar energy is absorbed and converted to thermal energy.

Recirculated Air - Air that is returned from a heated or cooled space, reconditioned and/or cleaned, and returned to the space.

Recirculation Systems - A type of solar heating system that circulates warm water from storage through the collectors and exposed piping whenever freezing conditions occur; obviously a not very efficient system when operating in this mode.

Rectifier - An electrical device for converting alternating current to direct current. The chamber in a cooling device where water is separated from the working fluid (for example ammonia).

Recuperator - A heat exchanger in which heat is recovered from the products of combustion.

Recurrent Costs - Costs that are repetitive and occur when an organisation produces similar goods or services on a continuing basis.

Recycling - The process of converting materials that are no longer useful as designed or intended into a new product.

Reflectance - The amount (percent) of light that is reflected by a surface relative to the amount that strikes it.

Refraction - The change in direction of a ray of light when it passes through one media to another with differing optical densities.

Refrigerant - The compound (working fluid) used in air conditioners, heat pumps, and refrigerators to transfer heat into or out of an interior space. This fluid boils at a very low temperature enabling it to evaporate and absorb heat.

Refrigeration - The process of the absorption of heat from one location and its transfer to another for rejection or recuperation.

Refrigeration Capacity - A measure of the effective cooling capacity of a refrigerator, expressed in Btu per hour or in tons, where one (1) ton of capacity is equal to the heat required to melt 2000 pounds of ice in 24 hours or 12,000 Btu per hour.

Refrigeration Cycle - The complete cycle of stages (evaporation and condensation) of refrigeration or of the refrigerant.

Refuse-Derived Fuel (RDF) - Fuel processed from municipal solid waste that can be in shredded, fluff, or densified pellet forms.

Regenerative Cooling - A type of cooling system that uses a charging and discharging cycle with a thermal or latent heat storage subsystem.

Regenerative Heating - The process of using heat that is rejected in one part of a cycle for another function or in another part of the cycle.

Relamping - The replacement of a non-functional or ineffective lamp with a new, more efficient lamp.

Relative Humidity - A measure of the percent of moisture actually in the air compared with what would be in it if it were fully saturated at that temperature. When the air is fully saturated, its relative humidity is 100 percent.

Reliability - This is the concept of how long a device or process can operate properly without needing maintenance or replacement.

Renewable Energy - Energy derived from resources that are regenerative or for all practical purposes can not be depleted. Types of renewable energy resources include moving water (hydro, tidal and wave power), thermal gradients in ocean water, biomass, geothermal energy, solar energy, and wind energy. Municipal solid waste (MSW) is also considered to be a renewable energy resource.

Renewable Energy Source - An energy source that is regenerative or virtually inexhaustible. Typical examples are wind, geothermal, and water power.

Resistance - The inherent characteristic of a material to inhibit the transfer of energy. In electrical conductors, electrical resistance results in the generation of heat. Electrical resistance is measured in Ohms. The heat transfer resistance properties of insulation products are quantified as the R-value.

Resistance Heating - A type of heating system that provides heat from the resistance of an electrical current flowing through a conductor.

Resistive Voltage Drop - The voltage developed across a cell by the current flow through the resistance of the cell.

Resistor - An electrical device that resists electric current flow.

Resource Recovery - The process of converting municipal solid waste to energy and/or recovering materials for recycling.

Retail Wheeling - An arrangement in which a utility transmits electricity from outside its service territory to a retail customer within its customer service territory.

Reversing Valve - A component of a heat pump that reverses the refrigerant's direction of flow, allowing the heat pump to switch from cooling to heating or heating to cooling.

Ribbon (Photovoltaic) Cells - A type of solar photovoltaic device made in a continuous process of pulling material from a molten bath of photovoltaic material, such as silicon, to form a thin sheet of material.

Roof Ventilator - A stationary or rotating vent used to ventilate attics or cathedral ceilings; usually made of galvanized steel, or polypropylene.

Rotor - An electric generator consists of an armature and a field structure. The armature carries the wire loop, coil, or other windings in which the voltage is induced, whereas the field structure produces the magnetic field. In small generators, the armature is usually the rotating component (rotor) surrounded by the stationary field structure (stator). In large generators in commercial electric power plants the situation is reversed. In a wind energy conversion device, the blades and rotating components.

Roundwood - Logs, bolts, and other round timber generated from the harvesting of trees.

Run-of-River Hydropower - A type of hydroelectric facility that uses the river flow with very little alteration and little or no impoundment of the water.

R-Value - A measure of the capacity of a material to resist heat transfer. The R-Value is the reciprocal of the conductivity of a material (U-Value). The larger the R-Value of a material, the greater its insulating properties.

-S-

Sacrificial Anode - A metal rod placed in a water heater tank to protect the tank from corrosion. Anodes of aluminium, magnesium, or zinc are the most frequently used metals. The anode creates a galvanic cell in which magnesium or zinc will be corroded more quickly than the metal of the tank giving the tank a negative charge and preventing corrosion.

Sealed Combustion Heating System - A heating system that uses only outside air for combustion and vents combustion gases directly to the outdoors. These systems are less likely to backdraft and to negatively affect indoor air quality.

Seasonal Energy Efficiency Ratio (SEER) - A measure of seasonal or annual efficiency of a central air conditioner or air conditioning heat pump. It takes into account the variations in temperature that can occur within a season and is the average number of Btu of cooling delivered for every watt-hour of electricity used by the heat pump over a cooling season.

Seasonal Performance Factor (SPF) - Ratio of useful energy output of a device to the energy input, averaged over an entire heating season.

Seasoned Wood - Wood, used for fuel, that has been air dried so that it contains 15 to 20 percent moisture content (wet basis).

Second Law Efficiency - The ratio of the minimum amount of work or energy required to perform a task to the amount actually used.

Second Law of Thermodynamics - This law states that no device can completely and continuously transform all of the energy supplied to it into useful energy.

Seebeck Effect - The generation of an electric current, when two conductors of different metals are joined at their ends to form a circuit, with the two junctions kept at different temperatures.

Selective Absorber - A solar absorber surface that has high absorbtance at wavelengths corresponding to that of the solar spectrum and low emittance in the infrared range.

Selective Surface Coating - A material with high absorbance and low emittance properties applied to or on solar absorber surfaces.

Semiconductor - Any material that has a limited capacity for conducting an electric current. Certain semiconductors, including silicon, gallium arsenide, copper indium diselenide, and cadmium telluride, are uniquely suited to the photovoltaic conversion process.

Sensible Cooling Effect - The difference between the total cooling effect and the dehumidifying effect.

Sensible Cooling Load - The interior heat gain due to heat conduction, convection, and radiation from the exterior into the interior, and from occupants and appliances.

Sensible Heat - The heat absorbed or released when a substance undergoes a change in temperature.

Series - A configuration of an electrical circuit in which the positive lead is connected to the negative lead of another energy producing, conducting, or consuming device. The voltages of each device are additive, whereas the current is not.

Series Connection - A way of joining photovoltaic cells by connecting positive leads to negative leads; such a configuration increases the voltage.

Series Resistance - Parasitic resistance to current flow in a cell due to mechanisms such as resistance from the bulk of the semiconductor material, metallic contacts, and interconnections.

Setback Thermostat - A thermostat that can be set to automatically lower temperatures in an unoccupied house and raise them again before the occupant returns.

Shading Coefficient - A measure of window glazing performance that is the ratio of the total solar heat gain through a specific window to the total solar heat gain through a single sheet of double-strength glass under the same set of conditions; expressed as a number between 0 and 1.

Sheathing - A construction element used to cover the exterior of wall framing and roof trusses.

Short Circuit - An electric current taking a shorter or different path than intended.

Short Circuit Current - The current flowing freely through an external circuit that has no load or resistance; the maximum current possible.

Sigma Heat - The sum of sensible heat and latent heat in a substance above a base temperature, typically 32 degrees Fahrenheit.

Silicon - A chemical element, of atomic number 14, that is semi-metallic, and an excellent semiconductor material used in solar photovoltaic devices; commonly found in sand.

Sine Wave - The type of alternative current generated by alternating current generators, rotary inverters, and solid-state inverters.

Single-Crystal Material - In reference to solar photovoltaic devices, a material that is composed of a single crystal or a few large crystals.

Single-phase - A generator with a single armature coil, which may have many turns and the alternating current output consists of a succession of cycles.

Sizing - The process of designing a solar system to meet a specified load given the solar resource and the nominal or rated energy output of the solar energy collection or conversion device.

Skylight - A window located on the roof of a structure to provide interior building spaces with natural daylight, warmth, and ventilation.

Slab - A concrete pad that sits on gravel or crushed rock, well-compacted soil either level with the ground or above the ground.

Slab on Grade - A slab floor that sits directly on top of the surrounding ground.

Smog - Air pollution associated with oxidants.

Solar Air Heater - A type of solar thermal system where air is heated in a collector and either transferred directly to the interior space or to a storage medium, such as a rock bin.

Solar Altitude Angle - The angle between a line from a point on the earth's surface to the centre of the solar disc, and a line extending horizontally from the point.

Solar Array - A group of solar collectors or solar modules connected together.

Solar Azimuth - The angle between the sun's apparent position in the sky and true south, as measured on a horizontal plane.

Solar Cell - A solar photovoltaic device with a specified area.

Solar Collector - A device used to collect, absorb, and transfer solar energy to a working fluid.

Solar Constant - The average amount of solar radiation that reaches the earth's upper atmosphere on a surface perpendicular to the sun's rays; equal to 1353 Watts per square meter or 492 Btu per square foot.

Solar Cooling - The use of solar thermal energy or solar electricity to power a cooling appliance. There are five basic types of solar cooling technologies - absorption cooling, which can use solar thermal energy to vaporize the refrigerant; desiccant cooling, which can use solar thermal energy to regenerate (dry) the desiccant; vapour compression cooling, which can use solar thermal energy to operate a Rankine-cycle heat engine; and evaporative coolers ("swamp" coolers), and heat-pumps and air conditioners that can be powered by solar photovoltaic systems.

Solar Declination - The apparent angle of the sun north or south of the earth's equatorial plane. The earth's rotation on its axis causes a daily change in the declination.

Solar Distillation - The process of distilling (purifying) water using solar energy. Water can be placed in an air tight solar collector with a sloped glazing material, and as it heats and evaporates, distilled water condenses on the collector glazing, and runs down where it can be collected in a tray.

Solar Energy - Electromagnetic energy transmitted from the sun (solar radiation). The amount that reaches the earth is equal to one billionth of total solar energy generated, or the equivalent of about 420 trillion kilowatt-hours.

Solar Fraction - The percentage of a building's seasonal energy requirements that can be met by a solar energy device(s) or system(s).

Solar Furnace - A device that achieves very high temperatures by the use of reflectors to focus and concentrate sunlight onto a small receiver.

Solar Gain - The amount of energy that a building absorbs due to solar energy striking its exterior and conducting to the interior or passing through windows and being absorbed by materials in the building.

Solar Irradiation - The amount of solar radiation, both direct and diffuse, received at any location.

Solar Mass - A term used for materials used to absorb and store solar energy.

Solar Module (Panel) - A solar photovoltaic device that produces a specified power output under defined test conditions, usually composed of groups of solar cells connected in series, in parallel, or in series-parallel combinations.

Solar Noon - The time of the day, at a specific location, when the sun reaches its highest, apparent point in the sky; equal to true or due, geographic south.

Solar Power Satellite - A solar power station investigated by NASA that entailed a satellite in geosynchronous orbit that would consist of a very large array of solar photovoltaic modules that would convert solar generated electricity to microwaves and beam them to a fixed point on the earth.

Solar Radiation - A general term for the visible and near visible (ultraviolet and near-infrared) electromagnetic radiation that is emitted by the sun. It has a spectral, or wavelength, distribution that corresponds to different energy levels; short wavelength radiation has a higher energy than long-wavelength radiation.

Solar Simulator - An apparatus that replicates the solar spectrum, and used for testing solar energy conversion devices.

Solar Space Heater - A solar energy system designed to provide heat to individual rooms in a building.

Solar Spectrum - The total distribution of electromagnetic radiation emanating from the sun. The different regions of the solar spectrum are described by their wavelength range. The visible region extends from about 390 to 780 nanometers (a nanometer is one billionth of one meter). About 99 percent of solar radiation is contained in a wavelength region from 300 nm (ultraviolet) to 3000 nm (near-infrared). The combined radiation in the wavelength region from 280 nm to 4000 nm is called the broadband, or total, solar radiation.

Solar Thermal Collector - A device designed to receive solar radiation and convert it into thermal energy. Normally, a solar thermal collector includes a frame, glazing, and an absorber, together with the appropriate insulation. The heat collected by the solar thermal collector may be used immediately or stored for later use.

Solar Thermal Electric Systems - Solar energy conversion technologies that convert solar energy to electricity, by heating a working fluid to power a turbine that drives a generator. Examples of these systems include central receiver systems, parabolic dish, and solar trough.

Solar Thermal Systems - Solar energy systems that collect or absorb solar energy for useful purposes. Can be used to generate high temperature heat (for electricity production and/or process heat), medium temperature heat (for process and space/water heating and electricity generation), and low temperature heat (for water and space heating and cooling).

Solar Transmittance - The amount of solar energy that passes through a glazing material, expressed as a percentage.

Solenoid - An electromechanical device composed of a coil of wire wound around a cylinder containing a bar or plunger, that when a current is applied to the coil, the electromotive force causes the plunger to move; a series of coils or wires used to produce a magnetic field.

Solenoid Valve - An automatic valve that is opened or closed by an electromagnet

Solid Fuels - Any fuel that is in solid form, such as wood, peat, lignite, coal, and manufactured fuels such as pulverised coal, coke, charcoal, briquettes, pellets, etc.

Solidity - In reference to a wind energy conversion device, the ratio of rotor blade surface area to the frontal, swept area that the rotor passes through.

Space Heater - A movable or fixed heater used to heat individual rooms.

Specific Heat - The amount of heat required to raise a unit mass of a substance through one degree, expressed as a ratio of the amount of heat required to raise an equal mass of water through the same range.

Specific Heat Capacity - The quantity of heat required to change the temperature of one unit weight of a material by one degree.

Specific Humidity - The weight of water vapour, per unit weight of dry air.

Specific Volume - The volume of a unit weight of a substance at a specific temperature and pressure.

Spectral Energy Distribution - A curve illustrating the variation or spectral irradiance with wavelength.

Spectral Irradiance - The monochromatic irradiance of a surface per unit bandwidth at a particular wavelength, usually expressed in Watts per square meter-nanometer bandwidth.

Spectral Reflectance - The ratio of energy reflected from a surface in a given waveband to the energy incident in that waveband.

Spectrally Selective Coatings - A type of window glazing films used to block the infrared (heat) portion of the solar spectrum but admit a higher portion of visible light.

Spillway - A passage for surplus water to flow over or around a dam.

Spinning Reserve - Electric power plant or utility capacity on line and running at low power in excess of actual load.

Split Spectrum Photovoltaic Cell - A photovoltaic device where incident sunlight is split into different spectral regions, with an optical apparatus, that are directed to individual photovoltaic cells that are optimised for converting that spectrum to electricity.

Split System Air Conditioner - An air conditioning system that comes in two to five pieces - one piece contains the compressor, condenser, and a fan; the others have an evaporator and a fan. The condenser, installed outside the house, connects to several evaporators, one in each room to be cooled, mounted inside the house. Each evaporator is individually controlled, allowing different rooms or zones to be cooled to varying degrees.

Spray Pyrolysis - A deposition process whereby heat is used to break molecules into elemental sources that are then spray deposited on a substrate.

Square Wave Inverter - A type of inverter that produces square wave output; consists of a DC source, four switches, and the load. The switches are power semiconductors that can carry a large current and withstand a high voltage rating. The switches are turned on and off at a correct sequence, at a certain frequency. The square wave inverter is the simplest and the least expensive to purchase, but it produces the lowest quality of power.

Squirrel Cage Motors - This is another name for an induction motor. The motors consist of a rotor inside a stator. The rotor has laminated, thin flat steel discs, stacked with channels along the length. If the casting composed of bars and attached end rings were viewed without the laminations the casting would appear similar to a squirrel cage.

Stack - A smokestack or flue for exhausting the products of combustion from a combustion appliance.

Stack (Heat) Loss - Sensible and latent heat contained in combustion gases and vapour emitted to the atmosphere.

Stagnation Temperature - A condition that can occur in a solar collector if the working fluid does not circulate when sun is shining on the collector.

Stall - In reference to a wind turbine, a condition when the rotor stops turning.

Stand-Alone Generator - A power source/generator that operates independently of or is not connected to an electric transmission and distribution network; used to meet a load(s) physically close to the generator.

Stand-Alone Inverter - An inverter that operates independent of or is not connected to an electric transmission and distribution network.

Standard Air - Air with a weight of 0.075 pounds per cubic foot with an equivalent density of dry air at a temperature of 86°F and standard barometric pressure of 29.92 inches of mercury.

Standard Conditions - In refrigeration, an evaporating temperature of 5°F, a condensing temperature of 86°F, liquid temperature before expansion of 77°F, and suction temperature of 12°F.

Standard Cubic Foot - A column of gas at standard conditions of temperature and pressure (32°F and one atmosphere).

Standby Heat Loses - A term used to describe heat energy lost from a water heater tank.

Starting Torque - The torque at the bottom of a speed (rpm) versus torque curve. The torque developed by the motor is a percentage of the full-load or rated torque. At this torque the speed, the rotational speed of the motor as a percentage of synchronous speed is zero. This torque is what is available to initially get the load moving and begin its acceleration.

Static Pressure - The force per unit area acting on the surface of a solid boundary parallel to the flow.

Steam - Water in vapour form; used as the working fluid in steam turbines and heating systems.

Steam Boiler - A type of furnace in which fuel is burned and the heat is used to produce steam.

Steam Turbine - A device that converts high-pressure steam, produced in a boiler, into mechanical energy that can then be used to produce electricity by forcing blades in a cylinder to rotate and turn a generator shaft.

Stirling Engine - A heat engine of the reciprocating (piston) where the working gas and a heat source are independent. The working gas is compressed in one region of the engine and transferred to another region where it is expanded. The expanded gas is then returned to the first region for recompression. The working gas thus moves back and forth in a closed cycle.

Stoichiometric Ratio - The ratio of chemical substances necessary for a reaction to occur completely.

Stoichiometry - Chemical reactions, typically associated with combustion processes; the balancing of chemical reactions by providing the exact proportions of reactant compounds to ensure a complete reaction; all the reactants are used up to produce a single set of products.

Stoker Boiler - A boiler in which fuel is burned on a grate with the fuel supplied and the ash removed continuously. Most of the steam is used for process heat, with the remainder being used for electricity if desired.

Storage Capacity - The amount of energy an energy storage device or system can store.

Storage Hydropower - A hydropower facility that stores water in a reservoir during high-inflow periods to augment water during low-inflow periods. Storage projects allow the flow releases and power production to be more flexible and dependable. Many hydropower project operations use a combination of approaches.

Storage Tank - The tank of a water heater.

Storage Water Heater - A water heater that releases hot water from the top of the tank when a hot water tap is opened. To replace that hot water, cold water enters the bottom of the tank to ensure a full tank.

Storm Door - An exterior door that protects the primary door.

Storm Windows - Glass, plastic panels, or plastic sheets that reduce air infiltration and some heat loss when attached to either the interior or exterior of existing windows.

Substation - An electrical installation containing power conversion (and sometimes generation) equipment, such as transformers, compensators, and circuit breakers.

Superconducting Magnetic Energy Storage (SMES) - SMES technology uses the superconducting characteristics of low-temperature materials to produce intense magnetic fields to store energy. SMES has been proposed as a storage option to support large-scale use of photovoltaics and wind as a means to smooth out fluctuations in power generation.

Superconductivity - The abrupt and large increase in electrical conductivity exhibited by some metals as the temperature approaches absolute zero.

Supplementary Heat - A heat source, such as a space heater, used to provide more heat than that provided by a primary heating source.

Supply Duct - The duct(s) of a forced air heating/cooling system through which heated or cooled air is supplied to rooms by the action of the fan of the central heating or cooling unit.

Supply Side - Technologies that pertain to the generation of electricity.

Swamp Cooler - A popular term used for an evaporative cooling device.

Synchronous Generator - An electrical generator that runs at a constant speed and draws its excitation from a power source external or independent of the load or transmission network it is supplying.

Synchronous Inverter - An electrical inverter that inverts direct current electricity to alternating current electricity, and that uses another alternating current source, such as an electric power transmission and distribution network (grid), for voltage and frequency reference to provide power in phase and at the same frequency as the external power source.

Synchronous Motor - A type of motor designed to operate precisely at the synchronous speed with no slip in the full-load speeds (rpm).

-T-

Tankless Water Heater - A water heater that heats water before it is directly distributed for end use as required; a demand water heater.

Task Lighting - Any light source designed specifically to direct light a task or work performed by a person or machine.

Temperature Coefficient (of a solar photovoltaic cell) - The amount that the voltage, current, and/or power output of a solar cell changes due to a change in the cell temperature.

Temperature Humidity Index - An index that combines sensible temperature and air humidity to arrive at a number that closely responds to the effective temperature; used to relate temperature and humidity to levels of comfort.

Temperature Zones - Individual rooms or zones in a building where temperature is controlled separately from other rooms or zones.

Temperature/Pressure Relief Valve - A component of a water heating system that opens at a designated temperature or pressure to prevent a possible tank, radiator, or delivery pipe rupture.

Tempering Valve - A valve used to mix heated water with cold in a heating system to provide a desired water temperature for end use.

Therm - A unit of heat containing 100,000 British thermal units (Btu).

Thermal Balance Point - The point or outdoor temperature where the heating capacity of a heat pump matches the heating requirements of a building.

Thermal Efficiency - A measure of the efficiency of converting a fuel to energy and useful work; useful work and energy output divided by higher heating value of input fuel times 100 (for percent).

Thermal Energy - The energy developed through the use of heat energy.

Thermal Energy Storage - The storage of heat energy during utility off-peak times at night, for use during the next day without incurring daytime peak electric rates.

Thermal Mass - Materials that store heat.

Thermal Resistance (R-Value) - This designates the resistance of a material to heat conduction. The greater the R-value the larger the number.

Thermocouple - A device consisting of two dissimilar conductors with their ends connected together. When the two junctions are at different temperatures, a small voltage is generated.

Thermodynamic Cycle - An idealized process in which a working fluid (water, air, ammonia, etc.) successively changes its state (from a liquid to a gas and back to a liquid) for the purpose of producing useful work or energy, or transferring energy.

Thermodynamics - A study of the transformation of energy from one form to another, and its practical application.

Thermoelectric Conversion - The conversion of heat into electricity by the use of thermocouples.

Thermography - A building energy auditing technique for locating areas of low insulation in a building envelope by means of a thermographic scanner.

Thermophotovoltaic Cell - A device where sunlight concentrated onto a absorber heats it to a high temperature, and the thermal radiation emitted by the absorber is used as the energy source for a photovoltaic cell that is designed to maximise conversion efficiency at the wavelength of the thermal radiation.

Thermopile - A large number of thermocouples connected in series.

Thermosiphon System - A solar collector system for water heating in which circulation of the collection fluid through the storage loop is provided solely by the temperature and density difference between the hot and cold fluids.

Thermostat - A device used to control temperatures; used to control the operation of heating and cooling devices by turning the device on or off when a specified temperature is reached.

Thermosyphon - The natural, convective movement of air or water due to differences in temperature. In solar passive design a thermosyphon collector can be constructed and attached to a house to deliver heat to the home by the continuous pattern of the convective loop (or thermosyphon).

Thin Film - A layer of semiconductor material, such as copper indium diselenide or gallium arsenide, a few microns or less in thickness, used to make solar photovoltaic cells.

Three-phase Current - Alternating current in which three separate pulses are present, identical in frequency and voltage, but separated 120 degrees in phase.

Tidal Power - The power available from the rise and fall of ocean tides. A tidal power plant works on the principle of a dam or barrage that captures water in a basin at the peak of a tidal flow, then directs the water through a hydroelectric turbine as the tide ebbs.

Tilt Angle (of a Solar Collector or Module) - The angle at which a solar collector or module is set to face the sun relative to a horizontal position. The tilt angle can be set or adjusted to maximise seasonal or annual energy collection.

Timer - A device that can be set to automatically turn appliances (lights) off and on at set times.

Timer (Water Heater) - This device can automatically turn the heater off at night and on in the morning.

Tip Speed Ratio - In reference to a wind energy conversion device's blades, the difference between the rotational speed of the tip of the blade and the actual velocity of the wind.

Tipping Fee - Price charged to deliver municipal solid waste to a landfill, waste-to-energy facility, or recycling facility.

Ton (of Air Conditioning) - A unit of air cooling capacity; 12,000 Btu per hour.

Topping-cycle - A means to increase the thermal efficiency of a steam electric generating system by increasing temperatures and interposing a device, such as a gas turbine, between the heat source and the conventional steam-turbine generator to convert some of the additional heat energy into electricity.

Torque (Motor) - The turning or twisting force generated by an electrical motor in order for it to operate.

Total Harmonic Distortion - The measure of closeness in shape between a waveform and it's fundamental component.

Total Heat - The sum of the sensible and latent heat in a substance or fluid above a base point, usually 32 degrees Fahrenheit.

Total Incident Radiation - The total radiation incident on a specific surface area over a time interval.

Total Internal Reflection - The trapping of light by refraction and reflection at critical angles inside a semiconductor device so that it cannot escape the device and must be eventually absorbed by the semiconductor.

Tracking Solar Array - A solar energy array that follows the path of the sun to maximise the solar radiation incident on the PV surface. The two most common orientations are (1) one axis where the array tracks the sun east to west and (2) two-axis tracking where the array points directly at the sun at all times. Tracking arrays use both the direct and diffuse sunlight. Two-axis tracking arrays capture the maximum possible daily energy.

Trailing Edge - The part of a wind energy conversion device blade, or airfoil, that is the last to contact the wind.

Transformer - An electromagnetic device that changes the voltage of alternating current electricity. It consists of an induction coil having a primary and secondary winding and a closed iron core.

Transmission - The process of sending or moving electricity from one point to another; usually defines that part of an electric utility's electric power lines from the power plant buss to the last transformer before the customer's connection.

Transmission and Distribution Losses - The losses that result from inherent resistance in electrical conductors and transformation inefficiencies in distribution transformers in a transmission and distribution network.

Transmission Lines - Transmit high-voltage electricity from the transformer to the electric distribution system.

Transmission System (Electric) - An interconnected group of electric transmission lines and associated equipment for moving or transferring electric energy in bulk between points of supply and points at which it is transformed for delivery over the distribution system lines to consumers, or is delivered to other electric systems.

Traveling Grate - A furnace grate that moves fuel through the combustion chamber

Trellis - An architectural feature used to shade exterior walls; usually made of a lattice of metal or wood; often covered by vines to provide additional summertime shading.

Trickle (Solar) Collector - A type of solar thermal collector in which a heat transfer fluid drips out of header pipe at the top of the collector, runs down the collector absorber and into a tray at the bottom where it drains to a storage tank.

True Power - The actual power rating that is developed by a motor before losses occur.

Tube (Fluorescent Light) - A fluorescent lamp that has a tubular shape.

Tube-In-Plate-Absorber - A type of solar thermal collector where the heat transfer fluid flows through tubes formed in the absorber plate.

Tube-Type Collector - A type of solar thermal collector that has tubes (pipes) that the heat transfer fluid flows through that are connected to a flat absorber plate.

Tungsten Halogen Lamp - A type of incandescent lamp that contains a halogen gas in the bulb, which reduces the filament evaporation rate increasing the lamp life. The high operating temperature and need for special fixtures limits their use to commercial applications and for use in projector lamps and spotlights.

Turbine - A device for converting the flow of a fluid (air, steam, water, or hot gases) into mechanical motion.

Turn Down Ratio - The ratio of a boiler's or gasifier's maximum output to its minimum output.

Two-Axis Tracking - A solar array tracking system capable of rotating independently about two axes (e.g., vertical and horizontal).

Two-Tank Solar System - A solar thermal system that has one tank for storing solar heated water to preheat the water in a conventional water heater.

-U-

Ultimate Analysis - A procedure for determining the primary elements in a substance (carbon, hydrogen, oxygen, nitrogen, sulphur, and ash).

Ultraviolet - Electromagnetic radiation in the wavelength range of 4 to 400 nanometers.

Unitary Air Conditioner - An air conditioner consisting of one or more assemblies that move, clean, cool, and dehumidify air.

Unvented Heater - A combustion heating appliance that vents the combustion by-products directly into the heated space. The latest models have oxygen-sensors that shut off the unit when the oxygen level in the room falls below a safe level.

Useful Heat - Heat stored above room temperature (in a solar heating system).

-V-

Vacuum Evaporation - The deposition of thin films of semiconductor material by the evaporation of elemental sources in a vacuum.

Valence Band - The highest energy band in a semiconductor that can be filled with electrons.

Vapour Retarder - A material that retards the movement of water vapour through a building element (walls, ceilings) and prevents insulation and structural wood from becoming damp and metals from corroding. Often applied to insulation batts or separately in the form of treated papers, plastic sheets, and metallic foils.

Vapour-Dominated Geothermal System - A conceptual model of a hydrothermal system where steam pervades the rock and is the pressure-controlling fluid phase.

Variable-Speed Wind Turbines - Turbines in which the rotor speed increases and decreases with changing wind speed, producing electricity with a variable frequency.

Vent - A component of a heating or ventilation appliance used to conduct fresh air into, or waste air or combustion gases out of, an appliance or interior space.

Vent Damper - A device mounted in the vent connector that closes the vent when the heating unit is not firing. This traps heat inside the heating system and house rather than letting it draft up and out the vent system.

Vent Pipe - A tube in which combustion gases from a combustion appliance are vented out of the appliance to the outdoors.

Vented Heater - A type of combustion heating appliance in which the combustion gases are vented to the outside, either with a fan (forced) or by natural convection.

Ventilation - The process of moving air (changing) into and out of an interior space either by natural or mechanically induced (forced) means.

Ventilation Air - That portion of supply air that is drawn from outside, plus any recirculated air that has been treated to maintain a desired air quality.

Vertical-Axis Wind Turbine (VAWT) - A type of wind turbine in which the axis of rotation is perpendicular to the wind stream and the ground.

Visible Light Transmittance - The amount of visible light that passes through the glazing material of a window, expressed as a percentage.

Vmp - Voltage at maximum power

Volt - A unit of electrical force equal to that amount of electromotive force that will cause a steady current of one ampere to flow through a resistance of one ohm.

Voltage - The amount of electromotive force, measured in volts, that exists between two points.

Volt-Ampere - A unit of electrical measurement equal to the product of a volt and an ampere.

-W-

Wafer - A thin sheet of semiconductor (photovoltaic material) made by cutting it from a single crystal or ingot.

Water Jacket - A heat exchanger element enclosed in a boiler. Water is circulated with a pump through the jacket where it picks up heat from the combustion chamber after which the heated water circulates to heat distribution devices. A water jacket is also an enclosed water-filled chamber in a tankless coiled water heater. When a faucet is turned on water flows into the water heater heat exchanger. The water in the chamber is heated and transfers heat to the cooler water in the heat exchanger and is sent through the hot water outlet to the appropriate faucet

Water Source Heat Pump - A type of (geothermal) heat pump that uses well (ground) or surface water as a heat source. Water has a more stable seasonal temperature than air thus making for a more efficient heat source.

Water Turbine - A turbine that uses water pressure to rotate its blades; the primary types are the Pelton wheel, for high heads (pressure); the Francis turbine, for low to medium heads; and the Kaplan for a wide range of heads. Primarily used to power an electric generator.

Water Wall - An interior wall made of water filled containers for absorbing and storing solar energy.

Water Wheel - A wheel that is designed to use the weight and/or force of moving water to turn it, primarily to operate machinery or grind grain.

Watt - The rate of energy transfer equivalent to one ampere under an electrical pressure of one volt. One watt equals 1/746 horsepower, or one joule per second. It is the product of Voltage and Current (amperage).

Watt (Electric) - The electrical unit of power. The rate of energy transfer equivalent to 1 ampere of electric current flowing under a pressure of 1 volt at unity power factor.

Watt (Thermal) - A unit of power in the metric system, expressed in terms of energy per second, equal to the work done at a rate of 1 joule per second.

Watthour (Wh) - The electrical energy unit of measure equal to 1 watt of power supplied to, or taken from, an electric circuit steadily for 1 hour.

Wattmeter - A device for measuring power consumption.

Wave Form - The shape of the phase power at a certain frequency and amplitude.

Wave Power - The concept of capturing and converting the energy available in the motion of ocean waves to energy.

Wavelength - The distance between similar points on successive waves.

Weatherization - Caulking and weatherstripping to reduce air infiltration and exfiltration into/out of a building.

Weatherstripping - A material used to seal gaps around windows and exterior doors.

Wheeling - The process of transmitting electricity over one or more separately owned electric transmission and distribution systems.

Wind Energy - Energy available from the movement of the wind across a landscape caused by the heating of the atmosphere, earth, and oceans by the sun.

Wind Energy Conversion System (WECS) or Device - An apparatus for converting the energy available in the wind to mechanical energy that can be used to power machinery (grain mills, water pumps) and to operate an electrical generator.

Wind Generator - A WECS designed to produce electricity.

Wind Power Plant - A group of wind turbines interconnected to a common utility system through a system of transformers, distribution lines, and (usually) one substation. Operation, control, and maintenance functions are often centralised through a network of computerised monitoring systems, supplemented by visual inspection.

Wind Resource Assessment - The process of characterising the wind resource, and its energy potential, for a specific site or geographical area.

Wind Rose - A diagram that indicates the average percentage of time that the wind blows from different directions, on a monthly or annual basis.

Wind Speed - The rate of flow of the wind undisturbed by obstacles.

Wind Speed Duration Curve - A graph that indicates the distribution of wind speeds as a function of the cumulative number of hours that the wind speed exceeds a given wind speed in a year.

Wind Speed Frequency Curve - A curve that indicates the number of hours per year that specific wind speeds occur.

Wind Speed Profile - A profile of how the wind speed changes with height above the surface of the ground or water.

Wind Turbine - A term used for a wind energy conversion device that produces electricity; typically having one, two, or three blades.

Wind Turbine Rated Capacity - The amount of power a wind turbine can produce at its rated wind speed, e.g., 100 kW at 20 mph. The rated wind speed generally corresponds to the point at which the conversion efficiency is near its maximum. Because of the variability of the wind, the amount of energy a wind turbine actually produces is a function of the capacity factor (e.g., a wind turbine produces 20% to 35% of its rated capacity over a year).

Wind Velocity - The wind speed and direction in an undisturbed flow.

Windmill - A WECS that is used to grind grain, and that typically has a high-solidity rotor; commonly used to refer to all types of WECS.

Window - A generic term for a glazed opening that allows daylight to enter into a building and can be opened for ventilation.

Windpower Curve - A graph representing the relationship between the power available from the wind and the wind speed. The power from the wind increases proportionally with the cube of the wind speed.

Windpower Profile - The change in the power available in the wind due to changes in the wind speed or velocity profile; the windpower profile is proportional to the cube of the wind speed profile.

Wingwall - A building structural element that is built onto a building's exterior along the inner edges of all the windows, and extending from the ground to the eaves. Wingwalls help ventilate rooms that have only one exterior wall which leads to poor cross ventilation. Wingwalls cause fluctuations in the natural wind direction to create moderate pressure differences across the windows. They are only effective on the windward side of the building.

Wire (Electrical) - A generic term for an electrical conductor.

Wood Stove - A wood-burning appliance for space and/or water heating and/or cooking.

Working Fluid - A fluid used to absorb and transfer heat energy.

Wound Rotor Motors - A type of motor that has a rotor with electrical windings connected through slip rings to the external power circuit. An external resistance controller in the rotor circuit allows the performance of the motor to be tailored to the needs of the system and to be changed with relative ease to accommodate system changes or to vary the speed of the motor.

-Y-

Yaw - The rotation of a horizontal axis wind turbine around its tower or vertical axis.

Yurt - An octagonal shaped shelter that originated in Mongolia, and traditionally made from leather or canvas for easy transportation.

-Z-

Zone - An area within the interior space of a building, such as an individual room(s), to be cooled, heated, or ventilated. A zone has its own thermostat to control the flow of conditioned air into the space.

Zoning - The combining of rooms in a structure according to similar heating and cooling patterns. Zoning requires using more than one thermostat to control heating, cooling, and ventilation equipment.

Bibliography

[1] Afgan, N. H., Carvalho, M.G. & Hovanov, N.V. Energy system assessment with sustainability indicators. *Energy Policy,* **28,** pp. 603-612, 2000.

[2] Afgan, N.H., Al Gobaisi, D., Carvalho, M.G. & Cumo, M. Sustainable energy management. *Renewable and Sustainable Energy Review,* **2**, pp. 235-286, 1998.

[3] Alcamo, J. (ed). *IMAGE 2.0: Integrated Modelling of Global Climate Change*. Kluwer, London, 1994.

[4] Alcantara V. & Roca J. CO_2 emissions and the occupation of the "environmental space": An empirical exercise *Energy Policy,* **27(9)**, pp. 505-508, 1999.

[5] Alternative Electricity Supply Scenarios 2020, *NTUA Report to EC DG-XVII*, 1993.

[6] Alternative energy scenarios for the European Community, *NTUA Report to EC DG-XVII*, 1991-1992.

[7] Anderson, K. B. *Conservation versus Energy Supply: An Economic and Environmental Comparison of Alternatives for Space Conditioning of New Residences.* PhD Thesis, Energy and Resources Group, University of California, Berkeley, 1987.

[8] Andersson M. & Karlsson B. Cost-effective incentives for co-operation between participants in the electricity market. *Applied Energy*, **54(4)**, pp. 301-313, 1996.

[9] Andersson M. Shadow prices for heat generation in time-dependent and dynamic energy systems. *Energy*, **19(12)**, pp. 1205-1211, 1994.

[10] *Annual Energy Outlook 1999*, DOE/EIA-0383(99), EIA, Washington, DC, December, 1998.

[11] APDC (Asian and Pacific Development Centre). *Integrated Energy Planing: A Manual*. Vol. 1: Energy Data, Energy Demand. René Codoni et al. (eds.). Asian and Pacific Development Centre: Kuala Lumpur, 1985.

[12] Atkins, P.W. *The Second Law*. W.H. Freeman: New York, 1984.

[13] Ayres, R.U. & Simonis U.E. (eds.). Industrial Metabolism: *Restructuring for Sustainable Development*. United Nations University Press: Tokyo, 1994.

[14] Babiker, M. Y., Reilly, J. M., Mayer, M., Eckaus, R.S., Wing, I. S. & Hyman R. C. *The MIT Emissions Prediction and Policy Analysis (EPPA) Model: Revisions, Sensitivities, and Comparisons of Results*. Report No. 71, MIT Joint Program on the Science and Policy of Global Change, February 2001.

[15] Backus, G., Amlin, J. & Kleeman, S. *Introduction to Energy 2020*, Systematic Solutions, Inc.: Fairborn, OH, USA, 1993.

[16] Baird S. *Energy Fact Sheet*. Energy Educators of Ontario, 1993. http://www.iclei.org/efacts/

[17] Bakken J. I. & Lucas N. Integrated resource planning and environmental pricing in a competitive and deregulated electricity market. *Energy Policy*, **24(3)**, pp. 239-244, 1996.

[18] Barker, T. Large-scale energy-environment-economy modelling of the European Union. *Applied Economics and Public Policy*, eds. I. Begg & S. G. B Henry, Cambridge University Press, 1998b.

[19] Barker, T. The use of energy-environment-economy models to inform greenhouse gas mitigation policy. *Impact Assessment and Project Appraisal*, **16(2)**, pp. 123-131, 1998a.

[20] Beaver, R. Structural comparison of the models in EMF 12. *Energy Policy*, **21(3)**, pp. 238-248, 1993.

[21] Bella, D. A. Technological Constraints on Technological Optimism. *Technological Forecasting and Social Change*, **14(3)**, pp. 15-20, 1979.

[22] Berthelemy, J.-C., Devezeaux de Lavergne J.-G. & Ladoux, N. *Melodie: An Energy-Economy Interaction Model for Long Term Planning*, 13th Congress of the World Energy Conference, Commissariat a l'Energie Atomique (CEA), September 1986, English translation: March 1989.

[23] Bevington, R. & Rosenfeld, A. Energy for buildings and homes. *Scientific American*, September 1990.

[24] Bhatia, R. *Economics, Modelling, Planning and Management of Energy*. World Scientific Publishing Co., 1990.

[25] Bleviss, D.L. & Walzer, P. Energy for motor vehicles. *Scientific American*, September 1990.

[26] Bosseboeuf D., Chateau B. & Lapillonne B. *Monitoring energy efficiency and CO2 abatment policies: What can we learn from indicators*. UNFCC Workshop best practices in PAM's, Copenhagen, April 2000.

[27] Brower, M. *Cool Energy: The Renewable Solution to Global Warming*. Union of Concerned Scientists: Cambridge MA, 1990.

[28] Buehring, W.A., Hamilton, B.P., Guziel, K.A. & Cirillo, R.R. *ENPEP: An Integrated Approach for Modelling National Energy Systems*, Argonne National Laboratory: France, February 1991.

[29] Burnham L., (ed.), *Renewable Energy*. Island Press: Washington, 1993.

[30] Burniaux, J. M., Martin, J.P., Nicoletti, G. & Oliveira-Martins, J. GREEN -- A multi-sector, multi- region dynamic general equilibrium model for quantifying the costs of curbing CO_2 emissions: a technical manual. *OECD Economics Department Working Papers,* No. 116, May, Paris, 1992.

[31] Capros, P. & Mantzos, L. *User's Manual of MIDAS.* Version 3.0, National Technical University of Athens: Athens, 1992.

[32] Capros, P., Georgakopoulos, P., Van Regemorter, D., Proost, S., Schmidt, T.F.N. & Conrad, K., European Union: the GEM-E3 General Equilibrium Model, *Economic and Financial Modelling*, special double issue, Summer/Autumn, 1997.

[33] Cecelski, E. From Rio to Beijing: Engendering the Energy Debate. *Energy Policy*, **23**(6), pp.88-110, 1995.

[34] Charters, W.W.S. Solar energy: current status and future prospects. *Energy Policy*, october 1991.

[35] Christiansson, L., *Diffusion and Learning Curves of Renewable Energy Technologies.* Working Paper, International Institute for Applied Systems Analysis, Laxenburg, Austria, 1995.

[36] Cirillo, R.R., C.M. Macal & Buehring, W.A. The use of non-linear models for energy planning in developing countries: ENPEP as an example. *Proc. of the 25th Intersociety Energy Conversion Engineering Conference*, **4**, pp. 360-363, 1990.

[37] Clarke, A. Wind energy. *Energy Policy*, october 1991.

[38] Consortium for International Earth Science Information Network (CIESIN). *Thematic Guide to Integrated Assessment Modeling of Climate Change* [online]. University Center; Mich., 1995. http://sedac.ciesin.org/mva/iamcc.tg/TGHP.html

[39] Cook, E. *Man, Energy, Society*. W. H. Freeman & Co. Publishers: San Francisco, 1976.

[40] Coon, R.W. The engineering of magnetic fusion reactors. *Scientific American*, **249(4),** pp. 38-45, 1983.

[41] de Kruijk, H. & van den Broek, M. *The EC Energy and Environmental Model EFOM - ENV specified in GAMS*. Petten, 1993.

[42] Devezeaux J.-G., Hammoudeh S. & Ladoux N., Melody: Jordan Final Report, CEA Working paper, 1989.

[43] DiPippo, R. Geothermal energy: electricity generation and environmental impacts. *Energy Policy*, october 1991.

[44] Dostrovsky, I., Chemical fuels from the sun. *Scientific American*, December 1991.

[45] Durant, W. & Durant, A. *The Lessons of History*.: Simon and Schuster: New York, 1968.

[46] EC: *European Energy to 2020: A Scenario Approach*, ECSC-EC-EAEC, Brussels, Belgium, 1996b.

[47] EC: *POLES 2.2*, Joule II Programme, EUR 17358 EN, Brussels, Belgium, December 1996a.

[48] EC: *The PRIMES Project*, Joule II Programme, EUR 16713 EN, Brussels, Belgium, August 1995a.

[49] Edmonds, J. & Reilly, J. *Global Energy: Assessing the Future.* Oxford University Press: New York, 1985.

[50] Edmonds, J., Wise, M. & MacCracken, C. *Advanced Energy Technologies and Climate Change: An Analysis Using the Global Change Assessment Model (GCAM).* Report prepared for the IPCC Second Assessment Report, Working Group IIa, Energy Supply Mitigation Options, PNL-9798, UC-402, Pacific Northwest Laboratories, Richland, WA, 1994.

[51] EIA: *Annual Energy Outlook 1997.* DOE/EIA-0383(97), Washington, DC, USA, December 1996b.

[52] EIA: *Assumptions for the Annual Energy Outlook 1997.* EIA/DOE, Washington, DC, USA, March 1996c.

[53] EIA: *The National Energy Modelling System: An Overview.* DOE/EIA-0581(96), Washington, DC, USA, March 1996a.

[54] Energy after Rio: Prospects and Challenges. UNDP. Energy and Atmosphere Programme. http://www.undp.org/seed/energy/

[55] *ETSAP. The New TIMES: a Model for the Millennium.* ETSAP news, 7(1), pp. 1-4, 2000. ECN Policy Studies, P.O. Box 1, 1755 ZG Petten, The Netherlands, www.ecn.nl/unit_bs/etsap/newslet/vol7-1/art-1.html

[56] ETSU: *An Appraisal of UK Energy Research Development & Dissemination, Volume I-VIII*, Strategic Studies Department, R 83, London, England, 1994.

[57] EUROSTAT. *Useful Energy Balance Sheets 1985.* EUROSTAT, Luxemburg, 1988.

[58] Farmer, R. (ed). *Gas Turbine World 1988-89 Handbook.* Pequot Publishing, Inc.: Fairfield, Connecticut, 1989.

[59] Fenhann, J. & Morthorst, P.E. *Energy Model for Denmark - EXPLOR - EDM - EFOM*, EUR 7284 EN, 1981.

[60] Fermi, E. *Thermodynamics.* Dover Publications, Inc.: New York, 1936.

[61] Fisher, J. *Energy Crises in Perspective.* John Wiley and Sons: New York, 1974.

[62] Flavin Ch. & Lensen, N. *Worldwatch Paper 100, Beyond the Petroleum Age: Designing a Solar Economy*, World Watch Institute, December 1990.

[63] Fluck, R.C. (ed). *Energy in World Agriculture.* Vol. 6. Elsevier Science Publishers: Amsterdam, The Netherlands, 1992.

[64] Ford, K.W., Rochlin, G.I. & Socolow, R.H. (eds). Efficient Use of Energy. Part I: a Physics Perspective. *AIP Conference Proceedings* No. 25, American Institute of Physics, New York, 1975.

[65] Fujii, Y. & Yamaji, K. Assessment of technological options. *The Global Energy System For Limiting The Atmospheric CO2 Concentration*, Japan, 1997.

[66] Fulkerson, W., Judkins R.R. & Manoj S. Energy from fossil fuels. *Scientific American,* September 1990.

[67] Galperin, A.L., *Nuclear Energy, Nuclear Waste.* Chelsea House Publishers: New York, 1992.

[68] Geiz D. & Kutzmark, T. Developing sustainable communitues – the furure is now. *Public Management Magazine.* International City/County Management Asssociation, Washington DC, 1998.

[69] Georgopoulou, E., Lalas, D. & Papagiannakis, L. A multicriteria decision aid approach for energy planning problems: the case of renewable energy option. *European Journal of Operational Research,* **103**, pp. 38-54, 1997.

[70] Gerking, H. Modelling of multi-stage decision making process in multi-period energy models. *European Journal of Operational Research,* **32(2)**, pp. 191-204, 1987.

[71] Goldemberg, J., Johansson, T.B., Reddy, A.K.N. & Williams, R.H. *Energy for a Sustainable World,* Wiley Eastern Limited: New Delhi, 1988.

[72] Golob, R. & Brus, E. *The Almanac of Renewable Energy.* Henry Holt: New York, 1993.

[73] Grabiel, F. *Theory of Energy Transfers and Conversions.* John Wiley & Sons, Inc.: New York, 1967.

[74] Griffin, J. M. & Steele, H.B. *Energy Economics and Policy.* Academic Press College Division: Orlando, FL, 1986.

[75] Grohnheit, P. E. Application and limitations of annual models for electricity capacity development. *Systems Modelling for Energy Policy,* eds. D. W. Bunn & E. R. Larsen, John Wiley & Sons: Chichester, U.K., pp. 89-116, 1997.

[76] Grohnheit, P.E. Economic interpretation of the EFOM model. *Energy Economics*, **13(2),** pp. 143-52, 1991.

[77] Groscurth H. M. & Schweiker A. Contribution of computer models to solving the energy problem, *Energy Sources*, **17(2),** pp. 161-177, 1995.

[78] Grubb, M., Edmonds, J. ten Brink, P. & Morrison, M. The cost of limiting fossil-fuel CO2 emissions: a survey and analysis. *Annual Review of Energy and the Environment*, eds. Socolow, R.H., Anderson, D. & Harte, J. vol. 18, Annual Reviews, California, pp. 397 –478, 1993.

[79] Grubler, A. Energy in the 21st century: from resources to environmental and lifestyle constraints, *Entropie*, **164/165**, pp. 29-34, 1991.

[80] Grubler, A. & Nakicenovic, N. *Long Waves, Technology Diffusion and Substitution.* International Institute for Applied Systems Analysis, PR-91-17, Laxenburg, Austria, 1991.

[81] Guilmot, J.F., *The EFOM Energy Model - Development to Answer Questions of Energy Supply (Le modele energetique EFOM: developpement d'un outil de reponse aux questions d'approvisionnement energetique),* EUR 9475 FR, 1984.

[82] Guilmot, J-F., McGlue, D., Valette, P. & Waeterloos, C., *Energy 2000.* Comission of the European Communities, 1986.

[83] Gyftopoulos, E.P., Lazaridis L.J. & Widmer, T.F. *Potential Fuel Effectiveness in Industry.* A report of the Energy Policy, Project of the Ford Foundation, Ballinger, Cambridge, MA, 1974.

[84] Gyftopoulos, E.P. & Beretta, G.P. *Thermodynamics: Foundations and Applications.* Macmillan Publishing Company: New York, 1991.

[85] Hafele, W. *Energy in a Finite World: Paths to a Sustainable Future.* Ballinger Pub. Co.: Cambridge, MA., 1981.

[86] Hafele, W., Energy from nuclear power. *Scientific American*, September 1990.

[87] Hake J.-F., Kleemann M. & Kuckshinrichs W. Modelling of energy-related emissions on a national and global level: an overview of selected approaches. *Advances in Systems Analysis: Modelling Energy-Related Emissions on a National and Global Level,* eds. J.-F. Hake, M. Kleemann, W. Kuckshinrichs, D. Martinsen, M. Walbeck, Konferenzen des Forschungszentrums Jülich, Band 15, Forschungszentrum Jülich, D-52425 Jülich, Germany, pp. 3-26, 1994.

[88] Hall, B.O., Biomass energy. *Energy Policy,* october 1991.

[89] Hamilton, B.P., Cirillo, R.R. & Buehring, W.A. ENPEP: an integrated approach to energy planning. *Proc. 1992 International Symposium on Energy, Environment, and Information Management*, Argonne National Laboratory, Argonne, Illinois, U.S.A., pp. 321-329 (Sept. 1992).

[90] Hamilton, L.D., Goldstein, G.A., Lee, J.C., Manne, A.S., Marcuse, W., Morris, S.C. & Wene, C.O. *MARKAL-MACRO: An Overview.,* Biomedical and Environmental Assessment Group, Analytical Sciences Division, Department of Applied Science, Brookhaven National Laboratory, Associated Universities, BNL-48377, November 1992.

[91] Hartnett, J.P. & Irvine, T.F Jr. eds. *Advances in Heat Transfer.* Academic Press: New York, 1985.

[92] Hatsopoulos, G. N. & Keenan, J.H. *Principles of General Thermodynamics.* Robert E. Krieger Publishing Company: New York, 1981.

[93] HDR: *Human Development Report 1995.* United Nations Development Programme (UNDP), Oxford University Press: New York, 1995.

[94] Heidarian, J. & Wu, G. *Power Sector Statistics for Developing Countries (1987-1991).* Industry and Energy Department, World Bank, Washington, DC, 1994.

[95] Henning, D. Cost minimisation for a local utility through CHP, heat storage and load management. *International Journal of Energy Research,* **22(8)**, pp. 691-713, 1998.

[96] Hoepfinger, E. & Huber, W. *EFOM 12C Case Studies - Candidate Technologies to Relieve the European Energy System – Germany.* EUR 8428 EN, 1983.

[97] Hohmeyer, O. *Social Costs of Energy Consumption: External Effects of Electricity Generation in the Federal Republic of Germany.* Springer-Verlag: Berlin, 1988.

[98] Holdren, J. P. Chapter V. Energy and human environment: the generation and definition of environmental problems. *The European Transition from Oil: Societal Impacts and Constraints on Energy Policy,* ed. G. T. Goodman, L. A. Kristoferson & J. M. Hollander, Academic Press: London, 1981.

[99] Holdren, J. P. *Integrated Assessment for Energy-Related Environmental Standards: A Summary of Issues and Findings.* Lawrence Berkeley Laboratory. LBL-12779. October, 1980.

[100] Holdren, J.P. Energy in transition. *Scientific American,* **263(3),** 156-163, 1990.

[101] Hollander, J.M. (ed.), *Annual Review of Energy and the Environment,* Annual Review Inc., 1992.

[102] Holman, J.P. *Thermodynamics*. McGraw-Hill Book Company: New York, 1969.

[103] Hope, C., Anderson, J. & Wenman, P. Policy analysis of the greenhouse effect. *Energy Policy,* **21(3)**, pp.56-76, 1993.

[104] Hourcade, J.C. et. al. Estimating the cost of mitigating greenhouse gases. *Climate Change 1995: Economic and Social Dimensions of Climate Change*. J.P. Bruce, H. Lee, & E.F. Haites (eds.), University Press: Cambridge, pp. 263-296, 1996.

[105] Houthakker, H.S. & Kennedy, M., *Directions in Energy Policy - A Comprehensive Approach to Energy Resource Decision-Making.* Ballinger Publishing Co., 1979.

[106] Howes, R. & Fainberg, A. *The Energy Sourcebook: A Guide to Technology, Resources and Policy*. American Institute of Physics, 1991.

[107] Hubbard, H.M. The real cost of energy. *Scientific American*, April 1991.

[108] Huber, W. et al., *EFOM Case Studies - The Escalating Supply Rationing*, EUR 8050 EN, 1982.

[109] Hyman, L.S. & O'Niell, D.C. Financing energy expansion: 1990-2020. *World Energy Council Journal*, December, pp. 7-12, 1995.

[110] IAEA: *DECADES Software Package (DECPAC), Volume 1: Overview and General Description of Design and Functions*, IAEA, DECADES 07, Vienna, Austria 1995b.

[111] IAEA: *The DECADES Project-Outline and General Overview*, IAEA, DECADES 01, Vienna, Austria, 1995a.

[112] IEA (International Energy Agency). *Biofuels.* IEA/OECD (Organisation for Economic Co-operation and Development), Paris, 1994.

[113] IEA (International Energy Agency). *CO_2 Capture and Storage in the Nature.* NG Project. Greenhouse Issues, **22**(1), 1996.

[114] IEA (International Energy Agency). *Energy Policies of IEA Countries: 1994 Review.* OECD/IEA, Paris, 1995.

[115] IEA (International Energy Agency). MARKAL Hard-Linked with MACRO, *ETSAP News,* Netherlands, November 1992.

[116] IEA (International Energy Agency). *Taxing Energy: Why and How.* Organisation for Economic Co-operation and Development (OECD)/IEA, Paris, 1993.

[117] IER: *Emission Reduction of Energy-Related and Climate-Relevant Trace Gases in the Federal Republic of Germany and in Baden-Wuerttemberg,* University of Stuttgart, Stuttgart, Germany, September 1995.

[118] IIASA: *A Comparative Assessment of Different Options to Reduce CO2 Emissions*, WP-92-27, Laxenburg, Austria, March 1992a.

[119] IIASA: *Inventory of Greenhouse-Gas Mitigation Measures, Examples from the IIASA Technology Data Bank*, WP-92-85, Laxenburg, Austria, November 1992b.

[120] Jensen, J. & Sørensen, B. *Fundamentals of Energy Storage*. John Wiley and Sons: New York, 1984.

[121] Johansson, T.B, Bodlund, B. & Williams, R.H. (eds.). *Electricity: Efficient End Use and New Generation Technologies, and their Planning Implications.* Lund University Press: Lund, 1989.

[122] Johansson, T.B., H. Kelly, Reddy, A.K.N. & Williams R.H. (eds.) *Renewable Energy: Sources for Fuels and Electricity.* Island Press: Washington, DC. & Covelo, California, 1993.

[123] Jusko, M.J., Buehring, W.A. & Cirillo, R.R. *Energy and Power Evaluation Program (ENPEP) Documentation and User's Manual.* Energy and Environmental Systems Division, Systems Analysis, Development and Evaluation Group, Argonne National Laboratory, August 1987.

[124] Kassler, P. *Energy for Development.* Shell Selected Paper, Shell International Petroleum Company, London, England, 1994.

[125] Katscher, W. *IKARUS-Instruments for Greenhouse Gas Reduction Strategies*. KFA Jülich, Interim Summary Report, 1993.

[126] Keenan, J. H. & Hatsopoulos, G. N. Basic thermodynamic considerations for a relativistic system. *A Critical Review of Thermodynamics*, ed. E. B. Stuart et al., Mono Book Corp.: Baltimore, 1970, pp. 417-419.

[127] Keenan, J. K. & Shapiro, A.H. History and exposition of the laws of thermodynamics. *Mechanical Engineering,* pp. 915-921, November 1947.

[128] Kestin, J. & Rice J.R. Paradoxes in the application of thermodynamics to strained solids. *A Critical Review of Thermodynamics*, eds. Stuart, E.B.,

Gal-Or, B & Brainard, A.J. Mono Book Corp.: Baltimore, pp. 276-280, 1970.

[129] Kleinpeter M. *Energy Planning and Policy*. John Wiley: Chichester, 1995.

[130] Kleinpeter, M. *Introduction to Energy Planning*. Metrica: Wien, 1989.

[131] Kneese A.V. & J. L. Sweeney (eds.) *Handbook of Natural Resources and Energy Economics,* Vol. III, Elsevier Science Publishers: Amsterdam 1993.

[132] Koomey J. & Krause, F. Introduction to Environmental Externality Costs, *CRC Handbook on Energy Efficiency,* CRC Press, Inc.: Berkley, CA, 1997.

[133] Koomey, J. *Comparative Analysis of Monetary Estimates of External Environmental Costs Associated with Combustion of Fossil Fuels.* Lawrence Berkeley Laboratory, LBL-28313, July, 1990a.

[134] Kram T. & Hill D. A multinational model for CO_2 reduction: Defining boundaries of future CO_2 emissions in nine countries. *Energy Policy,* **24(1)**, pp. 39-51, 1996.

[135] Krause, F. & Koomey J. G. *Unit Costs of Carbon Savings From Urban Trees, Rural Trees, and Electricity Conservation: A Utility Cost Perspective.* Lawrence Berkeley Laboratory. LBL-27311. Presented at the Conference on Urban Heat Islands, February 23-24, 1989 Berkeley, California. July, 1989.

[136] Krause, F., Bach, W. & Koomey, J. Energy Policy in the Greenhouse. Volume 1. *From Warming Fate to Warming Limit: Benchmarks to a Global Climate Convention*. El Cerrito, CA: International Project for Sustainable Energy Paths, 1989.

[137] Krause, F., Haites, E., Howarth, R. & Koomey, J. Energy policy in the greenhouse. Volume II, Part 1. *Cutting Carbon Emissions–Burden or Benefit? The Economics of Energy-Tax and Non-Price Policies.* El Cerrito, CA: International Project for Sustainable Energy Paths, 1993.

[138] Krause, F., Koomey, J., Becht, H., Olivier, D., Onufrio, G. & Radanne, P. Energy Policy in the Greenhouse. Volume II, Part 3C. *Fossil Generation: The Cost and Potential of Low-Carbon Resource Options in Western Europe.* El Cerrito, CA: International Project for Sustainable Energy Paths, 1994a.

[139] Krause, F., Koomey, J., Olivier, D., Radanne, P. & Schneider, M. Energy policy in the greenhouse. Volume II, Part 3E. *Nuclear Power: The Cost and Potential of Low-Carbon Resource Options in Western Europe.* El Cerrito, CA: International Project for Sustainable Energy Paths, 1994b.

[140] Lapp, R. E. & Andrews, H. L. *Nuclear Radiation Physics*, 4th ed. N.J.: Prentice-Hall, Inc., 1972.

[141] *LEAP - A Computerized Energy Planning System*, volume 1 Overview, volume 2 User Guide, volume 3 Technical Description, all for LEAP

Version 9001, Stockholm Environment Institute, Boston Center, Tellus Institute (formerly ESRG), Boston, 1990.

[142] Levine, M. D., Hirst, E., Koomey, J. G., McMahon, J. E. & Sanstad, A.H. *Energy Efficiency, Market Failures, and Government Policy.* Lawrence Berkeley Laboratory. LBL-35376. March, 1994.

[143] MacGregor, P.R., Maslak, C.E. & Stoll, H.G. *The Market Outlook for Integrated Gasification Combined Cycle Technology.* General Electric Company: New York, 1991.

[144] Manne, A. & Richels, R. *Buying Greenhouse Insurance - the Economic Costs of Carbon Dioxide Emission Limits.* MIT Press: Cambridge, 1992.

[145] Manne, A. *The Rate of Time Preference - Implications for the Greenhouse Debate".* Working paper, Stanford University, November, 1992.

[146] Manne, A.S. & Wene, C. O. *MARCAL-MACRO: A Linked Model for Energy-Economy Analysis.* Brookhaven National Laboratory, BNL-47161, 1992.

[147] Marcus W. *Making Ratepayers Pay: A Method for Determining Costs* of Externalities. Financial/Technical Supplement to IPPSO FACTO, February, 1992.

[148] Markvart, T.T. *Solar Electricity.* Wiley: West Sussex, England, 1994.

[149] Masters, C.D., Attanasi, E.D., Dietzman, W.D., Meyer, R.F., Mitchell R.W. & Root, D. H. World resources of crude oil, natural gas, natural bitumen, and shale oil. *Proceedings of the 12th World Petroleum Congress.* Houston, Texas, 1987.

[150] Mattsson, N. & Wene C.O. Assessing new energy technologies using an energy system model with endogenized experience curves. *International Journal of Energy Research,* **21**, pp. 385-393, 1997.

[151] *McGraw-Hill Encyclopedia of Science and Technology.* 7th edition, New York, 1992.

[152] McKibbin W.J. & Wilcoxen P.J. *The Theoretical and Empirical Structure of G-Cubed*, 1995a, http://www.eco.utexas.edu/faculty/Wilcoxen/papers.

[153] McKibbin, W. & Wilcoxen P. J. *The Theoretical and Empirical Structure of the G-Cubed Model,* Discussion Papers in International Economics No. 118, The Brookings Institution, 1995b.

[154] Meier, P. Energy Systems Analysis for Developing Countries. Vol. 222. *Lecture Notes in Economics and Mathematical Systems*, eds. M. Beckmann & W. Krelle, Springer-Verlag: Berlin, 1984.

[155] Meridian Corp. *Energy System Emissions and Materiel Requirements. The Deputy Assistant Secretary for Renewable Energy,* U.S. Department of Energy. February, 1989.

[156] Messner S. & Strubegger M. *Model-based Decision Support in Energy Planning.* IIASA Working Paper. WP-95-119. Laxenburg, Austria, 1995.

[157] Messner, S. & Strubegger M. *The Energy Model MESSAGE III,* Version 1.0, TEMAPLAN Group, Vienna, April 1990.

Subject Index

D

E

H

I

J

K

L

M

N

O

P

Q

R

S

T